# Rereading Orphanhood

Edinburgh Critical Studies in Victorian Culture
Series Editor: Julian Wolfreys
**Recent books in the series:**

*Rudyard Kipling's Fiction: Mapping Psychic Spaces*
Lizzy Welby

*The Decadent Image: The Poetry of Wilde, Symons and Dowson*
Kostas Boyiopoulos

*British India and Victorian Literary Culture*
Máire ní Fhlathúin

*Anthony Trollope's Late Style: Victorian Liberalism and Literary Form*
Frederik Van Dam

*Dark Paradise: Pacific Islands in the Nineteenth-Century British Imagination*
Jenn Fuller

*Twentieth-Century Victorian: Arthur Conan Doyle and the Strand Magazine, 1891–1930*
Jonathan Cranfield

*The Lyric Poem and Aestheticism: Forms of Modernity*
Marion Thain

*Gender, Technology and the New Woman*
Lena Wånggren

*Self-Harm in New Woman Writing*
Alexandra Gray

*Suffragist Artists in Partnership: Gender, Word and Image*
Lucy Ella Rose

*Victorian Liberalism and Material Culture: Synergies of Thought and Place*
Kevin A. Morrison

*The Victorian Male Body*
Joanne-Ella Parsons and Ruth Heholt

*Nineteenth-Century Settler Emigration in British Literature and Art*
Fariha Shaikh

*The Pre-Raphaelites and Orientalism*
Eleonora Sasso

*The Late-Victorian Little Magazine*
Koenraad Claes

*Coastal Cultures of the Long Nineteenth Century*
Matthew Ingleby and Matt P. M. Kerr

*Dickens and Demolition: Literary Afterlives and Mid-Nineteenth-Century Urban Development*
Joanna Hofer-Robinson

*Artful Experiments: Ways of Knowing in Victorian Literature and Science*
Philipp Erchinger

*Victorian Poetry and the Poetics of the Literary Periodical*
Caley Ehnes

*The Victorian Actress in the Novel and on the Stage*
Renata Kobetts Miller

*Dickens's Clowns: Charles Dickens, Joseph Grimaldi and the Pantomime of Life*
Jonathan Buckmaster

*Italian Politics and Nineteenth-Century British Literature and Culture*
Patricia Cove

*Cultural Encounters with the Arabian Nights in Nineteenth-Century Britain*
Melissa Dickson

*Novel Institutions: Anachronism, Irish Novels and Nineteenth-Century Realism*
Mary L. Mullen

*The Fin-de-Siècle Scottish Revival: Romance, Decadence and Celtic Identity*
Michael Shaw

*Contested Liberalisms: Martineau, Dickens and the Victorian Press*
Iain Crawford

*Plotting Disability in the Nineteenth-Century Novel*
Clare Walker Gore

*The Aesthetics of Space in Nineteenth-Century British Literature, 1843–1907*
Giles Whiteley

*The Persian Presence in Victorian Poetry*
Reza Taher-Kermani

*Rereading Orphanhood: Texts, Inheritance, Kin*
Diane Warren and Laura Peters

**Forthcoming volumes:**

*Her Father's Name: Gender, Theatricality and Spiritualism in Florence Marryat's Fiction*
Tatiana Kontou

*The Sculptural Body in Victorian Literature: Encrypted Sexualities*
Patricia Pulham

*Olive Schreiner and the Politics of Print Culture, 1883–1920*
Clare Gill

*Victorian Auto/Biography: Problems in Genre and Subject*
Amber Regis

*Gissing, Shakespeare and the Life of Writing*
Thomas Ue

*Women's Mobility in Henry James*
Anna Despotopoulou

*Michael Field's Revisionary Poetics*
Jill Ehnenn

*The Americanisation of W. T. Stead*
Helena Goodwyn

*Literary Illusions: Performance Magic and Victorian Literature*
Christopher Pittard

*The Ideas in Stories: Intellectual Content as Aesthetic Experience in Victorian Literature*
Patrick Fessenbecker

*Pastoral in Early-Victorian Fiction: Environment and Modernity*
Mark Frost

*Edmund Yates and Victorian Periodicals: Gossip, Celebrity, and Gendered Spaces*
Kathryn Ledbetter

*Literature, Architecture and Perversion: Building Sexual Culture in Europe, 1850–1930*
Aina Marti

*Oscar Wilde and the Radical Politics of the Fin de Siècle*
Deaglán Ó Donghaile

*Home and Identity in Nineteenth-Century Literary London*
Lisa Robertson

*Plotting the News in the Victorian Novel*
Jessica Valdez

*Manufacturing Female Beauty in British Literature and Periodicals, 1850–1914*
Michelle Smith

For a complete list of titles published visit the Edinburgh Critical Studies in Victorian Culture web page at www.edinburghuniversitypress.com/series/ECVC

Also Available:
*Victoriographies – A Journal of Nineteenth-Century Writing, 1790–1914*, ed. Diane Piccitto and Patricia Pulham
ISSN: 2044-2416
www.eupjournals.com/vic

# Rereading Orphanhood

Texts, Inheritance, Kin

Edited by Diane Warren and
Laura Peters

Edinburgh University Press is one of the leading university presses in the UK. We publish academic books and journals in our selected subject areas across the humanities and social sciences, combining cutting-edge scholarship with high editorial and production values to produce academic works of lasting importance. For more information visit our website: edinburghuniversitypress.com

© editorial matter and organisation Diane Warren and Laura Peters, 2020, 2022
© the chapters their several authors, 2020, 2022

Edinburgh University Press Ltd
The Tun – Holyrood Road, 12(2f) Jackson's Entry, Edinburgh EH8 8PJ

First published in hardback by Edinburgh University Press 2020

Typeset in 11/13 Adobe Sabon by
IDSUK (DataConnection) Ltd

A CIP record for this book is available from the British Library

ISBN 978 1 4744 6436 9 (hardback)
ISBN 978 1 4744 6437 6 (paperback)
ISBN 978 1 4744 6438 3 (webready PDF)
ISBN 978 1 4744 6439 0 (epub)

The right of Diane Warren and Laura Peters to be identified as the Editor of this work has been asserted in accordance with the Copyright, Designs and Patents Act 1988, and the Copyright and Related Rights Regulations 2003 (SI No. 2498).

# Contents

| | |
|---|---|
| Acknowledgements | vii |
| Series Editor's Preface | viii |
| Notes on Contributors | x |

Introduction: Rereading Orphanhood    1
*Laura Peters*

1. The Legal Guardian and Ward: Discovering the Orphan's 'Best Interests' in *Mansfield Park* and Mrs Fitzherbert's Notorious Adoption Case    10
   *Cheryl L. Nixon*

2. Orphanhoods and Bereavements in the Life and Verse of Charlotte Smith Richardson (1775–1825)    33
   *Kevin Binfield*

3. 'Like some of the princesses in the fairy stories, only I was not charming': The Literary Orphan and the Victorian Novel    56
   *Tamara S. Wagner*

4. Adoptive Reading    81
   *Kelly Hager*

5. No Place Like Home: The Orphaned Waif in Victorian Narratives of Rescue and Redemption    101
   *Harriet Salisbury*

6. Bodily Filth and Disorientation: Navigating Orphan Transformations in the Works of Dr Thomas Barnardo and Charles Dickens    121
   *Joey Kingsley*

7. The Limits of the Human? Exhibiting Colonial Orphans in Victorian Culture    142
   *Laura Peters*

8. Getting the Father Back: The Orphan's Oath in Florence Marryat's *Her Father's Name* and R. D. Blackmore's *Erema*    167
   *Peter Merchant*

9. Girlhood and Space in Nineteenth-Century Orphan Literature    186
   *Jane Suzanne Carroll*

10. 'The accumulated and single': Modernity, Inheritance and Orphan Identity    206
    *Diane Warren*

11. 'Something worse than the past in not being yet over': Elizabeth Bowen's Orphans, Exile and the Predicaments of Modernity    231
    *Ann Rea*

12. Orphans, Money and Marriage in Sensation Novels by Wilkie Collins and Philip Pullman    248
    *Claudia Nelson*

Coda: Rereading Orphanhood    268
*Diane Warren*

Index    270

*Acknowledgements*

Without the support of a number of people this volume would have remained an unrealised possibility. Thanks to Roehampton University, particularly Lynn Dobbs and Anna Gough-Yates, for a period of research leave which enabled this volume to be completed. Immense thanks to colleagues Jane Kingsley-Smith, Ian Haywood and Clare McManus for their support, feedback and endless cups of coffee. Many thanks to my co-editor Diane Warren for keeping faith in the project and being such a delight to work with. Finally, many thanks to my 'boys', Azzedine, Adam and Sami for their encouragement, patience and unlimited love.

This volume represents a tremendous collective effort. I should like to thank Alexandra Gray and Jennifer Jones for their work on the early stages of the project. I very much appreciate the intelligent, supportive and critically informed comments of Paráic Finnerty and Ben Dew. I should also like to thank my co-editor (Laura Peters) for her great insight and unflagging enthusiasm, as well as our contributors, for their persuasive and engaging chapters. Last (but most certainly not least) immense thanks are due to Richard and Daniel for their love, support, formatting help and their good-humoured tolerance of the family disruption caused by this project.

## Series Editor's Preface

'Victorian' is a term at once indicative of a strongly determined concept and an often notoriously vague notion, emptied of all meaningful content by the many journalistic misconceptions that persist about the inhabitants and cultures of the British Isles and Victoria's Empire in the nineteenth century. As such, it has become a by-word for the assumption of various, often contradictory habits of thought, belief, behaviour and perceptions. Victorian studies and studies in nineteenth-century literature and culture have, from their institutional inception, questioned narrowness of presumption, pushed at the limits of the nominal definition, and have sought to question the very grounds on which the unreflective perception of the so-called Victorian has been built; and so they continue to do. Victorian and nineteenth-century studies of literature and culture maintain a breadth and diversity of interest, of focus and inquiry, in an interrogative and intellectually open-minded and challenging manner, which are equal to the exploration and inquisitiveness of its subjects. Many of the questions asked by scholars and researchers of the innumerable productions of nineteenth-century society actively put into suspension the clichés and stereotypes of 'Victorianism', whether the approach has been sustained by historical, scientific, philosophical, empirical, ideological or theoretical concerns; indeed, it would be incorrect to assume that each of these approaches to the idea of the Victorian has been, or has remained, in the main exclusive, sealed off from the interests and engagements of other approaches. A vital interdisciplinarity has been pursued and embraced, for the most part, even as there has been contest and debate among Victorianists, pursued with as much fervour as the affirmative exploration between different disciplines and differing epistemologies put to work in the service of reading the nineteenth century.

Edinburgh Critical Studies in Victorian Culture aims to take up both the debates and the inventive approaches and departures from convention that studies in the nineteenth century have witnessed for the last half century at least. Aiming to maintain a 'Victorian' (in the most positive sense of that motif) spirit of inquiry, the series' purpose is to continue and augment the cross-fertilisation of interdisciplinary approaches, and to offer, in addition, a number of timely and untimely revisions of Victorian literature, culture, history and identity. At the same time, the series will ask questions concerning what has been missed or improperly received, misread, or not read at all, in order to present a multi-faceted and heterogeneous kaleidoscope of representations. Drawing on the most provocative, thoughtful and original research, the series will seek to prod at the notion of the 'Victorian', and in so doing, principally through theoretically and epistemologically sophisticated close readings of the historicity of literature and culture in the nineteenth century, to offer the reader provocative insights into a world that is at once overly familiar, and irreducibly different, other and strange. Working from original sources, primary documents and recent interdisciplinary theoretical models, Edinburgh Critical Studies in Victorian Culture seeks not simply to push at the boundaries of research in the nineteenth century, but also to inaugurate the persistent erasure and provisional, strategic redrawing of those borders.

Julian Wolfreys

# Notes on Contributors

**Kevin Binfield** is Professor of English and Director of Graduate Studies in English at Murray State University (Kentucky, USA). Most recently, he is co-editor, with William J. Christmas, of *Teaching Laboring-Class British Literature of the Eighteenth and Nineteenth Centuries* (New York: Modern Language Association, 2018). Most importantly, he is father to two adopted sons.

**Jane Suzanne Carroll** is the Ussher Assistant Professor in Children's Literature at Trinity College Dublin. Her teaching and research interests centre on nineteenth- and twentieth-century children's literature, spatiality and material culture in children's fiction. Her first monograph, *Landscape in Children's Literature* (Routledge, 2012) traces the development of literary landscapes in twentieth-century children's fantasy. She has also published on Susan Cooper, Terry Pratchett, J. R. R. Tolkien, M. R. James and Jules Verne.

**Kelly Hager** is Professor of English and Women's & Gender Studies at Simmons University in Boston, Massachusetts, where she teaches Victorian literature, children's literature and the history of feminism. She is the author of *Dickens and the Rise of Divorce* (2010) and of essays on Tennyson's *The Princess* and the school stories it inspired, Charlotte Mary Yonge, and canon formation and children's literature.

**Joey Kingsley** is a PhD student in English literature at the University of Rochester in New York state. She holds a BA in English from the College of the Holy Cross in Worcester, Massachusetts, and an MFA from Virginia Commonwealth University. Her work has appeared in *Blackbird*, *Salamander*, *The Adirondack Review*, *Unsplendid*, and elsewhere.

**Peter Merchant** is Principal Lecturer in English at Canterbury Christ Church University, UK, with interests in nineteenth-century fiction and in the field of literary juvenilia. He was a convener in 2012 of the bicentenary conference 'A Tale of Four Cities: Dickens and the Idea of "the Dickensian"', and then the co-editor, with Catherine Waters, of one of the volumes of essays resulting, *Dickens and the Imagined Child*. Among his more recent publications is the first critical edition of Thomas Anstey Guthrie's neglected novel *The Statement of Stella Maberly* (Valancourt Books, 2017); and he has work forthcoming on Anna Bonus Kingsford.

**Claudia Nelson** is Professor Emeritus of English at Texas A&M University. In addition to having produced six critical editions or co-edited collections of essays, she is the author of six books, most recently *Topologies of the Classical World in Children's Literature: Palimpsests, Maps, and Fractals*, co-authored with Anne Morey (Oxford University Press, 2019) and *Precocious Children and Childish Adults: Age Inversion in Victorian Literature* (Johns Hopkins University Press, 2012). Her monograph *Little Strangers: Portrayals of Adoption and Foster Care in America, 1850–1929* (Indiana University Press, 2003), won the Children's Literature Association Book Award.

**Cheryl L. Nixon** serves as Provost and Vice President for Academic Affairs at Fort Lewis College, Colorado. Her research explores literary representations and legal structurings of the family, focusing on the eighteenth-century rise of the novel. Her publications include *The Orphan in Eighteenth-Century Law and Literature: Estate, Blood, and Body* (2011), *Novel Definitions: An Anthology of Commentary on the Novel, 1688–1815* (2009), and the entry on 'Orphans' for Oxford Bibliographies. Working with students, she has curated rare books exhibitions for Boston Public Library, including 'Crooks, Rogues, and Maids Less than Virtuous: Books in the Streets of 18th-Century London.'

**Laura Peters** is Professor of English Literature and Head of the School of Humanities at Roehampton University. Specialising in Dickens, Victorian childhood and empire, she is the author of *Dickens and Race* (2013), and *Orphan Texts: Victorian Orphans, Culture and Empire* (2000), as well as numerous articles, and the editor of *Dickens and Childhood* (2012).

**Ann Rea** teaches twentieth-century British and Irish literature, the nineteenth-century novel and Jane Austen at the University of Pittsburgh at Johnstown. Her research interests include middlebrow fiction, as well as spy fiction and Elizabeth Bowen. She has recently published an article about spy novels focusing on Kipling's *Kim* alongside several of Eric Ambler's novels, as well as John le Carré's *The Spy Who Came in from the Cold*. She has another forthcoming article about Rachel Ferguson's *The Brontës Went to Woolworths* in the context of the early twentieth-century craze for spiritualism, as well as a piece about the 1930s aviatrix in the popular imagination. Her edited collection, *Middlebrow Wodehouse* has just been issued in paperback.

**Harriet Salisbury** has recently been awarded a practice-based PhD in Creative Writing, authoring an illustrated young adult novel set in the East End of London in the 1880s. This was conceived as a revisionist waif novel, exploring working-class communities and the rise of collective action. She studied Children's Literature under Michael Rosen at Goldsmiths University of London, and her interest in working-class experience stems from authoring an oral-history based book, *The War on Our Doorstep* (Ebury Books, 2012), researched and produced in collaboration with the Museum of London.

**Tamara S. Wagner** is Associate Professor at Nanyang Technological University, Singapore. Her books include *Victorian Narratives of Failed Emigration: Settlers, Returnees, and Nineteenth-Century Literature in English* (2016), *Financial Speculation in Victorian Fiction* (2010), and *Longing: Narratives of Nostalgia in the British Novel, 1740–1890* (2004). She has also edited collections on *Domestic Fiction in Colonial Australia and New Zealand* (2014), *Victorian Settler Narratives* (2011), and *Antifeminism and the Victorian Novel: Rereading Nineteenth-Century Women Writers* (2009). Wagner currently works on a study of Victorian babyhood entitled *The Victorian Baby in Print: Infancy, Infant Care, and Nineteenth-Century Popular Culture*.

**Diane Warren** is an independent scholar who is based in the UK. She is interested in modernist literature, especially work by Djuna Barnes, Sylvia Townsend Warner and Virginia Woolf, as well as echoes of modernism in the work of contemporary women writers. She is also interested in contemporary and early twentieth-century children's literature. She is the author of *Djuna Barnes' Consuming Fictions* (Ashgate 2008).

Introduction

# Rereading Orphanhood

*Laura Peters*

*How was a man to be explained unless you at least knew somebody who knew his father and his mother?* (Eliot 51)

*A character whose origins are unknown, [is] as a man without 'belongings'. He does not mean 'belongings' as property, but the record of birth and affiliation that affirms your legal and social status. Your genealogy 'belongs' to you and shows others where you belong. Without its guarantee of family history you have no identity or standing.* (Armstrong 11)

Once identified as the cornerstone of society, the family has been the subject of extensive and productive critical inquiry which has challenged its mythical status, extended its boundaries, and transformed our understandings of what is often referred to as the social building block. In a similar spirit, this collection examines the orphan figure in the long nineteenth century, from a range of perspectives, in order to explore the challenges such a figure posed for notions of kinship, inheritance, memory, the body, social reform, genre and the constitution of the human subject. In *Novel Politics: Democratic Imaginations in Nineteenth-Century Fiction*, Isobel Armstrong argues that 'illegitimacy becomes a nexus for democratic imagination because it challenges cultural certainties' (Armstrong 5). Illegitimacy and orphanhood are often intertwined: the lack of parents was often interpreted as symptomatic of a repressed scandal with regards to origins resulting in the orphan being ostracised from familial structures. This collection seeks to explore both the radical potential embodied in, and the shared problematic genealogy of, being outside heredity. The specific focus on orphanhood, whether legitimate or illegitimate, emphasises one whose existence is on the margins of familial and kinship structures and whose challenge is to develop relationships and an alternative family/kinship circle in order to see themselves recognised as human. As such the chapters, through a reading of orphan figures, illuminate the cultural, legal, social, emotional, scientific taxonomies that require negotiating well into adulthood. The chapters ensure the orphan is represented in larger current debates such as family law and inheritance, kinship studies, gender and writing, children's literature, memory, ethnicity and national belonging, neo-Victorianism and posthumanism.

While there has been critical work on the literary orphan figure, notably in studies by Laura Peters, David Floyd, Diana Pazicky and Maria Holmgren Troy et al., it is timely to revisit and reassess the significance of this figure. Since the publication of Peters' *Orphan Texts*, areas such as kinship, marriage and family studies have seen a surge in critical activity. Challenging the mythical status of the family has put every aspect under examination, *Rereading Orphanhood* both complements and extends this new work. Looking at the nature of the adult partnership at the heart of the family, Talia Schaffer's *Romance's Rival* offers a model of familiar marriage (companionate marriage) which is based on 'rational esteem'. Companionate marriage, firmly focused on the long-term future, offered an alternative to the model of desire-based romantic love that was primarily rooted in the present; companionate marriage challenges the desire model with one of caring and, at times, platonic partnership. Leonore Davidoff's *Thicker than Water*, explores 'alternative models of kinship' in order to decentre linear structures which advance patriarchal principles and genetic ties. Davidoff argues for family as 'a process' rather than a fixed set of relationships and pre-determined roles. Rachel Bowlby's *A Child of One's Own* seeks to foreground the act of parenting examining different concepts of parents beyond the biological arguing for parenthood as vital for community membership. Mary Jean Corbett's *Family Likeness* advocates a rethinking of Victorian family relations especially with regards to love within the family and incest. Other notable work by Eileen Cleere (*Avuncularism: Capitalism, Patriarchy and Nineteenth-Century English Culture*) and Holly Furneaux (*Queer Dickens: Erotics, Families, Masculinities*) seek to extend the understanding of family through notions of affiliation which read queer and/or extended kinship within the realm of the family. As Kelly Hager and Talia Schaffer argue in their introduction to an 'Extending Family' special issue of *Victorian Review*: 'The Victorian construction of family occurred in the wake of a long history of networks of affiliation that included cousins, friends, servants, neighbours, and connections' (Hager and Schaffer 19). Schaffer's *Romance's Rival* gestures towards how orphans may make use of such relationships to 'recover' from 'dangerous solitude' (Schaffer 170). *Rereading Orphanhood* demonstrates how this debate may be extended to allow for a more fully developed focus on the orphan figure. Read collectively the chapters illustrate how the orphan figure, and cultural discourses concerning orphanhood, complement these alternative readings of family and kinship structures by examining the ways in which orphan figures necessarily focus on the nature and limitations of kinship structures as they attempt to position themselves in social relations.

Nina Auerbach's 'Incarnations of the Orphan' published in *ELH* over forty years ago positioned the marginal, mutable and, at times, subversive orphan figure at the centre of literary endeavour, aligning orphanhood with the development of the novel as a genre. The orphan figure continues to intrigue both readers and writers. These chapters investigate the extent to which orphan figures can be understood as offering a radical and subversive cultural assessment: an analysis which extends Auerbach's initial investigations while also complementing recent work on the novel. Building on analyses of illegitimacy by Jenny Bourne Taylor and others, Isobel Armstrong examines the challenges illegitimacy poses to the family and the opportunity it offers for radical readings of nineteenth-century novels. Armstrong argues that illegitimacy disturbs notions of genealogy and inheritance which often perpetuated patriarchal and social power, frequently leading to perceptions of the novel as a bourgeois form. Illegitimacy and orphanhood were often conflated although there was not always a direct equivalence. Both figures embody a disruption of familial structures. Akin to the developing novel in the long nineteenth century, orphanhood problematises notions of genealogy and inheritance central to the genre in the form of influence, intertextuality and radical possibilities.

The chapters in the collection explore the cultural and social ramifications of orphanhood; it is much more than a biological issue. The extent to which orphan figures make visible the cultural role of inheritance, allied with their interest in self-invention and determination, locates them at a point of transition in many cultural exchanges. Orphans are critical in reflecting on the operation and limits of the family, especially in relation to memory and inheritance, and in making visible new kinship structures. This questioning is also apparent in analyses of the exchanges between orphan figures, the legal system and the nation.

While covering different literary forms across the long nineteenth century, the chapters coalesce around key themes of:

- gender, law and the body
- origins and originary narratives, including (il)legitimacy and being human
- memory, inheritance and recovering the past
- literacy, the novel and textual strategies
- the relationship of the past to colonisation and national identity
- construction of parenthood through adoption
- notions of community and kinship.

The focus of the collection is primarily on British and American writing but consideration is also given at times to writing from Canada and Switzerland. The collection traces the development of the orphan motif in both adult and children's literature, probing the genealogy of this figure from various perspectives, both canonical and non-canonical, and across a wide variety of genres.

The opening chapter, Cheryl L. Nixon's 'The Legal Guardian and Ward: Discovering the Orphan's "Best Interests" in *Mansfield Park* and Mrs Fitzherbert's Notorious Adoption Case', examines Jane Austen's *Mansfield Park* and the contemporary legal case *Seymour v Euston* to chart the changing perceptions in what constituted the best family for the orphan figure. Was the greatest importance to be given to family lineage and financial maintenance or to emotional care? By exploring the high-profile case of *Seymour v Euston*, Nixon's consideration of orphans from wealthy or landed families highlights the provisions made for these orphans, unlike those from poorer classes. Yet orphans from all classes have emotional needs; Nixon establishes how, increasingly, the love of a child was considered of paramount importance, even more so than the financial guardianship model. In examining Chancery cases and legal treatises, Nixon identifies that the guardian is responsible in law for the physical well-being, education and financial preservation of the orphan and their estate. In doing so, Nixon considers how a female orphan would have to negotiate with her guardian to ensure her own independence in these matters. Nixon charts how Austen's character Fanny, in *Mansfield Park*, negotiates a guardianship model in a family who do not love her, ultimately creating a new family defined by love. In doing so, Nixon's chapter identifies an increasing interest at the time in the 'best interests' of the orphan charting how guardianship evolves from an exercise of power to a duty to do well by the orphan.

Kevin Binfield's 'Orphanhoods and Bereavements in the Life and Verse of Charlotte Smith Richardson (1775–1825)' charts how another female orphan, Charlotte Richardson, negotiates her own orphanhood and the bereavement such orphanhood embodies in her writing. Considering a range of her verse, including little-known works, and archival records, Binfield explores the extent to which, for Richardson, orphanhood was an affective state and a social process. Ultimately orphanhood, for Richardson, was a lens through which to view others. Binfield argues that Richardson's works, both poetic and charity, are processes by which she supplants familial relationships she has lost.

Tamara S. Wagner's '"Like some of the princesses in the fairy stories, only I was not charming": The Literary Orphan and the Victorian Novel' explores how Victorian writers such as Charles Dickens, Wilkie Collins and Mary Elizabeth Braddon experiment with the form of the orphan narrative, based on the traditional foundling tale imbued with social criticism, such as exemplified in Dickens's *Oliver Twist*. At the heart of this narrative is the mystery of the orphan's origins as seen not only in *Oliver Twist* but also in Esther Summerson in *Bleak House*; the narrative then revolves around an exploration of family, kinship and relationships both in order to solve the mystery and to understand the extent to which the orphan remains outside these structures and to which the orphan's existence poses a threat to these structures. Wilkie Collins's 'No Thoroughfare' plays on the mysterious origins in multiple mistaken identities and doubles. Mary Elizabeth Braddon's *The Fatal Three* revisits the narrative of *Bleak House*, reworking the orphan as a threat and as a challenge to simplistic containment of the illegitimate within family structures.

Kelly Hager's 'Adoptive Reading' considers child orphans as readers whose reading helps them not only to survive but also to find belonging in imagined communities of readers. By exploring Lucy Maud Montgomery's *Anne of Green Gables*, E. Nesbit's *The Story of the Treasure Seekers* and *The Wouldbegoods*, Kate Douglas Wiggin's *Rebecca of Sunnybrook Farm* and Frances Hodgson Burnett's *A Little Princess*, all considered Golden Age classics, Hager looks at how the fictional orphan readers negotiate the ideology of the family. Enacting scenes from the texts, the children are shown to develop a reading strategy, 'adoptive reading' (Stauffer 86), which enables them to survive. In addition, the reading strategy also highlights the construction of an ideal concept of family which is rarely achieved. Rather these texts celebrate families which do not conform to this ideal, families which are adoptive, non-blood relation and inclusive.

Hager highlights how children's literature challenges and extends notions of both the family and childhood through a focus on the agency of the child readers.

Harriet Salisbury's 'The Orphaned Waif in Victorian Narratives of Rescue and Redemption' considers the link between family and class. Examining fourteen children's novels published by the Religious Tract Society (RTS), including well-known works by Hesba Stretton, 'Brenda' (Mrs Castle Smith), Mrs O. F. Walton and Silas Hocking alongside little-known authors such as Mary Howitt, L. T. Meade and others, Salisbury argues that these novels invert working-class structures of family, kinship and community by creating a larger religious familial group, the role of which is to embrace death. Following on from the children's domestic novel, what Salisbury terms 'waif novels' enhance our understanding of family and kinship structures of the impoverished classes in the urban centres by foregrounding how parental roles were assumed by siblings acting as 'parenting children'. These waif novels ultimately posit that poor families have chosen their marginalisation and that existing outside social structures puts their very presence within civilisation under threat.

Sharing the focus on the urban poor, Joey Kingsley's 'Bodily Filth and Disorientation: Navigating Orphan Transformations in the Works of Dr Thomas Barnardo and Charles Dickens' explores how Thomas Barnardo and Charles Dickens both focus on the bodily neglect of the poor orphan to highlight the loss of the family, in physical and moral terms. The dirty, uncared-for body of the poor orphan is a visual tool to point to the loss of resilience and Christian morals; Barnardo's photographs and Dickens's dramatic literary depictions create an image of a poor, uneducated, homeless child, verging on criminality and with an uncertain future. Redeeming this impoverished child body through appeals to middle-class charity and philanthropy, both Barnardo and Dickens work to recuperate this figure within a larger network of the larger Christian family and civilisation. Ultimately, Kingsley argues that Dickens and Barnardo differ in the agency demonstrated by the orphan figure they portray to achieve rehabilitation and moral transformation.

Also combining the visual and literary representation, Laura Peters's 'The Limits of the Human? Exhibiting Colonial Orphans in Victorian Culture' explores the concerns raised in Kingsley's chapter about the nature of civilisation through an examination of the definitions of being human in circulation at the time. By analysing the human zoos, with a specific focus on the exhibition of orphans from around the world and their literary counterparts, Peters explores discourses surrounding human/non-human/sub-human which were in circulation at the time in the developing discourses of evolution and scientific racism. Displaying orphans of other races alongside animals and the displaying of the lumpenproletariat within English society, calls into question the human status of these orphans. Without a traceable genealogy, these orphans fall outside the family of humans, highlighting how precarious the Victorians felt their evolutionary status was.

Peter Merchant's chapter, 'Getting the Father Back: The Orphan's Oath in Florence Marryat's *Her Father's Name* and R. D. Blackmore's *Erema*', explores how female orphan figures in Florence Marryat's *Her Father's Name* and R. D. Blackmore's *Erema*, liberated from the restraints of family and gender, undertake extensive travels to clear their deceased father's reputation. Through a consideration of how the dead are remembered and their reputations inherited, Merchant explores the importance of lineage and family reputation. Merchant also considers how the developing genres of detective story and sensation fiction provide an opportunity to reveal family skeletons and tainted inheritance through a narrative movement which inverts the orphan narrative's formulaic move from margins to social mainstream. Instead, the empowered female orphan protagonist, through cross-dressing, stage performance and impersonations, not only challenges gender norms but restores the public reputation of the patriarch, changing the way they are remembered. The reinstatement of the patriarch results in the orphans rejecting the 'mother' country choosing to return to other countries in a move from social mainstream back to peripheries.

Focusing also on female orphan protagonists, but those who remain in the domestic realm, Jane Suzanne Carroll's chapter, 'Girlhood and Space in Nineteenth-Century Orphan Literature', considers the female orphan figure in children's literature of the nineteenth-century as liminal figures, existing outside heteronormative family structures. Unlike Merchant's adult female protagonists, Carroll argues that because of their gender, child female orphan figures tend not to undertake lone adventures, rather they gain their knowledge and agency to affect wider society while in the domestic space in a family household. Carroll argues for the centripetal force of the narrative which draws the orphan girl into the still centre of the home space. The struggle these figures face is internal not only played out in the domestic space but of a personal and emotional nature. Considering six classic novels, Joanna Spyri's *Heidi*, Frances Hodgson Burnett's *A Little Princess* and *The Secret Garden*, L. M. Montgomery's *Anne of Green Gables* and *Emily of New Moon*, and Eleanor Porter's *Pollyanna*, Carroll argues that ultimately the female child orphan figures of the time, particularly those on the cusp of adulthood, are marginal figures whose liminality manifests itself both spatially, with the female protagonist continually drawn to borders and marginalised spaces, and spiritually as a figure bordering on the supernatural and/or sublime.

Diane Warren's '"The accumulated and single": Modernity, Inheritance and Orphan Identity' considers how the orphan figure, located at the interface of biology and culture problematises the issues of modernity and inheritance. Focusing on Djuna Barnes's *Nightwood* and Linda Grant's *When I Lived in Modern Times*, Warren explores how the past functions as both a burden and a resource, complicating the (cultural) orphan's search for kinship and a sense of home. The chapter also demonstrates that the influence of the long nineteenth century still inflects the experiences of twentieth-century orphan characters, undermining any attempt to break with the past. Rather, these adult orphans need to negotiate actively the role of inheritance to find kinship and an imaginative and emotional sense of home.

Ann Rea's '"Something worse than the past in not being yet over": Elizabeth Bowen's Orphans, Exile and the Predicaments of Modernity' considers Elizabeth Bowen's orphan protagonists in *The Last September, The House in Paris, The Death of the Heart* and *The Heat of the Day* as representative of characteristics of both the fractured nature of modern experience and the Anglo-Irish community at the time, namely a disrupted inheritance, problematic relationship to the past and the struggle to determine a future. In doing so, Rea draws parallels between orphanhood and modernism in that both embody a larger loss of culture and community. Rea traces how Bowen's own orphanhood is mirrored in her protagonists' dislocation and sense of loss. Ultimately, however, Rea demonstrates how Bowen's work embraces uncertainty and separation from older, now seen as false, belonging. Paradoxically, this state of uncertainty and dislocation is the necessary state enabling the forging of new connections. Often associated with modernity, Rea explores the legacy of imperialism on notions of memory, community and nation.

Working the fields of Victorian sensation and neo-Victorian literary studies, Claudia Nelson's 'Orphans, Money and Marriage in Sensation Novels by Wilkie Collins and Philip Pullman' reads Philip Pullman's Sally Lockhart trilogy against Wilkie Collins's *No Name* in order to highlight the way female orphan figures negotiate the world of finance in order to ensure domestic security. In these texts, domesticity is commodified and the female protagonists need to become entrepreneurs to secure the domestic space. In this, the ties of family to money are made explicit and the difficulties for female orphans are foregrounded. In this Nelson, like Nixon, explores how female orphans navigated a traditionally male space while illuminating problems with our inheritance, financial and memorial, of the past.

## Works Cited

Armstrong, Isobel. *Novel Politics: Democratic Imaginations in Nineteenth-Century Fiction*. Oxford University Press, 2016.

Auerbach, Nina. 'Incarnations of the Orphan.' *ELH* vol. 42, Fall 1975, pp. 395–419.

Bowlby, Rachel. *A Child of One's Own*. Oxford University Press, 2013.

Cleere, Eileen. *Avuncularism: Capitalism, Patriarchy and Nineteenth-Century English Culture*. Stanford University Press, 2004.

Corbett, Mary Jean. *Family Likeness: Sex, Marriage and Incest from Jane Austen to Virginia Woolf*. Cornell University Press, 2008.

Davidoff, Leonore. *Thicker than Water*. Oxford University Press, 2012.

Eliot, George. *Silas Marner*. Penguin, 1985.

Floyd, David. *Street Urchins, Sociopaths and Degenerates: Orphans of Late-Victorian and Edwardian Fiction*. University of Wales Press, 2014.

Furneaux, Holly. *Queer Dickens: Erotics, Families, Masculinities*. Oxford University Press, 2013.

Hager, Kelly and Schaffer, Talia. 'Introduction: Extending Family', *Victorian Review*, vol. 39, part 2, Fall 2013, pp. 7–21.

Pazicky, Diana Loercher. *Cultural Orphans in America*. University Press of Mississippi, 1998.

Peters, Laura. *Orphan Texts: Victorian Orphans, Culture and Empire*. Manchester University Press, 2000.

Schaffer, Talia. *Romance's Rival*. Oxford University Press, 2016.

Stauffer, Andrew, 'An Image in Lava: Annotation, Sentiment, and the Traces of Nineteenth-Century Reading.' *PMLA*, vol. 134, no. 1, January 2019, pp. 81–98.

Troy, Maria Holmgren et al. *Making Home: Orphanhood, Kinship and Cultural Memory in Contemporary American Novels*. Manchester University Press, 2014.

Chapter 1

# The Legal Guardian and Ward: Discovering the Orphan's 'Best Interests' in *Mansfield Park* and Mrs Fitzherbert's Notorious Adoption Case

*Cheryl L. Nixon*

Jane Austen places the guardian/ward relationship at the centre of *Mansfield Park*, using it to interrogate the proper place of the child in the affective family. In its dramatisation of Fanny Price's attempt to be accepted and valued by the adoptive Bertram family, *Mansfield Park* provides sustained engagement with the legal idea of the 'best interests' of the child. The concepts Austen addresses transform, over the course of nineteenth century, into a legal recognition of the need to protect the child's emotional welfare – not just physical and economic welfare – within family structure. In the novel, the child's emotional needs are emphasised by recreating Fanny as an orphan and dramatising her mistreatment by her surrogate family. In the early nineteenth century, legal questions concerning the emotional care of the child are similarly raised by turning to the orphan and emphasising his or her uncertain family status and need for a legal guardian. Unable to rely on the clarity of biological bonds, the guardian/ward relationship forces the law to define the foundations of the family: is the best family for the child one that emphasises familial lineage, legal protocol, bodily maintenance, economic trusteeship, or emotional care? A turn to *Seymour v. Euston* (1803–6), a scandalous case that involves the Prince Regent (later King George IV), his illegal wife Maria Fitzherbert, and her claims to the custody of an orphaned girl, reveals the radical nature of arguing for the emotional care of the child.

In both law and literature, the orphan becomes an important testing ground for new definitions of the family. Just as in *Mansfield Park*, *Seymour v. Euston* positions the emotional well-being of a young orphaned girl as paramount. In the case, the Court of Chancery is charged with locating the correct guardian for the orphaned

Mary Georgiana Emma Seymour (1798–1848), popularly known as Minney (or Minnie); it hears – and rejects – arguments that the emotional welfare of the child should determine the child's guardianship. Although Minney was cared for by Fitzherbert from infancy at the behest of her mother Lady Horatia Seymour, her guardianship is awarded to her uncles the Earl of Euston and Lord Henry Seymour. Minney's father's last will and testament names Euston and Seymour as guardians to his children; because Minney is born after the will is created, she is not named in it, creating an opening for her custody to be contested. In the Chancery proceedings, the vocabulary of emotional welfare – including the 'care', 'sensibility' and 'bonds' connecting Minney and Fitzherbert – is employed, debated and ultimately dismissed. Minney's custody is awarded to the uncles who have never cared for her. After a prolonged appeal process, the case is heard by the House of Lords, where, due to lobbying by the Prince Regent, the Chancery decision is overturned and a new 'compromise' guardian is named. That guardian, another of Minney's uncles, the Marquis of Hertford, and his wife the Marquess of Hertford assert that Minney remain with Fitzherbert. Although the *Seymour* case appears in print in the *Journals* of the *House of Lords* and is summarised in popular biographies, this essay brings newly discovered Chancery manuscript sources to a consideration of the case.

The *Seymour* case overtly articulates competing definitions of the family. A child-centred definition of the family is constructed by lawyers and witnesses who employ an emotional vocabulary of sensibility characteristic of fiction. Although convincingly argued, this emotional definition is rejected in favour of a precedent-following legal definition of guardianship. Through its practice of equity, the Court of Chancery oversaw the care of 'infants' (minors under the age of 21) and, more specifically, oversaw the care of the orphan by creating and regulating the guardian/ward relationship. Its definition of the orphan focuses on two foundations of power that define the guardian: the guardian's claim to the custody of the child, which ideally enacted the father's testamentary naming of the guardian in his last will, and the guardian's role as economic trustee, which focused on accounting structures created to manage the child's inheritance. The emotional welfare of the child was typically mentioned only briefly. *Seymour v. Euston* emphasises and complicates these issues. The case features a non-kin woman's emotional claim to guardianship against the men named as testamentary guardians. The future King of England makes Fitzherbert's claims economically attractive by promising the orphan a £10,000 inheritance. And, Fitzherbert advances the claim that her maternal care of the orphan should be recognised with custody, even when she is pointedly not the child's mother.

*Seymour v. Euston* evidences an attempt at employing a newly developing ideology of the family that does not become operative until the mid-to-late-nineteenth century. Similarly, like most late eighteenth- and early nineteenth-century novels focused on the orphan, *Mansfield Park* offers an emotional definition of the child that the law has not yet fully realised. Extending Ruth B. Yeazell's observation that 'Fanny Price is the only one of Austen's heroines to have a childhood,' Fanny is given a dramatic childhood of constructed orphanhood and kept in a suspended state of orphan dependency (77). From this seemingly powerless position, she is able to critique the family and, in particular, the guardian/ward family that needs an orphan in order to reassure itself that it *is* a family. *Mansfield Park* neatly summarises the legal concepts that define the activities of the eighteenth-century guardian, but positions them as concerns experienced by the orphan: the ward must worry about securing her own maintenance and education, the ward must negotiate with the guardian over his consent to her marriage, and the ward must search for nurturing maternal and paternal care. *Mansfield Park* embeds these legal concerns within elements of a formulaic guardian/ward plot: the heroine is outcast from her original family, often by real or symbolic orphaning; she experiences both rejection and acceptance as the ward adopted into a guardian family; she uses these experiences to form her understanding of the economic and emotional functions of the family; she reunites with and tests those ideas with members from her original family; and she ultimately creates her own definition of the family, often by marrying into and naturalising her guardianship family. This plot structures novels such as Fanny Burney's *Evelina* Elizabeth Inchbald's *A Simple Story,* and Charlotte Smith's *Emmeline*.

In his critique of 'generalizations about major shifts in family law – such as the movement from property to nurture in custody law', Michael Grossberg asks that those generalisations be 'reformulate[d]' in 'broader terms by trying to understand issues like child welfare or children's interests as constantly changing and dynamic concepts' (311). Historians such as Lynn Marie Kohm, Robert van Krieken, Mary Anne Mason and Holly Brewer have reconstructed the development of the legal doctrine of the best interests of the child, in which the needs of the child ultimately became paramount in law's determination of who should care for the child and how the child should be cared for. The best interests doctrine is developed within child custody law. The 1839 Custody of Infants Act codified the right of the mother to argue for the custody of her biological children against the claims of the father. The Act initiated what comes to be called the 'tender years' doctrine, which presumes that the mother should be given custody of her children, especially when they are under the age of 7; this is later replaced by the 'best interests' doctrine. Studies of child custody typically focus on the father's and mother's competing claims to custody, especially in twentieth-century divorce law; as a result, the nuclear family is positioned as playing a prominent role in creating new legal definitions of the child. However, in the eighteenth and early nineteenth centuries, child custody within the nuclear family remained clearly defined as the father's prerogative. The orphan and guardian are the figures that opened the family to definitional debate.

In the early nineteenth century, a legal understanding of protecting the welfare or acting in the best interests of the child is still under construction, and Austen uses familiar guardianship themes to perform a calculated appraisal of this developing definition of the child. *Mansfield Park* articulates a newly emergent meaning of the family by focusing on the emotional welfare of the ward and positioning it as a concern that can – and ought to – be independent of the economic structuring of guardianship. Unlike eighteenth-century heroines, Fanny is a ward who has no estate, no personal property, no 'surprise' inheritance, and no hidden wealthy parents – and yet, the novel argues that Fanny not only deserves to be treated as an equal family member but surpasses her guardianship family in propriety and morality. By creating a novel which experiments with reimagining the position of the orphan in the guardian/ward family, Austen not only enters emerging debates concerning the best interests of the child, but asks essential questions which help to structure our understanding of those debates: can the surrogate family provide a home for the orphaned or unwanted child, can the surrogate family redefine the family as centred on the emotional care of the child, and can the surrogate family help to determine who is the best person to care for the child, the mother-figure or father-figure? In dramatising and then answering these questions, Austen makes an obvious argument – a child should be cared for by those who love her – at a time when such an argument was not obvious.

*

The fictional Fanny Price and real Minney Seymour present opposite images of the orphan: Fanny is undesired and often neglected, while Minney is desired and even fought over. Although this opposition is extreme – Fanny cannot request a fire for her attic room, while Minney has the future king of England creating a £10,000 inheritance for her – the novel and case both recognise that 'welfare of the child' arguments demand that the child be seen as valuable and worthy of care. The orphan heightens this valuation of the child, as she can become an object of exchange that can be traded among non-biological families with competing claims. As *Seymour v. Euston* shows, the emerging ideology of the best interests of the child argues that the family that deserves the child is the one that can care for the child the best – or desires the child the most. But, as *Mansfield Park* reveals, the orphan is pressured to prove her worth in order to be desired by a family. Austen raises the stakes in the valuation of the child by depicting a child who does not prove her worth to her adoptive family. Importantly, however, Fanny does demonstrate her worth to the reader, allowing Austen to demonstrate that all children, no matter their apparent status or desirability, are worthy of care.

Although *Seymour v. Euston* and *Mansfield Park* contrast the desirable with the undesirable orphan, any orphaned, adoptive, or surrogate child occupies a contested familial space due to the shifting conceptual foundation of the family. In their fictional and factual articulation of this contested space, the case and the novel share several features. First, both fact and fiction attests to the negate-ability of the biological parent–child bond. Both feature parents that renounce their claim to their child; Fanny and Minney are 'given up' by their still-living mothers. In addition, both the novel and case chart the welfare of the child by charting the location of the child. No longer defined by biology, the surrogate child is open to shifting familial claims, and both Fanny and Minney circulate through a variety of family structures. Notions of care cannot be fully articulated and are, instead, stated as claims to custody. And, finally, this equation of the custody of the body with a care for the child's best interests opens up larger questions about who should provide that care and how that care can be evidenced. Both the novel and the trial dramatise the hope that the neglect of the child can be remedied by the desirability of the child. At first, neither Fanny nor Minney are awarded a family that recognises her best interests. However, failures to achieve the ideal family allow that ideal to be expressed and, for both, ultimately achieved. Not only does Fanny become increasingly central to the Bertram family and increasingly valued by her guardian Sir Thomas, she becomes a full member of the family when she marries her guardian's son Edmund. On appeal to the House of Lords, Minney is allowed to remain with her loving guardian, the only parental figure and only family she has known.

In both the trial and the novel, guardianship begins with the same event: the purposeful orphaning of the child through the removal of her from the biological family. The dates and events of *Seymour v. Euston* can be quickly reviewed: Minney is born in November 1798; both her parents, Lord Hugh Seymour and Lady Ann Horatia, die in 1801; her guardianship suit is entered into Chancery in 1803 and is decided in 1804; and the case is appealed to the House of Lords, where it is heard in May 1805. The case's defendants are Minney's uncles, George Fitzroy Earl of Euston, and Lord Henry Seymour; Euston is married to Minney's maternal aunt and already serves as the guardian and trustee of Minney's five siblings. Euston's testamentary guardianship of Minney is not clearly constructed because she is not named in her father's will. The case's plaintiff is Minney herself, as represented by her legal *prochein amy* or 'next friend', William Bentinck, who was Minney's father's friend and serves as his trustee. Protecting Minney's best interests, Bentinck argues on behalf of Fitzherbert, who has been entrusted with the custody of Minney. Minney's mother grew ill after giving birth, was advised to travel to Maderia, and left her sickly child behind; Fitzherbert has cared for Minney since she was two months old. Claiming that she has become a mother to Minney, Fitzherbert wants to maintain custody of Minney and, in order to do so, must be named her legal guardian. Thus, the case pits a mother-figure who has raised Minney against the legally named uncle-guardian who has had little familial contact with the child.

While focusing on the construction of the guardian/ward family, *Seymour v. Euston* reveals that the nuclear family is not stable and the biological parent/child relationship can be disassembled at will. Minney lacks a familial relationship with her parents. After giving birth to Minney in November 1798, her mother, Lady Horatia, 'being in a deep decline was advised to try the air at Madeira for the restoration of her health' (*Seymour v. Euston Journals* 2). Lord Hugh Seymour, Minney's father, arranges to accompany his wife. With her eldest son serving as a midshipman, and her next three sons away at boarding school, Lady Horatia must arrange for the care of her three underage children. She writes to Fitzherbert to express, as the court records explain, her 'extreme uneasiness on account of her children' (2). She takes two of her remaining children to Madeira, but decides that infant Minney should remain behind and be 'committed to the care of Mrs. Fitzherbert' (3). Lady Horatia writes Fitzherbert a letter, repeatedly cited in court, which states, '*little Minney is to be your child*' (3, italics original). The family never fully reassembles: Minney's parents spend early 1799 in Madeira, her father makes a brief return to London, and then they both travel to the West Indies;

Lady Horatia returns to England in May or June 1801 and dies on 12 July 1801; Lord Hugh dies in Jamaica on 11 September 1801. Other than the first two months of her life, Minney does not live with her biological parents. Her bodily custody and welfare have been entrusted to Fitzherbert.

Similarly, the first volume of *Mansfield Park* describes the displacement of the nuclear family, emphasising the physical, economic and emotional consequences of choosing to recreate the biological child as an orphan. Fanny experiences the trauma of being adopted without being desired. Frances Price has a 'superfluity of children' and asks her sisters, Mrs Norris and Lady Bertram, to help with the nine children's 'future maintenance' (3). Austen uses 'maintenance', the legal term for economic support, to define what the children need, and the decisions surrounding Fanny's custody are similarly described in economic terms. Deciding that 'poor Mrs. Price should be relieved from the charge and expense of one child,' the Bertrams take Fanny in, equating child custody with economic expense (3). Fanny is easily given up by her poor parents and is quickly forgotten; 'Of the rest she saw nothing, nobody ever seemed to think of her ever going amongst them again, even for a visit, nobody at home seemed to want her' (18). As soon as 'so benevolent a scheme' is created by Mrs Norris and the Lady Bertram, they try to trade Fanny off to one another (6). The Bertrams assume Fanny's custody, but later, when Lord Bertram's 'circumstances were rendered less fair than heretofore, by some recent losses on his West Indies Estate', Lady Bertram again tries to shift Fanny off onto Mrs Norris (20). This attempt is successfully repulsed by Mrs Norris, 'Here I am a poor desolate widow . . . with barely enough to support me in the rank of gentlewoman . . . – what possible comfort could I have in taking such a charge upon me as Fanny?' (25). Not only is Fanny an orphan charge, she is a undesirable 'charge' on Mrs Norris's and the Bertrams' accounts. Disavowed by her biological family, Fanny's surrogate family tries equally hard to disown her.

Fanny's guardian-uncle, Sir Thomas Bertram, defines Fanny by what she is not. Fanny may reside within his family, but must be aware that she is not part of it. Sir Thomas takes pains to meditate on 'the distinction proper to be made between the girls as they grow up'; the family must work to 'make [Fanny] remember that she is not a *Miss Bertram* . . . [T]hey cannot be equals. Their rank, fortune, rights and expectations, will always be different' (8). Knowing that she is defined in the negative, Fanny understands all too well the familial 'no place' she occupies; in an early conversation with Edmund, she states: 'I can never be important to any one', and '*Here*, I know I am of none . . . ' (23). Austen calls attention to this strategy of definition by negation when Mary Crawford, on trying to figure out Fanny's position, cannot place her into the familiar categories a young woman occupies. Unable to read Fanny's familial actions, such as dining with the Bertrams but speaking very little, Mary is confused by Fanny's social status. Mary pointedly asks 'Pray, is she out, or is she not?' (43) and pointedly concludes, 'Miss Price is *not* out' (46, italics original). Trying to determine whether Minney has been introduced into society, Mary's language also highlights Fanny's uncertain familial status: she is neither in nor out of the Bertram family.

Austen makes it clear that this devaluation of the ward is done at the expense of the stability of the family itself. The *Lovers' Vows* theatrical scenes illustrate the danger of neglecting the child, even if that child occupies an orphan position. Fanny is ignored until she is needed to participate in the play. When she is finally asked to join into the family theatrical, Fanny must say 'no' because she knows the play to be immoral, in exact opposition to her own definition of the family. Unable to explain that she disagrees with the play's morality and the Bertram children's embrace of its depiction of pre-marital relations, bastardy and abandonment, she can only state, 'You cannot have an idea. It would be absolutely impossible for me' (132). Her marginal, neither in nor out position allows her to more fully comprehend the definition of the family than those that are its full members, and to understand that even fictional definitions of the family have real meaning. Fanny remains true to her values, even if it means remaining marginal and, quite literally, off centre stage. Even Mrs Norris reminds her of her lack of familial place, labelling her 'very ungrateful indeed, considering who and what she is' (133). Fanny chooses to be no one within the play and the family, rather than join a family based on values she rejects.

Duplicating Fanny's circumstances, Minney is given to a guardianship family by her still-living biological parents, occupies an indeterminate position within several family structures, and is a sickly child whose physical well-being is directly affected by these familial locations. Only 7 years old at the conclusion of her trial, Minney is much younger than Fanny. Even the indirect critique of the family by the child, depicted so well by Fanny's moral judgement of the Bertrams and Prices, is impossible in Minney's case, as she gives no testimony at her trial and her familial experiences are represented only by the guardianship structures that attempt to claim her. Although a character equivalent to the orphan child that has no place, Fanny does have both a biological and a surrogate family, and does have a place, Mansfield Park. By imagining a ward that has an excess of family and place, but is still forgotten and neglected, Austen has created a withering portrait of the devaluation of the child within the family. Similarly, in *Seymour v. Euston*, the ward has an excess of parental claimants, but many seem more interested in their own status than in what is best for the child.

\*

By removing the daughter from the biological family and positioning her as an orphan, both *Mansfield Park* and *Seymour v. Euston* open the family up for redefinition. Both the novel and the case must address the physical custody of the orphan, but seek to enact a crucial translating of questions of custody into questions of care. However, both the novel and the case can only address those questions of care through the custodial structures of guardianship. Austen's novel addresses the question 'What does it mean to care for a child?' by dramatising another: 'What is the best familial place for the child?' *Seymour v. Euston* features the same conflation of questions: in order to determine the emotional care of the child, it must determine the guardianship home of Minney. As both *Mansfield Park* and *Seymour v. Euston* reveal, it proves easier to position a child in a family than to regulate how to care for that child.

Critics have long recognised that the family is *Mansfield Park*'s central ideological concern. Paula Marantz Cohen opens her exploration of the novel by stating, '*Mansfield Park* is Jane Austen's one novel in which the life of the family take precedence over the life of the individual' (669); David Kaufmann opens his by stating, '*Mansfield Park* is, above all, a novel not about the sanctity of marriage, but the sanctity of the family' (211); and, Johanna Smith opens hers by arguing that one of Austen's central goals is to reveal 'the constrictions of the family in the novel' (1). In her influential exploration of how '*Mansfield Park* tests the parameters of conservative mythology about the august gentry family' (96), Claudia Johnson analyses Fanny and Edmund's marriage, concluding 'it is precisely because familial love, here at least, appears to be the only legitimate arena for strong feelings that it is prone to incestuous permutations' (117). Much of the family-oriented criticism of *Mansfield Park* focuses on this near-incestuous marriage between Fanny and Edmund. In this criticism,

Fanny's experience becomes not one of orphaning, but one of the nuclear family. In her examination of the Fanny/Edmund union, Eileen Cleere surveys such criticism and concludes 'most critical work on *Mansfield Park* has depended on the primacy of the nuclear family and the metaphorical power of the nuclear family to account for Fanny Price's rise to power' (113). Cleere criticises this reliance on the nuclear family, arguing, 'I am convinced that more flexible models of family are needed' (114) and concluding, 'the revised family at Mansfield is an economic unit connected not by biology or affect, but by a collective sense of debt and repayment' (128). As Johnson and Cleere demonstrate, *Mansfield Park* is interested in more than the replication of the nuclear family; the novel proves to be most interested in the orphan-defined family's ability to simultaneously mimic and disrupt, and desire and critique, the nuclear family and its bonds.

Austen equates family structure with plot structure. Each volume of *Mansfield Park* creates a new familial position for Fanny, allowing a new consideration of how her welfare is determined by family location and a new recognition of the family's inadequacy in creating a proper space for the child. Each family situation seems to resolve the problems of the one preceding, only to then become more problematic. In addition to raising questions of family ideology, *Mansfield Park* raises questions concerning the narrative strategies the novel employs in shaping that ideology. In volume 1, Fanny occupies the margins of the Bertram family and is neglected by the surrogate mothers offered by Lady Bertram and Mrs Norris. In volume 2, Fanny becomes the family's central daughter-figure but remains misunderstood, given unwelcome attention by Henry Crawford. Unexpectedly, it is the surrogate paternal structures offered by Sir Thomas that empower the female ward. In volume 3, Fanny returns to the 'of none' position of a marginal person, but this dislocation occurs, most shockingly, in her biological family. The third volume allows a sustained erasure of the definition of both the biological and surrogate family. In each volume, the lack of child welfare becomes imagined as the no-place-ness of the orphan. *Mansfield Park* supports the best interests argument by critiquing Fanny's guardianship family – the Bertram family is unlikeable, absent and often cruel – without offering any viable alternative to it.

The *Seymour* trial similarly attests to the ease with which a child can be shifted among competing family structures. The opening of the case details Minney's movements from person to person and place to place. While awaiting the claim of Fitzherbert, the few-months-old

Minney is passed among her relatives; she stays in her maternal aunt's home and then her paternal uncle's, being 'taken to the house of the Earl of Euston, and after some stay there was removed to the house of Lord George Seymour' (*Seymour v. Euston Journals* 3). When the measles breaks out in Lord Seymour's home in February 1799 she is removed from that household, too. Fitzherbert then 'received the Appellant into her family, in which she has ever since resided and been treated as the child of Mrs. Fitzherbert' (3). As the case progresses, it shows a marked interest in charting the physical location of the child and, as in *Mansfield Park*, using that as evidence of the care or neglect of the child. For example, the case maps the movement of Minney and her nursemaid through London, describing the 'inconceiveable agony of mind' suffered by Fitzherbert when they did not return on time because they encountered Minney's aunt. Although this vignette is presented in the case to evidence Lord Hugh's recognition of Fitzherbert's custody of Minney, it also evidences how the case connects the emotional care of the child with the physical control of the child.

*Seymour v. Euston* articulates the argument that the orphan's care should dictate custody arrangements, rather than a custody claim dictating care. In the case, Chancery confronts two opposing constructions of guardianship, one claiming the bonds of law, the other claiming the bond of care, and the Court, on 21 December 1804, decides in favour of Euston and the bonds of law. This decision is not surprising; removing a child from a non-kin woman to give guardianship to an uncle claiming testamentary power follows all legal precedent at the time. A glance at a child custody case that is exactly contemporaneous to *Seymour v. Euston* reveals the ambitious nature of the case presented on behalf of Fitzherbert. Dayana Wright's 'Constructing Patriarchy: The Development of Interspousal Custody Law in England' examines the biological mother and biological father's competing claims to child custody. As Wright explains,

> Although the law of child custody eventually changed to reflect more closely the attitudes of domesticity and separate spheres, this did not occur at a time or in a manner that would allow us to identify a clear, linear relationship between the two. (253)

Focusing on a crucial precedent-setting decision in *De Manneville v. De Manneville* (1804), Wright positions the early nineteenth century as a time when the law re-asserts patriarchal familial rule as being more important than the best interests of the child.

Wright provides an in-depth analysis of the *De Manneville* case, which finds in favour of the father's right to control his children, no matter what his behaviour, against the claims of the mother. As she explains,

> Just when the courts were moving towards a more discretionary law that would accommodate the psychological and economic needs of all children, Mrs. De Manneville sued her husband, claiming an independent right to her child simply by virtue of her maternal tie [. . .] After *De Manneville*, the legal relationship of parent and child would be mediated through the legal relationship of the husband and wife. Judges would focus on the disruptive potential of interspousal custody disputes as the evil to be avoided, rather than on the good of settling custody under a meaningful welfare standard. Thus, as we see a shift from a property-based theory of custody to a best interests of the child theory slowly working itself out in the eighteenth century, the legal doctrine of coverture that defined the husband/wife relationship was superimposed onto the custody issue in ways that distorted, and preempted, a meaningful best interests analysis. (257–8)

Thus, the case defines child custody as an interspousal issue, not a child welfare issue. And, it becomes a precedent-setting case cited in child custody battles until child custody law is changed in 1839 with the Custody of Infants Act.

The *De Manneville* case tells a shocking tale that features a claim to custody that negates any consideration of the care of the child. The wealthy Mrs De Manneville is separated from her dissolute husband and has taken custody of their infant daughter. In 1804, as she sits breastfeeding her child, her husband forcibly enters the house, seizes the child and steals her away in an open carriage in bad weather. Mrs De Manneville seeks to regain custody of her child in the Court of King's Bench. She files a writ of habeas corpus, but is denied because, as Lord Ellenborough explains, 'a father was entitled by law to complete custody and control over the children of a marriage and could even prohibit all access by a mother to her children' (247). Mrs De Manneville turns to the Chancery Court, where Lord Eldon asserts that 'equity would not interfere with a father's right to custody unless the child had property and was in immediate danger of life and limb' (247). As Wright explains, 'The court at no time considered the interests of the child . . . although [Lord Eldon] mentioned the ill-usage Mrs De Manneville experiences, he made no reference to whether or not the child was a victim of similar treatment' (259). Similar to *Mansfield Park* and *Seymour v. Euston*, in the *De*

*Manneville* case the child's physical movement from person to person becomes the primary means of defining the child. Contradicting *De Manneville v. De Manneville*, *Seymour v. Euston* and *Mansfield Park* articulate a clear argument for the welfare of the child by emphasising the orphan's pressing need for care.

\*

The mother's independent claim to the guardianship of her biological child is not recognised until the passage of 1839 Custody of Infants Act. Over thirty years before the statutory recognition of the biological mother's familial role, *Seymour v. Euston* presents a *surrogate* mother's claim to custody by arguing for the welfare of the child. Audaciously, then, in 1803, a sensibility-based argument for child custody is being made on behalf of a person who could provide mother-*like* care. At a time when blood ties between mother and child were not worthy of legal protection, Fitzherbert's case argues that maternal love is essential to a child's well-being and that a non-biological mother figure can provide this love to an orphan. The boldness of this argument becomes even more apparent when it is realised that Fitzherbert is Catholic claiming that she is the best caregiver for a Protestant child. Fitzherbert marshals extraordinary evidence of her maternal care for the child, including depositions from three doctors, who argue that removing Minney from her care would be life-threatening to the child, and a deposition from the Prince of Wales, who supports her claim with his monetary promise.

As an alternative to the patriarchal power enshrined in testamentary guardianship, Fitzherbert's best interests argument emphasises the bond of sensibility created by maternal care. If the guardian/ward family is to be constructed on anything, her case asks, should it not be the emotional bond of mother and child? The case's State of Facts reproduces an early manuscript letter from Lady Horatia to Fitzherbert that states, 'I have written to Lady G. Seymour to tell her that little Minney is to be your Child – there never was any thing so kind & good as yourself' (*Seymour v. Euston* Court 13). Later, once Lady Horatia returns to England, Fitzherbert visits and 'offered to deliver up her charge'; Lady Horatia replies,

> Don't think I could be so unfeeling as to take her from you: it never was my intention you are more her mother than I now can be. No take her and do by her as you have done and rest assured that I shall never forget your kindness. (15)

In addition to submitting this State of Facts to the Master of Chancery, Fitzherbert submits manuscript Affidavits and Depositions that contain essentially the same material, although the language of sensibility is often added to the evidence in order to heighten its impact. For example, in the Affidavit dated 24 November 1804 this same conversation is described as:

> Lady Horatia (perceiving her emotion on the Idea of parting with the Child for which she this Deponent had then contracted a maternal affection) answered shedding tears dont think I could be so unfeeling as to take her from you. (7)

In structuring Fitzherbert's case, these documents implement a narrative strategy that moves from an economic account of the child's inheritance, to a general history of the child's familial situation, to a sensibility-driven claim to serve the child's best interests. As the legal narrative progresses, Fitzherbert assumes increasing maternal agency and explains that she considers Minney her 'adopted child' (16). Fitzherbert signifies her assumption of these maternal powers by giving a portrait of Minney to Lady Horatia, who, in turn, sends it to Lord Hugh; Lord Hugh never sees it due to his death, and the portrait is returned to Fitzherbert by Lord Euston's wife (16). The portrait's passage serves as a compelling symbol of the circulation of the child through her possible parents; the child in search of familial ownership is transferred through and out of the biological family, desired and claimed once again by the guardian. In the last pages of the State of Facts, Fitzherbert affixes the label of 'mother' to herself, describing that she:

> felt herself to be under an Obligation of the most solemn nature to discharge towards the Pl[ain]t[iff] to the utmost of her power all the Duties of a Mother to which she is now impelled by the Maternal Affection she bears towards the Pl[ain]t[iff] herself and she is therefore earnestly desirous to be permitted to continue the care and charge of the P[lain]t[iff]. (*Seymour v. Euston* Court 16)

Orphanhood enables contradictory constructions of maternity: is it at once duplicable and unique. The conversations and letters giving Fitzherbert custody of Minney attest to the transferability of motherhood and, yet, once maternal power has been assumed and practised, it creates emotional bonds that should never be broken – especially by the Court.

As these documents complete their definition of maternity, Fitzherbert powerfully connects the welfare of the child to Minney's physical health. In her State of Facts, she asserts that her sensibility empowers her to assess and meet the needs of an orphan who:

> is of a delicate constitution & her state of health is such as to require the most vigilant & unremitted care & observation. She is also of a very tender & affectionate disposition and having known no other mother that Mrs. Fitzherbert she is attached to her by as strong ties of affection as she could possibly have been to her natural Mother and there is every reason to apprehend that the separation of her from Mrs. Fitzherbert would deeply affect her mind and be attended with dangerous consequences. (*Seymour v. Euston* Court 17)

The doctors see this guardian/ward relationship as one of life and death. For example, William Fraser's Deposition of 24 November 1804 proclaims the 'fatal termination of the life of the said Infant can be avoided only by an uninterrupted series of the most vigilant attention by a person long accustomed to her' and that 'the Infant has continually experienced this kind of attention under the care of Mrs. Fitzherbert' (2). Fraser further attests to the 'great warmth of affection' between the two, noting the child's 'attachment' to her surrogate mother. Fraser makes explicit the connection between a delicacy of mind and body, explaining 'the Infants sensibility of mind [is] such that she could not bear to be separated from the said Mrs. Fitzherbert whom she . . . appears to love more than any person in the world' (2). Employing the language of sensibility, these documents evidence a larger cultural assumption that the family is an emotional structure in which parental love secures a child's health.

This application of the language of sensibility to the constructed mother/child relationship is repeated in the other physician's Depositions. On 20 November 1804 Gilbert Blanc explains that Minney 'possesses an uncommon degree of sensibility of mind and that she is attached by the warmest and tenderest affection to Maria Fitzherbert,' (1) and further argues that any 'seperation' of the two will 'endanger the life' of Minney, due to her 'peculiar frame . . . of mind and body' and her 'great natural sensibility' (2). Finally, on 24 November 1804, Sir Walter Farquhar connects the language of sensibility and maternity. Immediately after describing Minney as being 'full of sensibility,' he explains that 'the warm and parental attention shewn to her' by Fitzherbert was 'returned with a Love and Afection bordering on adoration' (2). He can only conclude that Minney would suffer a 'shock' if she were to be separated 'from one whom she loves as the fondest and most attached of Mothers' (2).

Although her case emphasises the bonds of sensibility as the foundation for the care of the orphan, Fitzherbert does not neglect to account for Minney's economic welfare. She explains that she:

> intends and is willing to undertake to continue to maintain and educate her in a manner suitable to her future fortune and expectations at her own expence in order that the whole Income of the Pl[ain]t[iff']s fortune may accumulate for her benefit. (*Seymour v. Euston* Court 16)

In addition, Fitzherbert plays a crucial role in securing the Prince Regent's £10,000 economic legacy for Minney, which contains an important stipulation:

> in case the pl[ain]t[iff] sho[ul]d be removed or taken from Maria Fitzherbert with whom she is therein stated to reside & under whose care she was placed by her dec[ease]d parents then the provision thereby made for her should not take effect. (10)

Because the Prince Regent's legacy resulted from a deathbed conversation with Minney's biological mother, the case argues, 'It may therefore be inferred that it was not merely the nurture of the Child during its earliest stage of Infancy that she meant to commit to Mrs. Fitzherbert but its future Guardianship or rather adoption' (16). Fitzherbert's guardianship enshrines the biological mother's dying wish, joins maternal care to royal favour, and uses the bonds of sensibility to combine emotional and economic care.

On 24 November 1804, the Prince himself offers a Deposition in support of Fitzherbert's maternal claims to Minney. He relates being summoned to Lady Horatia's deathbed, talking with her while the infant Minney sat on his knee, and reviewing Minney's guardian/ward history. The Prince recounts Lady Horatia's observation 'that Mrs. Fitzherbert must be more attached to the Child that she could be having hardly ever seen the Child and Mrs. Fitzherbert had had her constantly with her almost from her Birth.' He adds a dramatic conclusion to this conversation, explaining that Lady Horatia incorporates him into this guardianship family,

> I have something more Prince of Wales to say to you, recollect that it is the last request of a dying Mother and that is that you will take an Oath, and swear to me most solemnly, that you will be the Father and Protector through the life of this dear Child. (4)

The Prince interprets this as a confirmation of Fitzherbert's maternal role or 'wish that her said Daughter [. . .] should in the Event of her Death remain under the Care of Mrs. Fitzherbert' (5). The Prince's Deposition asserts the ideology of the best interests of the child; he wants Minney to 'remain in her present situation which [he] considers to be no less essential to her own Happiness and Welfare than to the fulfillment of the dying wish of her said Mother' (5).

*Seymour v. Euston* seems undeniable in its simplicity: Minney's best interests are best served by Fitzherbert. The proof supporting that claim is similarly clear; Fitzherbert can be read as arguing: I was given custody of Minney by her mother; I serve as Minney's mother; I have secured Minney's emotional, physical and economic well-being. Fitzherbert can even claim that the Prince Regent endorses her definition of the family as correct. However, Fitzherbert's argument is built on an assumption that the family is first and foremost an emotional structure – an assumption that is up for debate in the early nineteenth century. Furthermore, Fitzherbert assumes that the family is structured to serve the child and that maternal love is a legally recognised emotion. Clearly, Fitzherbert loves Minney as her own child, but love is an element of the family that is not recognised by guardianship law. It is only on appeal to the legislative branch of the House of Lords that love for the orphaned child is affirmed.

*

Which family is most concerned with 'welfare of child': the biological or the surrogate? Both the case and the novel are at pains to argue that the nuclear family should be equated with the best interests of the child, while presenting evidence to the contrary. In both, the biological family remains an ideal, while the guardian/ward family is operative. When in Chancery, *Seymour v. Euston* decided in favour of the biological bond, supporting the father's legal right to control his children through his last will. When at Mansfield Park, Fanny similarly privileges the biological family. But, after returning to Portsmouth, Fanny quickly realises that her biological family is more flawed than her surrogate family. The emotional best interests of Minney reside in the guardian/ward family; the same is true of Fanny and her surrogate family. For all that Fitzherbert creates a compelling image of surrogate maternal care, Chancery counters her arguments by following the testamentary orders of the deceased father. The claims of Fitzherbert, a non-kin mother-figure, are dismissed until re-evaluated by the House of Lords. Similarly, *Mansfield Park* not only dramatises but furthers the father-figure's control of his family: Sir Thomas's patriarchal power is recognised by Fanny and that recognition is rewarded by Sir Thomas. Austen's construction of the Bertram family furthers this legal definition of the family.

Sir Thomas's patriarchal power has been well charted by critics. Lionel Trilling famously calls Fanny 'the daughter of Sir Thomas's stern heart' and argues that although his faults are easily catalogued, 'Of all the fathers of Jane Austen's novels, Sir Thomas is the only one to whom admiration is given' (137). This understanding of Sir Thomas as a conservative protector of family order is echoed in later criticism, such as David Kaufmann's statement that Sir Thomas is 'the hierarchical, patriarchal head of the family, who, by his very presence, sets things aright' (221). More recently, following Edward Said's well known critique, Sir Thomas's patriarchal powers have come under heavy fire due to their colonialist source. For example, Susan Fraimen argues,

> [I]t seems all-too-obvious that in Mansfield Park, slavery functions . . . not as a subtext wherein Austen and Sir Thomas converge but, on the contrary, as a trope Austen introduced to argue the essential depravity of Sir Thomas's relationship to other people. (813)

For all that this patriarchal power is 'depraved,' a sympathetic reading of Sir Thomas's power comes not from Austen or the reader, but from Fanny herself. In his evolving relationship with Fanny, Sir Thomas asserts patriarchal power that would have been legally recognised, but he also increasingly uses it to create an affective bond with Fanny – and Fanny appreciates Sir Thomas's newly emotional definition of the family.

The second volume of *Mansfield Park* signals a sharp change in Fanny's familial status and explores whether the orphan should be placed at periphery or centre of the family. Because Fanny recognises the 'best interests' of the family in her rejection of the *Lovers' Vows* theatricals, her 'best interests' are considered and she is accepted into the family. With his unexpected return from Antigua and his re-entrance into the family, Sir Thomas brings with him a new affective family philosophy in which he envisions the family as all-inclusive emotional structure that emphasises care. He defines the family as a 'circle' that includes Fanny (161); he expresses a new 'kind'-ness and 'tenderness' towards Fanny (159–60). Fanny's decision to not participate in the play is recognised; and Sir Thomas sees Fanny's moral centrality to the family after Edmund offers his praise:

> Fanny is the only one who has judged rightly throughout, who has been constant. Her feelings have been steadily against it from first to last. She never ceased to think what was due to you. You will find Fanny every thing you could wish. (168–9)

Shockingly, the orphan proves to be the member of the family most deserving of respect and affection. Fanny's acceptance of her 'no place' in the *Lovers' Vows* scenes secures her a place in the family; as Edmund explains, 'your uncle never did admire you till now – and now he does' (178). Fanny moves from being unwanted to being 'indeed the daughter he wanted' (431).

When Maria and Julia leave home, and later become embroiled in scandal, Fanny becomes a desired source of stability. Although this occurs through the principle of substitution – 'Fanny's consequence increased on the departure of her cousins' (184) – Fanny takes the place of the daughter. Ultimately, due to Sir Thomas's acceptance, the substitute daughter achieves familial and social status greater than the biological daughters. The earlier neglect of Fanny is replaced with an active seeking of her presence:

> [T]he only young woman in the drawing room, the only occupier of that interesting division of a family in which she had hitherto held so humble a third, it was impossible for her not to be more looked at, more thought of and attended to, than she had ever been before; and 'where is Fanny?' became no uncommon question, even without her being wanted for any one's convenience. (184)

Fanny's value as a daughter-figure is overtly acknowledged, such as when Lady Bertram observes, 'I am very glad we took Fanny as we did, for now the others are away, we feel the good of it.' Importantly, Sir Thomas sanctions this emotional definition of their relationship by stating, '[S]he is now a very valuable companion. If we have been kind to *her*, she is now quite as necessary to *us*' (259).

Fanny's new centrality to the family is perhaps best depicted in scenes detailing her hosting the first ball held at Mansfield Park. Fanny understands that her new social standing is an extension of her new familial standing, 'She could hardly believe it. To be placed above so many elegant young women! The distinction was too great. It was treating her like her cousins!' (250). As she prepares for the ball, Fanny receives a necklace from Henry Crawford, transmitted by his sister Mary, and a necklace from Edmund. Unexpectedly, she has received an excess of attention, and she must choose which chain to thread through a cross pendant given to her by her brother William. Although she feels obliged to recognise Henry and Mary's attention and wear that chain, she is relieved that Edmund's chain is the only one that fits through her pendant. Her biological and surrogate families are united; she can connect her two family structures and place herself at their centre. At the ball, she wears both chains, plus the cross. Her neck is encircled with symbols of her desirability.

At the opening of volume 3, Fanny chooses to exercise her newfound power against Sir Thomas, denying him one of his most important guardianship powers. Fanny refuses Henry's marriage proposal, a proposal that Sir Thomas approves of on economic grounds: 'Here is a young man wishing to pay his addresses to you, with everything to recommend him; not merely situation in life, fortune, and character, but with more that common agreeableness, with address and conversation pleasing to every body' (285). Sir Thomas reminds her of the failings of her biological family, 'The advantage or disadvantage of your family – of your parents – your brothers and sisters – never seems to have had a moment's share in your thoughts on this occasion' (288). He ends his lecture by calling attention to the fact that she is not his child, but that he hoped she would have acted as such. 'You do not owe me the duty of a child', he says, implying that she, as his ward, does. (289). Fanny decides that she must construct her family – both her present and her future family – on her own emotional terms. Knowing that her moral reading of Henry and his illicit relationship with Maria Bertram must be correct, Fanny chooses to reject her guardian/ward family rather than tacitly accept and perhaps perpetuate its corrupt emotional practices. She can only hope that Sir Thomas will come to feel, as she does, 'how wretched, and how unpardonable, how hopeless and how wicked it was, to marry without affection' (293). By rejecting Henry's proposal and Sir Thomas's pressure, she affirms the possibility of an emotional restructuring of the patriarchal family.

Fanny is sent to her biological family in Portsmouth, a return that is both an extension of her guardian's power and an assertion of her own. Sir Thomas conceives of the 'scheme' (335) in an attempt to remind Fanny of the superiority of her surrogate family:

> He certainly wished her to be heartily sick of home before her visit ended; and that a little abstinence from the elegancies and luxuries of Mansfield Park, would bring her mind into a sober state, and incline her to a juster estimate of the value of that home of greater permanence, and equal comfort, of which she had the offer. (335)

In contrast, Fanny imagines herself as finally achieving a truly central place in the family, rather than being a mere substitute placed in a surrogate space. The prospect of returning home encourages Fanny to feel the most intense emotions she has yet experienced,

> The remembrance of all her earliest pleasures, and of what she had suffered in being torn from them, came over her with renewed strength, and it seemed as if to be home again, would heal every pain that had since grown out of separation. To be in the centre of a circle, loved by so many, and more loved by all than she had ever been before, to feel affection without fear or restraint, to feel herself the equal of those who surrounded her . . . This was a prospect to be dwelt on with a fondness that could be but half acknowledged. (336)

She compares the judgemental reproach of the guardian/ward family with the undemanding love of the biological family.

If the novel is seen as, in part, a meditation on the meaning of the family, this comparison between the surrogate and biological is essential. Importantly, Austen empowers her heroine to make that comparison. The Portsmouth section asserts the orphan's ability to judge the family and her position within it. However, Fanny's image of a loving circle secured by biology proves to be an expression of idealised sensibility. Fanny's return is described in the terms of a physical assault: 'Fanny was almost stunned' (347). The smallness of house can barely contain the large family's overwhelming activity, and Fanny cannot help but think, 'It was the abode of noise, disorder, and impropriety. No body was in their right place, nothing was done as it ought to be. She could not respect her parents' (354). Fanny compares the Price household's chaos to Mansfield Park's control:

Yet she thought it would not have been so at Mansfield. No, in her uncle's house there would have been a consideration of times and seasons, a regulation of subject, a propriety, an attention towards everyone which there was not here. (348)

Her one requirement, 'Would they but love her, she should be satisfied', is pointedly left unsatisfied (343). Even Fanny's 'every feeling of duty, honour, and tenderness' are left 'wounded' by her mother's and sisters' words and actions (352). Fanny quickly realises that her expectations for familial care will be left unmet, 'Before the week ended, it was all disappointment' (353). Her biological family neglects to love her, much as her guardianship family has. Rather than occupy the centre of her biological family, Fanny inhabits, once again, a familial 'no place'.

Fanny's return to the biological family allows Austen to highlight its absence of emotional bonds, the very bonds that the surrogate family also lacked but was able to develop. With the return to Portsmouth, Austen forces Fanny to ask, 'What is the basis of the family?' Biology does not secure the emotional bonds that will, in turn, secure care for the best interests of the child. The guardianship family, with its emphasis on custody rather than care, does not seem to serve the best interests of child either. Neither family is perfect, neither family meets Fanny's expectations, and neither family places the welfare of its children as its first consideration. Fanny has set a care-focused standard for what a 'good' family is, and the family should be changed to meet those demands rather than Fanny revising her standards. When forced to choose the family that best meets her needs, Fanny chooses the guardian/ward relationship as the one that best serves the orphaned child.

Both *Mansfield Park* and *Seymour v. Euston* argue for a more careful consideration of the best interests of the child, but both define what is best for the child by noticing its absence. By arguing for the careful attention to the child's welfare, both position the orphan at the centre of the family – but, revealingly, this argument is made by noticing the child's peripheral position. The novel and the case are united in making an argument that in the family – perhaps most pressingly in the guardian/ward family – the child's welfare should be monitored, protected and used to define the family itself. Both use the surrogate family to construct an idealised family in which the orphan occupies the centre, valued by a mother-figure or father-figure. The orphan's imperfect family experiences provide evidence for the need to reconstruct family meaning. Both *Mansfield Park* and *Seymour v. Euston* reconstruct the family according to a seemingly obvious principle that is not obvious to early nineteenth-century law: all families should be structured around the loving care of a child.

## Works Cited

Abramowicz, Sarah. 'English Child Custody Law 1660–1839: The Origins of Judicial Intervention in Paternal Custody'. *Columbia Law Review*, vol. 99, no. 5, June 1999, pp. 1344–92.

Austen, Jane. *Mansfield Park*. [1814]. Oxford University Press, 2003.

Cleere, Eileen. 'Reinvesting Nieces: *Mansfield Park* and the Economics of Endogamy'. *Novel: A Forum on Fiction*, vol. 28, no. 2, Winter 1995, pp. 113–30.

Cohen, Paula Marantz. 'Stabilizing the Family System at Mansfield Park'. *ELH*, vol. 54, no.3, Autumn 1987, pp. 669–93.

Fraimen, Susan. 'Jane Austen and Edward Said: Gender, Culture, and Imperialism'. *Critical Inquiry*, vol. 21, no.4, Summer 1995, pp. 805–21.

Grossberg, Michael. *Governing the Hearth: Law and Family in Nineteenth-Century America*. University of North Carolina Press, 1988.

Johnson, Claudia L. *Women, Politics, and the Novel*. University of Chicago Press, 1988.

Kaufmann, David. 'Closure in *Mansfield Park* and the Sanctity of the Family.' *Philological Quarterly*, vol. 65, no.2, Spring 1986, pp. 211–29.

Said, Edward. *Culture and Imperialism*. Penguin Vintage, 1994.

*Seymour v. Euston*. Court of Chancery: Manuscript Case Documents. The National Archives, Kew. C 13/83/7.

*Seymour v. Euston. Journals of the House of Lords*, Vol. XLV. His Majesty's Stationery Office, 1805–6.

Smith, Johanna M. 'My Only Sister Now: Incest in *Mansfield Park*'. *Studies in the Novel*, vol. 19, no.1, Spring 1987, pp. 1–15.

Trilling, Lionel. 'Mansfield Park', in *Jane Austen: A Collection of Critical Essays*, ed. Ian Watt. Prentice Hall, 1963, pp. 124–40.

Wright, Danaya C. 'De Manneville v. De Manneville: Rethinking the Birth of Custody Law under Patriarchy'. *Law and History Review*, vol. 17, no. 2, 1999, pp. 247–307.

Yeazell, Ruth B. 'The Boundaries of *Mansfield Park*'. *Representations*, vol. 7, Spring 1984, pp. 133–52.

Chapter 2

# Orphanhoods and Bereavements in the Life and Verse of Charlotte Smith Richardson (1775–1825)

*Kevin Binfield*

*Poems Written on Different Occasions* (1806), the first volume published by Charlotte (née Smith) Richardson of York (1775–1825), is the poet's subjective record of losses, lamentations and attempts at self-consolation; her second volume, *Poems Chiefly Composed During the Pressure of Severe Illness* (1809), continues many of the themes of bereavement while marking Richardson's expanding social sphere and perspective.[1] Both volumes, supplemented by archival materials, afford a chance to consider the ways in which sustained and repeated bereavement may be understood not only as a material status but also as an affective and social process, a moral standpoint and a trope constructed within a larger series of losses that in Richardson's case includes bastardy, orphanhood, widowhood and parental bereavement. Far from jealously guarding her bereavement and distinguishing her own case as unique, Richardson developed bereavement as a lens through which she viewed others, seeing in them, as in herself, bereavements that were actual, feared and conjectured. Her social impulses, in both text and action, may have been inspired by the various York charitable institutions from which she benefited; but, in Richardson's case, the institutions did not erode or erase her individual identity – a danger that Cheryl L. Nixon sees in charitable institutions created for poor orphans in particular (Nixon 40). Rather, read alongside the totality of print and manuscript records of Richardson's life (many from York charitable institutions), her writings demonstrate her navigation of social relations, her increasing civic engagement beyond expected spheres, and, eventually, her redefinition of her own orphanhood through her adult actions.

\*

Richardson's entry into the world was defined for current and later readers by her self-appointed 'editor', Catherine Cappe (1744–1821). In her preface to Richardson's first volume, Cappe writes, 'Charlotte Smith was born in the year 1775, under circumstances the most unfavourable' (vii). Cappe was widely regarded for her activity in York charities, including the Grey Coat Girls School, the York Dispensary and the York Female Friendly Society.[2] Cappe's 1806 and 1809 prefaces, and the biographical sketches of Richardson therein, provide useful glosses on several of the poems in the volumes but leave a fair number of gaps, wrought in part by Cappe's construction of Richardson as meditating piously on adversity while depending upon religion and active charity to set her on a path towards stability, health and usefulness. To fill those gaps, I consider Richardson's volumes alongside pertinent archival and print records.

Smith was born on 5 March 1775 in the parish of All Saints, Pavement, in York. Neither the baptismal register entry for Charlotte, nor the one for her brother John, christened 18 November 1776, lists a father, although surrounding entries identify other children of single mothers as 'bastards' (York, All Saints, PR/Y/ASP 1). Later, however, both Charlotte and John were listed as bastards. In both cases, bastardy, though absent from early records, accompanied them through their lives.[3] Richardson remained largely silent on the absence of a father, breaking that silence only a few times. In a poem addressing a query by her friend, Mary Smith, into her orphaned state, Richardson writes, 'A tender father's care I never knew, / One only parent blest my early years', although 'memory whispers – They are in the grave' ('To M. Smith. The Inquiry', *Occasions* 27). Her entry in the Admission Register of the York Female Friendly Society (a benefits society established for girls who went into service after training in the Grey Coat Girls School), however, lists as parents 'Wm & Hannah Smith Peter the Little York' (YFF/1/1, p. 3). The 30 March 1804 baptismal entry for her son, Robert Harling Richardson, identifies Richardson as 'Charlotte Daur of William & Hannah Smith' (York, St Michael, PR/Y/MB 7). The question of Richardson's bastardy is important for several reasons, including her apparent attempt to construct a parentage, the motives for which are not difficult to imagine. As Cappe's writings make clear, respectability and reputation mattered for the poor women who were the focus of Cappe's concern. Richardson's poetry also indicates the great care she took with her character.

Cappe describes the salutary effects of a Sunday school education upon Smith ('Preface', *Occasions* vii), but little else is known about her childhood apart from sparse accounts of her activities in the Grey Coat School Minute Books. Smith's admission to the School in 1787 provides evidence of the family's poverty (York Charity Schools, pp. 206 and 214). She entered the school during a period of transition, when a group of women, led by Cappe, assumed its management to address problems caused by girls leaving the school to go into service without the moral and social skills necessary to avoid dangers faced by young women in service, especially with regard to the conduct of male employers and the need to guard their character so as to remain employable.

Smith left the School in July 1790 for service in the family of Charles Pinder, a shoemaker in Jubbergate (YFF, *Admissions*, YFF/1/1, p. 3). The death of Smith's mother in November 1790 compounded problems that she encountered in her first few positions. The first two poems of the 1806 volume contemplate the mother's moral influence on the daughter through difficult circumstances, and several of the poems composed prior to her marriage reflect her awareness of moral danger as an unmarried orphan.

On 31 October 1802, Smith left service to marry Robert Richardson, a cordwainer, (York, St Mary, PR Y/M Bp. S. 10) and move with him into College Street in the parish of St Michael-Le-Belfrey. Soon after Richardson's recovery from a serious illness, her husband manifested symptoms of consumption (Cappe, 'Preface', *Occasions* xv.). Their son, Robert Harling Richardson, was born on 29 March 1804, but Richardson's husband died shortly after, in June 1804 (York, St Michael, PR Y/MB 7).

*

Cappe visited Richardson during her husband's final illness and later during her son's illness. During the latter visit Cappe 'became acquainted with the poetical talents of the Author', having read 'He Sleeps', Richardson's meditation upon her husband's death. Cappe was 'struck by the piety of the sentiments' and 'affected by the pathos with which they are expressed'.[4] Discovering that Richardson had filled a volume of manuscript poems over several years, Cappe conceived an idea to publish a selection of the poems via subscription to raise funds sufficient to enable Richardson to open a school for her and her son's 'joint support' ('Preface', *Occasions* xvi–xvii, xix).

Cappe advertised the subscription in national periodicals, describing Richardson's circumstances and providing samples of her verse: nearly 900 persons subscribed.

*Poems Written on Different Occasions* comprises pieces that Richardson had written between 1790 and 1805. The chronological arrangement and Richardson's clear indication of periods of composition make it possible to link Richardson's intellectual and emotional states to events in her life. The volume begins with orphanhood. 'Elegy on the Death of a Tender Indulgent Mother, Who Quitted a World of Sin and Sorrow, on Friday, November 5, 1790' consists of nine quatrains, each in the common measure, lamenting the death of Hannah Smith. An unidentified speaker frames the poem and sets the scene in the first and final quatrains, while the intermediate seven quatrains are spoken by 'Sad Lucy', taking her way by night through the churchyard. Lucy speaks to herself:

> 'Ah! hapless maid,' she wept and cried,
> 'Of friends thou art bereft;
> 'Soon as thy tender parent died,
> 'An Orphan thou wert left'. (ll. 5–8)

The third quatrain, in Lucy's own voice recalls the scene of her mother's death, providing in turn another frame for the next three quatrains, in which Lucy quotes her mother's dying words. As the mother bids her children 'Adieu', she foresees the hardships that they are likely to endure but implores them to remain firm in their virtues: '"Should fortune prove to you severe, / "Still, let your ways be true"' (ll. 15–16). The central quatrain of the poem is the mother's recommendation that her children place all their confidence in God, making his word their guide, as he will protect their innocence and provide for their wants (ll. 17–20). The mother's final words, in the next quatrain, foresee the family's being reunited in heaven, using a trope of completion to describe death: '"My happiness will be complete – / "We ne'er shall part again!"' (ll. 23–4). The two succeeding quatrains are in Lucy's voice again. The penultimate quatrain may be read as Lucy's return to the full measure of grief prior to returning home:

> 'For ever will my streaming eyes,
> 'With ceaseless tears o'erflow
> 'All worldly pleasure I despise,
> 'My heart is fill'd with woe'. (ll. 29–32)

Richardson's choice to have her own thoughts and words spoken by a persona, 'Sad Lucy', might be read as Richardson's availing herself of the persona (in this case, a doubling and layering of voices) as a poetical device to denote a bereavement and alienation so intense that she is lost even to herself. Overall, the poem is balanced among speakers and subjects, with a pivotal point in the middle quatrain – a pious redirection which the mother offers but which Lucy fails fully to embrace.

The poem sets the stage for Richardson's contemplations on bereavement over the next several years. In the fourth poem in the volume, 'Prayer for Safety and Protection', the mother's injunction has been embraced and acted upon, as 'The Author', according to Cappe's footnote, 'was at this time in her 19th year, and was thrown amongst associates whose example and conversation were in every respect low, corrupt, and ruinous' (Cappe, *Occasions* 15, fn). In 'Prayer', the author, in unqualified first person, utters to God a prayer that echoes the mother's language in the earlier poem, imploring God to 'write thy laws within my heart, / And plant thy statutes there' (ll. 11–12).

The second poem in the 1806 volume, 'The Orphan's Prayer, When Distressed by Great Unkindness in the Year 1792', takes up the injunction spoken by the mother in the 'Elegy'.[5] That injunction, to place confidence in God and to base her behaviour and ground her hopes on God's word, takes the form of narrative, request and speculation on a future state, before concluding with an imperative, directed to God, to 'Remember then the Orphan's prayer'. Composed prior to the more famous 1800 song of the same title, *The Orphan's Prayer: A Pathetic Ballad*, with words by M. G. ('Monk') Lewis and music set by Harriet Abrams, the poem anticipates the song's condemnation of the brutality of society's ignoring an orphan's pleas. The orphaned speaker-poet expresses her disappointment in 'worldly friends' (l. 1), their 'unkindness' (l. 8), her friendlessness and poverty (l. 9), and her being 'by the proud and wealthy scorn'd' (l. 10). That which is 'worldly' (l. 1) or 'earthly' (ll. 13 and 20) merits no reliance as they 'frown' (l. 1) or 'fade and die' (l. 13); Richardson seeks rather to place all her reliance on God as 'Father' (l. 3) and 'faithful friend' (l. 16).

Whereas in the 'Elegy' Lucy is frozen in helpless bereavement, in 'The Orphan's Prayer' Richardson claims her own agency to a limited degree by imploring God to follow through on his commitment to her ('Remember then the Orphan's prayer'), following much the same trajectory as described by the dying mother in the 'Elegy'. Stylistically, 'The Orphan's Prayer' builds upon and moves a step beyond the 'Elegy'. Written in octosyllabic sexains, the poem joins the common measure found in the 'Elegy' with couplets that conclude each sexain. Epistrophe – in this case, the conclusion of each sexain with the words 'the Orphan's prayer' – combines with the sexain structure to convey not only an insistence on Richardson's part but also glimpses of the beginnings of her own moral agency.

The fifth poem in the 1806 volume, 'Elegy on the Death of an Only and Beloved Brother' (1799), written in elegiac stanzas, is more formal in tone and expansive in structure than the preceding poems. Richardson, now bereft entirely of family, does not fall back upon the traditional consolations recommended by her mother, and she is completely abandoned by her previous sense of moral agency manifested in the final imperative line of 'The Orphan's Prayer'; rather, she imagines her deceased brother's soul as an efficacious agent, an angel acting as guide in place of a distant God:

> O, best of brothers, from thy blest abode
>     Still view thy sister with an angel's love!
> Direct and guide her in the ways of God,
>     That she may meet thee in the realms above!
> In that dread hour, when earthly joys shall fade,
>     When I, th' appointed course of life have trod,
> Guide me, blest spirit! through Death's awful shade,
>     Then waft my soul to heaven, to meet my God! (ll. 37–44)

The poems composed between the death of her brother in 1799 and her marriage in 1802 show Richardson's struggle to find comfort, guidance and support. In the majority, she apostrophises either God or, more abstractedly, 'Religion'. In several poems, such as the elegy on her brother, 'Religion' is personified and addressed in the second person; often, God is set at a distance in third person. At this point, her ambivalence about God's distance parallels her doubts about her personal agency. Her adversities often lead her to abrogate her own personal agency; any possibility of her agency is left to a conditional future. We see such a gesture in 'On My Recovery from Sudden Illness, Nov. 13, 1800': 'O while I shall my life enjoy, / Grant that I may that life employ, / In works of righteousness' (ll. 13–15). In the poem, a brief glimpse of a contingent personal agency ('while I shall my life enjoy') yields quickly to a passive receptivity: 'Give me my sinful state to see, / And draw me nearer still to thee, / And fill my soul with peace!' (ll. 16–18). Even 'Death' is personified as acting upon her 'with friendly hand' (l. 20).

The theme of feeling contingent and unmoored continues in 'To M. Smith. The Inquiry' (also composed in 1800), which recollects Charlotte's response to Mary Smith – herself an orphan, a schoolmate from the Grey Coat School, and, it proved, a lifelong friend – who had earlier enquired, 'Where do your parents dwell?' (l. 1). The poem, the first in the volume addressed to a living person, describes Charlotte's utter bereavement and the concomitant difficulty to assume her own agency. Like the 'Elegy' on her mother, 'Inquiry' incorporates a frame that allows the poet to speak at length upon her orphanhood. The elegiac stanzas move from Mary's question to Charlotte's tearful response, 'I have no parents . . . Nor am I, by the ties of blood allied / To one kind being in this world below' (ll. 5–8). The third stanza demonstrates the ambivalence of her early years, continuing a frequent theme of the subsuming or consuming of one state of being by its opposite:

A tender father's care I never knew,
One only parent blest my early years;
Beneath a mother's fost'ring shade I grew
From infancy to youth – devoid of tears. (ll. 9–12)

After another stanza that amplifies her childhood bliss despite the absence of a father and another stanza of adult moralising upon the 'phantom' character of childhood bliss, Richardson's oppositional formula takes on an almost volta-like character as her tale moves towards her mother's illness and death: 'And into sorrow turn'd my happiness' (l. 24). Yet, 'One tender tie remain'd – a brother dear' (l. 33). Despite his lot of 'Chill penury and sickness', his patient, pious resignation allowed him to forget 'all his wants and sorrows . . . For love divine sustain'd his youthful mind' (ll. 39–40).

At this point, in a movement similar to the return to a framing speaker in 'Elegy', the poet returns to Mary, and we are reminded that the poem is revisiting a conversation:

– Forgive these tears, my Mary, – you have known
Those agonizing pangs that pierce the heart;
You too have wept o'er a lov'd parent's tomb,
And felt what 'tis from those we love to part. (ll. 45–8)

Despite this evident sympathy and what could otherwise have been rendered as an alliance forged from shared grief, Richardson fails to embrace the social moment; rather, she stands alone in a bleak and contingent 'Now', incapable of agency or connection:

> – Now, on the world's bleak waste, I stand alone,
> An unprotected orphan I am left;
> To me, the names of kindred are unknown,
> Of each endearing comfort, I'm bereft! (ll. 49–52)

I am tempted to read in these two stanzas the victory of a social system that valorised family over all else; however, when I consider the material realities of Charlotte Smith and Mary Smith, both orphaned young women in domestic service, I must understand the helplessness and alienation that Charlotte Smith clearly was feeling. Cappe's footnote describes Smith's circumstances during this period: 'The Writer was at this time unkindly treated by her Mistress, and not having any home, or a relation in the world to assist her, found her spirits unusually depressed' (*Occasions* 24, fn). Smith's consolation, as in earlier and later poems, is a supplanting of familial sources of guidance and joy (a dead mother and brother) by an abstracted 'heavenly Father', who 'Will not, without a cause, his children grieve, / His promises support and cheer my mind, / And countless mercies I from him receive!' (ll. 57–60). The theme of the supplanting divine father expands in later poems in the volume to fulfil the roles of family and friends (see, for example, 'Written under Great Doubt, and Anxiety of Mind, 1801', p. 39, l. 12, and 'To an Acquaintance, on Her Marriage – Accompanied by a Small Present, 1802', p. 47, ll. 23–4), although Richardson's ambivalence often shows through.

Even at this early point, Richardson's ideal of divine protection interweaves with an awareness of the role played by charitable institutions. Two poems celebrate institutions – 'Ode Addressed to the Grey Coat School; The former scene of my happiest days' and 'Ode on Visiting The Retreat, Near York; A House erected by the Society of Friends, for the reception of Insane Persons'. The first combines nostalgia and benediction:

> Blest be the spot, where Charity presides,
> Where Pity, for the Orphans' wants provides,
> And gently strives to cheer the drooping mind
> Of those who erst in want and mis'ry pin'd . . . (ll. 1–4)

Oddly, I think, but perhaps in keeping with her propensity for treating social and moral entities not as persons or groups but as abstracted personifications, Richardson downplays the paedeutic character of the poem. In fact, she refers to human agents in only three lines – in blessing the 'gen'rous souls' (l. 41), addressing the 'Dear honour'd Guardians of my infancy' (l. 48), and blessing 'the generous Founders of the Grey Coat School' (l. 60). Only 'Guardians' could be read as referring to her teachers; her greatest praise and her benediction are reserved for those 'Founders' whose charity made the School possible.

The Grey Coat School offered a 'tranquil, calm retreat' (l. 29), protection for 'white rob'd Innocence' (l. 35), and a place for fostering dispositions essential for a girl intended for domestic service – 'Mild, unassuming Modesty, / Content and smiling Industry' (ll. 37–8). But the School also offered a setting where:

The kindred Virtues love to meet,
(Religion leads the train)
And listens to the Orphan's song,
Whilst Echo doth the notes prolong . . . (ll. 30–3)

The 'Echo' is best understood as the similar songs of other orphans (such as Mary Smith) admitted to the School. The 'Echo' eventually resounded in solidarity among a number of the girls into their later lives, as the records of another institution, the York Female Friendly Society, suggest. And, as we shall see, 'kindred Virtues' enacted by women on behalf of girls is echoed later in Richardson's poem on female charity coming to the aid of Margaret Russell, the orphaned 'Tawny Girl'. The generally positive tone of this irregular ode resounds in the alexandrines that conclude all stanzas but one and orientate all that came before in those stanzas towards piety, praise and benediction.

Poems composed from 1802 to 1804 reveal a period of joy in Richardson's life, marked by her marriage to Robert Richardson. Those joys recast her fears and sorrows. During her own dangerous illness, Richardson expresses fears for her husband's bereavement but shifts from identifying God as her all-in-all (as she had, in 'Invitation to the Sacrament', [58, l. 48]) towards seeing her husband in that role. In 'Addressed during my own Severe Illness, to the Kindest of Husbands', composed in elegiac stanzas, she offers to him, a prospective widower, the consolation of the end of her pains (l. 9) and a vision of her 'increasing joy' in Heaven (l. 14). She concludes with a new version of completeness. Just as in her pious yet whimsical 'Valentine. To R. R. Written Extempore, Feb. 14, 1802' (44–5), here her husband supplants God in the role of family and friend: 'In thee the lover and the friend combine' (l. 27).

After 1804, as Robert slowly succumbed to consumption, Richardson's poems express her fears over a new bereavement, shifting after his death into elegies and meditations upon widowhood. 'After the Death of my Dear Husband, 1804' employs language similar to her meditations upon orphanhood. The poem begins, 'Bereft of all I lov'd below' (l. 1), continues with diction of joys overturned and a desire for 'Calm resignation' (l. 26) and 'meek submission' (l. 29), and ends with a prayer for 'needful aid' (l. 37). On occasion, Richardson reached beyond general literary forms (such as elegy) and sought specific literary models for expressing her grief. For example, her poem 'The Widow' takes as its inspiration James Montgomery's poem of the same name. 'The Widow' employs Richardson's customary personifications and abstractions in depicting the grief of the new widow and young mother, but the infant is a new, real actor in the scene of despair. He feels what the mother feels without understanding the reasons, and, with his cries, 'Bids each maternal feeling rise' (l. 52). The next few lines hint at the emergence of a new social model for Richardson in dealing with her bereavements. Her social (in this case, maternal) obligations to comfort her child comfort her in turn:

> In him she sooths her wounded mind,
> She feels her grief's excess reprov'd,
> Views the sweet pledge still left behind,
> The image of the saint she lov'd.
> Though of her dearest hopes bereft,
> Yet, thankful for the treasure left,
> She bends to Heav'n with gratitude sincere,
> And learns to trust, be patient, and revere. – (ll. 53–60)

Although her later verse does not always continue this moral vision of herself as mother (her later anxieties at times recast motherhood in terms of worry), in this poem, the maternal plays the most active and powerful role. Whereas earlier Richardson had described God as 'a faithful Friend, / A Father, and a Guide' ('To an Acquaintance', p. 47, ll. 23–4), here 'Religion' in a maternal role comforts Richardson and teaches her patience in and reverence for a distant, entirely non-parental God:

> She points her to yon realms above
> Where dwells the spirit of her love,
> Instructs her how to bear the chast'ning rod,
> And in Affliction's furnace, glorify her God. (ll. 63–8)

Most of the poems in the 1806 volume (and some in the 1809) are fraught with Christian piety or consolation, some even to the point of objectionability, yet Richardson's editor clearly approved. 'Prayer for my Afflicted Child, July 1805', for example, begins by invoking God's aid for her ailing son. The verse form is ambitious, combining into each eight-line stanza one hymnal measure (quatrain rhyming *abab*) with what is either two tetrameter couplets or a quatrain rhymed *ccdd* in tetrameter. The effect of the first half of the stanza is a sense of wavering; the second half of each stanza gestures towards resignation with the removal of some measure of uncertainty. The fourth stanza careens uncomfortably towards resigned acceptance of an unspeakable 'Thy will be done':

> But if, (for well thou knowst, O Lord)
>     His future life would be,
> Such as by thee would be abhorr'd,
>     A life of infamy:
> If he thy sacred laws would slight,
> And in the part of vice delight,
> O save him from this dreadful doom,
> And snatch him from the ills to come! (ll. 25–32)[6]

The last couplet in each stanza drives to a finality in both form and content; this stanza offers no exception. The resignation of a widow faced with her son's illness, his medical expenses and no income to pay for his treatment must be understood in the context of helplessness, solitude, poverty and the prospect of the workhouse, just as the situations of Mary Smith and Charlotte Smith discussed above must be understood materially.

For a time, Richardson created elegiac verses intended to temper joy (which she treats as an earthly attachment) and evoke pre-emptive grief and resignation in others. Following 'Prayer for my Afflicted Child,' Richardson addresses a poem 'To Mrs. P\_\_\_\_, North Street'. Writing in elegiac stanzas, she describes in general terms the newly married addressee's 'happy state' and 'felicity', and recalls her own 'past images of bliss'. The tension between the expectations for future bliss felt by Richardson early in her marriage and the underlying reality suggested by the elegiac stanzas presages an end to Mrs. P\_\_\_\_\_'s 'happy state':

> You too, my Anna, when your sand is run,
>     Must quit the object of your tend'rest love,
> Or else with tears bedew a husband's urn,
>     And all a widow'd mother's anguish prove.
> If such your lot, O may that gracious God
>     Who makes the Widow his peculiar care,
> Support you under his chastising rod,
>     Until the perfect joys of Heav'n you share. (ll. 25–32)

But such were the models of consolation available to her. Christian meditations, such as those of Elizabeth Singer Rowe, taught such perspectives: 'With a holy contempt let me survey the ample round of creation . . . ' (Rowe 17). Richardson, orphaned, widowed and plagued by illness, sought, through poetical and moral inversions, divine purposes for such adversity – 'chastisement'. We should see in such poems Richardson's attempts to bridge the space between herself and others. She sees in Anna P. the same prospects and the same possible disappointments as she had experienced; similarly, in 'To my Infant Asleep', she sees in her son 'Sorrow's child' (l. 13), echoing her earlier self-description as 'child of sorrow'.

\*

The funds raised from the 1806 volume (which went into two editions) enabled Richardson to open a small school in College Street. By 1808, she was suffering from a debilitating abscess, which forced her to close the school and threatened her life (Cappe, 'Preface,' *Illness* iii). Again, a subscription was advertised and superintended by Cappe beginning in the summer of 1808. As Richardson was near death, the original aim of the subscription was to provide for what her friends believed would be her orphaned son (Cappe, 'Letter', pp. 217–18). The 1809 volume (which also went into two editions), raised a sum sufficient to carry Richardson through her illness and recovery and to re-open her school. Like the 1806 volume, it contains elegies and contemplations on her orphaned and bereaved state, but a shift in Richardson's perspective is discernible, as the poems in the 1809 volume are more varied and engage social, moral and psychological spheres beyond the constrained subject positions and themes of an orphan, a widow and a mother concerned for her health and for her child.

The shift, however, would not be evident in looking only at the first poem, 'The Child of Sorrow', which echoes not only her 1806 phrasing but also an established literary formulation. During the last half of the eighteenth century, 'the child of sorrow' featured in drama, poetry and moralistic prose. In *The Troubles of Life* (1795), one of the Cheap Repository Tracts, 'the child of sorrow' is described thus:

> There are some persons who seem to have everything made against them; they have had neither the success in business, nor yet the health of other men, and they have experienced also their full share of affecting deaths in their family, and at length they meet with some additional calamity, whereby their grey hairs are brought down in sorrow to the grave. (8)

Richardson's poem, written in long hymnal octaves (doubled long hymnal stanzas), which tend to heighten the formality and solemnity of the regular hymn by drawing it out and suggesting the durability of the state described therein, moves in a fashion topically similar to 'To Mrs. P____', recounting early bright prospects followed by loss and affliction. The bright prospects were, she suggests, 'transient visions' (l. 9), produced not only by some degree of external obscuring but also by her own imagination:

> In youth's fair morn when first I threw
>     My eyes across life's checker'd road,
> On airy pinions fancy flew,
>     With gay delight my bosom glow'd.
> Each scene to me could joy impart,
>     While hope still promis'd bliss to-morrow,
> Ah little reck'd my foolish heart,
>     I e'er should be the child of sorrow! (ll. 1–8)

Richardson's use of the passive voice in much of the poem reduces any sense of her personal agency in alleviating her grief and suffering. Her situation is static, as the epiphoral 'child of sorrow' concluding each stanza suggests. Instead, personified abstractions such as 'Calm Resignation' (l. 23) and 'Hope' (l. 24) heal and cheer her while leaving her in her circumstances as a 'child of sorrow'.

Although in a number of poems Richardson expresses her anxiety at the prospect of the death of her son during his illnesses, in regard to the effect of her own death on her son, she is remarkably unperturbed, which seems even more unusual given her earlier attempts to console her husband over what she feared was her impending death. 'A Prayer, in the Immediate Prospect of Death, March, 1808' was composed during an especially dangerous illness for Richardson – the persistent abscess that had plagued her for many months. The records of disbursements paid to her by the York Female Friendly Society indicate that she was debilitated from early February through mid-October of 1808, at which point she experienced a modest recovery and was beginning to benefit from the proceeds from the subscription for the second volume. Although Richardson describes her recovery in 'Self-Examination, on Recovery from Severe Illness, October, 1808' (*Illness* 121–2), the abscess eventually had to be opened surgically in March 1809 (Tuke to Copsie, Tuke/1/6/1/6/25).

'A Prayer' is a sombre, contemplative poem. Its ambitious form reflects its formality. Each of the six stanzas approximates the Spenserian. Eight decasyllabic lines rhyme *ababbcbc*; however, instead of concluding with an alexandrine, each stanza ends in a single fourteener, rhyming *c*. Read in light of her previous poems, the formal choice suggests an extension of her earlier use of the elegiac stanza, which she had early set in quatrains and later doubled into octastiches. Adding a third rhyme sound in lines 5–8 in each stanza amplifies the elegiac form, adding to its seriousness while retaining a progression from the first four lines; the fourteener distinguishes her stanzas in tone from most uses of the Spenserian, while the additional length suggests her willingness to have the prayer carry on to the length it deserves.

The first two stanzas, with humility and praise, address God (once again) in distant forms as creator, destroyer and knower of all. In the third stanza, however, Richardson invokes God as 'Father' while she makes her request, referring to herself in the third person, echoing but inverting the self-distancing 'Lucy' in 'Elegy': 'Might she be spar'd, in Wisdom's paths, her darling child to train' (l. 27). But she imagines God-as-Father merely in the capacity of, she hopes, granting her request to stay his hand, to spare her life for the sake of her child. In the next stanza, as she foresees her death, she pointedly absents God from the care of her child:

> Yet were to me this last request deny'd,
> And this weak frame to Death's cold arms consign'd,
> A parent's loss will amply be supply'd,
> For to my Mary is that task assign'd:
> She'll shield from vice his tender op'ning mind,
> And plant the seeds of every virtue there;

She'll teach him to be just, humane, and kind,
And G – – -m, too, the sacred trust will share,
And o'er his growing years will watch with pious care. (ll. 28–36)

Should God choose to 'slay' her, to use her word from line 5 of the first stanza, Richardson removes from God the responsibility for protecting her son from vice and guiding him onto virtuous paths; she employs passive constructions for both her and God from the point of God's putative denial of her prayer. Instead, human agents – her friend Mary Smith and John Graham, Rector of St Mary Bishophill Senior – would act in all of the moral roles which, for herself, in previous poems dating back to 1790, she had asked God to fulfil. Although in the next stanza she returns to her earlier vision of God as moral guide, asking him to guard her son from temptation, in the raw preceding stanza's replacing herself as mother and God as father with Mary Smith and John Graham she points to her increasing appreciation of the efficacy of human agents, known primarily through social institutions.

Even while bedridden, beset by illness, and experiencing pain from which 'opium's aid alone' grants her 'a short repose' (as she writes in 'Stanzas, Written in April, 1808, When Still under the Pressure of Severe Illness', ll. 15–16), she turns towards temporal friends, not only as comforts to her, but also as comforts to others and as agents of moral progress. Moreover, many of the poems from her months of serious illness address others' suffering, and she takes stances, at times, of comforter and moral instructor. From the narrower perspective of orphan and widow, she enlarges her view and engages, at least through poetry, in an active sympathy.

Poems reflective of her enlarging sympathetic sphere include 'On the Death of Goldfinch, Chained in a Cage. Addressed to his Young Mistress, from the Groves of Elysium. May, 1808' (in which she gently chastises a woman who kept a goldfinch), 'On the Death of the Rev. Wm. Wood, of Leeds. Addressed to the Rev. C. Wellbeloved, May, 1808' (in which she comforts a York clergyman on the death of his friend), 'After Reading Clarkson on the Abolition of the Slave Trade, August, 1808', and 'Addressed to Mr. Clarkson, Sept. 1808'. The latter two poems follow a pattern begun in 1807, after interval of illness, in which Richardson took up social causes, such as calling for the abolition of the slave trade and the election to Parliament of William Wilberforce.

*

In the years following her second volume, Richardson, having recovered from surgery to drain her abscess and using funds raised by the sale of her books, re-opened her school. She continued to write poetry, enlarged her social sphere, and participated in several of the charitable institutions in York. Her writing and social engagement brought her within the circle of friendship of the Tuke family, leaders in many Quaker charitable endeavours in Yorkshire. Her correspondence with the women of the Tuke family shows her having been welcomed into a sphere of amiability, intimacy and mutual concern.

Richardson was active in civic and religious charities until her decline in health in 1822, following the death of her son in Bradford (*Yorkshire Observer*). Until that time, she continued as an enrolled member of the York Female Friendly Society and in 1818, was appointed a Visitor by the Society, with responsibilities for evaluating need and providing care for its members (YFF, Committee Mins 21 May 1818, YFF/1/9, p. 16). As the appointed Registrar of another charity, the York Society for the Encouragement of Faithful Female Servants, she enrolled members and ensured that networks of mutual aid, moral guidance and intellectual improvement for women in service were maintained (York Society, Rules, DD/BW/Y/39, p. 3).

Both of Richardson's final known texts address orphanhood primarily in terms of human agency. The story of Margaret Russell (1806–1821), a poor mulatto girl who, with her mother, moved to York from Warrington following her father's death, was widely known within York during the later Regency years. An anonymous account of Russell's life, *The Tawny Girl; Or, The History of Margaret Russell*, was published in two editions in York by William Alexander (husband of Ann Tuke Alexander, with whom Richardson occasionally corresponded). Alexander's *Annual Monitor* for 1829 contains a brief memoir of Margaret Russell and a poem, 'Stanzas on the Decease of Margaret Russell', written by Richardson some years before (126–31). Richardson's themes and diction echo those of her earlier poems – orphanhood, bereavement, the need for moral guidance and perseverance along paths of virtue. But another theme is subjoined – Richardson's indignation at the treatment of the orphaned girl, recalling and casting in new light her expressed indignation at society's treatment of the orphan in 'The Orphan's Prayer'. Russell's initial application in 1814 for admission to a York 'school that had recently been established for the instruction of children of the labouring classes', was rejected on a presumption of the bad effects of 'her wandering life and probably dissolute habits'; that decision was later reversed, and Russell excelled in her studies until her mother's decline in health affected her attendance (*Tawny Girl* 13–14).⁷

Nevertheless, public outrage over her denied admission remained, evident in *The Tawny Girl*, Alexander's memoir, and Richardson's poem. Richardson sees in poverty a right to relief and assistance, and, as in her earlier poems, she notes that it is a woman who recognises need and provides relief:

> In happy hour one female saw
> The wanderer in her wretched plight;
> And long'd this hapless child to draw
> From scenes which would each virtue blight.
> How warm and eloquent was prayer,
> While pleading in Compassion's name,
> That 'TAWNY' might those blessings share,
> To which her miseries laid a claim. (ll. 13–20)

Although Richardson lauds Russell's maintaining piety despite adversity, she locates agency and efficacy in addressing Russell's poverty and in securing for her the 'blessings / To which her miseries laid a claim' primarily with women acting from charity, morality and social obligation.

Richardson's final text is her wonderfully conversational will, which she wrote on her own. In it, she muses on what ought to be mentioned in a will ('I purpose leaving some articles of furniture to the Girls, must they also be named separately?'), mentions the visits of friends, hopes that her unpublished poems may be printed and the proceeds used to fund charitable work, and disposes of her estate (valued at £450) in both expected and surprising ways. In a clear display of wanting to give back (as I expected in reading her will), she bequeaths substantial gifts to a number of charities – the Grey Coat School, the York Infirmary, the York Dispensary, the Sunday Schools, as well as a number of missionary charities. But I want to conclude this chapter with attention to two passages in particular, both of which demonstrate the extent to which orphanhood, bastardy and bereavement shaped Richardson's life and her efforts to shape what remained of her in meaningful, though curious, ways.

The first passage includes two related bequests: 'To Margaret Wrightson the Sister of my late Husband £10, free from the controul of her Husband, also my wearing apparel' and 'To Robert Harling Richardson the Son of my Husband's Brother £20' (f. 19). Robert Harling Richardson was not only the name of her own son but also the name of the bastard son of her husband's sister, Margaret: 'Robert Harling Illegitimate Son of Margaret Richardson Baptized Jan 9 1805' (Scrayingham, PR/SCR/6). Two months later, on 4 March 1805, Margaret Richardson married Thomas Wrightson, a tanner from St Margaret's Walmgate, in the parish church at Dunnington (Dunnington, PR/DUN/5,). I feel comfortable in inferring that Margaret trusted her surviving brother with the care of her son (Richardson identifies this Robert Harling as the son of her late husband's brother); nevertheless, the significance of Richardson's bequests remains. In a society in which bastardy was a lifelong blemish, made clear earlier in this chapter by reference to John Smith's burial register entry and the administrative documents regarding Richardson's will, Richardson chose not to let bastardy influence her bequests.

The second passage is the most striking with regard to Richardson's ongoing engagement with orphanhood and bereavement:

> I know not that I ever mentioned to you having paid last year £5 to the Church Missionary Society as part of £30 to be paid for having a Ceylonese Boy named after my dear Son. Should I die before the rest has been paid it must be taken from what is left. (f. 19)

The practice of paying the Church Missionary Society to rename a child in one of the overseas regions in which the Society maintained missions is described in a handful of religious publications of the time. In the 1822 *Proceedings of the Church Missionary Society*, the practice is referred to in reports on missions to Sierra Leone and Ceylon, and those contexts reveal the Society's financial motives. The Sierra Leone report specifies that the practice was to replace or expand the original subscription funding scheme for the Africa School Fund:

> This Fund, so far as Sierra Leone is concerned, no longer exists on its original plan; the maintenance and education of all the Children of the Colony being otherwise secured: but, on the plan mentioned in former Reports, of receiving from Benefactors who may wish to name an African Child the sum of 30*l.* to be appropriated to its future benefit, various Young Persons have been named at their baptism. (55)

Such benefactions were typically recorded in ledgers reported for the *Proceedings* from associations outside London. In fact, the next two reports of the Church Missionary Society document Richardson's benefactions: '*School Fund*. Mrs Charlotte Richardson, for *R. H. Richardson*, (1st year) . . . [£]5 0[s] 0[d]' (*Proceedings, 1824–1825*, n.p.) and '*School Fund*. Mrs Charlotte Richardson, for *R. H. Richardson*, (2d year) . . . [£]5 0[s] 0[d]' (*Proceedings, 1825–1826*, n.p.).

The intention of the Society in offering such a scheme for donations was clearly to provide for the education of the children. It would be consistent with Richardson's earlier poems, her work as a teacher, her civic engagement and other bequests to educational charities that she would want to provide for the education of a child who otherwise lacked access to instruction. What she offered, in poetry and action, in the last several years of her life was charity as an avenue to set others on their way forward.

Richardson's poetry, her correspondence and the institutional documents that mark her life reveal her efforts to cope with a lifelong series of absences and losses in meaningful ways. It is possible to discern a number of general patterns in her moving from the familial to the social, from the imaginary to the material, and from patience to action. Particular patterns emerge, too, in her endeavouring to form new relationships to supplant those of which she was bereft – an imaginary father for an absent real father, God for a mother, a brother for God, a husband for blood family, a son for a husband, and a Ceylonese boy for her dead son. But do those patterns of movement take shape as an actual trajectory? I believe that they do. Richardson understood that orphanhood, widowhood, bereavements and adversities were outside individuals' hands. She further understood them as the effects of God's purifying and chastising rod. Her earlier writings manifest her reaction to the rod as patient, silent and solitary suffering. But as she benefited from and participated in the York social institutions of her time, inhabiting not only the material reality of institutional effect but also its discourse – both of which, as we have seen, were largely woman-centred and woman-motivated – she came to insist that any penury, social alienation and moral vulnerability that resulted from those bereavements and adversities could be – must be – subject to human mitigation through active sympathy, charity and mutual aid.

## Notes

1. Hereafter, I will cite Richardson's volumes as *Occasions* and *Illness*, referring only to the first editions of each volume. Also, throughout this chapter, I will use 'Smith' to refer to Charlotte Smith as a person

prior to her marriage and 'Richardson' to refer to her as an author and as a person subsequent to her marriage. I should also here distinguish between the subject of this chapter and two other poets with whom she has been confused, Charlotte Caroline Richardson and Charlotte Turner Smith.
2. Roger Sales devotes the bulk of his 1999 essay, 'The Maid and the Minister's Wife: Literary Philanthropy in Regency York', to Cappe and her philanthropic agenda as it facilitated and shaped Richardson's publications. For a larger study of Cappe that describes her combining Christianity and feminism into practical social activism, see Helen Plant's *Unitarianism, Philanthropy and Feminism in York, 1782–1821: The Career of Catherine Cappe*.
3. Burial records classify her mother, Hannah Smith, as 'A Single woman Descent not known' (York, St Cuthbert, PR/Y/CU 3) and her brother as 'Illegitimate Child of the late Hannah Smith of this Parish' (York, St Cuthbert, PR/Y/CU 4). Probate documents from 1825 relating to Richardson's will identify her as 'Widow & a bastard'. There was also some question regarding the administration of her will 'on account of the deceased having died a Bastard' (Nicholl to Lawton, f. 19).
4. Cappe's having been struck by 'He Sleeps' and her use of the passive voice in describing Richardson's comportment demonstrate the extent to which Cappe focuses on bereavement, helplessness and resignation in defining Richardson. 'He Sleeps' is entirely about the poet's ephemeral loss and divine consolation. The poet describes wandering around her husband's grave, memory offering no consolation but rather making her 'sorrows flow afresh' (78, l. 8). In subsequent stanzas, her fears and sorrows emerge in her emotional responses to a divine voice she thinks she hears. She makes no mention of her son or her fears for his future; her sorrows are purely those of a widow bereft of all familial and social comfort, finding solace only in her husband's repose and in God's promise of peace to those who maintain a faithful resignation through temporal trials.
5. 'The Orphan's Prayer' was much anthologised, generally in abridgement, as in James Plumptre (ed.), *A Collection of Songs, Moral, Sentimental, Instructive, and Amusing*, Vol. 1 (London: F. C. and J. Rivington, 1806), pp. 371–2. In later years, it was reproduced, without attribution or with malicious misattribution, in a number of volumes, such as a thematic miscellany, *Pathetic English Poetry, with Some Original Pieces Never Before Published; For the Use of Schools, and Young Persons in General* (Plymouth: R. Bond, 1830), p. 15. A three-stanza version was published in *History of the Orphan Asylum, in Philadelphia; With an Account of the Fire, in Which Twenty-three Orphans Were Burned* (Philadelphia, PA: American Sunday School Union, 1832), pp. 50–1. It also appears in a number of Christian hymnals and song books. It is misattributed to a 'Miss Carter', as 'The Orphan's Prayer. Words by

Miss Carter' in *Taylor's Sacred Minstrel; or American Church Music Book: A New Collection of Psalm and Hymn Tunes, Adapted to the Various Metres Now in Use*, ed. Virgil Corydon Taylor (Hartford, CT: J. H. Mather and Company, 1847), p. 259. It is misattributed to a 'P. M'. in *The Christian Hymn-Book, a Compilation of Psalms, Hymns, & Spiritual Songs Original and Selected. By A. Campbell and Others. Revised and Enlarged by a Committee* (Melbourne: Thomas Smith, 1869), pp. 575–6.

6. The final poem of the first edition of the 1809 volume, 'Epitaph, on Jane Brown, Aged Two Years and a Half, Who Died Feb 14, 1809' revisits the circumstances of parental bereavement while eliding any mention of the parents of the dead child and any mention of God's agency. The theme is similar to that in 'Prayer'. 'Epitaph' is a single quatrain with a moral objectionable to modern readers – a tacit validation of Death's snatching away Jane Brown before sin or grief could assail her:

> Ere Sin its poison could convey,
> > Or Grief's tempestuous storms arise,
> Death snatch'd this tender bud away,
> > And bade it blossom in the skies. (p. 136)

7. The school may have been the Manor School, opened in 1812 to educate poor children.

## Works Cited

Cappe, Catherine. 'Mrs. Cappe's Letter on Charlotte Richardson.' *The Athenaeum*, vol. 4, September 1808, pp. 217–18.

Dunnington (Parish). Register of Marriages, 1615–1994. PR/DUN/5. York. Borthwick Institute for Archives.

Lewis, M. G. and Harriet Abrams. *The Orphan's Prayer: A Pathetic Ballad*. Lavenu, 1800.

*The Missionary Register for MDCCCXXVI. Containing the Principal Transactions of the Various Institutions for Propagating the Gospel: with the Proceedings, at Large, of the Church Missionary Society*. L. B. Seeley & Son, 1826.

Montgomery, James. *Memoirs of the Life and Writings of James Montgomery*. ed. John Holland and James Everett., vol. II. Longman, Brown, Green, and Longmans, 1855.

Nicoll, Iltid. Manuscript letter to George Lawton. 17 November 1825. *Exchequer and Prerogative Courts of the Archbishop of York, Probate Index, 1688–1858*, vol. 173, f. 19. Documents of administration in the Matter of the Estate of Charlotte Richardson, January 1826. York. Borthwick Institute for Archives.

Nixon, Cheryl L. *The Orphan in Eighteenth-century Law and Literature: Estate, Blood, and Body*. Ashgate, 2011.

Plant, Helen. *Unitarianism, Philanthropy and Feminism in York, 1782–1821: The Career of Catherine Cappe*. Borthwick Paper 103. York: Borthwick Institute for Archives, 2003.

*Proceedings of the Church Missionary Society for Africa and the East. Twenty-Second Year. 1821–1822*. London, 1822.

*Proceedings of the Church Missionary Society for Africa and the East. Twenty-Fifth Year. 1824–1825*. London, 1825.

*Proceedings of the Church Missionary Society for Africa and the East. Twenty-Sixth Year. 1825–1826*. London, 1826.

Richardson, Charlotte. Manuscript Will. *Exchequer and Prerogative Courts of the Archbishop of York, Probate Index, 1688–1858*, vol. 173. Documents in the Matter of the Estate of Charlotte Richardson, January 1826. York. Borthwick Institute for Archives.

Richardson, Charlotte. *Poems Chiefly Composed During the Pressure of Severe Illness*. Wilson, 1809.

Richardson, Charlotte. *Poems Written on Different Occasions*. Wilson, 1806.

Richardson, Charlotte. 'Stanzas on the Decease of Margaret Russell', *The Annual Monitor, and Memorandum Book*, no. 17, 1829, pp. 126–31.

Richardson, Charlotte. 'Written after hearing a Lecture from St. John, 9th Chapter, verse 25, "Whereas I was blind now I see". – Sunday evening, March 28, 1819', *Yorkshire Gazette*, 8 October 1819, p. 4.

Rowe, Elizabeth. *Devout Exercises of the Heart, in Meditation and Soliloquy, Prayer and Praise*. M. Luckman, 1790.

Sales, Roger. 'The Maid and the Minister's Wife: Literary Philanthropy in Regency York', in *Women's Poetry in the Enlightenment: The Making of a Canon, 1730–1820*, ed. Isobel Armstrong and Virginia Blain, St Martin's Press, 1999, pp. 127–41.

Scrayingham (Parish). Register of Baptisms and Burials, 1778–1813. PR/SCR/6. York. Borthwick Institute for Archives.

*Tawny Girl; Or, The History of Margaret Russell*. 2nd edition, William Alexander, 1823.

*The Troubles of Life*. Cheap Repository Tracts. Marshall, 1795.

Tuke, Mary Maria to Favilla Copsie, 23d of 3d Month, seventh day, 1809. Tuke Papers. York. Borthwick Institute for Archives. Tuke/1/6/1/6/25.

York, All Saints, Pavement (Parish). General Register, 1739–1809. PR/Y/ASP 19. York. Borthwick Institute for Archives.

York Charity Schools. *Committee of the Blue and Grey Coat Schools Minute Books, 1770–1789*. YCS 2/1/2. York. Borthwick Institute for Archives.

YFF (York Female Friendly Society). Committee Minutes for 21 May 1818. 'Resolutions, Memorandums &c belonging to the Private Fund of the York Female Friendly Society.' *Female Friendly Society Papers, 1795–1883.* YFF/1/9. York. York Explore Library and Archives.

YFF (York Female Friendly Society). *Admission Registers, 1788–1899.* YFF/1/1. York. York Explore Library and Archives.

YFF (York Female Friendly Society). *Private Memorandum Book.* Female Friendly Society Papers, 1795–1883. YFF/1/8. York. York Explore Library and Archives.

York, St Cuthbert (Parish). *General Register, 1709–1795.* PR/Y/CU 3. York. Borthwick Institute for Archives.

York, St Cuthbert (Parish). *Register of Baptisms and Burials, 1795–1812.* PR/Y/CU 4. York. Borthwick Institute for Archives.

York, St Mary Bishophill Senior (Parish). *Register of Marriages, 1754–1810.* PR Y/M Bp. S. 10, York. Borthwick Institute for Archives.

York, St Michael-Le-Belfrey (Parish). *General Register, 1779–1812.* PR/Y/MB 7. York. Borthwick Institute for Archives.

*Yorkshire Observer.* No. 28, 24 May 1823.

York Society for the Encouragement of Faithful Female Servants. *Rules and Subscriptions, 1820*, DD/BW/Y/39. Doncaster. Doncaster Archives.

Chapter 3

# 'Like some of the princesses in the fairy stories, only I was not charming': The Literary Orphan and the Victorian Novel

*Tamara S. Wagner*

In Victorian fiction, orphans embody vulnerability, while dramatising personal growth within a changing social panorama. They express social and cultural anxieties in an age of increasing mobility and uncertainty, define a need for good homes and families by exemplifying the effects of their absence, and in becoming adopted into unusual households, they question conventional domestic arrangements. The literary orphan's mystery of origins becomes channelled into investigations of early memories, child development and campaigns for the protection of children. Dickens's *Oliver Twist* (1838) influentially transforms traditional foundling tales into an account of child rescue, and yet Oliver's incorruptibility remains an incongruity in the text's social criticism. The complex narrative situation of Dickens's *Bleak House* (1853) self-consciously engages with the resulting epistemological impasse, addressing the orphan's shifting meaning in Victorian culture, while externalising the simultaneity of the *Bildungsroman* and the social panorama in the nineteenth-century novel. Esther Summerson describes herself as an unwanted child, 'orphaned and degraded from the first of these evil anniversaries [her birthdays]' (*Bleak House* 26), in juxtaposition with the omniscient narrator's metaphors of orphanhood to describe a society of disconnected individuals. 'No Thoroughfare' (1867), co-written by Dickens and Wilkie Collins, hinges on mysteries of origins in a convoluted plot of mistaken identities and sensationalised doubles, and yet it is also one of the notably few narratives that feature the Foundling Hospital centrally in the text and one of the first to describe the difficulties of adoption before its legalisation.

Whereas Dinah Craik's thesis novel about adoption, *King Arthur* (1886), becomes oddly fissured by the sustained narrative power of the orphan's mysterious origins, late-Victorian sensation novels challenge this plot device in order to dismantle readers' expectations. Thus, in Mary Elizabeth Braddon's *The Fatal Three* (1888), the secret of an adopted child's parentage destroys families across generations. Yet with a direct intertextual reference to *Bleak House*,[1] Braddon also critically reworks the orphan's role as a potential threat in sensation fiction. The ambiguities of the vulnerable, yet often mysterious, Victorian orphan still determine persistent clichés surrounding both the Victorians and orphans in literature.

Victorian orphan narratives combine the structures of the traditional foundling tale with social criticism. Throughout the century, the mystery of an orphan's origins remains an important driving force in fiction. However, it retains its thematic significance precisely by becoming redefined through a self-reflexive engagement with narrative structure itself. In narratological terms, such emplotment ensures that the orphan narrative is at once cohesive (that it works as a narrative) and that it can and indeed needs to be reconstructed or updated. Nina Auerbach has influentially stressed that the 'figure of the wandering orphan, searching through an alien world for his home, has fascinated generations of novelists', so that 'we find the orphan emerging as the primary metaphor for the dispossessed, detached self' (395).[2] According to Monika Fludernik, the Victorian orphan is among the most recognisable and 'basic narratological types' (119). Novelists, however, also variously utilised this figure as a vehicle to express a range of concerns. The then still emergent figure of the literary orphan child – now perhaps the most iconic figure of Victorian literature – facilitated investigations into changing social and more specifically family structures and dynamics. Nineteenth-century orphan narratives explore differing notions of family and the extent to which the orphan belongs in a (variously extended or also redefined) family or remains outside it.

Recent research on the Victorian family has newly explored its versatility and extendibility, questioning traditional categorisations of what constituted normative or non-normative family constellations at the time. Holly Furneaux speaks of 'the expandability of Victorian kin in, for example, widespread practices of non-biological adoption', which 'demonstrates that "families of choice" and "elective affinities" have a long and emotionally rich history' (14). Kelly Hager and Talia Schaffer similarly stress the need that we investigate how family formation in Victorian Britain operated as 'a permeable, flexible, and shifting configuration' (7). Considering the potentially radical nature of the novel as a genre in the nineteenth century, Isobel Armstrong foregrounds the orphan's role as part of this radicalness, suggesting that illegitimacy works as 'the growing point of a democratic imagination' (30). An 'invariant element of the novel of this era,' the Victorian family is 'defined through its other, illegitimacy' (Armstrong 6). Claudia Nelson has made a similar point in her discussion of adoption, arguing that nineteenth-century adoption narratives routinely use alternative household arrangements 'as a way of critiquing other sorts of family relationships' (*Family* 146). Consequently, the figure of the orphan becomes an increasingly visible and versatile feature in literature. In addition, Victorian writers might have capitalised on the orphan's popularity and effectiveness to showcase social issues, but they also critically reacted to the clichés that soon came to be associated with this recurring figure. Largely due to its easy commodification as an icon – and, often literally, as a poster child – of various social reforms, the orphan became sentimentalised, and contemporary detractors of the supposed usefulness of sentimental literature as a 'moral lever' already maintained that perhaps 'far from conscience-creating outward-oriented action, emotional expenditure on fictional people threatened to inoculate readers against the more obdurate facts of real suffering' (Burdett 585). As a result, novelists strove to rework expected narratives, often specifically to challenge emergent clichés.

The emplotment of orphan narratives became more self-conscious and intertextual. Contrasting key texts such as *Oliver Twist*, *Bleak House*, 'No Thoroughfare', *King Arthur* and *The Fatal Three* let us map how Victorian literature generated and exploited the fascination with the orphan. These nineteenth-century narratives capitalise on the popularity and flexibility of this figure while reworking pervasive paradigms. With growing self-reflexivity, these texts tackle established patterns to express particular preoccupations with society and often with narrative form itself. *Bleak House* dismantles expectations of sentimentalised orphans and their identification as the ideal resolution in foundling tales, answering questions that *Oliver Twist* raises, but largely leaves unanswered. 'No Thoroughfare' plays with the easily clichéd significance of the double in orphan narratives, literalising the figure of the *Doppelganger*, yet if this creates a potentially sensational imposter plot, the focus firmly rests on the social problems and ethical issues embodied and ultimately, in this text, expunged by the illegitimate orphan. *King Arthur* allots unprecedented attention to the adoptive parents, while resorting to the foundling tale as an adjustable framework for adoption narratives. Conversely, *The Fatal Three* trades on, yet also redeploys, the sensational potential of the orphan figure in order to challenge attitudes to and representations of adoption. Braddon thereby self-consciously redirects the literary significance of orphaned characters. If the literary orphan child as an iconic figure is a peculiarly Victorian creation, the Victorians were keenly aware of its flexible embodiment.

\*

The iconic Victorian orphan is a downtrodden, abused and frequently ragged child, who is rescued in a consummate realisation of adoption fantasies that reinstates the importance of family affection or social justice. Thus, orphaned characters in nineteenth-century fiction are peculiarly free and flexible in their movement across the social panorama, and yet the most memorable examples are restored to lost homes or positions. On the one hand, this movement – often presented as a rags-to-riches story that might involve several experiences of rags or of riches – reflects class mobility as well as the vulnerability and anxiety that this mobility brought with it. Oliver Twist, having been 'badged and ticketed' (*Oliver Twist* 4–5) in the workhouse, is rescued repeatedly from a series of abandonments and abductions that encapsulate the uncertainties of a changing social system. On the other hand, Oliver's recognition and adoption by Brownlow hinge upon a fortuitously solved mystery of origins. This plot development keeps resurfacing throughout nineteenth-century fiction, although it begins to be treated more self-reflexively. Dickens's next novel, *Nicholas Nickleby* (1839), for example, contains a less exuberant resolution that nonetheless turns on the solved mystery of a putative orphan's identity as a lost middle-class child, while simultaneously illustrating the looseness with which the term 'orphan' was used at the time. Dotheboys Hall is full of unwanted orphans, including illegitimate offspring, stepchildren, disabled children, as well as the stolen boy, Smike, Ralph Nickleby's presumably dead son:

> there were the bleared eye, the hare-lip, the crooked foot, . . . ; and there were young creatures on whom the sins of their frail parents had descended, weeping even for the mercenary nurses they had known, and lonesome even in their loneliness. (*Nicholas Nickleby* 188)

Believed dead by his father, Smike longingly eyes any letters directed to the school 'with a sickly hope that one among them might relate to him' and a look that 'told a long and very sad history' (*Nicholas Nickleby* 78). Smike's adoption into his cousin's family constitutes a 'dreadful retribution' for Ralph Nickleby (*Nicholas Nickleby* 789). Conversely, the titular hero of Dickens's most autobiographical *Bildungsroman*, *David Copperfield* (1850), moves from being the sheltered child of a well-off widowed mother to becoming a resented stepchild and a child labourer, to be reclaimed as a member of the middle classes by his great-aunt. In *Bleak House*, Dickens self-consciously rejected this pattern, both in order to render the orphan a better embodiment of social injustice and to upend familiar narrative patterns. But if Dickens rewrote established plotlines, partly through parody and partly through self-reflexive criticism, the iconic Victorian orphan nonetheless persisted and continued to develop.[3]

In fact, while this figure encompasses several definitional characteristics, the divergences from the pattern chart how the orphan's portrayal negotiated both changing social realities and readers' expectations. Reflecting real-life indeterminacies in the terminology at the time, the Victorian orphan became the epitome of the vulnerable child. Not all orphaned protagonists are 'parochial orphans' or even know that they have 'got no father or mother', like Oliver Twist (12). Esther Summerson, in *Bleak House*, wonders at the absence of 'a black frock' or 'mama's grave' (25). This conspicuous absence generates a mystery, while the child 'set apart' as her mother's 'disgrace' (*Bleak House* 26) also reminds us that orphanhood was a common euphemism for illegitimacy. There is considerable evidence, for example, that illegitimate middle-class children tended to be raised as informally adopted orphans, at times in the same household as their legitimate half-siblings.[4] In the same vein, social reformers considered '"orphan" to be the most charitable term available that can encompass the complexly multivalent "whole idea" of children without parents' (Nixon 6). Discussing the 'orphan' as a figure that can 'be found in plenitude' in Victorian writing, Laura Peters speaks of the persistent 'link between orphanhood [and] illegitimacy' (6) in public discourse. Novels played into this association, transforming the attendant mysteries of origins into sensational detective plots.[5]

In nineteenth-century discourse on orphans as superfluous waifs, their presumed illegitimacy became itself invested with a larger metaphorical potential. This interpretation of superfluity implied that orphans – identified therein as homeless street children – had no legitimate claim to their existence. Referring to this particular interpretation of the 'orphan' in the Victorian imagination, Peters argues that 'the lived experience of the orphan during this time' was characterised by poverty, state intervention and the stigmatisation of illegitimacy (6). Scripted as an 'outsider without origin', this representative orphan 'embodies excess' (Peters 49). Similarly, Lydia Murdoch's study of what she terms 'imagined orphans' stresses that 'most institutionalized children were not orphans' and draws attention to the

> common phrases used to describe poor children [which] accented their alleged separation from parents and lack of connection to established, stable communities. They were 'waifs and strays', or 'nobody's children', or 'street arabs' who wandered nomadically through the urban landscape. (Murdoch 2, 1)

The same slipperiness informed the term 'foundling' – a slipperiness that was reinforced by the official designations used by the Foundling Hospital. As Rachel Bowlby has pointed out, 'the infants taken into the Foundling Hospital were not technically foundlings. They had not been left somewhere and picked up by good luck, but were brought in deliberately by mothers (or someone connected with a mother)' (Bowlby 92). Those depositing these infants were encouraged to include a token or memento. In return, they were issued with an official receipt, which allowed them to inquire after – and possibly to reclaim – their child. Precisely such a memento promises a story of concealed origins and fortuitous reclamation, but if this narrative arc is realised in several Victorian works of literature and art – most famously in *Oliver Twist* and, with a startling twist, in 'No Thoroughfare', as we shall see – in reality parental reclamations were extremely rare.[6] The superfluous orphan that epitomised excess in political economy consequently had a peculiarly fraught, yet creative relationship with the 'valued orphan' of narrative emplotment (Nixon 6).

Two diametrically opposed ideas of the orphan thus competed in Victorian narratives, although increasingly, self-conscious literary experiments addressed this disjunction. Traditionally, research on the Victorian orphan nonetheless reflects this split. Cultural histories have concentrated on the 'orphan' as an interchangeable term for a waif or street child. These studies reconstruct real-life conditions to assess how popular culture – including the so-called 'waif fiction' (Nelson, *Family* 56) produced by social reformers – captured, or failed to capture, these conditions.[7] By contrast, close readings, often informed by narratology, analyse the mysteriously lost child's narrative functions in canonical literature. These discussions favour versions of the

*Bildungsroman* that detail a central orphaned character's individual growth. Orphanhood often operates as an extreme version of the vulnerability of childhood or as a metaphor for an existential sense of abandonment, an 'orphan condition' as 'a state of mind that [...] informs some part of everyone's imagination' (Hochman and Wachs 14). Even a cursory look at the most important orphan narratives reveals that we need a more balanced approach to appreciate the literary orphan's full significance. The texts under discussion expand and develop the orphan narrative, tracking shifts in attitudes towards childhood, parenting, illegitimacy, social responsibility, middle-class rescue fantasies and adoption.

\*

Dickens's *Bleak House* features an impressive cast of orphan figures. It is a novel about parental as well as social responsibility that indicts society through an extended metaphor of orphanhood. The failure to care for society's most vulnerable members is literalised by a spectrum of individual abandonments, while satirised false philanthropy exposes patronising behaviour towards the poor. Esther's father, Captain Hawdon, alias Nemo (literally, Nobody), dying of an overdose of opium, leaves 'no more track behind him, that any one can trace, than a deserted infant' (*Bleak House* 159). Orphanhood is at once an existential condition, scripted as a peculiarly modern development in its intensity, and a real-life concern. When the superficial Skimpole exclaims that Ada, a parentless heiress, cannot possibly be termed 'an orphan' because she 'is the child of the universe', the novel's exemplary philanthropist, the Guardian, drily rejects such sophistry: '"The universe", he observed, "makes rather an indifferent parent, I am afraid"' (*Bleak House* 84). Yet if society is arraigned for its general indifference, the novel is also full of neglectful parents. The most conspicuous among these parental failures is indisputably Mrs Jellyby, who declares 'public duties' to be her 'favourite child' (*Bleak House* 353–4). In contrast to the far-off objects of her 'Telescopic Philanthropy', the street child Jo is 'not a genuine foreign-grown savage; he is the ordinary home-made article' (*Bleak House* 669). While indicting self-serving charity, this insistence on Jo's lack of an interesting background simultaneously divorces orphanhood from any mysterious inheritance. Similarly, Esther's *Bildungsroman* curiously revives in order to eschew an expected mystery of origins. The full significance of Dickens's narrative experiment for the changing literary emplotment of orphan narratives, in fact, cannot be appreciated without a renewed attention to these parallel plots.

In *Bleak House*, Dickens resolves a central epistemological problem of his earlier novel about an orphan: *Oliver Twist*. Once the mysterious foundling is identified as belonging to the middle classes, the inheritance plot pushes aside the indictment of the Poor Laws. This parish boy's 'progress', stopped short by his fortuitous rescue, hence fails to exemplify social problems. Harold Bloom speaks of

> a conflict between the propagandistic intent and the dramatic action of the novel. One of Dickens' strongest arguments against the new Poor Law is the way it breeds criminality. . . . But the story of the novel depends on the opposite notion: the image of an invulnerable goodness persisting unstained through all attempts to deprave it. (n.p.)

Arguably, the revelation that the persecuted waif is a lost child belonging to the middle classes might have presented an additional shock-effect for a bourgeois reader. Nonetheless, while it remains a central conundrum whether this identification reinforces or undermines social criticism in *Oliver Twist*, Dickens plays out competing discourses on the orphan against each other in *Bleak House*.[8]

The orphan as a recognisable narratological type that needs to be newly understood becomes at once a main theme and a new opportunity for social criticism. In the figure of Jo in particular, Dickens insists on presenting a street waif 'in uncompromising colours'. The text dwells extensively on Jo's exterior, indicting the implied reader for expecting anything else:

> Dirty, ugly, disagreeable to all the senses . . . Homely filth begrimes him, homely parasites devour him, homely sores are in him, homely rags are on him; . . . Stand forth, Jo, in uncompromising colours! From the sole of thy foot to the crown of thy head, there is nothing interesting about thee. (*Bleak House* 669)

This is direct, straightforward and relentlessly realistic. Much has been written on Dickens's fictitious street sweep as a cultural icon (Murdoch 20–1), yet with the character of Jo, Dickens did not only attack social irresponsibility or realistically describe a street child. He rewrote two separate predominating orphan narratives of the time: waif fiction and the valued orphan's mystery of origins. *Bleak House* thus dramatises the rejection of a familiar narrative arc. In a comical sub-plot that parodies the narrative's overarching plot of detection, Mrs Snagsby suspects that because her husband compassionates a ragged boy and gives him money, the child must be his illegitimate son. This parodic detective plot – a comical character 'pursu[ing] her object of detecting and confounding her false husband' (*Bleak House* 765) – upends common plot developments in orphan narratives while playing with the emergent interest in detective stories in the 1850s.[9] Simultaneously, this sub-plot reinforces the rejection of the mystery of origins as a narrative driving force in Esther's story.

Dickens alternately employs parody and stark realism to transform the conventional emplotment of an orphan's abandonment and adoption. The text reworks the expected orphan narrative on three counts: in resituating foundling tales within the social realities of Victorian Britain; in eschewing both inheritance plots and adoption fantasies; and in parodying the newly popular detective plots. When Esther describes herself as seemingly a typical literary orphan, but with a significant difference, she at once expresses the subtle irony that renders the tonal shifts in her narrative so intriguing and initiates the novel's revision of the orphan narrative: 'I was brought up, from my earliest remembrance – like some of the princesses in the fairy stories, only I was not charming – by my godmother. At least I only knew her as such' (*Bleak House* 24). Prosaically introducing the character's illegitimacy, Dickens situates the orphan figure in everyday realities. Explicit references to fairy tales pervade Dickens's rewriting of orphan tales. Most memorably perhaps, Aunt Betsy 'vanishes like a discontented fairy' at David Copperfield's birth (*David Copperfield* 22). She might be an eccentric godmother-figure (indeed, she only intends to be godmother to a girl who is never born), but she nonetheless steps in between David and his abusive stepfather at a decisive moment, effecting a fairy-tale-like rescue. In pointed contrast, Esther's godmother forms one of the false mother-figures who signal maternal absence in Dickens's fiction, anticipating Mrs Dorrit and Miss Havisham in what has been termed their distorted 'moral agenda' in adopting infants (Novy 119).[10]

In a second parodic sub-plot, the ridiculous Guppy, Esther's unwelcome admirer, sets himself up as a detective figure attempting to discover the 'mystery about Miss Esther Summerson's birth and bringing up' with the explicit intention of thereby establishing 'a sort of claim upon Miss Summerson' (*Bleak House* 429). Yet the secret itself does not generate narrative tension. At the first appearance of 'My Lady Dedlock (who is childless)', she watches 'a child, chased by a woman, running out into the rain to meet the shining figure of a wrapped-up man' – a sight that puts her 'quite out of temper' (*Bleak House* 18). The parenthesis signals a potentially mysterious prehistory. The juxtaposition with Esther's wonder over the absence of 'mama's grave' (*Bleak House* 25), however, establishes a connection fairly early, as does the introduction of the nameless law-writer, whose writing Lady Dedlock recognises. When the details are revealed, moreover, the focus is immediately on the impossibility of maternal reclamation. Through Guppy, Lady Dedlock discovers that her seemingly stillborn illegitimate child has been 'reared . . . in rigid secrecy' by her sister. Esther may appreciate that she 'had not been abandoned by [her] mother' (*Bleak House* 539), but this is only half of the novel's reworking of the 'foundational narrative' of 'the abandoned and adopted child' (Taylor 295). In her study of adoption narratives, Marianne Novy mentions *Bleak House* as 'the novel that gives the fullest sympathy to a birth mother' (119). The mother grieves for lost opportunities, passionately asking for 'kisses for the last time,' whereas her child wonders over 'the mother's voice, so unfamiliar and so melancholy' to her because in her 'childhood [she] had never learned to love and recognise [it], had never been sung to sleep with, had never heard a blessing from, had never had a hope inspired by' (*Bleak House* 538). Yet if Esther's unnecessary orphanhood sentimentalises mothering by exemplifying its loss, the impossibility of a relationship with her rediscovered mother short-circuits any reunion. Esther spells out this rejection of revealed origins as a resolution when she puts a stop to Guppy's unsolicited investigations. He hopes to gain 'the means of advancing [Esther's] interests and promoting [her] fortunes by making discoveries' (*Bleak House* 570) after his curiosity is aroused by Lady Dedlock's portrait, which bears a striking resemblance to Esther. This repeats, in order to rewrite, the significance of the portrait in *Oliver Twist*: a striking affinity between a streetwaif and the painting of a young lady in Brownlow's house. Brownlow's investigations lead to the discovery of Oliver's parentage and his inheritance. In pointed contrast, Guppy's parodied reconnaissance is exposed as unpleasant meddling that fails to realise fortunes:

> I presume that you founded that belief upon your general knowledge of my being an orphan girl. . . . You could make no discovery in reference to me that would do me the least service or give me the least pleasure. I am acquainted with my personal history, and I have it in my power to assure you that you never can advance my welfare by such means. (*Bleak House* 570)

Esther's interpolated *Bildungsroman* instead upends the expected emplotment. The inadvertently deserted child can neither be reunited with her mother nor benefit from any fortuitous inheritance plot.

Far from promising helpful intervention, the godmother masks an illegitimate relationship – a common strategy in everyday life, as we have seen. In the same vein, adoption fantasies are evoked only to be dismissed as both impractical and undesirable. The Guardian is neither Esther's biological father – despite the 'idle dream' of Esther's 'earliest history' (*Bleak House* 95) – nor does he realise his fantasy of raising an ideal wife for himself by befriending an orphan. Instead, Esther's husband remains a shadowy and unusually heroic character precisely to underscore how the unwanted child, scorned for illegitimacy by the most hypocritical characters, makes an ideal match and becomes the mother of two girls, doubles of herself. The dark-haired young doctor who stars in an offstage shipwreck, who models the right behaviour towards the poor and suffering as well as to the illegitimate, embodies the perfect resolution in Esther's narrative. Their 'two little daughters' (*Bleak House* 911) – unnamed, as if not to obscure their function as symbols of reclaimed childhood and motherhood – mark how Esther's *Bildungsroman* has come full circle. In a twofold doubling, they are a recompense for her own mother's loss and her loss of a mother. That there are two of them indeed closes the insistent doubling of dead and dying babies in the novel with an almost comical crescendo.

In *Bleak House*, the insistent doubling of the lost child – the putative orphan Esther – connects the *Bildungsroman* (Esther's retrospective narrative) to timely social criticism (the present-tense account of the omniscient narrator) to forge a reworked orphan narrative by welding together two opposing nineteenth-century interpretations of the orphan as a social problem and as an expression of individual opportunity. Whereas the foundling plot of *Oliver Twist* competes with the social criticism, in *Bleak House*, Dickens's self-conscious reworking of the resulting ambiguity generates the narrative structure itself. Dickens maps out Lady Dedlock's loss in an obsessive textual return to her presumably dead baby. Esther's doubles thus range from the doll she buries – whereby she '[u]nwittingly . . . repeats in literal form the psychological drama enacted by her own mother on her own birthday: a mother burying her dead baby' (Dever 90) – to the brickmakers' dying baby. Strengthening the symbolism while generating a detective plot, this infant is covered with a handkerchief marked 'Esther Summerson', a handkerchief that Lady Dedlock hides in a drawer, where a detective eventually finds it. In addition, as the illegitimate middle-class child is projected onto a spectrum of suffering infants, several 'orphaned' characters become doubled in their own children to symbolise reclaimed childhood. Thus, Ada's baby, whose 'errand' is 'to bless and restore his mother', even though he is too late to be the 'great aid' she would have needed to save his father, is also a second Richard and thereby presents the happier offspring of two orphans, while he also calls Esther his second mother. Her mothering is thus doubled in an extended reconstitution of an ideal, non-normative family: 'I call him my Richard! But he says that he has two mamas, and I am one' (*Bleak House* 911, 859, 913). Conversely, Mrs Jellyby's daughter Caddy makes up for her own neglected childhood and symbolically repeats the reclaiming of baby Esther when she tends to her diminutive disabled baby (named after Esther), dreaming of 'projects . . . for little Esther's education, and little Esther's marriage, and even for her [Caddy's] own old age as the grandmother of little Esther's little Esthers' (*Bleak House* 710). In Dickens's novel, these forms of reclamation or rebirth determine the resolution despite the gentle parody of emergent detective plots. In pointed contrast, sensation fiction foregrounds the narrative potential of the orphan's mystery of origins, often specifically to complicate the literary uses of adoption before its legalisation. The orphan's double – or the orphan as double – resurfaces in complex imposter plots that threaten to explode the containment of illegitimacy in family structures. In particular, adoption no longer offers a straightforward resolution.

\*

Adoption forms a convenient denouement for orphan narratives. In the second half of the nineteenth century, however, popular fiction addressed practical issues, including the inconveniences or dangers of adoption, often with the intention of criticising the absence of adequate laws regulating the practice. Legal adoption was not possible in Britain until the passage of the Adoption of Children Act in 1926. This is precisely why nineteenth-century novels employ informal adoption as a means to express anxieties surrounding identity formation, the future of the nation, as well as the shifting definition of the Victorian family. As Tess O'Toole has pointed out, the 'lack of a legal framework with which to legitimize an adoption made such reconfigurations of the family both more flexible and more tenuous than modern adoptions and, thus, arguably more closely aligned with fiction than would otherwise be the case' (18). Increasingly, novelists rendered the very absence of legal regulations central to their narratives. Geraldine Jewsbury's *The History of an Adopted Child* (1853) was the first novel to tackle adoption explicitly, although its ambiguous use of the term also exemplifies how our current understanding differs from that predominating in Victorian Britain. Adopting a child could refer both to legally unrecognised non-biological adoption and to the care of young children by relatives other than their birth parents. Thus, the main character considers herself 'an adopted child' because she 'did not live with [her] own parents', but is instead cared for by her grandparents, although she is subsequently also adopted by an unmarried woman who randomly takes a fancy to her (1). At the end of the century, by contrast, Craik produced in *King Arthur* a thesis novel conceived for the purpose of addressing the need for adoption laws. Yet ultimately this agenda becomes entangled in a mystery of origins – with its attendant inheritance plot – testifying to the continued power of this emplotment.

Like orphanhood, the term adoption was used loosely. Victorians often spoke of adopting an orphaned relative, which might or might not involve a legal guardianship, bequeathed in a will. The term might likewise refer to taking in an otherwise unwanted child on impulse, as David Copperfield's great-aunt decides to do when she rescues the boy from his stepfather. After 'step[ping] in between [David and his stepfather] . . . for ever', Miss Trotwood announces to her lawyer that she has 'adopted' the child and wants the best for him: 'to make the child happy and useful' (*David Copperfield* 206, 214–15). She vehemently rejects the suggestion that she might have 'a mixed motive' in doing so: 'A mixed fiddlestick!' (*David Copperfield* 215). In the same novel, a destitute 'orphan nephew and niece' are said to have been 'adopted in their childhood' by Mr Peggotty (*David Copperfield* 32). Similarly, in a straightforward rescue that also marks the resolution at the end of *Oliver Twist*, for example, 'Mr Brownlow adopted Oliver as his own son' (451). By contrast, Aunt Reed does not 'adopt [Jane] of her own accord' when her husband's sister leaves an orphaned baby in Charlotte Brontë's *Jane Eyre* (84). This does not prevent Mrs Reed from subsequently presenting herself as the child's 'benefactress . . . the pious and charitable lady who adopted her in her orphan state' (Brontë 79). These adopted orphans are presented as victims of social or family circumstances and expectations, with adoption either featuring as a rescue or as exacerbating their isolation.

In addition, adoption not only at times fails as a resolution and instead accentuates orphanhood; conversely, mysteries of origins as a recurrent driving force in orphan narratives can prevent closure. The final twist of Craik's thesis novel renders it an insightful case study of the persistent attraction of mysterious origins and lost heirs. Craik (née Mulock) was herself an adoptive mother.

She married George Lillie Craik in 1865 and four years later they adopted a 9-month-old baby girl who had been left at the workhouse. In *King Arthur*, Craik highlights the lack of legal protection of such children by provocatively pointing out that Britain's legislation lagged behind that of the United States of America, where state legislatures had begun passing adoption laws from the mid-century onwards.[11] In the novel, the American doctor who delivers the baby acts as a useful mouthpiece when he asserts that, if he were at home, his wife would 'make [him] adopt it – as we can and often do in America' (Craik 35). Briefly, a starkly vilified birth mother sells her (legitimate) newborn, who is raised by idealised adoptive parents. After a minute detailing of their exemplary parenting, however, Arthur – named after one of the most famous foundling figures in myth or history – turns out to be the missing heir to a nobleman's estate. Middle-class nurture may have rendered him the ideal ruler of the estate (standing in, rather clumsily, for the British Empire), yet this undercuts the novel's interest in adoption laws. Instead, his adoptive father is deemed right in considering that 'in his old age [he himself] would need all his own money; he must not be stinted in anything for the sake of a son – who was not his son' (Craik 116). Within the same logic, Arthur receives his biological father's inheritance. This improbable twist pushes aside realist detail in favour of extended metaphors about future generations. The continued power of the orphan's mystery of origins here interrupts what might otherwise have become the most important adoption novel of the age. Even as Craik dramatises the adoptive mother's constant fear that her son might be taken away from her, the mystery of the foundling's origins nonetheless drives the narrative.

*King Arthur* may ultimately remain ambiguous about issues of inheritance and the respective rights and responsibilities of adopted children and their biological and adoptive parents, but the text is both an important example of a Victorian adoption narrative and evidence of the persistent popularity of the orphan's mysterious origins in fiction. In Craik's novel, this plot device derails the central theme (the need for legal adoption), ironically while attempting to package a particular message in a popular narrative framework. Symptomatically, by the end of the century, lost infant heirs had become an easily parodied cliché. In *The Importance of Being Earnest* (1895), Oscar Wilde pokes fun at the motif: 'To be born, or at any rate bred, in a hand-bag' and thus to be found by a 'charitable gentleman who had a first-class ticket' at the station's cloakroom certainly seems 'to display a contempt for the ordinary decencies of family life' (ll. 631–2, 616–17, 633). The play's denouement parodies narratives involving foundlings and sentimental reunions – at once summing up the most prevalent tropes of the Victorian orphan narrative and pinpointing how clichéd they had become.

\*

Despite these undeniable clichés, the literary uses of orphanhood continually diversified in the course of the nineteenth century. Sensation fiction, in fact, often deliberately upended adoption as a narrative resolution precisely in order to reject clichéd plot developments. 'No Thoroughfare', co-written by Dickens and Collins, showcases the reworking of a classic foundling plot as a sensational narrative of detection. The self-conscious rewriting is already signalled by a shift in class alignments. The traditional tale of swapped infants is moved into an everyday, middle-class milieu. A main character learns that he is not the heir he thought he was. But not only is the heirship transformed into the inheritance of a wine business, owned by a single woman who has had a child out of wedlock. Similarly, the narrative presents the Foundling Hospital as a praiseworthy charity while nonetheless using it as the source of an inadvertent imposter plot. There is consequently an intriguing duality about the Foundling Hospital in the text. It is at once a well-functioning modern institution with exemplary employees and a mysterious place. This continues Dickens's endeavour to weld together the orphan's role in social criticism and the sustained narrative power of a mystery of origins, which is now combined with a sensational plot of mistaken identities. Informed by the widespread popularity of sensational writing at the time, 'No Thoroughfare' capitalises on the anonymity and illegitimacy associated with the Foundling Hospital, even as it is praised as an institution that provides nurturing care to the embodiments of a social problem.

Illegitimacy has been identified as '[o]ne of the most fascinating topics for [sensation] writers' and a 'subject that is especially central to Wilkie Collins's life and books' (Simpson 115). Vicky Simpson terms sensation fiction 'a dynamic forum for Victorians to map out new ideas about the family in the midst of social and political change' (115), and Armstrong further connects the representation of illegitimacy to 'a social imaginary that is fired by an analytic narrative of the dispossessed at the deepest level' (29). Armstrong speaks of the 'double outsider status for mother and child' (7). In 'No Thoroughfare', part of the sensationalism (and the radical undercurrent of this foundling hospital tale) rests in the representation of the fallen woman as a financially successful businesswoman and, in this capacity, as the empowered saviour of unwanted orphans. The self-made woman legally bequeaths her business and property along a doubly illegitimate line.[12] This notably creates her supposed son's moral dilemma, as he is indeed her legal heir, but not her biological child. Thus, the narrative interest shifts to the question of what (adoptive) parenthood means: Is he or is he not her son, if she believes him to be so? Her tragedy – since her project to rescue her biological child fails – is simultaneously that of the adoptive and of the birth mother.

The narrative encapsulates the shift from a sentimentalised Dickensian orphan to the sensationalised foundling whose revealed origins rarely present a straightforward solution or rescue. The opening scene concentrates on a distraught birth mother obsessively lingering in front of the Foundling Hospital. The infant is conspicuously absent. Eschewing readers' expectations of a vilified desertion, the mother appeals to a nurse to breach the rules and reveal the name that has been given her child. Twelve years later, the lady visits the Foundling Hospital, urging a different employee to point out the child of that name. The brief interaction with the boy, Walter Wilding, shows him to be an idealised orphan, polite, grateful and eager to please. Another twelve years later, the adult Walter reflects on his gratitude to and genuine love for the deceased woman, whom he now believes to have been his biological mother: 'the dear parent to whom my heart was mysteriously turned by Nature when she first spoke to me, a strange lady' (Dickens and Collins 548). Wilding himself considers this reclamation 'quite a romantic adventure' (Dickens and Collins 557), but this interpretation is replaced by a much more convoluted, sensational tale of mistaken identities and inadvertent imposture.

Seldom realised in real life, reclamations from the Foundling formed 'a powerful collective fantasy' (Taylor 300).[13] 'No Thoroughfare' capitalises on this fantasy only to demystify it. A former nurse accidentally reveals that, in the narrative's prehistory, the anonymous lady's biological child is adopted as an infant and the name promptly given to a new foundling. This foundling (Wilding in the narrative) now considers himself an imposter, mourning 'the treasured delusion from which he had been awakened so cruelly – of the lost memory which had passed from him like a reflection from a glass' (Collins 579). But if the adoptee's distress condemns the revelation of biological origins, the narrative incongruously derives its main interest from the mystery surrounding the doubled foundlings. 'No Thoroughfare' thus oscillates between asserting the superior importance of nurture and toying with false clues in suggesting that the adoptive mother's own biological child might meanwhile have turned into a criminal character. Wilding's lawyer sums up the most straightforward interpretation of the situation:

> I should comfort myself with remembering that I had loved that poor lady whose portrait you have got there – truly loved her as my mother, and that she had truly loved me as her son. All she gave to you, she gave for the sake of that love. (Dickens and Collins 562)

But the revelation turns out to be fatal to Wilding, who suffers from a possibly hereditary heart disease. Although his business partner, George Vendale, suspects the vicious Obenreizer – guilty of forgery and attempted murder – of being the lost heir, the seeming clues are so obtrusively misinterpreted that the final twist does not come much as a surprise: Vendale, ignorant that he is adopted, turns out to be the original Walter Wilding. Only a hypocrite like Obenreizer, intensely self-conscious about his own background as a Swiss peasant, expects that Vendale would therefore consider himself 'an impostor, without name or lineage, disguised in the character of a gentleman of rank and family' (Dickens and Collins 655). Instead, Vendale welcomes the disclosure because it fulfils his 'dear dead friend's last wish on earth' in finding the right heir and, in addition, 'make[s] him prouder than ever of his peasant-wife', Obenreizer's niece (Dickens and Collins 655).

A narrative that takes two foundlings as its heroes and portrays the fallen woman both as a loving mother and as a successful businesswoman who wants to ensure that her child inherits her fortune, 'No Thoroughfare' finds new venues for conventional orphan plots. While mysteries form a source of sensation, several questions significantly remain unanswered. It becomes irrelevant who Wilding's biological parents are or who Vendale's father might have been. The Foundling Hospital instead becomes the orphan's point of origin. No similarity, moreover, is ever traced between Vendale and his birth mother. Instead, her portrait only inadvertently reveals that Wilding is not the infant deposited at the Foundling in the opening chapter. While indisputably trading on mysterious origins, the narrative ultimately reaffirms ties forged through adoption. Most importantly, the adoptive parent's nurture is thereby identified as the decisive element in the protagonists' character formation. In 'No Thoroughfare', the question about inherited character simply adds to the false clues by misleading us to suspect that the heir might have turned into a villain. In a radical dismissal of genealogy that underscores Armstrong's identification of illegitimacy as 'a heuristic device for examining its challenge to cultural norms, exclusion, social abjection, and perceived inequality' in Victorian fiction (5), this text asserts a prioritisation of nurture that erases the significance of the orphan's origins.

By contrast, precisely by trading on the orphan's sensational potential, Braddon's *The Fatal Three* simultaneously explores an abandoned child's psychological distress and specifically cautions against concealing an adoptee's antecedents. The mysterious origins of Fay (or Fanny) Fausset, alias Vivian Faux, drive the plot. Within a larger exposure of hypocrisy, the illegitimate child is a victim of social mores, but this representation is complicated by her role as a figure of retribution that destroys two families across generations. While challenging readers' expectations of sentimentalised orphans and instead capitalising on the sensational potential of concealed origins, Braddon nonetheless ensures the reader's sympathy with the orphan figure. Fay's childhood memories establish her as a recognisable literary orphan child in the tradition of Oliver Twist, Jane Eyre and Esther Summerson. Through intertextual references, Braddon charts an alternative emplotment that condemns all concealment.

Upending the narrative use of adoption as a pat ending, *The Fatal Three* opens up with the lengthy discussion of 'the adoption of an orphan girl' into a 'temple of domestic peace', which might not 'be quite as peaceful when a new presence was among them': '"It is very dreadful", sighed Mrs Fausset, as if she was speaking of an earthquake. "We have been so happy alone together – you and I and Mildred"' (Braddon 4, 7, 4). The word 'adoption' is insistently reiterated, as the text posits the moral responsibility that Mr Fausset takes on, and further, the incongruity between the promised integration into the family and Fay's alienation. The reference to an 'earthquake' is comical, exposing Mrs Fausset's selfishness. The 'temple of domestic peace' is likewise evoked in a tongue-in-cheek fashion, and yet the teenage adoptee does not make her integration easy. Despite her instantaneous friendship with the Faussets' much younger biological daughter Mildred, the adopted child remains a disruptive presence, which is exacerbated by Mrs Fausset's jealous suspicions that Fay might be her husband's illegitimate daughter because of a slight resemblance between the two girls. Fay is sent abroad, and the narrative re-opens decades later, depicting an idealised family comprising Mildred, her husband George, and an idolised daughter. After the daughter's tragic death – which George interprets as a punishment, much to his wife's confusion – Mildred accidentally discovers that her husband has been married before and recognises in her predecessor's picture her supposed half-sister Fay. The novel thus participates in controversies surrounding the Deceased Wife's Sister Act, which proscribed a widower's marriage to his wife's sister as incestuous, i.e. within forbidden degrees of affinity.[14] Mildred believes she has committed incest, leaves her husband, and engages in reconnaissance work on Fay's tragic orphan narrative. The vivid sketches of Fay's childhood and youth draw on contemporary theories of memory, especially early childhood memories, evoking the childhood chapters of *David Copperfield*, *Great Expectations* and *Jane Eyre*, with their mix of emotional intensity and peculiar glimpses of remembered items. Sharing the feelings of isolation and abandonment with earlier orphan figures, Fay suggests that the difference in her financial circumstances as 'that so-called orphan' exacerbates rather than alleviates her suffering (Braddon 143): 'they all hate me all the same; perhaps because I have a little more money than most of them; perhaps because I am nobody – a waif and stray – able to give no account of my existence' (Braddon 241). Like the embittered Miss Wade in *Little Dorrit*, whose interpolated account of self-hatred adds to Dickens's wide-ranging exploration of illegitimacy and orphanhood, Fay is an illegitimate heiress who feels despised by the world.[15] This friendless rich waif nurtures resentment and self-hatred until her suicide in the late stages of pregnancy drives her husband temporarily insane.

The piecemeal revelation of her death, birth and, ultimately, her parentage teases the reader with false clues. The mysteries of origins thus become the fulcrum on which the detective plot turns. In a direct invocation and inversion of *Bleak House*, rediscovered letters reveal that Mildred's aunt is Fay's biological mother. Miss Fausset is an unmovable, self-righteously pious spinster highly reminiscent of Esther's aunt, whom she cites out of context in an old letter to her now deceased brother: 'Do you remember those words in *Bleak House*? "Your mother, Esther, is your disgrace, and you were hers". So it is with that girl and me. Can love be possible where there is this mutual disgrace?' (Braddon 308). The quotation is heavily ironic considering Lady Dedlock's longing for her presumably dead baby. Instead, in a conflation of the missing mother and the hardhearted aunt who denies any blood-relationship, Miss Fausset is selfishly 'willing to break two hearts rather than hazard [her] own reputation' (Braddon 318). Not only could she have 'made [her] daughter's life happy' – and the text stresses, in an effective sweeping away of any social considerations, that she simply 'would not' (Braddon 321) – but despite repeated appeals to her knowledge of Fay's antecedents, she likewise refuses to lift the suspicion of inadvertent incest from Mildred's marriage. The condemnation is uncompromising:

> How could she [Mildred] be sorry for this woman who had never been sorry for others; who had let her child travel from the cradle to the grave without one ray of maternal love to light her dismal journey! She remembered Fay's desolate life and blighted nature. (Braddon 319)

Throughout the narrative, Fay may be presented as a threat to family life, with the adoptee scripted as an intruder, a superfluous extra child and an equally superfluous first wife. An undeserved outcast, she is a realistically described, psychologically disturbed character, and a sensationalised, Gothic figure. At the end of the novel, however, she is reinterpreted as the victimised orphan, whose life has been 'blighted' by social hypocrisy and injustice. Braddon evokes a deliberate misquotation from *Bleak House* to remind the reader of the classic emplotment of the suffering orphan. Simultaneously, she rewrites the character of Esther Summerson by tracing the lasting psychological damage of an emotionally abused orphan girl. In Braddon's late-Victorian sensation novel, Dickens's orphan narratives feature as intertextual shortcuts to harness readers' familiarity with a particular emplotment, which may then be redirected in self-reflexive engagements with emergent psychological theories and changing social attitudes. This at once consolidates the representative and still iconic significance of Dickens's orphan figures, while showcasing how they can be – and have been repeatedly since the nineteenth century – redeployed in diverse ways to push literary experimentation as well as social agendas.

\*

The Victorian orphan has become unnecessarily clichéd in the popular imagination. Ironically, its iconic status has overshadowed the figure's versatility. Yet nineteenth-century authors were highly aware of and often explicitly tackled the conceptual fluidity of the literary orphan and thereby transformed this figure. For the Victorians, the figure of the orphan primarily symbolised the vulnerability of childhood and, as such, it was easily sentimentalised, yet it also served as a usefully flexible figure to showcase pressing issues of the time. This duality created problems for the realist representation of the idealised, but suffering – or ideal, because suffering – orphan child. Sentimentalised young orphans seemed curiously immune to social circumstances, while the mysteries of origins complicated their role especially in reform writing. One important way to tackle the resulting ambiguities was a more in-depth focus on psychological development, and thus orphan narratives centrally assisted in the exploration of childhood, memory and trauma in fiction. While Oliver Twist is notoriously incorruptible, for example, orphans whose childhood – if not their entire development – has been 'blighted', as Braddon puts it in *The Fatal Three*, embody specific social and legal concerns that directly pertained to the experience of orphanhood: the social regulation of illegitimacy and the lack of laws governing adoption.

Orphan narratives thus self-reflexively reshaped expected patterns, creating aesthetically and culturally insightful experiments. In particular, adoption no longer worked as a simple resolution or pat ending. Challenging the easy containment of the illegitimate through the reconstitution of family structures, sensation novels frequently employed the figure of the double to play out the adoptee's potential as a threat, while nonetheless engendering sympathy for the victimised orphan. In an ironic twist that concludes 'No Thoroughfare', the inadvertent imposter's putatively legitimate business partner turns out to be the missing orphan, while the murderous villain embodies, articulates, and through his death, ultimately expunges hypocritical attitudes to illegitimacy. However, if the informality and secrecy of adoption at the time certainly facilitated such narrative mysteries, their exposure in sensation fiction could also explicitly condemn the lack of transparency, as we have seen in Braddon's conscious rewriting of Dickensian orphanhood. Throughout the nineteenth century, novelists continued to sentimentalise as well as to sensationalise orphan protagonists, but in the most self-conscious moments, their narrative functions were critically addressed and redirected. Even if the most memorable literary orphans of the period seemingly fit into a clichéd iconography, it is vital that we appreciate the variety, flexibility and self-reflexivity of their narratives.

### Notes

1. Braddon challenges popular orphan narratives through several levels of intertextual references. A character's appropriation of specific 'words in *Bleak House*' referring to Esther's supposed 'disgrace' through her mother is among the most explicit of such references (Braddon 308), as we shall see.
2. Auerbach argues that an examination of the orphan 'may give us another perspective on the English novel, both as a genre in itself and as a reflection of the culture it simultaneously embodies and repudiates,'

but this is precisely why 'the orphan seems to represent a vital strain in the novel' (395).
3. A Victorian orphan figure is usually introduced as a young child who becomes neglected or mistreated by villainous characters, an uncaring society, or both. In several cases, the protagonist is rescued and adopted, often by a relative who has been looking for the long lost child. Several of these child protagonists, from Dickens's Oliver Twist and Charlotte Brontë's Jane Eyre to Sara Crewe in Frances Hodgson Burnett's *A Little Princess* (1905), are originally of middle-class origins and have been cheated out of an inheritance or their presumably proper place in society. The paradigm continues, often in children's literature, although increasingly the inheritance plot is rejected in favour of fortuitous adoption. Examples range from film adaptations of *The Little Princess* to such Disney classics as *Pete's Dragon* (1977; remade in 2016) or *Meet the Robinsons* (2007), or also *Little Orphan Annie*, originally conceived as a comic strip in 1924, inspired by James Whitcomb Riley's 1885 poem 'Little Orphant Annie', to become a Broadway musical in 1977.
4. Some well-known real-life examples include George Henry Lewes, who gave his name to his wife's illegitimate children by Thornton Hunt; Edith Nesbit adopting two of her husband's illegitimate children by Alice Hoatson; and Lillie Langtry's daughter, who was told she was her niece. See also Frost on the 'fictitious identity' of the child in working-class households (Frost, *Lamb* 295). In fiction, examples range from Henry Fielding's *Tom Jones* (1749) to Dr Thorne's adoption of his illegitimate niece in Trollope's *Dr Thorne* (1858) and the illegitimacy sub-plot of Mary Cholmondeley's *Diana Tempest* (1893). Armstrong evokes Pip, in Dickens's *Great Expectations*, as 'an honorary illegitimate child', who is 'virtually co-opted into illegitimacy' (31).
5. Several protagonists of Victorian canonical fiction, from Arthur Clennam in Dickens's *Little Dorrit* (1857) to the eponymous hero of George Eliot's *Daniel Deronda* (1876), are ignorant of or in doubt about their possible illegitimacy. In Dickens's *The Old Curiosity Shop* (1841), an exploited servant girl is her mistress's illegitimate daughter.
6. Roach has suggested that between 1840 and 1860, out of 834 infants admitted, only 26 were reclaimed (n. 30).
7. Nelson describes waif fiction as 'a widely read genre that combined pathos with an earnest desire to improve society' (*Family* 56). On the representation of the NSPCC (National Society for the Prevention of Cruelty to Children, founded in 1884) in Victorian literature see also Flegel, *passim*.
8. Dickens scholars have tended to diagnose the resulting inconsistency as an expression of bourgeois anxiety (Baldridge 184), yet it is also evidence of Dickens's commitment to romance structures within his realism (Tillotson 87–105).

9. The sensation novel began to emerge in the 1850s, with the early works of Wilkie Collins and Mrs Henry Wood.
10. Novy argues that 'Aunt Barbary and Miss Havisham, even Aunt Reed, have moral agendas in their treatment of their adopted children, agendas that in some cases build on commonplaces of Victorian culture' (119).
11. The Massachusetts Adoption of Children Act was passed in 1851.
12. 'Reading against dominant paradigms of patriarchal inheritance and women's marginalized financial status', Lana Dalley and Jill Rappoport have recently stressed the need that we 'explore women's capacity to function as active economic agents' in Victorian texts (16, 25).
13. Emma Brownlow King's painting *The Foundling Restored to Its Mother* (1858), purpose-painted to adorn the walls of the London Foundling Hospital, powerfully portrays such a reclamation. Its depiction of the 'restoration of child to mother (and mother to child)' realises 'the dream [of a] moment of recognition and reunion, with the mother's happy return,' a dream that simultaneously 'involved a fantasy not just of the mother's improved material situation, but of her moral improvement too' (Bowlby 98–9). See Taylor (298–302); Bowlby (97–102). Bowlby argues that King's 'picture resonates with two novels published in the same period': George Eliot's *Silas Marner* and Emily Brontë's *Wuthering Heights* (99–100).
14. Known as Lord Lynhurst's Act, passed in 1835, the law was repeatedly under attack and generally flouted, but in Britain marriage to a deceased wife's sister was only legalised in 1907. The novel has primarily been read in the context of this controversy (see Pedlar 127).
15. In an embedded narrative in *Little Dorrit*, Miss Wade recounts how her illegitimacy renders her an angry and revengeful outcast. Miss Wade feels drawn to the foundling Tattycoram, inducing her to run away from the friendly, but patronising Meagles. In the same novel, Arthur Clennam discovers his concealed illegitimacy. The character of Fay is likewise remarkably similar to the suicidal and insanely jealous first wife in Collins's *The Law and the Lady* (1875).

## Works Cited

Armstrong, Isobel. *Novel Politics: Democratic Imaginations in Nineteenth-Century Fiction*. Oxford University Press, 2016.

Auerbach, Nina. 'Incarnations of the Orphan'. *ELH*, vol. 42, no. 3, 1975, pp. 395–419.

Baldridge, Cates. 'The Instabilities of Inheritance in *Oliver Twist*'. *Studies in the Novel*, vol. 25, no. 2, 1993, pp. 184–95.

Bloom, Harold. *Charles Dickens*. Chelsea House, 2013. Google Ebook: https://books.google.com.sg/books?id=rZhbAgAAQBAJ&printsec=fron

tcover&source=gbs_ge_summary_r&cad=0#v=snippet&q=incorruptibl e&f=false (accessed 11 September 2017).

Bowlby, Rachel. *A Child of One's Own: Parental Stories*. Oxford University Press, 2013.

Braddon, Mary Elizabeth. [1888]. *The Fatal Three*. Stroud: Sutton Publishing, 1997.

Brontë, Charlotte. *Jane Eyre*. [1847]. Penguin, 2006.

Burdett, Carolyn. 'Emotions', in *The Oxford Handbook of Victorian Literary Culture*, ed. Juliet John. Oxford University Press, 2016, pp. 580–97.

Craik, Dinah Maria Mulock. *King Arthur: Not a Love Story*. Bernhard Tauchnitz, 1886.

Dalley, Lana and Rappoport, Jill. 'Introducing Economic Women', in *Economic Women: Essays on Desire and Dispossession in Nineteenth-Century British Culture*, ed. Dalley and Rappoport. Ohio University Press, 2013, pp. 1–21.

Dever, Carolyn. *Death and the Mother From Dickens to Freud: Victorian Fiction and the Anxiety of Origins*. Cambridge University Press, 1998.

Dickens, Charles. *Bleak House*. 1853. Oxford World's Classics, 1998.

Dickens, Charles. *David Copperfield*. 1850. Oxford World's Classics, 2008.

Dickens, Charles. *Dombey and Son*. 1848. Oxford World's Classics, 2008.

Dickens, Charles. *Great Expectations*. 1861. Oxford World's Classics, 2008.

Dickens, Charles. *Little Dorrit*. 1857. Oxford World's Classics, 2012.

Dickens, Charles. *Nicholas Nickleby*. 1839. Oxford World's Classics, 2008.

Dickens, Charles. *Oliver Twist*. 1838. Penguin, 2003.

Dickens, Charles. *Our Mutual Friend*. 1865. Penguin, 1997.

Dickens, Charles and Collins, Wilkie. 'No Thoroughfare'. *Christmas Stories by Charles Dickens*. 1867. Oxford University Press, 1996.

Flegel, Monica. *Conceptualizing Cruelty to Children in Nineteenth-Century England: Literature, Representation, and the NSPCC*. Ashgate, 2009.

Fludernik, Monika. *An Introduction to Narratology*. Routledge, 2009.

Frost, Ginger. '"The black lamb of the black sheep": Illegitimacy in the English Working Class, 1850–1939'. *Journal of Social History*, vol. 37, no. 2, 2003, pp. 293–322.

Frost, Ginger. *Victorian Childhoods*. Praeger, 2009.

Furneaux, Holly. 'Children of the Regiment: Soldiers, Adoption, and Military Tenderness in Victorian Culture'. *Victorian Review*, vol. 39, no. 2, 2013, pp. 79–96.

Furneaux, Holly. *Queer Dickens: Erotics, Families, Masculinities*. Oxford University Press, 2009.

Golding, Robert. *Idiolects in Dickens: The Major Techniques and Chronological Development*. Macmillan, 1985.

Hager, Kelly and Schaffer, Talia. 'Extending Families', *Victorian Review* [Special Issue], vol. 39, no. 2, 2013, pp. 7–21.

Hochman, Baruch and Wachs, Ilja. *Dickens: The Orphan Condition*. Fairleigh Dickinson University Press, 1999.

Jewsbury, Geraldine. *The History of an Adopted Child*. Grant and Griffith, 1853.

Murdoch, Lydia. *Imagined Orphans: Poor Families, Child Welfare, and Contested Citizenship in London*. Rutgers University Press, 2006.

Nelson, Claudia. 'Adoption, Fostering, and the Poor'. *Victorian Review*, vol. 39, no. 2, 2013, pp. 57–61.

Nelson, Claudia. *Family Ties in Victorian England*. Praeger, 2007.

Nixon, Cheryl L. *The Orphan in Eighteenth-Century Law and Literature: Estate, Blood, and Body*. Ashgate, 2011.

Novy, Marianne. *Reading Adoption: Family and Difference in Fiction and Drama*. University of Michigan Press, 2005.

O'Toole, Tess. 'Adoption and the "Improvement of the Estate" in Trollope and Craik', in *Imagining Adoption: Essays on Literature and Culture*, ed. Marianne Novy. University of Michigan Press, 2001, pp. 17–33.

Pedlar, Valerie. *'The most dreadful visitation': Male Madness in Victorian Fiction*. Liverpool University Press, 2006.

Peters, Laura. *Orphan Texts: Victorian Orphans, Culture and Empire*. Manchester University Press, 2000.

Roach, Catherine. 'The Foundling Restored: Emma Brownlow King, William Hogarth, and the Public Image of the Foundling Hospital in the 19th Century'. *British Art Journal*, vol. 9, no. 2, 2008, pp. 40–9.

Simpson, Vicky. 'Selective Affinities: Non-Normative Families in Wilkie Collins's *No Name*'. *Victorian Review*, vol. 39, no. 2, 2013, pp. 115–28.

Taylor, Jenny Bourne. '"Received, a blank child": John Brownlow, Charles Dickens, and the London Foundling Hospital – Archives and Fictions'. *Nineteenth-Century Literature*, vol. 56, no. 3, 2001, pp. 293–363.

Tillotson, Kathleen. 'Oliver Twist'. *Essays and Studies*, vol. 12, 1959, pp. 87–105.

Wagner, Tamara S. '"We have orphans ... in stock": Crime and the Consumption of Sensational Children', in *Nineteenth-Century Childhood and the Rise of Consumer Culture*, ed. Dennis Denisoff. Ashgate, 2008, pp. 201–15.

Wilde, Oscar. *The Importance of Being Earnest*. 1895. Ebook: https://www.gutenberg.org/files/844/844-h/844-h.htm (accessed 1 November 2016).

# Chapter 4

# Adoptive Reading
## Kelly Hager

Consider these characters: Oswald Bastable (and his five brothers and sisters), Sara Crewe, Anne (of Green Gables) and Rebecca (of Sunnybrook Farm). Orphans all, at least in the nineteenth-century sense of the term,[1] and also voracious, impressionable and, to use the parlance of our day, interactive readers. This chapter is about the coping strategies and pragmatic uses these orphan readers make of and take from their books, as well as the effects of that admittedly uncritical – relying as it does on projection and identification – reading. The co-incidence of all these orphans (all these fictional children in need, at least according to the novels and the culture that produced them, of a family) that act out and upon their reading in direct and very result-oriented ways indicates something significant about how they read and about what that kind of reading gets them.

Left largely on their own and to their own devices after their mother's death, the six Bastable children seek to 'restore the fallen fortunes of the ancient House of Bastable', a phrase that reveals how their reading defines and dictates their actions, reminiscent as it is of the books they have read (2). The title of E. Nesbit's first novel about the Bastable children – *The Story of the Treasure Seekers* (1899) – suggests its plot, but what the title doesn't indicate is that participatory reading is their strategy for finding treasure,[2] nor does it indicate the more significant subject of the novel, which is discovering not treasure, but how to remedy their orphaned state. As Oswald, the eldest boy and the novel's narrator, says,

> we were the Treasure Seekers, and we sought it high and low, and quite regularly, because we particularly wanted to find it. And at last we did not find it, but we were found by a good, kind Indian uncle. (*The Wouldbegoods* 137)

Similarly, Frances Hodgson Burnett's (riches-to-)rags-to-riches story, *A Little Princess* (1905), depicts in quasi-fantastic fashion the power of reading as a coping strategy, enabling Sara Crewe to endure abuse, neglect, hunger and alienation. But the real pay-off of Sara's belief that '*Everything's* a story' comes when, in true fairy-tale fashion, she's rescued from her life of servitude by the fairy godfather figure that lives next door (89). He not only raises her status from drudge to princess and moves her from the rat-filled servants' quarters to his spacious and opulently furnished house next door, but, and the novel suggests more importantly, in restoring her domestic fortunes, he ensconces her within not just one, but two families. Sara is 'adopted' by Mr Carrisford, her father's best friend (the novel's diction, significantly, equates ties of affection with those of blood), and the fact that he himself has been embraced by his lawyer's own 'Large Family'[3] means that when he becomes Sara's guardian, he gives her two families, one with him, and another with that 'Large Family'.

Like Sara's predilection for equating the fortunes and misfortunes that befall her with things she's read about, Anne Shirley, too, seems unable to understand her life in anything but literary terms. 'My life is a perfect graveyard of buried hopes', she says, when Marilla tells her that her hair's not likely to turn from the red she hates to 'another color when she grew up'. 'That's a sentence I read in a book once', she explains, 'and I say it over to comfort myself when I'm disappointed in anything' (39). That habit of approaching her life in terms of literature proves to be such an undeniable (albeit strange) attraction to the bachelor/spinster brother and sister who find her on their hands that they adopt her. 'I can feel already that I'm wondering what on earth she'll say next. She'll be casting a spell over me, too. She's cast it over Matthew already', Marilla 'mutter[s] to herself' halfway through Anne's first day at Green Gables (37). And while Rebecca Randall's aunts take her in out of a sense of obligation, not because they're enamoured of her habit of acting out scenes from the novels and poems she's read (which she does at the drop of a hat), it is Rebecca's reading, just as it is the Bastable children's and Sara's and Anne's, that creates the community of friends that cluster around her in Kate Douglas Wiggin's 1903 novel; it is the irresistible way she makes play novel – her novel-play, we might say – that puts her at the centre of all the text's adventures and provides her with a loyal band of followers. That play not only endears her, eventually, to her maiden aunts, in a plot that anticipates Montgomery's, but it also, the novel implies, leads her to the man who will become her husband.[4]

These orphans, then, engage in what Andrew Stauffer calls 'adoptive reading', a phrase I find so resonant and so apt that I've taken it for my title. Tracing the way nineteenth-century readers annotated their copies of Felicia Hemans's poems, Stauffer reveals the 'layering of common and individual experience' at work in their reading and the very specific and (literally) text-based ways they link what they're reading to what they've experienced in their own lives (86). In Hemans's poetry, Stauffer observes, 'readers found a language for their own baffled hearts and an almost ritualised unpacking of emotion like a chant or spell whereby the book becomes a source of expression when one's own words fail' (90). While Stauffer's readers are actual, and the links they make between their lives and the poems they read are discernible in the marginalia of their copies of Hemans's volumes of poetry, the readers I'm concerned with here are fictional, and the links they make between their lives and the texts they read (stories, poems, novels, fairy tales, history books) are discernible in their diction, their play, and their way of understanding and engaging with their worlds and the characters that people those worlds. But both the actual nineteenth-century readers – who left traces of the uses they made of Hemans's poetry in their volumes of her poems – and these fictional Golden Age children – who use what they read as scripts for their adventures and as guides to the situations they encounter – are employing those 'books as objects of use, as interfaces providing occasions for interaction' (Stauffer 81). That is, they respond to what they read as if it has reference to and relevance for them, as if it's something to be engaged with directly, something they can use and apply to and in their own lives.

The 'adoptive and adaptive' way they read is, Stauffer would point out, not unlike the way our students, 'who often want literature to be relatable', sometimes read (86, 83). But that kind of reading is also at work, as Stauffer shows, in the poetry of Felicia Hemans herself, when she 'fills in the gaps [of something she's read], expanding the reference by investing it with personal emotion drawn from her recent experience' as well as in the annotations that nineteenth-century readers made in early editions of her poems (83). Stauffer takes that kind of reading seriously; he sees it as an important addition and corrective to our understanding of nineteenth-century reading practices. Similarly, 'by focusing on how nineteenth-century novels invite readers to feel as though they have come to know unreal persons, places, and incidents in unexpectedly intimate and durable ways', Elaine Auyoung 'demonstrate[s] that 'uncritical' reading can be an object of study that repays serious critical attention' (3). Accordingly, I point to the significance of playing by the book as an important addition to our understanding of children and their reading practices in the Golden Age[5] (or, perhaps more accurately, the way children's reading practices were understood and constructed by Golden Age writers) and an indication of the cultural work these novels are doing with respect to the ideology of the family. Acting out scenes from their favourite novels and poems and 'tak[ing] them to illuminate the world' (the phrase is Jonathan Culler's) is not, in these novels, quixotic behaviour they need to grow out of but rather a reading strategy that enables them to find a kind of family, a community and a sense of belonging (5). What is more, their 'active, invested, adoptive reading' enables them to survive in both domestic and economic terms. (Stauffer 95). I seek, then, to shed light on the way childhood reading was constructed and construed in the period we celebrate as the Golden Age of children's literature and to uncover the connection between that kind of reading and the way these classic texts for and about children contributed to the era's valorisation of the nuclear family, even as they depict and celebrate decidedly non-normative forms of family.

Crucial to my exploration here is the tight – if at times ironic, given how often the genre places orphans front and centre – link between children's literature and the notion of family. More often than not, family is either the goal of the child protagonist's quest – the *telos* of the plot of a work of children's literature – or the setting – the background or ethos that frames and defines the child and the text in which she figures. But that notion of family needs also to be contextualised in terms of the emergence in the eighteenth century of what we now recognise as the modern family, and it's equally important to remember that such an idea of family was not universal. Indeed, children's literature in the long nineteenth century (not to mention before and after) is full of non-normative families presented as domestic ideals, and the novels I'm concentrating on here, Golden Age classics from the US and the UK, shed some light on the ideology of family to which they're responding and, at the same time, helping to shape. That ideology was 'painstakingly performed, reconstructed, challenged, and extended' in the nineteenth century, and that performance, reconstruction, challenge and extension is at work in the four novels that are my focus here (Hager and

Schaffer 14–15). That ideology is performed with particular clarity in the topos of the orphan figure, suggesting, as that bereft child so clearly does, that the nuclear family is the norm and that a child without both parents is bereaved of something crucial and important. But that ideology is also reconstructed and extended in the families these novels ultimately celebrate, all of which are, to some degree or another, non-normative. All of these novels begin with fractured families and children orphaned in some form or fashion, and they all end with families made whole, albeit almost always in unconventional, usually non-biological arrangements, arrangements that suggest how pliable the notion of family is, at least in these novelists' hands.

The family at the centre of *The Treasure Seekers* is composed of the six Bastable children and their widowed father and marked most prominently by the absence of both parents (their mother is dead, while their father is usually away on business and distracted by financial worries when he is home). At the end of the novel, the Bastables and their father are about to move in with their (rich) maternal uncle, a figure who makes their family whole and financially sound. The rather normative and biological nature of that family is reshaped and extended in the second novel in the series, however, when the six Bastables and two other children (the son and daughter of 'an old college friend' of Mr Bastable's) go to the country for the summer to live with the uncle of the child who lived next door to the Bastables (before they moved in with their rich great-uncle, that is) (109). That individual, routinely referred to not by name but by extended relation, if you will, as 'Albert-next-door's-uncle', is the closest thing the series has to a paternal figure, and it's crucial to the link I'm tracing here between reading and family that he is a novelist. As such, he has patience with and sympathy for the way the Bastable children play. It is 'Albert-next-door's-uncle', in fact, 'who first taught us how to make people talk like books when you're playing things', Oswald relates (115–16). In both the first and the second novels in the series, the family that gets the most attention is composed of this avuncular bachelor figure and a set of children with the scantest of (and absolutely no biological) connections to him. And while the construction of this family appears, I realise as I struggle to describe it, improbable and incredibly ad hoc, its composition is, in Nesbit's hands, organic and benevolent. Their father's evident love for his children notwithstanding, it is Albert-next-door's-uncle that spends the most time with the children in the first two novels, provides the most consistent care for them, disciplines them, and tells them stories, and it is to him they constantly and routinely turn when they are in trouble. They seem to belong to and with him more than they do with any of their biological kin.

The uneasy, deficient relationship between blood relations is at work in *Rebecca of Sunnybrook Farm*, too. Rebecca Randall is the second of seven children. When the novel opens, her father has been dead for three years, and she is on the way to live with her mother's older sisters, two spinsters who have 'invited her [though her "self-contained, well-behaved, dependable" older sister was their first choice] to be a member of their family and participate in all the advantages of their loftier position in the world' (23). The novel's language is key here; she is not just invited to live with her aunts, which she does for the duration of the novel, but 'to be a member of their family'. One could argue that she is already, as their niece, a member of their family, and it's crucial to this novel's ideology of family at the outset that it is a matter of invitation, not blood (or happenstance and shared proclivities, as it is in Nesbit's series). However, the family at the end of the novel is composed of Rebecca, her remaining three siblings (one has married, one has died, one is living with a widowed cousin), her mother and her youngest aunt (Jane), and they are all to live in her aunts' house, which the eldest aunt (Miranda) wills to Rebecca. This is the narrator's description of that home and that family, at novel's end:

> It was home; her roof, her garden, her green acres, her dear trees; it was shelter for the little family at Sunnybrook; her mother would have once more the companionship of her sister and the friends of her girlhood; the children would have teachers and playmates. (224–5)

Rebecca is, at the age of seventeen, the matriarch of the family, and it is her maternal grandfather's house that will protect and nurture the family she presides over. Biological family is valorised here, to be sure, but in an oddly virginal way, with Rebecca's mother returned to her girlhood and Rebecca's father all but erased. Further, this version of family is created as a result of that initial invitation to Rebecca to become a part of her aunts' family.

Rebecca is also, early on in the novel, unofficially but most affectionately adopted by a childless couple, the Cobbs, who are animated as much by sympathy for the cold reception Rebecca initially gets from her Aunt Miranda as they are by their admiration of her literary bent. The Cobb family both performs and challenges the normative ideology of family. On the one hand, Jeremiah Cobb calls his wife Sarah 'Mother' even though she 'was mother only to a little headstone in the churchyard where reposed "Sarah Ann, beloved daughter of Jeremiah and Sarah Cobb, aged seventeen months"'; he calls her 'Mother' because 'the name of mother was better than nothing, and served at any rate as a reminder of her woman's crown of blessedness' (69). Motherhood is presented here as both a kind of requirement ('the *name* of mother was better than nothing') and a mark of holiness, as if a child was both necessary[6] and divinely sent. Yet calling his wife 'Mother' is deemed an 'old-fashioned habit,' a phrase and a judgement that suggests that perhaps the novel's ideas of family are more advanced than those of Mr Cobb (69). In referring to himself as Rebecca's 'old uncle Jerry', he also has recourse to a biological relationship to describe a tie of affection. That understanding is echoed by Rebecca's (biological) Aunt Jane, who calls Rebecca 'an old maid's child' when happily recounting the skills she's been teaching her niece (73). The novel thus holds up the biological, nuclear family as the norm and standard and, simultaneously, makes it clear – in ways that feel earned in terms of the plot and are emotionally satisfying – that recent acquaintances can quickly attain the status of aunt and uncle and that a niece might more accurately be thought of as 'an old maid's *child*'. The bonds established between Rebecca and the Cobbs and between Rebecca and her gentle Aunt Jane are affectionate, sustaining and mutually supportive; they embody and illustrate the kind of instruction and care a family is supposed to provide. They're also animated and characterised by their appreciation of Rebecca's literary habits. The narrator makes special mention of the 'joy' Jane takes 'in certain quiet evenings when Miranda went to prayer meeting; evenings when Rebecca would read aloud Hiawatha or Barbara Fritchie, The Bugle Song, or The Brook' (118). Mrs Cobb is convinced that Rebecca's poetry is not only 'as good' as Longfellow's 'A Psalm of Life,' but also 'consid'able clearer' (86). It's important to note here, too, that biological families do not, in this novel, often live up to the standard set by the Cobbs and Aunt Jane.[7]

Biological families rarely appear in *A Little Princess*, though they certainly loom large in the novel's plot and are among its primary concerns. Sara's mother died when she was born, seven years before the novel begins, and while she loves her father 'more than all the world ten times over', when the novel opens, he is taking her to boarding school in London, a transition she has been dreading all 'her short life' and one that marks the rupture of their little nuclear family (25, 6). Sara has grown up with the awareness that she, like all the other British children she knows in India, will be separated from her parents because 'the climate of India was very bad for children, and as soon as possible they were sent away from it' (6). 'She had seen other children go away', the narrator tells us in the novel's opening chapter,

> and had heard their fathers and mothers talk about the letters they had received from them. She had known that she would be obliged to go also, and . . . she had been troubled by the thought that [her father] could not stay with her. (6)

At Miss Minchin's Select Seminary, Sara is surrounded by children separated from their parents.[8] Being what the narrator calls 'a motherly young person', she turns them into a kind of family (29). Most explicitly, she tells the spoiled baby of the school, Lottie, 'I will be your mamma. We will play that you are my little girl. And Emily [Sara's doll] shall be your sister' (34). 'There were' also and crucially (for the plot and for the novel's ethos with respect to the construct of family) 'several [intact biological] families in the square in which Miss Minchin lived, with which she had become quite familiar in a way of her own', the narrator tells us in a chapter soon after Sara's father dies. In the novel's happy ending, Sara becomes a part of one of those families. Indeed, the familial warmth (and material privilege) that ensconces Sara at the novel's beginning is matched by the same domestic warmth and privilege at the end, and while the father–daughter tie is replaced with a foster[9] uncle–niece relationship (not unlike the celebration of the avuncular we see in Nesbit and Wiggin), the novel's Cinderella plot makes the family Sara finds at the end of the novel seem more like the stuff of fairy tale than a verisimilitudinous representation of family at the turn of the century.

Anne Shirley echoes that sense of a domestic dream come true when she exclaims to Matthew, 'It seems so wonderful that I'm going to live with you and belong to you' (13). And that fairy tale, similarly, takes a while to come true. Indeed, family in *Anne of Green Gables* is not, at least at the outset and on the surface of the novel, a very flexible or inviting structure. Matthew and Marilla set out to adopt a boy (not a girl) from the orphan asylum, and they want the boy not to be a member of their family but to help sixty-year-old Matthew with the farm. Even when Marilla assures her best friend, the interfering but good-hearted Rachel Lynde, that they want a boy who will be 'of some use in doing chores right off', Rachel is aghast. 'I think you're doing a mighty foolish thing – a risky thing, that's what. You don't know what you're getting. You're bringing a strange child into your house and home and you don't know a single thing about him' (7). The novel's, or at least Marilla's, scepticism about family in general becomes clear when Marilla replies that 'there's risks in people having children of their own if it comes to that – they don't always turn out well' (8). Anne's experiences as an orphan girl farmed out to various families to help with their children bears out Marilla's scepticism. Only eleven when the novel begins, she has already been exposed to the reality of unhappy marriages, abusive husbands, and unwanted and neglected children.[10] Nevertheless, Anne enters the novel starved for home and family and overcome by the idea 'of coming to a really truly home', while the novel's end finds her happily ensconced in a home and with people that are 'really truly' hers in every sense (20). 'I love you as dear as if you were my own flesh and blood', Marilla tells her, 'and you've been my joy and comfort ever since you came to Green Gables' (310). 'I'd rather have you than a dozen boys', Matthew assures her, calling her 'my girl – my girl that I'm proud of' (306). Anne has grown up at Green Gables, she has been loved and disciplined and educated and nurtured in it and by its owners, and her salary as a teacher will enable Marilla to keep it, for the heart attack that kills Matthew at the novel's end is brought on by news that the bank that holds 'every cent of our money' has failed. Without Anne's financial help, Marilla would be forced to sell the family home (317).

How that home (and more to the point, that family) come to be Anne's has, as I suggest above, much to do with the kind of reader she is, and the same is true for all the orphans I'm focusing on here. While Marilla initially insists they send Anne back to the orphan asylum since she's not the (useful) boy they asked for, Matthew wants to keep her because, as he puts it, 'she's a real interesting little thing. You should have heard her talk coming from the station' (31). Her talk coming from the station is characteristic of her speech (and her nature), and it reflects her reading, with references to marble halls and worldly goods and a confession that she liked to imagine things about the other children in the asylum. 'Perhaps the girl who sat next to you was really the daughter of a belted earl, who had been stolen away from her parents in her infancy by a cruel nurse who died before she could confess', she breathlessly recounts (14). That her imaginings come from her reading is made explicit when she relates that her red hair is her 'lifelong sorrow' and goes on to explain that she 'read of a girl once in a novel who had a lifelong sorrow, but it wasn't red hair. Her hair was pure gold rippling back from her alabaster brow' (18). Anne is stamped as a reader, characterised by her understanding of her life in terms of the books she's read and by the literary allusions that mark her even her casual conversation. We see in her speech, her actions and her approach to the world how what she's read 'infiltrates and informs her life', to borrow Rita Felski's apt phrase (10).

In her manifesto, *Uses of Literature*, Felski chides critics who 'fail to do justice to the specific ways in which [works of literature] infiltrate and inform our lives' and who don't consider a text's 'ability to traverse temporal boundaries and to generate new and unanticipated resonances' (10). 'We are', she insists, 'sorely in need of richer and deeper accounts of how selves interact with texts' (11). Similarly, Elaine Auyoung proposes that we consider how 'novels invite readers to feel as though they have come to know unreal persons, places and incidents in unexpectedly intimate and durable ways' and that we think about that kind of reading 'as an effect whose persistence suggests that producing it is fundamental to the craft of fiction', rather than dismissing it as 'nonintellectual, even regressive' (3, 2). Like Stauffer's reclamation of 'adoptive reading', these critics take seriously the identificatory habit of reading that characterises my orphan-readers. In considering how the Bastable children, Rebecca Rowena Randall, Sara Crewe and Anne Shirley act out and upon their reading, I join these critics in that recuperative work.

Take, for instance, the literary dinner to which the Bastable children treat the uncle they have just met, a dinner straight out of *Children of the New Forest*, where they pretend to be eating 'the deer we had slain in the green forest with our trusty yew bows' and put the pudding on the floor, as befits the 'wild boar at bay' ('very hard indeed to kill, even with forks') it is impersonating. That scene of (extremely) active, participatory reading not only charms their uncle and shows him in a very sympathetic light ('the Uncle was very fierce indeed with the pudding, and jumped and howled when he speared it'), but it also leads him to reverse his original opinion of their domestic situation (123). Indeed, the evening he spends with them is such a success that his disgust at the 'shocking bad dinner!' their father had given him the night before and the aspersions he casts on their father's business capabilities turn into sympathy for the family's plight and an offer to invest in Mr Bastable's business (118). That his reversal has much to do with the children's reading practices is made clear in several ways.[11] He exclaims to their father the very next day, right after this literary 'play-dinner', that they are the 'jolliest little cubs I ever saw', remonstrates with Mr Bastable for not introducing him to the children at the outset, and suggests he'll be able to help him out with his business after all (122, 127). What is more, the enthusiastic way he enters in to this adventure novel brought to life suggests that he is at heart a naïve reader himself, so adept is he at carving the 'deer' and alive to the 'fact' that, as he puts it, 'game was always nicer when you had killed it yourself' (123). [12]

In his recuperation of the annotative, adoptive reading practices of Hemans's first readers, Stauffer calls attention to the fact that he is countering the 'general suspicion of personal, appropriative responses to literary works wherein literature is valued for being relatable', and I want to highlight the fact that the Bastables' uncle also counters that suspicion (94). While he is disturbed by the fact that the children are not in school, he does not associate their truant state with their identificatory reading practices. He does not dismiss them as naïve, untutored readers but rather delights in the way they pull their reading right down to the nursery floor. He is also delighted by them. He sees in Dora, the eldest Bastable child, 'the image' of his deceased sister (the Bastables' mother), 'and as to young Oswald, he's a man!' (127). At the novel's end, he brings them all to live with him, 'and, please God, it'll be a happy home for us all', he trusts (131). That benediction cements the connection between the (re)formation of family and a mode of reading that links the fictional with the actual, but there is more. After this announcement, Oswald tells us

> the Uncle took us all over the house, which is the most comfortable one I have ever been in. There is a beautiful portrait of Mother in Father's sitting-room. The Uncle must be very rich indeed. This ending is like what happens in Dickens's books; but I think it was much jollier to happen like a book, and it shows what a nice man the Uncle is, the way he did it all. (131)

It also shows what kind of reader the Uncle is, we might argue, since he arranges an ending that resembles that of a novel. That ending is, then, capped off by the extension and stabilisation of their family (that 'beautiful portrait of Mother' constitutes her only appearance in the novel, but, as Oswald puts it in the novel's second paragraph, 'if you think we don't care because I don't tell you much about her you only show that you do not understand people at all') and characterised by the link it establishes between the actual and the fictional.

Oswald thinks there's nothing remarkable or at all questionable about his literary approach to life. For instance, he 'felt quite certain that the books were right, and that the best way to restore fallen fortunes was to rescue an old gentleman in distress' (68).[13] He and his siblings approach books as if they were a kind of manual for, if not daily life, then treasure seeking and play in general (not to mention conversational patterns, modes of address and turns of phrase). Anne Shirley and her friends exhibit the same approach when they act out Tennyson's poem 'Lancelot and Elaine'; after studying the poem in school, 'the fair lily maid and Lancelot and Guinevere and King Arthur had become very real people to them' (231). Sara Crewe, too, reads in a way that makes plain her 'own attachments, investments, and vulnerabilities as a reader' (Felski 10). What is more, she is the protagonist of a novel that is unabashedly romantic and even quasi-fantastic in its depiction of those 'attachments, investments, and vulnerabilities'. Sara finds consolation in imagining her life in terms of the books she's read, and that mode of reading is not just a coping strategy. It also proves to be anticipatory, and it has actual, tangible results, for it brings her, as I suggest above, a real, if somewhat irregular family. The novel makes this clear in two ways, in particular.

Sara's habit of looking at the families that live in the same square as the school (the families that surround the school, we might say) links her love of stories with the novel's tendency to marginalise, yet explicitly include, the valorised domestic: 'when [Sara] passed houses whose windows were lighted up, she used to look into the warm rooms and amuse herself by imagining things about the people she saw sitting before the fires or about the tables' (91). Coming from a place with rooms that are anything but warm – for Sara's attic rooms are literally cold, and the rooms of the school are figuratively so – Sara is drawn to the inviting firesides and mealtime tableaux of the families that are 'lighted up' and framed in their windows, as if on display. She's comforted by the sight, strangely enough, and she makes up stories about the cosy domestic scenes she spies on. She's particularly intrigued by the only intact biological family we learn any particulars about, the family that will eventually become her own extended family, the Carmichaels (aka the Large Family).

The Carmichaels are, to be sure, an actual family (in the world of the novel, that is), but they are also a fictional family and a good example of the way Sara creates families from and by her reading. Not unlike the way she turns the mean girls of Miss Minchin's into a more sisterly set of companions by telling stories and narrating her own reading to them, Sara turns the actual Carmichaels into the fictional Montmorencys and gives them 'names out of books – quite romantic names', in fact:

> The fat, fair baby with the lace cap was Ethelberta Beauchamp Montmorency; the next baby was Violet Cholmondeley Montmorency; the little boy who could just stagger and who had such round legs was Sydney Cecil Vivian Montmorency; and then came Lilian Evangeline Maud Marion, Rosalind Gladys, Guy Clarence, Veronica Eustacia, and Claude Harold Hector. (91)

The narrator participates in romanticising this family as much as Sara does, exclaiming that there is 'a stout, rosy mother, and a stout, rosy father, and a stout, rosy grandmother', that

> the eight children were always either being taken out to walk or to ride in perambulators by comfortable nurses, or they were going to drive with their mamma, or they were flying to the door in the evening to meet their papa and kiss him and dance around him and drag off his overcoat and look in the pockets for packages . . .

that, 'in fact, they were always doing something enjoyable and suited to the tastes of a large family' (91). Such exuberant, incredulous language, composed as it is of absolutes and happy adjectives and adverbs, adds to the novel's simultaneous celebration of and disbelief in the idea of a happy family. It's almost too good to be true, how rosy and happy and affectionate the Carmichael/Montomorency family is; they're described as a kind of domestic fairy tale come true.

But, it's crucial to note, the Carmichael family is *almost* too good to be true. Like the warm and cosy furnishings Sara imagines for her attic, which Ram Dass then supplies, the domestic fantasy Sara imagines about the Carmichaels is in fact true, and it turns out to be a domestic fantasy that will include her. In addition, the fairy tale that the Carmichaels' invent about Sara comes true. For 'the Large Family', the narrator tells us, 'was as profoundly interested in her as she was in it', and they decide that while she seems to be a servant and an orphan, 'she is not a beggar, however shabby she looks' (94). When they share their imaginings about 'the-little-girl-who-is-not-a-beggar' with Mr Carrisford, he begins to wonder if the little girl he is looking for is in a similar situation (94). That is, he begins to wonder if the story the Carmichaels imagine about Sara is the reality of the orphan he is desperate to find. It is, of course, and more, for Sara is the orphan daughter of his best friend, and her reality is not just similar to the story the Large Family imagines about her; it is that story. Moreover, the ending to her story is the stuff of fairy tale ('she will be more a princess than she ever was – a hundred and fifty thousand times more', her friend Ermengarde exclaims), and the plot of her riches-to-rags-to-riches life is 'a story which was quite as wonderful as any Sara herself had ever invented, and which had the amazing charm of having happened to Sara herself' (180, 181).

The way these 'emphatic experiences' (the phrase is Felski's) of literature come true is perhaps the most literal example of the pattern I'm exploring here between naïve, identificatory reading and the establishment of a solid, secure family structure, and so it's perhaps no accident that they appear in a novel that takes up the debate over ways of reading head on (20). When Ermengarde visits Sara in the attic she's been relegated to, she is initially, if only mildly, critical of Sara's naïve equation of the fictional and the actual and of her tendency to make up stories about what she experiences, of her tendency to turn everything into a story, in other words. 'Oh, Sara!' she exclaims, 'You *are* queer' (88). But Sara's reply (in addition to the fact that Ermengarde is not, even loyal Sara has to admit, very smart, and does not like books at all) makes it clear where this novel stands in the debate: 'I – I can't help making things up. If I didn't, I don't believe I could live . . . I'm sure I couldn't live here' (88). Approaching her life as if it were a story (the inverse but hardly the opposite of finding a corollary between what she reads and what she experiences) is a coping strategy and one that's quite effective in enabling Sara to survive all the abuse Miss Minchin heaps upon her. Just a page later Ermengarde has come over to the other side of the debate and is entranced by the way Sara and her fellow-servant play Bastille; 'It is the prisoner in the next cell', Sara says 'quite dramatically' when Becky knocks on the wall:

> 'Listen, the two knocks meant, "Prisoner, are you there?"'
> She knocked three times on the wall herself, as if in answer.
> 'That means, "Yes, I am here and all is well."'
> Four knocks came from Becky's side of the wall.
> 'That means', explained Sara, '"Then, fellow-sufferer, we will sleep in peace".' (89)

Ermengarde does not find this 'queer'; rather, she 'quite beamed with delight' and exclaims 'O, Sara! It is like a story!' (89). Converted to Sara's habit of naïve, associative reading in just a few short moments, Ermengarde also articulates what we might call the book's mantra, for life, the way Sara approaches it, is indeed like a story, and a story, in Hodgson Burnett's hands, which bears a very close resemblance to the events of her characters' lives. Sara goes even farther: 'It *is* a story', she insists. '*Everything*'s a story. You are a story – I am a story. Miss

Minchin is a story' (89). Not you are in a story, I am in a story, Miss Minchin is in a story; not the metafictional awareness of their status as characters, but rather a recognition of the story their lives are.

'If reading cannot help but involve moments of recognition', Felski writes, 'the question we face is not how to avoid such moments, but what form they might take' (38). She goes on to recount her experience of reading a Hilary Mantel novel

> only to be floored by the shock of the familiar. In Mantel's account of a Catholic girl growing up in a grimy northern English town and winning a scholarship to an elite grammar school, I found a history unnervingly close to my own. (39)

Her analysis of that moment of recognition makes it clear why finding ourselves in what we read is anything but naïve and uncritical and why it helps Sara, for instance, to cope:

> Recognizing aspects of ourselves in the description of others, seeing our perceptions and behaviors echoed in a work of fiction, we become aware of our accumulated experiences as distinctive yet far from unique. The contemporary idiom of 'having an identity' owes a great deal to such flashes of intersubjective recognition, of perceived commonality and shared history. (39)

Or as Deidre Lynch puts it, 'the [affective] attachments that have connected Anglo-American readers to the institutions of English are crucial to the history of private life, because the aesthetic sphere is a site for the dramas of individuals' identity formation' (11).[14] Lynch's formulation helps us see that comparing a generous new acquaintance to Aladdin, as Rebecca does, assuming that the newspaper advertisement promising 'MONEY PRIVATELY WITHOUT FEES' has been placed by 'a Generous Benefactor, like in Miss Edgeworth', as one of the Bastable children does, pretending to be a princess 'scattering largess to the populace', as Sara does, are all ways in which they act out their understanding of the world they live in and the place they hold in it, an understanding based in large part on what they read, and an understanding they can extend from the text to themselves because of 'the clarity with which a form of life is captured' in that text (Nesbit 62; Hodgson Burnett, *Princess* 43; Felski 39). It is, in other words, not the sign of an unsophisticated reader but rather of an effective text. That recognition is 'typically triggered', Felski explains, 'by a skillful rendition of the densely packed minutiae of daily life' (39). Or as Elaine Auyoung puts it, 'novelists bring their object "home to us in all its concrete particularity" in part by selecting details that are literally close to home' (13).

Auyoung's analysis of how a novelist creates 'fiction [that] feels real', to paraphrase the title of her important book, makes it clear, in fact, that the way these orphan-readers read and the uses they make of their reading are illustrations of precisely how realistic fiction works. That is, 'approaching the words of a literary text not as bearers of interpretive meaning but as cues that prompt readers to retrieve their existing embodied knowledge, to rely on their social intelligence, and to exercise their capacities for learning', as Auyoung does, allows us to see that when Rebecca describes her emotions in the language of a novel she's read, she is not being quixotic but rather learning from fiction how to articulate her feelings, linking her 'existing embodied knowledge' of her state of mind to textual 'cues' (18, 23). 'I am thrilling with unhappyness this morning', she writes to her mother. 'I got that out of Cora The Doctor's Wife whose husband's mother was very cross and unfealing to her like Aunt M. to me' (35). In the phrase 'like Aunt M. to me', we see Rebecca 'rely on [Cora The Doctor's Wife] to make sense of persons and events in her everyday life' (Auyoung 16). Auyoung's subject is how fiction works to make itself legible and lively to its readers; how it manages to create that strange but delightful and absorbing effect of seeming more real than our own lives, at times; how we come to think of the characters we read about as if they were real people. My concern is how a reader of fiction uses that reading to make her life legible to herself, but the process is, as I argue above with respect to Sara's coping strategies, the same. Rather than finding themselves in a book, as Felski did in reading Hilary Mantel and as Hemans's first readers did in annotating her verses, the fictional readers I'm concerned with find books (Sara would say stories) in themselves. That is, they understand what they experience in terms of books they've previously read, whereas nineteenth-century annotaters of Hemans (and Hemans herself) recognise themselves in what they are currently reading.

'We looked at each other, speechless with surprise and delight, like in books', Oswald writes, describing their reaction when, digging for buried treasure, they find a half-crown (12).

> I have read of people looking at a loss for words, and dumb with emotion, and I've read of people being turned to stone with astonishment, or joy, or something, but I never knew how silly it looked till I saw Noël standing staring at the Editor [who has just offered him a guinea for his poems] with his mouth open

he remarks in regards to another treasure-seeking expedition (31). 'So now we thought it was time to do something to rouse him from the stupor of despair, which is always done to heroes when anything baffling has occurred', he says, again with reference to his brother Noël (40). Consider these moments in light of one of Auyoung's examples of another fictional reader 'retrieving embodied knowledge':

> the narrator of *The Mill on the Floss* notes that, whenever Maggie reads *The Pilgrim's Progress* and comes to the sentence about Christiana 'passing "the river over which there is no bridge,"' an image of the Floss comes to Maggie's mind. (6)

That's how she understands the moment in Bunyan, by relating it to something she's familiar with in her own life. What Oswald is doing is, again, the inverse: understanding a moment in his life by relating it to something he's read. Oswald's recognition of one-to-one correspondences between the life he lives and what he has read is the recognition upon which realist representation depends. As Auyoung explains, 'realist writers cue readers to think about fictional characters and incidents in the same way that they think about persons and events in real life' (18). That's how they 'overcome the limits of their artistic medium': 'by engaging their readers' knowledge', for 'verbal artists can make us 'feel things' only if there is some intimate, preexisting connection between their verbal medium and our senses' (18, 13). Or as Felski puts it, 'we cannot help linking what we read, at least in part, to what we know' (37).

In the later eighteenth century, Lynch argues, literature began to be understood as 'something to be taken personally, by definition', and 'in the period's records of reading ... recourse is had to the stickier, subjectivity-saturated language of involvement and affection' (8, 10). That these orphan-readers take the literature they read so personally is tangible evidence of that moment in the history of reading, and the stickiness of their response to what they read (the way their reading sticks to and with them, not to mention the way it adheres to their speech patterns and attracts others to them) is part and parcel of that involved and intimate relationship with their reading. Adoptive readers all, they adopt what they read, and they are adopted because they read.

## Notes

1. As Laura Peters reminds us, 'in Victorian culture the term [orphan] referred to one who was deprived of only one parent' (1). The Bastable children's father is alive and lives with them, absent though he is from

most of *The Treasure Seekers*' plot and pages; Sara Crewe's father is alive for the first third of the novel and very much a part of its plot, if not its pages; Rebecca Randall has a mother, with a romantic backstory of her own, while both of Anne Shirley's parents died when she was three months old.

2. Noel, the poet of the family, suggests 'Let's read all the books again. We shall get lots of ideas out of them' as a way of figuring out how to go treasure-seeking. The ideas that follow range from posing as highwaymen and robbing people on Blackheath, based on the penny dreadfuls Oswald has read, to using a divining rod, which Alice, Noel's twin, has 'often read about', and digging for buried treasure (5). Indeed, when they dig for buried treasure, they predict what they will find and how they will find it in such detail it seems as if they are reading from a script: 'an ancient parchment has revealed to us the place of concealment', Alice says, going on to explain that 'when we have dug deep enough, we shall find a great pot of red clay, full of gold and precious jewels' and alerting her siblings that they 'were just coming to the underground passage that leads to the secret hoard, when the tunnel fell in' (9, 11).

3. The term is Sara's, given to the affectionate Carmichael family because it is so big, comprised as it is of eight children, two parents and a grandmother.

4. While the novel never makes their eventual marriage explicit, the parallels Mr Ladd, the novel, and Rebecca draw between their relationship and the story of Aladdin and the 'Adorable Princess' who accepts his proposal make their future relationship quite clear. It is the way she acts out and upon her habits of reading that first endears her to the Cobbs, too. 'Did you watch her face when we went into that tent where they was actin' out Uncle Tom's Cabin? And did you take notice of the way she told us about the book when we sat down to have our ice cream? I tell you Harriet Beecher Stowe herself couldn't 'a' done it better justice', exclaims Mrs Cobb (77). This elderly couple quickly take on the role of surrogate parents, providing both unlimited and unconditional affection, as well as good advice and quiet, loving correction.

5. The phrase 'Golden Age' refers to the mid-nineteenth to early twentieth-century period that, in Marah Gubar's words, 'witness[ed] an unprecedented explosion of high-quality children's fiction and poetry, not to mention an unparalleled proliferation of children's periodicals and the emergence of children's theater' (212, n2).

6. Similarly, the narrator tells us that, thanks to Rebecca, Aunt Jane's 'life now had a motive utterly lacking before' (117).

7. The novel can't seem to help but privilege the biological family, however, even as it reveals its limitations and presents so clearly the benefits of affectionate, rather than consanguineous, ties. After musing over his successful efforts to help Rebecca cope with her aunt's 'hector and abuse' of her, he concludes, 'Mirandy Sawyer would be a heap better

woman if she had a little gravestun to remember, same's mother 'n' I have,' suggesting that he's a better parent than she is because he's been one biologically, albeit only for 17 months (76). As he exclaims to his wife soon after, 'We've known what it was to hev children, even it 't was more 'n thirty years ago' (78).
8. It's not clear why most of the children are at Miss Minchin's. Sara seems to be the only one there because of the climate in India, and indeed, the fact that parents rarely visit the school suggests her classmates' parents were, unlike Sara's father, eager to break up their families by sending their children to boarding school. Lottie Legh, for example, whose mother, like Sara's, is dead, 'had been sent to school by a rather flighty young papa who could not imagine what else to do with her' (30).
9. The word 'foster' is especially apt here, combining as it does the connotations of both 'nurture' and the adjectival 'stand-in'.
10. The number of superfluous children in the novel is heart-rending. When Anne arrives at the orphan asylum, she learns 'they didn't want me [there], either; they said they were overcrowded as it was. But they had to take me' (42).
11. I don't mean to speculate about the novel that Nesbit didn't write and claim that if the children had not revealed themselves to be such delightfully naïve readers, their happy ending would have been denied them. But it is textually true that they intervene at a critical moment, catching the uncle as he leaves and inviting him to have dinner with them the next night. Indeed, it is hard to believe that after telling Mr Bastable that what his 'business wanted was not capital but management', the uncle would have returned his visit to his deceased niece's family (118, 119). Certainly Mr Bastable, who 'saw him to the door and let him out, and then went back to the study, looking very sad' could not have expected (or wanted) to see him again, much less become the recipient of his generosity and a member of his household (121).
12. In this respect, he seems to have more than a little in common with Albert-next-door's uncle, who 'is more like us, inside of his mind, that most grown-up people are. He can pretend beautifully', Oswald enthuses (115).
13. He and his siblings finds inspiration and guidance even in books they don't particularly admire; 'We had just been reading a book by Dick Diddlington – that's not his right name, but I know all about libel actions, so I shall not say what his name is really, because his books are rot. Only they put it into our heads to do what I am going to narrate' (13).
14. She goes on to argue, in a move that underscores the links I'm drawing between associative reading and the formation of a nurturing family, that 'because encountered, for example, in the form of 'the Family Shakespeare' or 'the Sir Walter Scott birthday book', the canon [of English literature] has mediated the relationships that define home' (11).

## Works Cited

Auyoung, Elaine. *When Fiction Feels Real: Representation and the Reading Mind*. Oxford University Press, 2018.

Culler, Jonathan. *Theory of the Lyric*. University of Chicago Press, 2015.

Felski, Rita. *Uses of Literature*. Wiley-Blackwell, 2008.

Gubar, Marah. *Artful Dodgers: Reconceiving the Golden Age of Children's Literature*. Oxford University Press, 2009.

Hager, Kelly and Talia Schaffer. 'Introduction: Extending Families', *Victorian Review*, vol. 39, no. 2, Fall 2013, pp. 7–21.

Hodgson Burnett, Frances. *A Little Princess*. [1905]. Penguin, 2002.

Lynch, Deidre. *Loving Literature: A Cultural History*. University of Chicago Press, 2015.

Montgomery, L. M. *Anne of Green Gables*. 1908. Penguin, 2017.

Nesbit, E. *The Story of the Treasure Seekers and the Wouldbegoods*. 1899 and 1900. Palgrave Macmillan, 2013.

Peters, Laura. *Orphan Texts: Victorian Orphans, Culture and Empire*. Manchester University Press, 2000.

Stauffer, Andrew. 'An Image in Lava: Annotation, Sentiment, and the Traces of Nineteenth-Century Reading'. *PMLA*, vol. 134, no. 1, January 2019, pp. 81–98.

Wiggin, Kate Douglas. *Rebecca of Sunnybrook Farm*. 1903. Penguin, 2005.

Chapter 5

# No Place Like Home: The Orphaned Waif in Victorian Narratives of Rescue and Redemption

*Harriet Salisbury*

At the beginning of *Christie's Old Organ, or, 'Home Sweet Home'* (1874), a man known as old Treffy sits alone in his attic, turning the handle of his barrel organ. A little ragged boy called Christie creeps up the lodging-house stairs to listen, drawn by the strains of the familiar tune: 'Home, Sweet Home'. This is the last song his mother sang to him as she lay dying, before uttering her final words: 'I'm going home, Christie' (Walton 6–7). The parentless child, cheerless lodging house and identification of death with home situate *Christie's Old Organ* within a strand of children's literature known as the 'waif' or 'street Arab' novel, which flourished from the mid-1860s until the early twentieth century.

Most waif protagonists are orphans; either literally parentless or, following Laura Peters' definition: 'deprived of only one parent [or] "bereft of protection, advantages, benefits, or happiness, previously enjoyed" (*OED*)' (Peters 1). There has been limited critical attention paid to this fertile genre of orphan literature, despite waif books having been the bestsellers of their age, with continuing readerships persisting through the twentieth century (Rose 2001) and, among evangelical groups in particular, into the twenty-first. For the purposes of this chapter, I will consider the following (non-exhaustive) group of thirteen books as exemplifying the genre. They are: *The Story of Little Cristal* (1863) by Mary Howitt; *Jessica's First Prayer* (1865), *Pilgrim Street* (1867) *Little Meg's Children* (1868) *Alone in London* (1869), and *Lost Gip* (1873) by Hesba Stretton; *Nothing to Nobody* (1873) and *Froggy's Little Brother* (1875) by 'Brenda' (Mrs Castle Smith); *Christie's Old Organ* by Mrs O. F. Walton (1874), *Scamp and I* by L. T. Meade (1875),

*Her Benny* (1879) by Silas Hocking; *Dust, Ho!, or, Rescued from a Rubbish Heap* by Mabel Mackintosh (1891) and *Mollie's Adventures* by May Wynne (1903).

The books I have selected are from a range of waif authors, with due weight given to the prolific and popular Hesba Stretton, along with examples from other well-known writers within the genre ('Brenda', Mrs O. F. Walton and Silas Hocking), and from authors who seem to have produced just a single waif narrative (Mary Howitt, L. T. Meade, Mabel Mackintosh and May Wynne). Most waif novels are set in London but I have included novels set in Liverpool (*Her Benny*), and Manchester (*Pilgrim Street*). I have also looked for the earliest and latest examples of the genre: at just thirty-two pages, *Little Cristal* is more tract than novel, but is identified by Gillian Avery as setting off a 'literature of social conditions', following the publication of Mayhew's *London Labour and the London Poor* in 1861.[1] At the other end of the scale, *Mollie's Adventures* (1903) grafts a racy story about a kidnapped child onto a waif narrative where children gum matchboxes in a Hoxton cellar in a 'pre-education act London' (Avery 117).

In the development of children's literature, waif novels follow on from what Naomi Wood calls the 'children's domestic novel', which focuses on a concern for 'the internalization of discipline, however difficult the process might be' (Wood 120). Children's books are, of course, inherently concerned with both discipline and the domestic, but the waif novel departs from familiar portrayals of middle-class children helping (or learning noble suffering from) poor villagers, to focus entirely on the urban working classes. Set in the slum areas of England's industrialised cities, these novels create an emotional charge from detailed descriptions of crowded living conditions and entrenched poverty. They feature un-parented children who are struggling and failing to survive on their own and point towards an ideal of domestic comfort through repeated depictions of its absence. Waif novels add to our understanding of Victorian families in fiction by their presentation of families where absent or infantilised adults are largely replaced by oddly mature, parenting children. These atypical families place the books within an evolving field of literary research, covered by a 2013 special issue of the *Victorian Review* focusing on 'Extending Families', ed. Kelly Hager and Talia Schaffer (Hager and Schaffer 2013), and more recently in Schaffer's *Romance's Rival*, which looks at the place of companionate love within our ideas of family and marriage (Schaffer 2016).

According to Leonore Davidoff, from the 1780s onwards:

> Various religious affiliations may have been divisive on the surface, but they were united in the value all put on a code of morality closely linked to the idealization of the family and home as the prime site of affection as well as duty, a foretaste of the Heavenly Home. (Davidoff 6)

The key to understanding the domestic narrative of the waif novel is this theology of mid- to late nineteenth-century evangelism. At least two waif narratives (*Little Cristal* and *Jessica's First Prayer*) literally echo the evangelical conversion experience in a narrative structure that bears witness to what Bebbington refers to as the three 'r's: ruin – an acceptance of the fallen state of man; redemption – the acknowledgement of the sacrifice of Christ; and regeneration – the requirement that true believers are born again through a personal and emotional engagement with the Holy Spirit (Bebbington 134–6). Conversion and spiritual renewal are the most significant narrative element in waif novels, and other key themes such as isolated protagonists, validation of the domestic, love of nature and care for young children, copious tears and glorification of death, reflect elements within the evangelistic belief system.

The novels effectively present two routes out of brutish and brief lives within city slums. One is contained within the evangelical elision of Heaven with home; this offers suffering children the everlasting happiness of life-in-death, under the rule of a perfect Father, in a place where there is no disease, poverty or pain. The other route is the rescue and removal of 'chosen' children by an appropriate person or institution where evangelistic fervour is combined with transformative financial resources. In the majority of waif novels, both these routes – the one offering rescue and the other redemption – are pursued.

Although waif writers varied in their personal beliefs – from the Quaker Mary Howitt to Methodist preacher Silas Hocking – these books were produced by evangelical publishing houses, for a religiously inclined book-buying public. Both Walton and Stretton were published by the Religious Tract Society (RTS), founded after the death of John Wesley with a mission to produce books with an emphasis 'on scriptural truth and some account of a sinner's way to salvation, to be narrated in a plain and direct prose style' (Butts and Garrett 9). The other significant waif novel publisher (of Brenda, L. T. Meade and Mackintosh) was John F. Shaw, who also seems to have specialised in evangelistic books.[2]

Waif narratives explicitly point to the possibilities opened up by evangelical conversion, showing this as means by which even the poorest of society may live blessed lives of harmony and content. This regenerative doctrine is ideal territory for children's literature, being easy to grasp without recourse to expert elucidation or complex doctrinal ideas. Instead, it demands a fundamentally personal and emotional engagement with God, one that requires a return to the childish state; the phrase 'born again' meaning, literally, re-entering of the state of infancy. In waif novels, adults are led to this state by the simply articulated faith of a child, whose helplessness is signalled not just by youth, but by poverty, an absence of parents and lack of home comforts. Helplessness is thus validated over the competence of adults, whose faith is shown as dulled or inactive, and in need of renewal.

Friendships that transcend barriers of age occur in all waif novels; these allow contrasting adult and child perceptions to be explored. In *Little Cristal*, the young hero visits the countryside with an elderly bird-catcher called Ephraim. Cristal calls his companion's attention to the glories of nature and this leads the old man to recall long-ago lessons taught by his mother, and to 'understand anew' the stories from his now pawned Bible and hymn book. (Howitt 9). In *Her Benny*, Nelly befriends an old nightwatchman called Joe Wragg, and he later sets up a Sunday School, telling attendees:

> '[Nelly] used to come an' ax me all sorts o' questions. Bless yer, that little girl had real speretuel [sic] insight . . . I tell 'e, mates, every one of the questions helped to lead out o' darkness into the light.' (Hocking 165)

As old Treffy puts it in *Christie's Old Organ*: 'I was as dark as a heathen till Christie came to me, and read to me out of his Bible, and talked to me of Jesus, and put it all so clear to me' (Walton 83). Even toddler Mollie, stolen by hop-pickers and relocated to Hoxton, recites prayers and hymns learned at her mother's knee to her new friends, revealing: 'the old, old story of a Saviour's love, in the simple words that made it so plain to a baby mind' (Wynne 54).

Simple belief contrasts with adult doubt, for example, in *Christie's Old Organ*, when Treffy thinks he cannot be redeemed because: 'I've been so bad, Christie; it doesn't seem likely He'd do it for me . . . there's such a deal of sin on my soul' (Walton 42). In *Lost Gip*, Sandy asks the father of his friend John Shafto if he really believes 'as Lord Jesus Christ 'ud do all they say He'll do for a poor boy in the streets, without shoes to his feet or a cap to his head'. After this, Mr Shafto begins to feel 'a strange new sense of shame', for, despite professing to believe Christ had died for all, 'when this poor, untaught boy stood before his face, demanding of him if he really believed these things, he dared not say that he did' (Stretton, *Lost* 79, 85).

But the portrayal of children within the waif novel is more complex than a binary contrast between innocence and experience. They were written at a time of increasing industrialisation, when old certainties were being challenged. Within such destabilised times, Adrienne Gavin has suggested 'childhood becomes a matter of particular cultural concern', and in the late nineteenth century, children appeared both 'as victims who need greater protection from abuse', and as 'semi-feral victimizers who make the streets unsafe for adults and signal society's disintegration' (1).

It is not only the narratives of these books but also the names by which they became known that shed light on this uneasy discourse about the poor. The term 'street Arab' is far more recent than 'waif', appearing in the 1840s in the writing of Lord Ashley (better known by his later title, Lord Shaftesbury), and Scottish educational reformer Thomas Guthrie, specifically addressing the issue of poor urban children. Kimberley Reynolds finds in the writings of Shaftesbury a reflection of social concerns about 'a separate territory inhabited by primitive hordes that infused Victorian social discourse'. She relates this 'othering' of the poor to Plotz's 'domestic orientalism'; it is used as a means of placing children outside society by 'designating them inferior and in need of regimes of discipline and education intended to be "civilizing"' (Reynolds 257, 260).

Shaftesbury talks of 'Arabs of the metropolis' which are 'the wild colts of the Pampas, not the sober nags of the paddock; the lasso . . . must be the instrument of their capture'. He describes London children 'as bold, and pert, and dirty as London sparrows' and so plentiful that the streets 'teem with them like an ant's-nest'. He says we are tempted to ask 'whether these nondescripts ever had a parent?' and when we visit the 'receptacles' where they are 'spawned' we cannot help but question their 'points of resemblance to the rest of mankind' (Shaftesbury 140, 127–9). Guthrie describes ragged boys as 'wild as desert savages' and also seems to have desert horses in mind, when he says: 'These Arabs of the city are wild as those of the desert, and must be broken in' (Guthrie 12, 19).

The word 'waif' generally means a person 'who is without home or friends; one who lives uncared-for or without guidance'. In its legal use, it refers to 'an article washed up on the seashore, an animal that has strayed' (*OED*). It is therefore bound up in issues of property and ownership that are intimately connected to the nineteenth-century conception of family, when marriage 'united two individuals in one person, and English law defined that person as the husband' (Stocking 198).

In waif novels, husbands are missing or dead, sunk in lethargy, in prison, or brutal alcoholics. Often no husband is mentioned and many waif children must be presumed illegitimate. Isobel Armstrong has examined the link between illegitimacy and the radical within nineteenth-century novels, with the radical defined as 'that which cuts to the root of things, reconceptualises roots'. The rootlessness of the waif child thus poses 'a challenge to the democratic imagination' because 'once you are placed outside the law your status as a fully human being can be questioned' (Armstrong 5). This was literally the case with waifs in the Middle Ages, when a waif was a female outlaw: 'as women were not sworn to the law . . . they could not properly be outlawed, but were said to be waived' (Wharton 478–9).[3]

Like the tracts they replaced, waif novels were explicitly produced to counter the radical effects of licentious or political reading matter. Avery has suggested it is 'ironical that the evangelicals, who so mistrusted works of imagination, should throughout the century produce the juvenile fiction that sold' (Avery 115). However, evangelicals, while waiting for the Almighty to bring about the conversion of the world, believed themselves authorised to employ 'techniques offered by the modern world such as sailing ships and printing presses to disseminate the gospel' (Bebbington 138). The success of the waif novel – widely read in Sunday schools and disseminated to readers of all classes through circulating libraries – may have contributed to increased rates of literacy, but their suspicion of indiscriminate reading is internalised in their pages. In *Alone in London*, old Oliver runs a newspaper stall and uses his newspapers as covers for orphan Tony's bed, but they are never studied. The subject of their nightly reading is the New Testament, referred to as: 'the life of the Master, who was so intimately dear to the heart of old Oliver' (Stretton, *Alone* 48). Christie also comes to regard the Bible or, as Mrs Walton calls it, 'the Book of books' as having: 'a word for every need, and a message for every soul. There was peace for the sin-burdened, comfort for the sorrowful, rest for the weary, counsel for the perplexed, and hope for the dying' (Walton 83).

When *Jessica's First Prayer* was published in book form in 1897, after serialisation in *Household Words*, Shaftesbury himself wrote to commend the book for its 'simplicity, pathos, and depth of Christian feeling'. He also praised its author's 'minute, and accurate, knowledge of that class, its wants, and its capabilities' (Lomax, 'Reclaiming' 95). The book's success was immediate and stratospheric. It sold 60,000 copies within two years, and 400,000 by 1885. It touched a chord with readers high and low; alongside Shaftesbury, Queen Victoria, Florence Nightingale and Augustus John enjoyed it and Tsar Alexander II is said to have demanded a copy be placed in every school in Russia (Lomax, *Writings* 54–5). In 1871, Stretton recorded that she had met a missionary from Feejee [sic] and 'a black man from Liberia who both knew my books' (Lomax, 'Telling' 132). Sales were estimated to have reached 2.5 million by 1911, the year of Hesba Stretton's death (Rickard 224). Like the earlier tract, *Little Christie*, this novel's structure leads the reader through the evangelical stages of ruin, rescue and redemption.

At the start of the novel, Jessica – who was once a fairy when 'mother played at the theatre' – is shivering and in rags. Her father is never mentioned and her mother remains firmly offstage, disappearing entirely before the end of the story. Her lack of maternal concern for her daughter is summed up in Jessica's first utterance to Mr Daniel, a coffee-stall holder. Explaining why she is hanging around in the rain, she says: 'mother's been away all night, and she took the key with her'. Her mother's past as an actress is a well-worn Victorian code for prostitution, and mother and daughter live in 'a hayloft over the stable of an old inn', accessed via 'a wooden ladder, whose rungs were crazy and broken, and which led up through a trip-door in the floor of the loft'. It is not clear how, or even why, this arrangement might require a key; the loft contains

> only a litter of straw for the bedding, and a few bricks and boards for the furniture. Everything that could be pawned had disappeared long ago, and Jessica's mother only lamented that she could not thus dispose of her child. (Stretton, *Jessica* 64, 9, 25–6)

Jessica's titular prayer occurs after she has been found hiding in a chapel to listen to the services. In answer to the minister's questions, she tells him: 'I never had any father'. In reply, he tells her: 'God is your father ... He knows all about you, because He is present everywhere. We cannot see Him, but we have only to speak, and He hears us, and we may ask Him for whatever we want' (Stretton, *Jessica* 54–5). Jessica looks at the minister's little girls, then at her own ragged clothes and muddy feet, and asks: 'Will he let me speak to Him as well as these fine children that are clean and have got nice clothes?' When this is affirmed, she shuts her eyes, bends her head to her hands and says: 'O God! I want to know about You. And please pay Mr. Dan'el for all the warm coffee he's give me'.

Tears stand in the minister's eyes as he adds his 'Amen' (Stretton, *Jessica* 55–6).

E. Nesbit wrote to a friend, that after reading *Jessica's First Prayer* to her maid: 'I felt my eyes smart and my throat go lumpy towards the finish. Pathetic simplicity is a grand gift in writing' (Briggs 241). This is Shaftesbury's 'simplicity and pathos' in action, harking back to one of Charles Wesley's hymns, lisped by many a schoolchild:

> Gentle Jesus, meek and mild,
> Look upon a little child;
> Pity my simplicity,
> Suffer me to come to Thee. (Henson 187)

At the end of the story, Jessica almost succumbs to fever alone in the hayloft, but is discovered by Mr Daniel who – in a metaphorical 'still small voice' experience (1 Kings 19:12) – hears 'a faint, small voice through the nicks of the unceiled boarding above his head'. Confident that God has sent him, Jessica asks what He has said. Daniel replies 'He told me I loved a little bit of dirty money better than a poor friendless, helpless child'. Reflecting that 'You're more fit for heaven than I ever was in my life', he tells Jessica. 'I've been kneeling down Sunday after Sunday when the minister's been praying, but all the time I was thinking how rich some of the carriage people were'. In a rare departure from her child's voice, Jessica reminds him of what the minister says: 'Herein is love, not that we loved God, but that He loved us, and sent His Son to be the propitiation for our sins'. She then prays to God to 'make Mr Daniel's heart soft, for Jesus Christ's sake, Amen' (Stretton, *Jessica* 78–80).

Removed to Mr Daniel's room, where she is attended by the minister, Jessica recovers after telling God: 'I asked You to let me come home to heaven; but if Mr Dan'el wants me, please to let me stay a little longer'. Mr Daniel's faith is restored and he tells the minister, 'the questions this poor little creature has asked me have gone quicker and deeper down to my conscience than all your sermons'. Emphasising the superior qualities of simple faith, he tells the minister that despite 'hearkening to you every blessed Sabbath, I was losing my soul, and you never once said to me, though you saw me scores and scores of times, "Standring, are you a saved man?"' (Stretton, *Jessica* 92, 90).

Although only a coffee-stall holder, Mr Daniel's ability to rescue Jessica depends on his wealth. As Jessica recovers, he uses his savings of nearly £400[4] to rent 'a little house for himself and his adopted daughter' having first made enquiries about her mother who 'never appeared again in her old haunts' (at least, not until the author resurrected her in a sequel called *Jessica's Mother*, around 1900). With the restoration of the domestic ideal, Jessica and Mr Daniel walk each day to the coffee stall to serve customers. They also attend services at the chapel, where Jessica's elevated situation is signalled by the fact that she now occupies a pew, like the minister's daughters (Stretton, *Jessica* 93–4).

Jessica's status as orphan-waif has a number of functions within this narrative. It means there is no claim on her loyalties, and no one to prevent her from moving out of her social class and into a different one. The narrative offsets the negative associations of her rags, muddy feet and poverty by focusing on the pathos of her isolation, youth and vulnerability, the sight of which reduces the minister to tears. The lone state of the orphan child also acts as a barrier within this narrative – as it does in other waif novels – setting a child (or group of siblings) apart from the surrounding degradation. In her study of the concepts of purity and dirt in the formation of religious and cultural taboos, Mary Douglas notes that 'Holiness is the attribute of Godhead. Its root means "set apart"'. Part of holiness is 'keeping distinct the categories of creation. It therefore involves correct definition, discrimination and order'.

The Greek goddess of the hearth is associated with the correct ordering of domesticity, family and home, and Victorian respect for this order is referenced by Elizabeth Thiel, who quotes an 1872 Disraeli speech where he states: 'England is a domestic country. Here the home is revered and the hearth is sacred' (Thiel 4). Within the waif novel, this revered space metamorphoses into all kinds of deviant forms as children occupy precarious spaces in attics and cellars; sleep beneath stairways, in graveyards and under upturned boats, or make their abode in communal night shelters or lodging houses. But whatever the location of home and however lowly it may be, waif characters stand apart and above the surrounding masses, suggesting their presence within the slum is, in itself, a form of mis-categorisation. They are out of place, and their apartness is signalled by character traits absent in the surrounding community: innate honesty and truthfulness, a desire to care for little children and re-establish domestic order, and a great propensity for tears.

At the start of *Lost Gip*, a boy called Sandy, all of whose infant siblings have died young, is desperate to look after and protect a soon-to-be-born baby. The reader is introduced to his milieu: a narrow street with heaps of 'rotting fruit, potato-pairings, and decaying cabbage leaves' and a 'busy spirit vault' (gin shop) at each end of the street. Here, the sun doesn't merely shine, but like a vengeful Old Testament God, it 'smites down upon the closely built houses', which are 'so shut out of sight that those who live in them feel no shame, and no fear of being seen by anyone less wretched than themselves'. Their shame, and fear of being looked on evokes man's fallen state and attempts to hide from God in the Garden of Eden, suggesting the responsibility for their condition lies with the fallen slum-dweller. Descent from the ideal domestic to an unnatural and animalistic state is made clear in the revelation that half the children born there 'die before they have lived out their twelve months of misery', yet their funerals 'excite no notice' because mothers 'seem to have lost their natural love for their little ones' (Stretton, *Lost* 7–9). The trope of the unnatural mother, bereft of tender feelings towards her own child, has already been seen in the abandonment of Jessica, and I will return to it in an examination child death as the culminating event of the waif narrative. But alongside the absent father, the uncaring mother leaves a space ready to be taken up by the nurturing waif child.

Sandy stands apart from the surrounding 'almost naked children', looking on with an abstract and anxious expression until he hears a feeble cry which indicates the arrival of his sister. Tears start into his eyes but he brushes them off hastily 'lest anybody should see them'. Symbolically, he passes his jacket through the window to wrap the baby in, and the bundled child is delivered into his care. The mother is 'too inveterate a drunkard to take much interest' and leaves Sandy to look after his sister, until the day she accidentally mislays her on a drunken spree. Like Jessica, Sandy has not a single friend within his slum surroundings. But during his search for Gip, he meets a religious and well-spoken crippled boy called John Shafto who, although very poor, appears as 'almost a gentleman' to Sandy, who will later take his friend's place after John's early death. (Stretton *Lost* 9–10, 16, 38).

Separation is shown as a physical removal in *Little Meg's Children*, as Meg and her brother Robin look down from an attic room to the pavement below where 'a number of children of every age and size, but all ill-clothed and ill-fed, were crawling about, in and out of the houses'. The childrens' cries and shrieks came up to them 'in their lofty seat' but their mother (who lies dead on a bed next to them) has not let them play outside, and the children they observe are 'mostly strangers'. When Robin moves to close the gap by mentioning that their absent father also drinks, Meg moves into a motherly role, telling her brother: 'Father doesn't get drunk often; and you mustn't be a naughty boy and talk about it'. Meg then makes tea, undresses Robin and the baby and 'when all her work was over, and the fire put out' puts herself to bed (Stretton, *Little* 21–2, 25, 27). The making and serving of meals and the taking on and off of garments (even the poorest children seem to own nightclothes) validate the domestic and underline the difference between these orphans, and the disordered lives of the people who are figuratively and literally below them.

Similarly, the orphan boys of *Froggy's Little Brother* have spent their lives in the same attic room, apparently surrounded by strangers. When they look down on the 'miserable inhabitants of the squalid houses opposite', where the pavement holds 'swarms of dirty little gutter-children', there are no signs of recognition, no indication the ragged brothers identify (with) them, or have any inclination to join their play. After returning from work with food and fuel to make his brother porridge, Froggy signals a commitment to domestic order by his decision to 'mend up his jacket, and comb his hair' so he can apply for an errand boy's job. He is 'very handy with his needle, and could patch and darn almost as neatly as a girl', so Froggy sits 'in his shirtsleeves with his hair over his eyes and his lips pouting a little', drawing the too-long thread out over his shoulder with every stitch (Brenda, *Froggy* 105–6). While marriage unites two individuals, Froggy appears to be amalgamating an entire family within his eleven-year-old person, as he juggles his roles as head of household, breadwinner, cook, carer, seamstress and putative errand boy.

Care for younger children is not confined to girls, or even older children, and is presented as a mark of difference, a sign of the evangelical child. In contrast to Froggy, the similarly aged Dick in *Scamp and I*, is a 'throw-all-care-to-the-winds' little fellow who has 'often been idle' leaving the daily grind of mending shoes in a dark cellar to his younger sister Flo. Just eight years old, she is

> a very little girl in any other rank of life, but in this St Giles's cellar she was a woman. She had been a woman for a whole year now; ever since her mother died . . . she had put childish things away and taken on herself the anxieties, the hopes, and fears of womanhood. (Meade 18, 107)

Both Froggy and Dick are taken up by older boys who wish to exploit their innocence and lead them into a life of thieving. While Froggy resists, Dick's inability to embrace domesticity and hard work signals an innate weakness of character, and he ends up in Reformatory school.

Waif novels explicitly identify God with an absent father. Some even characterise him as a mother figure. In *Lost Gip*, John Shafto says that 'all this world is like one large room to God; and He is among us, like a mother is with her children' (79). In *Pilgrim Street*, Tom discovers, after his father returns from prison to claim him, that the word father has two sounds. One is 'full of gracious comfort, and of peace passing all understanding . . . But the other sound was one of shame and misery, and dread'. Seeking entrance to a cathedral – which is symbolically covered in scaffolding – Tom is forbidden to enter by a verger who calls him a ragamuffin and sends him away, signalling Tom's alienation both from society and from an established religion clearly in need of repair. Lying in the cathedral's shadow, 'though a constant stream of people were passing to and fro before his eyes, yet he was alone'. But fixing his eye on 'a patch of pale blue wintry sky', he grows calmer in spirit, and 'with a deeper and stronger feeling that it was true, he said in his heart, "I have another Father, my Father in heaven!"' (Stretton, *Pilgrim* 110, 111).

Dust and dirt are everywhere in the slums. According to Douglas, the presence of these elements harnesses both literal and symbolic meanings. 'Where there is dirt there is system. Dirt is the by-product of a systematic ordering and classification of matter, in so far as ordering involves rejecting inappropriate elements' (Douglas 44). In *Dust Ho!*, an entire family live by collecting rubbish and this common profession is shown as deeply concerning, inspiring instinctive rejection. As Carrie walks along one morning with her loaded sack, 'many a well-to-do servant, attending upon the milkman, looked at her for a moment in scorn and amazement, wondering that such a creature should be allowed to walk in their street' (Mackintosh 15).

In contrast, the countryside is shown as not only a healthy but a profoundly religious place that reaffirms God's natural order. At the end of *Froggy's Little Brother*, after an outing to the countryside, readers are told: 'Such an experience is better than all the sermons and books in the world' for teaching children 'the love of God and the beauty of all his works' (Brenda, *Froggy* 189). That is a message not easily found in the dirt and squalor of the city. Even an outing to Temple Gardens, in *Little Meg's Children*, sees young Robin awestruck by at the sight of chrysanthemums, asking: 'Is it gardens, Meg? Is this Temple Gardens?' as he reaches 'with outstretched hands as if he would fain gather them all into his arms' (Stretton, *Little* 49). In *Pilgrim Street*, wooded glades are described as 'stretching far away, like the long aisles of some grand cathedral', and after gazing at the sky, Tom says: 'He is smiling at us now. God smiles at us. I never saw my father smile at me, never! But God loves us dearly' (Stretton, *Pilgrim* 139, 141).

The strong emotional reactions of waif children – towards vulnerable brothers and sisters, nature, and, of course, God – are part of an evangelistic creed. Margaret Cutt suggests this 'expression of individual impulse, so long suppressed by the moralists' and the foregrounding of emotional release in books for children as part of a religious lesson signalled that 'the expression of emotion by the young was coming into favour' (Cutt 23). Little Cristal's engagement with the countryside and its 'golden sunrise [and] masses of opal-coloured cloud' prefigures his conversion, when he instinctively kneels before a stained-glass window showing Christ blessing young children. As the sun shines through it, 'all at once, he saw that his little dirty hands, his breast, and all his poor clothes, were covered with a glorious light as of rubies and emeralds and transparent topaz, all purple and red, and green and gold'. His reaction is religious emotion in action: '"It is the blessing!" thought poor Cristal. Oh, how happy he was! How he loved the Saviour, how he thanked Him in his simple child's heart!' (Howitt 2, 14). In contrast, when Christie talks of God to old Treffy, the older man can only repeat that he 'can't feel it', so 'whilst Christie was walking in the sunshine, Old Treffy was still groping on in the shadow' (Walton 42).

Instinctively evangelical waif children, including Cristal, are mostly destined for an early grave, and it is largely from such deaths that waif novels gained their reputation as 'tearjerkers'. In Flora Thompson's account of growing up in rural Oxfordshire in the 1880s, she says: 'many tears were shed in the hamlet over the poor neglected slum children of *Christie's Old Organ* and *Froggy's Little Brother*' (Thompson 251). Tears, according to Douglas, are unlike other 'unclean' bodily effusions as they are 'naturally pre-empted by the symbolism of washing. Tears are like rivers of moving water. They purify, cleanse, bathe the eyes' (Douglas 155). Within these narratives, tears signify a softening of the heart and childlike submission to the circumstances. When Froggy is told of the death of his father, he says:

> 'I know he's in a Better Land, and never can't speak to me no more; but I'm thinking as how I'd just like to see his face once again, and touch his hand as I did mother's when she was gone.'

After this, 'the little heart seemed well-nigh to bursting with the first keen pangs of the orphan's loneliness, and he sobbed aloud, wailing bitterly for some minutes'. The nurse attending him has to hide her own tears, but her emotion signals that she is a woman 'who has tried and proved to herself the abiding love of Jesus' (Brenda, *Froggy* 22–3). When the strangely named waif orphan Daddy Long Legs[5] realises that a soldier she has just met is the long-lost brother of her friend, they both experience the other extreme of emotional happiness as she throws herself to the ground, 'sobbing and crying as if her heart would break; the little drummer-boy grown so tall, leaning over her, sobbing like a child' (Brenda, *Nothing* 161).

The emotional catharsis of death is not applied equally within the waif narrative, even when it comes to the early deaths of children. As shown in *Lost Gip*, whole communities can regard the funerals of the young with a stoicism bordering on indifference. When Benny's little friend Debs dies in *Froggy's Little Brother*, her father sits with an empty gin bottle and her mother weeps, but she is gently chided by a Greek chorus of neighbours who tell her: 'I wouldn't fret about it overmuch if I was you'; 'We don't likes to lose 'em when we've got 'em . . . but depend upon it, children's best out of it all!' and 'We've had seven, and we've buried 'em all, and we thank the Lord for it now' (Brenda, *Froggy* 120–1).

Davidoff makes clear that this representation is not rooted in fact. She points to studies by Linda Pollock that show child death as 'an occasion for intense anguish, no matter how many living children remained', and by Anthony Fletcher, whose examination of parental responses to child death show that 'parental love and affection was constant, powerful and virtually invariable from 1600 to 1914' (Davidoff 315–16). But within the waif novel, this calm reaction fulfils two roles. It emphasises the dehumanised responses of the average slum-dweller, and allows the author to remind us that when death occurs in such a world, it is not an occasion for sadness. Brenda's readers are told: 'Happy little Deb! Who need to have wept for her?' In her coffin, she is 'calm and peaceful' with 'all the suffering gone out of her old woman's face, all her cries hushed, all the wrinkles smoothed away' (Brenda, *Froggy* 121). Contrast this with the death of a young, middle-class midshipman in *Nothing to Nobody*. The news of his death 'fell upon the family as an overwhelming blow, far too bitter for any words of mine to describe' (Brenda, *Nothing* 127). Sorrow over this loss leads to the death of the boy's mother, but neither she, nor the reader, are chided out of their sympathy by the author.

Middle-class death and death in the slums are clearly different, as only the latter functions as an escape from a life of misery. Death under these conditions can be, paradoxically, a kind of wellness. When orphan Flo is mortally injured in an accident, she is told by middle-class Miss Mary that there are two ways of getting well. One is 'getting well to be ill again by and by – to suffer pain again, and sickness again – that is the earthly way'. However, there is a better way: 'a way of getting so well, that pain, and sickness, and trouble, and death, are done away with for ever – that is the heavenly way'. On realising that would mean going to Jesus to 'live up in the gold streets wid Himself', Flo considers this 'wonderful news' and is possessed of 'a sudden and great joy' at the thought that 'He was coming himself to fetch her – she should lie in His arms and look in His face, and be always with Him' (Meade 204–5). The crippled John Shafto in *Lost Gip* spends much of the book telling his friend Sandy that he must take his place as his mother's son after his death. His final words, just after Sandy has found his lost sister Gip, are: 'Lost and found! Dead and alive again! Rejoice with me! He is saying that' (Stretton, *Lost* 117).

In *Froggy's Little Brother*, Benny succumbs to the same fever that carried off his friend Debs. During his final days, Froggy nurses him tenderly, and sings hymns depicting death as a wonderful journey to a brighter and better city:

> Soon in the golden City
> The boys and girls shall play,
> And through the dazzling mansions
> Rejoice in endless day;
> O Christ, prepare Thy children
> With that triumphant throng
> To pass the burnished portals,
> And sing th' eternal song.    (153)

As they share a pillow 'for the last time in the poor garret', Brenda informs her readers that 'The world's loneliness seemed to be there, and poverty very deep, but ah! The two little brothers were not really alone; they were not really poor!' Having been told that Jesus himself is present and watching over them, we are exhorted: 'Little children, pray for that presence – pray that Jesus may come and abide with you, then you can never be very lonely, or very sad!' Benny dies after uttering his final words: 'everybody's going home' (Brenda, *Froggy* 154, 183).

Death is a welcome transition because God can provide a far better home than any earthly parent, cladding his children in robes of purest white, allowing them to walk on golden streets, and saving them from sadness, sickness and hunger. A popular 1886 painting by G. F. Watts shows an angelic maternal figure whose dark wings encircle a peaceful-looking baby, with closed eyes and parted lips. Clasping one of the baby's hands, to her face, the angel bends low and smiles sadly; her other hand holds a small, shining circlet over the child's head. The maternal figure tells us that death is nothing to be feared, and the title – *Death Crowning Innocence* – presents it as a 'crowning achievement', offering the message that the best deaths are those that occur in infancy, when the child is as yet untainted by the sins of the world. As a hymn quoted in *Pilgrim Street* has it:

> 'Here in the body pent,
> Absent from Him I roam;
> Yet nightly pitch my moving tent,
> A day's march nearer home!' (Stretton, *Pilgrim* 145)

As a single waif orphan, Jessica takes on the roles of both the rescued and the redeemed, recovering from her near-death experience to live a comfortable life in a proper home. Little Cristal gets redemption without rescue, although he dies 'more resplendent than any earthly monarch' with the court where he lives filled with the glory of the Lord's blessing which seems 'to stream down on him in the light of all the precious stones and all the gold in the world' (Howitt 30). But after these singular children, waif novel orphans began to appear in groups of two or three siblings. This meant that the cathartic death of one child could lead directly to the restoration of domestic order, the dying child effectively saving the others through his or her 'sacrificial' death.

In *Little Meg's Children*, the death of the youngest of three children (only ever referred to as 'baby') is the catalyst for a series of reconciliations and a release from the slums for the surviving children. After Meg's fallen neighbour Kitty is revealed to be Posy, the long-lost daughter of Meg's employer, Mrs Blossom, Posy's hardened heart is softened as Meg helps her pray for forgiveness. After 'a storm of tears and sobs', she tells her mother, 'God'll hear me and have mercy on me, I'm going to be your Posy again!' Meg's father, long missing at sea, then returns; he too has found God during his travels and has signed the pledge. Leaving the squalid court behind, both reunited families embark on a new life as emigrants (Stretton, *Little* 63–4, 144–52).

*Lost Gip* also ends with a life overseas. The Gip of the title is rediscovered when Sandy goes to fetch a street preacher for his dying friend, John Shafto. His sister has been picked up off the streets and is about to be sent abroad with a group of children emigrating to Canada, but Sandy finds her as they are saying goodbye. This plants an idea in Mr Shafto's head, and when his house (situated in the middle of a graveyard) is subject to compulsory purchase by a railway company, he tells his wife that with the money, they will take Sandy and Gip – who have replaced their dead child – and begin a new life. The last time the family are seen, they have achieved the rural idyll; Sandy is 'driving a yoke of oxen in a strong substantial wagon, with Mrs Shafto and little Gip seated comfortably in the back' (Stretton, *Lost* 145–7).

Flo's faith brings her the friendship of a respectable working-class woman called Mrs Jenks, along with the saintly and aristocratic Miss Mary, for whom Mrs Jenks works. Both sit with her as she lies dying, with her soul 'washed white in the blood of the Lamb'. Her death is 'a quiet passing into a better Land' and her last words are ''tis h'all glory'. Soon after, Mrs Jenks is reunited with her errant son to whom Flo has written; her simple letter having effected conversion and repentance from his thieving past. Miss Mary says that God has told her to take care of Flo's brother Dick, first led astray by young Jenks, but now reformed. Flo's redemptive death thus enables the rescue of other waifs (Meade 205).

At the end of *Pilgrim Street*, Tom dies trying to rescue his criminal father who has set fire to a factory. His last words dwell on a brief criminal episode in his own past, as he says: 'The body dies and is buried; but if we are born of God we shall live forever . . . I was a thief, and the son of a thief, but Jesus gave me power to become one of the sons of God'. His little brother Phil is then adopted by a kindly policeman whose harsh faith has been softened by Tom's exemplary conversion and death. Having saved 'a good sum of money', he rehouses both Phil and an entire poor but religious family called the Pendletons in two cottages in the cemetery next to Tom's grave (Stretton, *Pilgrim* 183, 189).

A clergyman and doctor arrive too late to save Froggy's brother Benny, but they arrange for Froggy's admission to a Home for Boys, where he is to learn the suitably symbolic trade of a carpenter. Soon after his admission, a policeman brings in a boy of four or five, called Billy. The child has no mother and, in a repetition of the event that leaves Froggy and Benny orphans at the start of the book, his father has just been knocked down and killed on the street. On being presented to the Home's trustees, the boy produces a nut from his pocket and proceeds to eat it 'taking small bites at a time, much after the fashion of marmozet [*sic*] monkeys in the Zoological Gardens' (Brenda, *Froggy* 193). This demonstration suggests this waif animal will not be wild and savage, but a tame, caged one, and he is given into the care of Froggy as his new brother.

The book ends with an appeal to its readers to send 'pennies and shillings to help schools, and Homes, and Kindergartens' and to respond to appeals 'to enable poor little East End children to have a day in the country' (Brenda, *Froggy* 199). This is no suggestion readers should agitate or work towards lasting social change, simply a request they donate to institutions working among the poor. In case it is not already clear that the major beneficiaries will be those working within them, we are told:

> As we hope to partake in the same citizenship in the one Everlasting City, let us take care how we disregard our pastor's pleading, for when we are arraigned at the Last Day before the Judgement Seat of Christ we will be held responsible for the little souls that enter His Presence there, maimed and scarred and ignorant for the want of care, and love and teaching which we on earth have denied them. (Brenda, *Froggy* 198)

For all their hand-wringing descriptions of poverty and sorrow, the message of the waif novel is that individual orphan bodies are not important, what matters is that we remember: 'these children may be street Arabs, but they have immortal souls' (Brenda, *Froggy* 198). As long as saved souls reach their true home in heaven we, as their saviours, will be able to answer for our actions on the Day of Judgment.

## Notes

1. In many respects, Mary Howitt's dreamy and fanciful 'little Cristal' also anticipates MacDonald's similarly named 'little Diamond' from *At the Back of the North Wind* (1871).
2. An 1880 book, *The Sword of Bardwell*, includes praise for the firm from four evangelical periodicals, assuring readers that each John F. Shaw book has been 'written with a higher purpose', is 'pure in its tone, and scriptural in its teaching', and takes seriously the ability to 'influence for good or ill the future of the rising generations' (Phipps 1880: n.p.).
3. The original meaning of waif is un-gendered, but perhaps because of this later meaning, we tend to think of waifs as feminine.
4. Mr Daniel's savings of nearly £400 are the equivalent, according the National Archives Currency Converter, of five-and-a-half-years' wages for a skilled tradesman in the 1860s. This unlikely fortune for a coffee-stall holder is partially explained by a reference to 'his savings-bank book and his receipts for money put out at interest' (Stretton, *Jessica* 54–5).

5. Printed outside copyright in the US, in 1874, the Daddy Long Legs of *Nothing to Nobody* seems a likely inspiration for Jean Webster's 1912 bestseller *Daddy Long Legs*. Webster shifts the name from her young orphan heroine to a benefactor, whose surname 'Smith' matches Brenda's actual surname.

## Works Cited

Armstrong, I. *Novel Politics: Democratic Imaginations in Nineteenth-Century Fiction*. Oxford University Press, 2016.

Avery, G. *Childhood's Pattern: A Study of the Heroes and Heroines of Children's Fiction. 1770–1950*. Hodder & Stoughton, 1975.

Bebbington, D. 'Evangelical Theology in the English-Speaking World during the Nineteenth Century.' *The Scottish Bulletin of Evangelical Theology*. vol. 22, no 2, 2004, pp. 133–50.

'Brenda' (Castle Smith, G.). *Nothing to Nobody*. [1873]. John F. Shaw, 1898.

'Brenda' (Castle Smith, G.) *Froggy's Little Brother*. John F. Shaw, 1875.

Briggs, J. *A Woman of Passion: The Life of E. Nesbit, 1858–1924*. New Amsterdam Books, 1987.

Butts, D and Garrett, P. *From the Dairyman's Daughter to Worrals of the WAAF*. Lutterworth Press, 2006.

Cutt, M. N. *Ministering Angels*. Broxbourne, Five Owls Press, 1979.

Davidoff, L. *Thicker Than Water: Siblings and Their Relations, 1780–1920*. Oxford University Press, 2012.

Douglas, M. *Purity and Danger*. 1966. Routledge, 2002.

Gavin, A. E. (ed.). *The Child in British Literature: Literary Constructions of Childhood, Medieval to Contemporary*. Palgrave Macmillan, 2012.

Guthrie, T. *A Plea for Ragged Schools: Prevention Better than Cure*. John Elder, William Collins, and James Nisbet, 1847.

Hager, K. and Schaffer, T. 'Extending Families' [Special Issue]. *Victorian Review,* vol. 39, no. 2, 2013, pp. 7–21.

Henson, G. W. *Hymns We Love*. Hall Mack Co., 1935.

Hocking, S. *Her Benny*. Frederick Warne & Co., 1879.

Howitt, M. *The Story of Little Cristal*. Alfred W. Bennett, 1863.

Lomax, E. 'Reclaiming the Outcast: A Study of the Writings of Hesba Stretton in Their Social and Cultural Context'. PhD thesis, De Montfort University, 2003.

Lomax, E. *Writings of Hesba Stretton: Reclaiming the Outcast*. Ashgate Publishing Ltd, 2009.

Lomax, E. 'Telling the Other Side: Hesba Stretton's "Outcast" Stories'. *Popular Children's Literature in Britain*, ed. J. Briggs, G. Butts and M. O. Grenby. Ashgate Publishing, 2008.

Mackintosh, M. *Dust, Ho!, or, Rescued from a Rubbish Heap*. 1891. John F. Shaw & Co., 1903.

Meade, L. T. *Scamp and I*. John F. Shaw & Co., 1875.

Peters, L. *Orphan Texts: Victorian Orphans, Culture and Empire*. Manchester University Press, 2000.

Phipps, K. *The Sword of de Bardwell*. John F. Shaw, 1880.

Reynolds, K. 'Froggy's Little Brother: Nineteenth-Century Evangelical Writing for Children and the Politics of Poverty'. *The Oxford Handbook of Children's Literature*, ed. J. L. Mickenberg and L. Vallone. Oxford University Press, 2011.

Rickard, S. L. G. '"Living by the pen": Hesba Stretton's Moral Earnings'. *Women's History Review*, vol. 5, no. 2, 1996, pp. 219–38.

Rose, J. *The Intellectual Life of the British Working Classes*. Yale University Press, 2001.

Shaftesbury, Lord. 'The Second Annual Report of the Ragged School Union'. *The Quarterly Review*, vol 7, 1847, pp. 127–41.

Schaffer, T. *Romance's Rival: Familiar Marriage in Victorian Fiction*. Oxford University Press, 2016.

Stretton, H. *Jessica's First Prayer*. [1865].The Religious Tract Society, 1907.

Stretton, H. *Alone in London*. The Religious Tract Society, 1869.

Stretton, H. *Little Meg's Children*. [1868]. The Religious Tract Society, 1939.

Stretton, H. *Pilgrim Street*. [1878]. The Religious Tract Society, 1930.

Stretton, H. *Lost Gip*. [1873]. The Religious Tract Society, 1881.

Thiel, E. *The Fantasy of Family: Nineteenth-Century Children's Literature and the Myth of the Domestic Ideal*. Routledge, 2008.

Thompson, F. *Over to Candleford*. Nonpareil Books, 2009.

Walton, Mrs O. F. *Christie's Old Organ*. [1874]. The Religious Tract Society, 1890.

Wharton, J. J. S. *The Law Lexicon, or, Dictionary of Jurisprudence*. Spettigue and Farrance, 1887.

Wood, N. 'Angelic, Atavistic, Human: The Child of the Victorian Period'. *The Child in British Literature: Literary Constructions of Childhood, Medieval to Contemporary*, ed. A. E. Gavin. Palgrave Macmillan, 2012.

Wynne, M. *Mollie's Adventures*. W. R. Russell and Co., 1903.

Chapter 6

# Bodily Filth and Disorientation: Navigating Orphan Transformations in the Works of Dr Thomas Barnardo and Charles Dickens

*Joey Kingsley*

In a photograph circulated by the Anglo-Irish philanthropist Dr Thomas Barnardo in 1874, a young girl, costumed to appear as a newspaper seller, peers out from under a nest of dishevelled hair, an unkempt dress bunched in the rear exposing her bare legs and feet (Fig. 6.1). The image depicts Florence Holder (Murdoch 13; Barnardo, *Florence*), one of over 100,000 poor and orphaned children who overwhelmed the streets of London in 1867, a year after Barnardo opened 'Dr Barnardo's Homes' for 'absolutely destitute' children who wandered 'homeless, frequently diseased, and usually starving' without 'parents or friends' (Barnardo, 'Volume' 4). Although Florence clutches a white pamphlet in her hand, her smudged face diverts the viewer's gaze. One of nearly a dozen doctored images distributed by Barnardo to solicit fiscal contributions to his 'welfare charities' (Mile 261), this photograph reveals the nineteenth-century orphan's power to elicit 'Pity and Compassion' (Mile 261) from the upper and middle classes who feared contracting homelessness, physical filth or moral disease. Nineteenth-century reformers drove a philanthropic movement aimed at helping orphans by persuading well-off patrons, who feared a fall from social grace, that fiscal contributions could distance them from the aura of dirt, hunger and death surrounding orphans.

The threat of death does not discriminate along class lines, however, and parents of every class feared being plunged into penury. In both cities and rural areas, every class of family was susceptible to contracting a number of highly contagious illnesses ('diphtheria, measles, scarlet fever, pneumonia, and small pox') caused by unsanitary

Figure 6.1 Florence Holder posed as a newspaper seller (June 1874). Barnardo's Film and Photographic Archive, London (Admission Album 1/1, no. 16).

living conditions, poor nutrition and a lack of hygiene (Davin 17). The reality of death in the mid-nineteenth century ensured that the upper classes were surrounded by an increasingly visible class of street children who had lost parents due to death, abandonment or illegitimacy. Thus surrounded, the more comfortable middle and upper classes developed a fear of orphans who served as reminders of the lower class's high birth rates and overcrowding. In the hierarchy of children, orphans thus remained at the bottom, but wielded enormous power over the upper classes who feared them.

In the nineteenth century, the loss of a parent due to illness, neglect or accidental death radically reclassified children, situating them farther beyond the domestic and social rituals of the traditional family. In both images and descriptions of Victorian England, orphans wander independently beyond the reach of adults. In the depictions of orphans produced by Dr Barnardo and Charles Dickens, orphans find a kind of extended family in the company of other orphans. Cottage homes, prisons, workhouses and asylums forge orphan communities according to age, class, disability, financial position, legitimacy, race, religion, sex and crime. Both photographic representations and dramatic descriptions of orphan life broadcast an image of the orphan as a poor, uneducated and possibly criminal child with a lost past and an uncertain future. Happiness was not even considered a 'prime ingredient' for lower-class children until the 1830s (Cunningham 92). Left to the mercy of the viewers and readers who pitied them, Victorian orphans were defined by external signs of suffering (dirt, torn clothing, emaciated bodies, coughing) and their circumstances were interpreted by audiences whose desire to maintain social standing encouraged them to associate orphanhood with misery. For well-intentioned reformers like Barnardo and Dickens, presenting children as unhappy beings with mysterious pasts was advantageous; they were plot holes to be filled by wealthy imaginations. The only certain thing that an audience could glean from these representations was the subjects' loss of family, a fate which could befall anyone, allowing the audience to define orphans according to what they themselves were *not* – poor or dead.

Of course, not all orphans came from poverty and many children had one living parent. Despite the popular image of Victorian orphans as famished outcasts, many came from good homes and attentive parents who, even if they were poor, cared for their children faithfully. In their charitable work, however, both Barnardo and Dickens embraced the public stigma against orphans in order to aid them. By presenting wealthy patrons with images of hungry children, they capitalised on the upper classes' fear, hoping that it would turn to compassion, yield donations and ultimately enable the children's rehabilitation. The donors, in turn, could feel superior, yet beneficent, insulated once more in a sense of safety that never existed. Among the 59,800 children Barnardo rescued in his lifetime, Florence Holder demonstrates how effective fabricated representations could be in the economy of charity. Exaggerated portraits elicited donations regardless of whether they honestly represented the children's true conditions.

Mediums like photography and writing are particularly suited to storytelling. Although the artist shapes the narrative, the mechanisms of interpretation disengage the viewer or reader from the work's means of production. For instance, the self-referential nature of a photograph, as Lindsay Smith argues, ensures that its appearance 'overrides its methods of production' and forces the viewer's attention towards stray or extraneous details (Smith, 'Photographic' 173). In their photographs and writing, Barnardo and Dickens together seek a journalistic stance akin to witness, tasking an upper-class audience with inventing a narrative for those child subjects whose appearances they have already symbolically linked with death and illness in generous detail: sour expressions, dirty clothes, bare feet and exhaustion. Whether in photographs, pamphlets, speeches or novels, the viewer is so distracted by the children's appearances that shock and pity, the desired effects, override any initial dismay at the reformers' unprincipled staging and framing. Ideally, this departure from truth allows the reformer to seek a higher truth: that children without parents should not be sentenced to sleep and starve and eventually die in the streets. Heightened melodrama thus becomes a vehicle for children's advocacy by prizing children's welfare over completely faithful representation.

The photographic medium can divorce orphans from the context of their lives entirely, presenting viewers with shocking details that may not be derived from life but nevertheless accurately communicate their emotional traumas. Lindsay Smith comments that the 'more deliberately aestheticized hand-generated medium' of photography can produce more 'visually shocking' images by detaching them from a referent, thereby introducing the possibility of invention (Smith, 'Photographic' 167). And, indeed, some of Barnardo's photographs do project a story whose details mislead the viewer. In some cases, Barnardo's photographs altogether eliminate public recognition of the loving (albeit compromised) parents who tried to secure better lives for their children by sending them to his institutions (Murdoch 17). In reality, many respectable children who had lost one or both parents were forced into charitably funded institutions due to a diminished family income, not parental neglect. By staging the photograph of Florence Holder, Barnardo provides her with an invented past that virtually erases her family, linking her misfortunes to parental absence, thereby denying their very existence. Florence's mother, upon seeing Barnardo's work, exclaimed that her daughters had been 'sent into the Homes as clean and comfortable as [she] could make them' (Murdoch 12). Florence's sister, too, travelled throughout London on the sides of Barnardo's collection boxes, which announced her as 'a little waif of London, rescued from the streets, six years old' (Murdoch 12). Who could be more beseeching than a half-starved, scruffy six-year-old or a girl mulishly hawking papers in an economy of literacy that so far eluded her? How could people cushioned with plenty refuse the donation box when starvation and spiritual hunger were at stake?

Separated from their families, Victorian orphans stand outside traditional family structures but find belonging in an extended family of other orphans whose bodies share similar bruises. Orphans swarm Dickens's novels, demonstrating the ways in which physical hardship, such as a lack of food or a bed, can lead to moral strength and inner resourcefulness. In order to arouse compassion in an indifferent upper-class readership, however, Dickens must also show how orphans suffer the blame for their own illness and defilement at the hands of the law. As the childhood death toll climbed to 21,000 in 1858 in London alone (Markel 674), Dickens implored readers to save the 'tens of thousands' (Mile 260) of 'spoilt children of the poor in this great city' (260) whose 'Poverty and Sickness' (260) 'rock their wretched cradles, nail down their little coffins, pile up the earth above their graves' (260). The social diseases of poverty and sickness stigmatised orphans. Like Barnardo's visual records, Dickens's literary portraits provide a quasi-journalistic testimony of the neglect suffered by orphans whose existence, the upper classes believed, nursed the urban squalor created by people seeking work in rapidly developing factories (Collins 194, 531). These depictions intended to awaken 'the seamy side of modern civilisation' (Batt 27) operate on the premise that physical decay breeds moral dissolution, deserving punishment. Dickens's orphans are symbolically cleansed through bathing rituals, as in *David Copperfield* (1850) when David's bath by means of 'taps of water-butts' (47) sees him violently 'soaped, and kneaded, and towelled, and thumped, and harrowed, and rasped' (47), only to be delivered into the hands of Mr Pumblechook, whom he compares to a 'sheriff' (47). Following his rigorous bath, David assumes for himself a criminal identity, understanding that adult authorities consider him tainted. Through physical renewal, the abused waifs of Dickens's novels convincingly bolster the Victorian argument that outward cleansing ('Wash him!' 'Heat the bath!') (Dickens, *David Copperfield* 167) can uncover self-reliance and industriousness, which then may encourage respectable apprenticeship and recalibrate the moral compass of even the most transgressive youth. Cleansed by the power of honest work, orphans like David find redemption in physical cleanliness as they strive for upward mobility.

Transformation narratives like David's reassure the reader that charitable giving *does* create real, authentic change in the lives of orphans. In an advertisement for Barnardo's Home for Working and Destitute Lads, the boy E.E.J.M., 'once a little vagrant' leaning against a tree, is pictured toiling happily at his workbench, 'now a little workman' (Murdoch 37). The clean complexions and calm gazes of orphans in Barnardo's 'after' images reinforce the power of industry to evoke emotional change (Morris, 'Plea' 660–1). The inherent nature of transformational 'before' and 'after' photographs assures the viewer that the invented narrative is not only the correct narrative, but also the intended one. A photograph (Batt 56–7) of boys in a shoemaker's shop shows them seated in rows, calmly working away, immersed in what appears to be placid and divine introspection. By the late 1890s, Barnardo's young charges were employed in his various workshops making brushes, mats, harnesses and shoes, as well as wooden, tin, tailored and printed goods (Ash 91). The sweat of manual labour mirrors the sweat of spiritual conversion as if 'the nearness and reality of Divine help and protection' as Barnardo's biographer John Herridge Batt testifies, 'is borne in upon the mind and heart that is stayed upon God' (Batt 12). These snapshots of industrial training demonstrate how the virtues of silence, obedience and industriousness encourage the resilience required for inner transformation. The silent photograph, devoid of the subject's own thoughts and feelings, invites the reader to connect industriousness and obedience – core virtues of the Victorian period – with cleanliness. In his 1904 biography of Barnardo, Batt includes a photograph of 'young tinsmiths at work' beneath the announcement 'Technical Training!' (57). Overseen by the master tinsmith, the boys in smart uniforms attend to the equipment, making pitchers, pots and watering cans, fully immersed in their domestic tasks. At home in the shop, they want for nothing, the image implies. Barnardo's advertisements circulate the idea that labour is akin to godliness and children set to industrial tasks toil in pursuit of moral rectitude. Labour aligns with Christian redemption in Dickens's *Great Expectations* (1861), too, as the orphan Pip becomes apprenticed to the blacksmith Joe. For him, labour entails symbolic punishment *and* purification. He must 'roll up [his] shirt sleeves and go into the forge' (Dickens, *Great Expectations* 99), emerging from the world of fire feeling 'dusty with the dust of the small coal' but aware of the 'tolerable zeal' with which he works 'against the grain' of his feeble 'sense of the virtue of industry' (Dickens, *Great Expectations* 99). Orphans at work support the Victorian ideal of resilience, which reformers can nurture in spite of children's innate wickedness.

In correlating bodily impurity with poverty – and, as an extension, moral degeneracy – Barnardo and Dickens reaffirm the idea that class can 'be read from the body' (Swain and Hillel 45) and outward cleansing can lead to divine redemption. In another of Barnardo's images, sloppily dressed Francis Coot leans against a wall, outfitted with rough boots, a hat and a satchel – a flimsy container for his meagre property. John Maloney sits on a rock, propped up by a straw basket, eating a hunk of bread, his open shirt revealing his thin frame

(Wagner and Lloyd 26). Low to the ground, he grimaces, looking vulgar. These boys' sickly appearances reinforce their despondency, a lack of inner verve suggesting moral deficiency and a sluggish intellect. As long as their bodies sustain signs of parental abandonment and spiritual lack, orphans fulfil the upper classes' expectations that the lower classes deserve misery. And, thus excluded from rituals that would usually be overseen by parents or servants (eating, bathing, sleeping, learning, working), orphans embody the physical and spiritual contamination virtually unknown to the more solvent and educated higher classes.

By working in the medium of photography, Barnardo captures isolated moments in the lives of his orphans, freezing them in time. The effect of a snapshot ensures that the child subjects are severed from any backstory or context that would illuminate their inner lives and communicate their understanding of their own predicament. The audience interprets the photographs in order to assemble a narrative about the orphans' embodied experience based solely on external signifiers. The viewer infers their emotional states from their physical appearances, but cannot understand the orphans' thought processes, true feelings or inner conflicts. Dickens, in contrast, works with words, moulding the text to suit his characters' unique personalities and singular predicaments. Description facilitates a three-dimensional effect in which the reader can experience the orphans' daily traumas by proxy through the medium of the narrator.

The textual medium allows Dickens to represent an orphan's own account of orphanhood rather than that composed solely by a non-orphan of the middle class. In *David Copperfield*, for example, David relates that he feels 'twenty times more wretched, to know how unselfishly mindful' (415) his aunt is of him, and 'how selfishly mindful he is of himself' (415). This self-awareness precipitates his self-knowledge, which confirms for David an identity of deserved degradation. David admits to the reader that his 'dirt and dust' (*David Copperfield* 158) and 'tangled hair' (158) make him feel 'quite wicked' (158) and he is 'hungry, thirsty, and worn out' (163). Dickens appeals to the middle class's superiority by painting orphans as participants in their own demonisation. Their inner monologues and verbal comments present a three-dimensional representation of childhood in which the reader serves as proxy, narrating the orphan's own thoughts and thus imagining himself or herself as an orphan. Sore from travelling to find his aunt, David's body ('acute pains in my limbs' 'so tired and low') becomes 'very faint and sleepy' after he is 'enrobed' in clean linens and fed 'broth one tablespoon at a time' because he is 'actually starving' (169). Dickens's portrait of the orphan's filth and bodily decline – and the ritual kindnesses that follow – gestures towards the fact that he intends to dramatise the orphan's story in order to redeem outcast, abused, infirm, deaf-mute, disabled and abandoned child bodies. The first-person narrator allows David to claim agency over his physical neglect and to serve as a representative of a larger family – the extended family of orphans everywhere. And, by extension, the textual medium also allows Dickens to present the orphan David as a mouth piece for an entire caste of children who are constantly in touch with other children and the adults who shame, abuse and rescue them. Dickensian orphans achieve salvation not only by recognising the sour conditions of their bodies, but by explicitly evaluating the roles that they play in their own oppression and challenging the reader to do the same. When they place themselves in relation to others, the children can see themselves as other, too.

In *The Politics of Focus: Women, Children and Nineteenth-Century Photograph*, Lindsay Smith speculates that critics of Barnardo were troubled by the ways in which visual deceptions forwarded a 'sham identity' based in children's labour (Smith, *Politics* 124). Barnardo's costuming and stereotyping are extensions of this same strategy that Dickens launches: in order to gain the attention of the middle classes, orphans must be seen as disgraceful enough to warrant any attention at all, but also eligible for redemption through work. The East End Juvenile Mission founded by Barnardo claimed to 'rescue the *Destitute* and *Neglected* Boys and Girls found wandering, homeless and friendless, throughout the great Metropolis' and to shelter them in 'Homes' where they could be 'educated and taught various branches of Industry' and 'carefully instructed in the Word of God' (Wagner and Lloyd 21). Children could attain spiritual or moral cleansing in private homes where they were taught a trade or through grueling labour in state-run, English workhouses made possible by the 1834 Poor Law Amendment Act. Witness to images of despair, the public assumed the moral burden of protecting and punishing (for their own good) those whom it deemed responsible for depravity – namely, children – by putting them to work. In this way, Barnardo's advertisements function as Christian testimonials to the fruits of common labour, insinuating that the destitution and neglect to be found in the 'great city' obscure the education and industry 'carefully' undertaken by the higher classes.

In Barnardo's orphan narratives, physical health parallels moral strength. The juxtaposition of Barnardo's before-and-after images invites the viewer to gauge the effectiveness of Barnardo's homes based on the improved moral conditions of the children who appear clean, fed and occupied. The viewer's role in this assessment determines the degree to which a narrative of redemption stimulates charitable donations, but it also offers a speculative argument in favour of children's labour in service to national interests and the economy of the British empire. In one photograph, a geography instructor delivers a lesson to boys seated at desks. A globe, symbolic of the manifest opportunities provided by conquest, captivates the children's attention. Their focus implies that 'careful' instruction can prove 'useful' to the upper classes whose wealth hinges on the labour of the lower classes. The image further suggests that physical health encourages 'wise' decisions along 'the path' to a practical future. In another image, Freddie, the supposed infant in one image, 'grows older' as 'wise guidance and careful training' shape his character along a 'path to a self-reliant and useful future' (ad from Barmouth, 1936, for Dr Barnardo's Homes). Barnardo's rhetoric of exertion ('careful', 'training', 'mould', 'direct', 'useful') links orphans with productivity, quantitatively framing their worth in terms of economic output and justifying the existence of welfare charities by speculating on the contributions that children can make towards national progress. Potential for economic productivity, then, becomes a sign of moral fibre, linking the orphan's physical body to his or her identity as someone capable of being saved.

Dickens, too, exploits physical health as an indicator of moral resolve. David Copperfield's physical state ('you are very well physically') (*David Copperfield* 232) provides an avenue for his aunt's encouragement of his spiritual development. She admonishes him, 'I want you to be ... I don't mean physically, but morally' a 'firm fellow' with 'resolution', 'determination' and 'strength of character that is not to be influenced' (232). David then feels 'ashamed', confessing, 'She had so far improved me' (302). David's desire to do right by his aunt demonstrates his commitment to the sense of right and wrong that she instils in him. Thus, 'physical proportions' and 'moral nature' serve as the barometers by which the reading public can measure the power of physical and moral rehabilitation (*Bleak House* 21). Because the identity of Dickens's Victorian orphan hinges on the child's shame, middle class readers are permitted to equate physical neglect with poverty and vice. When orphans express dismay at their own bodies, they invite a pitying or fearful gaze, thereby implicating themselves as perpetrators in the crime of poverty, too. They risk writing the public's judgement upon themselves by assuming moral responsibility in order to be pardoned.

Like Barnardo, Dickens arranges scenarios in which children must incriminate themselves in order to achieve candidacy for the middle and upper classes' attention. Like Pip whose body ('He's a young 'un, too, but looks bad, don't he?') (*Great Expectations* 97) underscores his criminality and guilt ('the pilfering,' 'an oppressed conscience') (14), David Copperfield's coarse desire for money ('I told him humbly that I wanted money, and that nothing else was of any use to me') (*David Copperfield* 160) identifies him as lower class. As these orphans recognise the reality of their position, they align themselves with the urban filth that the upper classes associate with iniquity. In doing so, they both gain respectability through the work of bettering themselves and are forced to acknowledge their perceived lack of respectability. When they are ranked among the destitute, they become pliable candidates for self-edifying reformers like Dickens and Barnardo.

One irony of orphanhood is that adults – and the law – held orphans to the same standards of behaviour unanimously valued in children from stable homes: obedience, silence and industriousness. In the middle and upper classes' view, the absence of parental support did not excuse bodily filth, despondency, theft or sleeping outdoors. As if to keep death at bay, the upper classes held orphans to nearly unattainable standards, despite knowing that maintaining cleanliness and good behaviour was difficult without resources. In this way, the upper classes created a dynamic in which they could police orphans while also embracing charitable giving meant to ease their suffering. This irony reveals the upper classes' intractable fear of death, which reinforced their disdain for orphans who might be daring enough to survive starvation and poor weather. In a sense, charitable giving validated the upper classes' desire to be above death itself.

For instance, when Dickens's characters contemplate their lawlessness, they confirm their wickedness. Pip wonders whether his poor performance at his lessons with Mr Murdstone will send him to prison: 'Whether it was a criminal act I had committed? Whether I should be taken into custody, and sent to prison? Whether I was at all in danger of being hanged?' (*Great Expectations* 59). This childish uncertainty renders Pip pitiful enough to garner attention, but vulgar enough to require punishment. The adults must assume direction over his care if he is to be reformed and become an example of the upper classes' generosity. Similarly, Mr Bumble oversees Oliver Twist's morning bath outside for fear of his 'catching cold' (*Oliver Twist* 10) and props him up as an example of sin and disobedience during 'prayer-time' (10) to save the other children's souls. Simply put, orphans must be kept alive for them to be redeemed. Despite the fact that he is sheltered in the workhouse, Oliver's rootlessness prevails because he fears the 'mercy' of the adults who oversee him. Oliver's fear of death highlights the extent to which Dickens utilises the emotional and physical torment of his orphan characters to breed anxiety in readers whose entertainment capitalises on their dread of dying. The egregious punishments doled out to Oliver reinforce the idea that punishment can lead to redemption, but that death might be preferable to the conditions of the workhouse. Pip's reflection linking criminality and death force the reader to question whether it is 'right' to virtually sentence a child to death in prison or the poor house. Would it be possible to fund an alternative solution? Could displaced children be cleared from the streets and placed in safer communities out of the public eye where they could be taught morality?

Nineteenth-century orphans perform their displacement in Barnardo's photographs. In one image, a young boy, J. B., 'once friendless and forlorn on the streets' (Barnardo, 'Volume' 60), perches on a wooden post draped with a dirty cloth. His tattered trousers reveal knobby knees; he scowls. In another image, five young girls look out over a caption announcing them 'Fruits of Neglect – The Raw Material' (13). In yet another, a barefoot boy in a ripped, fraying coat haphazardly holds copies of *The Daily News*, his glazed eyes implying vapidness. These are the 'outcasts of vice-cursed populations, naked starved, shelterless, friendless' (Batt 24) – 'nobody's children' (Wagner and Lloyd 21) who '"don't live nowhere"' (Batt 24). Seated, contorted or crouched on rocks and wooden posts, the children pose low to the ground amid raw materials (boxes, barrels, shipping crates) as if to suggest that they are not yet fully human but natural elements waiting to be moulded from the landscape. Like the young girls whose caption objectifies them as 'The Raw Material' with which reformers must work, the children photographed near raw materials accrue significance when they intersect with industrial objects.

The moniker 'Nobody's Children' effectively divorces abandoned children from their pasts, renders them illegitimate, and alienates them from the rest of society. This manipulation of language fosters disorientation ('no body') and directs attention to the role that Victorian reformers played in the public shaming of their young charges. Both literary and visual representations of orphans catalogue their confinement and punishment at the hands of brutish adults. The puritanical efforts of adults, Bernardi suggests, were contrived to sanitise them of immorality but, instead, unveil their own leading roles in the children's criminal behaviour (445–73). In keeping with his support of the Custody of Children Act, which ensured rights for children who previously 'could be ill-used and corrupted' by 'a bad parent or a bad guardian' ('Dr. Barnardo') the glazed eyes and shredded clothing of Barnardo's subjects imply that they have been '[s]tarved, beaten, prisoned, drugged, tormented, slain' (Morris, 'Plea' 61) and '[d]ashed to death on the stones of the street' (Morris, 'Meliora' 658). And, yet, in the workhouses, children and their parents are 'victim of a systematic course of treachery and deception' in which they are deprived of food, abused, ('a tremendous shake,' 'a kick,' 'a tap on the head, with his cane') (*Oliver Twist* 3) and segregated to prevent reproduction and 'decrease the surplus population' (*A Christmas Carol* 10). The image of the workhouse highlights the violence done to children by the system designed to both save them and resolve their threat to society. By the mid-1800s, Frost reports, many thought the workhouses unsuitable places for children and by the end of the century approximately 'ten thousand pauper children' (129–30) lived in homes operated by private charities. However, children of the workhouses, many of whom were orphans (Frost 124), endured hunger, exhaustion and abuse. The food, limited education, sleeping quarters and work provided in the workhouses (Frost 123) provided a solution whereby children might work to survive, swapping physical labour for basic needs. Efforts to relocate children from workhouses to 'homes' transitioned them back into pseudo-familial environments. And, yet, these efforts still systematically reinforced the untouchability of the upper classes and the filth of the lower classes.

Within the economy of charity, the workhouses function as institutions of suffering where children punished into acknowledging their wickedness are forced to express their fear of adults and themselves. The written medium allows Dickens to play into the public's fear of street children and fully dramatise the criminality of his orphan characters. When poor orphans express horror at their own bodies, for example, they incriminate themselves in their own poverty and become suitable candidates for salvation. Their need for money is especially linked to horror. Pip says, 'I was in mortal terror of myself ... I had no hope of deliverance ... I am afraid to think of what I might have done on requirement, in the secrecy of my terror' (*Great Expectations* 26, 12). When David Copperfield tries to sell his jacket to a shopkeeper, the man yells, 'Get out of my shop!' and scolds him, saying, 'don't ask for money; make it an exchange' (*David Copperfield* 160). David then reflects, 'I never was so frightened in my life, before or since' (*David Copperfield* 160). In such scenes, orphans are shamed by adults for needing money and, as a result, see themselves as both victims and criminals. Even though he had slept on the ground after a hard day's work and awoken to trudge twenty-three miles, David is shamed and silenced by the shopkeeper, even though he appears to David like a 'drunken madman' (*David Copperfield* 160). Both Dickens and Barnardo campaign for reform by exploiting orphans who demonstrate an understanding of their own debasement, fulfilling charitable donors' desire for them to feel deserving of their misery on moral grounds. However, when orphans voice their own fear of themselves, Dickens's readers experience a sense of horror facilitated by the medium itself. Because a narrator sees and hears the children's pain, the reader is able to serve as both a witness and an active participant in their so-called deserved suffering. Then, just as the orphans' self-directed horror names them the ultimate consequence of others' indifference, it makes them eligible for aid, if not love.

Orphans documented in 1873 in Wandsworth Prison look resigned to the large, wooden signs crudely hung around their necks, identifying them by number: Thomas Savage (4193), Edmund Harker (6342), John Hearn (5722) and William Sayers (5049) (Wagner and Lloyd 27). Inspired by Barnardo's advertising methods, these mugshot-style portraits concentrate on the face and upper body, directly addressing the boys as if they were criminals. This objectification translates criminality in both Barnardo's 'realistic' photographs and Dickens's journalistic fiction. Oliver Twist is painted as a criminal who has been 'badged and ticketed . . . a parish child – the orphan of the workhouse – the humble, half-starved drudge – to be cuffed and buffeted through the world – despised by all, and pitied by none' (*Oliver Twist* 1). Without the tether of home, he roams ('buffeted') like a prisoner ('cuffed') caged by his own vices, which render him ineligible for tenderness ('despised by all', 'pitied by none') (1). He seems swept up in violent winds of misdirection. The close third-person narrator brokers Oliver's inner thoughts as he seems to describe his imprisonment within the workhouse and, more dramatically, his prescribed fate. Wearing the physical signs ('half-starved') of his neglect, he is marked like cargo ready to be shipped ('badged', 'ticketed') (1). This identifies him as a vehicle of economic opportunity – a promising candidate for rehabilitation and productivity. However, opposite the young boy hugging his knees to his chest in Barnardo's famous image '"Lost!" Alone in the streets of London' (Wagner and Lloyd 23), Oliver is described as well-kept. The boy featured in 'Lost', in contrast, hides his face above his shrunken ribcage. This child has not even earned a sign and, 'lost' in the swell of humanity, represents the need for the orphan's salvation. His stance insinuates to the audience that he has been self-imprisoned; he is so unfortunate that he has learned self-disgust. Unlike Oliver Twist, who is virtually imprisoned, this boy seems imprisoned in his own body, his only home. He hugs his knees to his chest as though protecting himself, but his ribs (like prison bars) clearly show how little he has to lose. He has not been ticketed; he is not in transit; he is empty, unworthy of mobility. Instead, he sits in the street as people bustle around him. Barnardo's images reveal the extent to which his 'calculated narrative uses' of photography create an element of suspension (Smith, 'Politics' 125). Badged and tagged, the orphans are suspended in time, caught between coming and going, crouching like stray animals. The bestial, exotic otherness of these children, Smith suggests, almost sabotages their chance at salvation due to their 'unknowable alien qualities' (125). Dickens's characters, too, are often depicted as 'other' than human, lingering in doorways, halfway between shelter and the streets. These representations reaffirm the idea that orphans are simply part of the landscape – the 'raw material' from which model morality may be chiselled.

By depicting orphans in transitional stages and positioning them near the ground, such descriptions and advertisements confirm the orphan's identity as irrelevant. The orphan figures in turn internalise the social fears and class hierarchies that are projected onto them by the upper classes. The appearance and positioning of their bodies maintains their sense of their own inferiority while simultaneously eliciting pity in a voyeuristic audience. In an early 1870s illustration of the 'shilling baby', a 'little waif' who 'had been left there by an inmate' (Wagner and Lloyd 24), a baby in rags crawls through a doorway, headed into the road. Without earthly parents or a heavenly Father, such a child fallen from grace becomes a fixture of the streets. Victorian orphans who lie prostrate in doorways, on floors, or on cobblestones assume positions of supplication that imply guilt, deformity and prayer. When they make themselves filthy on the ground, they gesture towards their knowledge of their own wickedness. In *David Copperfield* (1850), the orphan Emily expresses her longing to 'crawl to the door-step, in the night, kiss it, lay [her] wicked face upon it, and theer be found dead in the morning' (595). Emily is an extreme case, as she seeks to remove her 'wicked' body entirely. However, her imagined release (or annihilation) from the pressures of reality illuminates the singularity of her torture, through which Dickens's readers can equate self-inflicted death with physical diminishment ('crawl', 'wicked face', 'found dead') (*David Copperfield* 595) and read her desire for death as a desire for entrance into the saving light of religion ('door-step', 'be found', 'the morning') (595). In effect, she calls on the reader to physically pull her up out of the street and save her. Barnardo and Dickens capitalise on the sensational powerlessness of these children by suggesting that they *want* to be saved, thereby reasserting the power of the middle and upper classes, which condescend to aid those orphans whose suffering is most visible and most vocal.

In images from 1874, Barnardo's young boys sink against walls or sacks or curl on the ground pitifully, looking vulnerable. In his 'before' snapshot, Thomas Bayes can be seen sitting awkwardly against a heap of wooden boxes and barrels. In the 'after' image, he poses with his right hand stuffed squarely in his pocket, one arm propping his chin up against a wall plastered with copies of *The Daily News*. Here, the child's body – erect, thoughtful, clean, proud – insinuates his ownership over his body and his fate. His posture suggests the evolution of an inner life; his rehabilitation can be read in his upright back, lack of visible sores, and proximity to the written word. His stance implies that philanthropy has the potential to tag children and send them off to be remade in private homes, imitating family life, as opposed to state-run workhouses where rehabilitation was akin to torture.

The stances assumed by children in Barnardo's and Dickens's work contribute to the sense of disorientation and flux defining Victorian orphanhood. In *Bleak House* (1853), the crossing-sweep Jo with his 'grimy tears' dies of pneumonia and, in death, his tortured body that has been haunting doorways becomes a symbol of middle-class negligence. Jo laments, 'How unfortnet do you want fur me to be? I've been a chivied and a chivied, fust by one on you and nixt by another on you, till I'm worried to skins and bones' (*Bleak House* 660). Much like the despondent stares of children in Barnardo's photographs, Jo's harassed body challenges the reader to take up the mantle of generosity by admonishing him or her to identify with Jo's purity. He haunts the houses and doorways to which he is never admitted. Meant to penetrate the hardened shell of a dispassionate audience, Jo's body symbolises the abuse of an entire class. In a public speech in which he advocates on behalf of the poor, Dickens presents a similarly sick child when he offers this recollection published in *The Medical Pickwick: A Monthly Literary Magazine of Wit and Wisdom* in 1921:

> there lay, in an old egg-box which the mother had begged from a shop, a little feeble, wasted, wan, sick child. With his little wasted face, and his little hot worn hands folded over his breast; and his little bright, attentive eyes, I can see him now, as I have seen him for several years, looking steadily at us. (Mile 261)

Dickens's public attempt to convert the masses functions similarly to Barnardo's photo testimonials in that he gestures to a 'real' child whose condition is replicated in his fiction. The sick child appears as pure as Jo, subject to the whims of a cruel world. His 'bright, attentive eyes' shine despite his 'feeble, wasted, wan' (Mile 261) body, a reminder of his curiosity and intellect, his potential for recovery. Dickens's reference to his own moral awakening ('I have seen him for several years, looking steadily at us') (261) includes him in the class to which he preaches as well. The child signifies the middle and upper classes' deliberate remove from the children who plague them. In setting the child within his sights, Dickens asserts his responsibility for the child's seemingly inevitable death.

Transformation images validate the open doors of Barnardo's homes by suggesting that the disorientation of street children is temporary. Narratives of orphan travel or imminent displacement imply that social betterment is possible and spiritual rehabilitation occurs when orphans are removed from poverty or embark on personal quests that lead them away from sites of suffering. These fringe positions push Dickens's characters into disorienting self-knowledge that trumps the histories assigned to them by others. While Barnardo's 'after' images project newly invented identities on rescued children, their inability to physically speak in their photographs mutes the full range of their experience. Barnardo's costuming exaggerates their physical suffering, placing them at the whims of a photographer despite the fact that they are free to move as they please. In contrast, Dickens's orphans often construct their own self-mythology via a first-person narrator. And, even when a close (seemingly first) third-person narrator describes them, their small bodies battle incredible hardships – hunger, sleep deprivation, filth, illness, death – that lend them a mythic, self-made quality. These literary orphans ultimately find a sense of home as they move from place to place, evolving as they go. While Barnardo's children move from 'Home' to the workhouse, or between multiple privately funded 'homes' they find 'not an imitation of a home, but several real homes' (Batt 72). In fact, Dickens's orphans often find more loving care when they are taken in and cared for by others. This process transitions them from recipients of information, help, or basic resources into informed, helpful and resourceful people. Dickens imagines his 'chilled and desolate' child characters (like Oliver Twist left 'alone in a strange place') conjuring their divorced families through memories, imaginings, or distant objects (*Oliver Twist* 23).

Without homes or in between homes, these orphans must become their own homes, isolating themselves within bodies that often sustain profound disorientation. Standing in the graveyard above his parents' tombs, Pip thinks his father 'a square, stout, dark man, with curly black hair' and imagines his mother as 'freckled and sickly' from the character and inscription of her headstone, from which he lifts his fanciful history (*Great Expectations* 1). His imaginings underscore his disorientation, as the appearance of escaped convicts interrupts the intimate moment, symbolically shattering his dream of a unified, gentle-hearted family. It is important to note that this invented family *is* a dream developed by the orphan, a fictional history narrated in order for the child to create a sense of self and express his need for belonging. Dickens thus positions Pip as both the owner of his story and a tenant who dwells within it. David Copperfield finds home in his own imagined backstory, too, summoning his mother's unknown 'youth and beauty', imagining her 'weeping by the fire, and my aunt relenting to her' to summon the 'courage to go on' (*David Copperfield* 158). David's ensuing conversion at the hands of his aunt occurs only after the reader witnesses his horror at himself and comes to feel a desire for belonging. As an educated, middle-class narrator of his own story, David crafts for himself a narrative of positive transformation: hard luck and unfortunate circumstances can lead to luck and redemption. But, even though his transformation story entails his own fortitude and strength, Dickens also accommodates the middle class by suggesting that David's survival is aided by their morality. David's inclusion in the middle class – and his association with middle-class people – provides a reassuring narrative for middle-class readers suspicious of orphans and those who champion them.

When orphan children acknowledge their imperfections through physical posturing or self-reflection, they reinforce the upper classes' fear of catching orphanhood through association with filth and illness. When reformers place orphans in scenes of 'useful toil and healthy happiness' (Batt 28), their seemingly industrious contributions to society validate the middle and upper classes' self-edifying philanthropy. Thus, bodily transformation *and* spiritual transformation reaffirm the widespread belief that work brings self-respect and respectability. Dickens draws on both when he beseeches readers in 1921:

> This is the pathetic case, which I have to put to you; not only on behalf of the thousands of children who annually die in this great city, but also on behalf of the thousands of children who live half-developed, racked with preventable pain, shorn of their natural capacity for health and enjoyment. If these innocent creatures cannot move you for themselves, how can I possibly hope to move you in their name? (Mile 262)

In many orphan narratives, the orphan's clean, strong body becomes a visible sign of his or her new sense of purpose or dedication to the empire. Dickens shames the upper classes by insinuating that they are guilty of being immune to suffering but might be redeemed by helping to return children to their 'natural capacity for heath and enjoyment'. Thus, Dickens calls on the wealthy to change their hearts. And, when this audience believes that orphans might be cleansed of pain and deformity merely by donating, they prioritise morality. As Barnardo's missions testifies, workers in his Homes like the 'East End Juvenile Mission' testified that they were 'increasingly assured that the secret of a radical transformation [was] to be found alone in a TRUE CHANGE OF HEART' (Wagner and Lloyd 21). Just as the testimonial of Barnardo's East End Juvenile Mission visually links hallmarks of good health with inner goodness to elicit donations, Dickens calls on a larger public conscience to promote the respectable upper classes as responsible gatekeepers of morality. A genuine change – a true transformation of body and spirit in which morality becomes a choice motivated by strong feelings of desire – could persuade patrons that the 'charity' they made possible provided not *just* charity but moral transformation as well.

Victorian representations of redeemed orphans necessarily rehabilitate child bodies fallen from grace in order to claim legitimacy for charitable enterprises. Neither Dickens nor Barnardo is able to denounce the indifference of the upper classes without relying on visual or written rhetoric rendering orphan children suspect, filthy, broken or morally bankrupt – and deserving of better – so that their transformations convey the external signs of health that inner change can bring. In order to cultivate a philanthropic attitude among the middle and upper classes, these reformers identify the orphan's loss of respectability with an ability to attain self-respect once recognition of their personal filth helps them to place themselves within a class of renegade others.

Despite the troubling nature of many depictions of Victorian orphans, the British public, as Shurlee Swain and Margot Hillel observe (2010), was mostly untroubled by the staged nature of Barnardo's before-and-after illustrations. His ad campaigns drew donations by cultivating a sense of duty in middle- and upper-class reformers whose bloated sense of moral superiority drove them to pity orphans and eventually pushed them to donate. In contrast, Dickens's testimonials of child neglect buoy a sense of superiority among readers whose empathy is inevitably offset by a fear of laziness, grime, drunkenness, coarseness, lewdness, sickness and overcrowding. Dickens appeals to an audience that can only be steered towards philanthropic acts by descriptions of defilement that display orphans as unproductive slouches whose transience and beggary contaminate respectable people.

The extent to which Barnardo and Dickens capitalise on the upper and middle classes' contempt for the poor may be seen in their assertion of orphan stereotypes in which a sanctimonious, precarious middle class cares for orphans out of fear of social decline. The child's body remade in writing and photography ultimately yields a sense of displacement that encompasses a larger, more spiritual – and therefore more pressing – bewilderment. Then, the wan faces, tattered clothes, uncombed hair and sickly pallor of London's nineteenth-century orphans beg divine redemption as well as physical cleansing. And, as the literary and visual advertisements for orphan welfare seek to recalibrate the thinking of rich and poor alike, Barnardo and Dickens demonstrate how catering to the self-righteous sensibilities of the oppressive upper classes manipulates the identity of the Victorian orphan so that the loss of biological family, as well as the eventual discovery of a 'made' family, may be seen through a lens of compassion and good will.

## Works Cited

Ash, Susan. *Funding Philanthropy: Dr. Barnardo's Metaphors, Narratives and Spectacles.* Oxford University Press, 2016.

Barnardo, Dr Thomas J. *Florence Holder.* Barnardo's, 1874.

Barnardo, Dr Thomas J. 'Volume of News-cuttings on the Death of Dr. Barnardo'. *Daily News*, 21 September 1905. https://archive.org/details/b28981972/page/n3 (accessed 30 October 2017).

Batt, John Herridge. *Dr. Barnardo: The Foster-Father of 'Nobody's Children'. A Record of an Interpretation*. S. W. Partridge & Co., 1904.

Bernardi, Milena. 'Children and the Dark Side of Charles Dickens'. *History of Education & Children's Literature*, vol. 8, no. 1, 2013, pp. 445–73.

Collins, Philip. *Dickens and Crime*. Macmillan, 1994.

Cunningham, Hugh. *The Children of the Poor: Representations of Childhood since the Seventeenth Century*. Oxford University Press, 1992.

Davin, Anna. *Growing Up Poor: Home, School, and Street in London, 1870–1914*. Rivers Oram Press, 1996.

Dickens, Charles. *Bleak House*. Oxford University Press, 1996.

Dickens, Charles. *A Christmas Carol – A Ghost Story of Christmas*. Wisehouse Classics, Kindle edn, 2015.

Dickens, Charles. *David Copperfield*. Penguin Books, 1994.

Dickens, Charles. *Great Expectations*. Bantam Books, 1986.

Dickens, Charles. *Oliver Twist*. Open Road Media, Kindle edn, 2015.

Frost, Ginger S. *Victorian Childhoods*. Praeger, 2009.

Markel, Howard. 'Charles Dickens' Work to Help Establish Great Ormond Street Hospital, London'. *The Lancet*, vol. 354, no. 9179, 1999, pp. 673–5. Science Direct. https://doi.org/10.1016/S0140-6736(98)10108-3 (accessed 22 August 2019).

Mile, Ira S. *The Medical Pickwick: A Monthly Literary Magazine of Wit and Wisdom*, vol. 7, The Medical Pickwick Press, 1921, pp. 260–2.

Morris, Sir Lewis. 'Meliora', in *The Works of Sir Lewis Morris*. Kegan Paul, Trench, Trubner & Co. Ltd., 1907.

Morris, Sir Lewis. 'A Plea for the Children', in *The Works of Sir Lewis Morris*. Kegan Paul, Trench, Trubner & Co. Ltd, 1907.

Murdoch, Lydia. *Imagined Orphans: Poor Families, Child Welfare, and Contested Citizenship in London*. Rutgers University Press, 2006.

Smith, Lindsay. 'Photographic Simulation and Nineteenth-century Expression'. *Criticism*, vol. 54, no. 1, 2012, pp. 167–74. http://www.jstor.org/stable/23133924 (accessed 15 June 2019).

Smith, Lindsay. *The Politics of Focus: Women, Children, and Nineteenth-Century Photography*. Manchester University Press, 1998.

Swain, Shurlee and Hillel, Margaret. *Child, Nation, Race, and Empire: Child Rescue Discourse, England, Canada and Australia, 1850–1915*. Manchester University Press, 2010.

Wagner, Gillian, Lloyd, Valerie and The National Portrait Gallery. *The Camera and Dr. Barnardo: An Exhibition*. Barnardo School of Printing, 1974.

Williams, Valerie. 'London Narratives in Photography 1900–35', in *The Camden Town Group in Context*, ed. Helena Bonett, Ysanne Holt and Jennifer Mundy. Tate Research Publication, 2012. http://www.tate.org.uk/art/research-publications/camden-town-group/valerie-williams-london-narratives-in-photography-1900-35-r1104366 (accessed 7 July 2019).

Chapter 7

# The Limits of the Human? Exhibiting Colonial Orphans in Victorian Culture

*Laura Peters*

In 2018, at the age of fifteen, Swedish teenager Greta Thunberg started protesting in front of the Swedish parliament about the need to take urgent action to address climate change. From this sole protest grew an international campaign, Fridays for Future, a weekly strike by school children, in a number of countries around the world, to compel adults to act on climate change. Fridays for Future has been awarded Amnesty International's Ambassador of Conscience 2019. As a direct result, a number of countries have recognised climate change as an emergency, including the UK parliament. The courage and conviction of children marching to call for action has captured the collective imaginary; the children are celebrated as having clarity of vision, untainted by a consumerist mentality which has led to the current situation. Children are seen as the embodiment of hope and of the future; it is their generation that will inherit the damaged environment brought about by regressive adult consumption and policies.

Within this context, the need for posthumanism, or the move to de-centre humans as the apex of all development, is clear. Critical of the 'speciological chauvinism' (Ellis 139) of the Anthropocene, posthumanism looks to challenge the sense of autonomy from and domination over nature by replacing consumptive notions of progress with values 'conducive to the long-range survival of humans and of other life-forms, biological and artificial, with whom we share the planet and ourselves' (Hayles 291). Yet concerns about posthumanism's use of the term human as a monolithic category gives rise to criticism that it lacks engagement with the history of humanism and its problematic relationship to matters of race. Historically, those who have struggled to find recognition of their difference under the term human, specifically racially diverse peoples, colonised subjects, women and even children, find themselves doubly marginalised by a posthumanist discourse that identifies all humans as equal humans. In reality, the experience of those historically excluded from this category is not one of achieving equality. Zakiyyah Jackson argues that racism 'remains one of the most powerful and resilient technologies for delimiting and policing the border between the "fully" human and the "nonhuman"' (Jackson 15). It is also the case that these same, marginalised and impoverished peoples are most vulnerable to the devastating effects of climate change.

Similarly, while it is children who are driving Fridays for Future, children have not always been celebrated as the embodiment of hope and of the future. Historically, childhood has been a much-contested category. While the Romantics celebrated the cult of the child in which childhood was seen as a particularly charged state of innocence, at one with nature, the Victorians tended to view children as less developed than adults. In evolutionary discourses, the figure of the child was seen to embody a state of underdevelopment and/or degeneration of specific races as discussed below. Uniting these strands, this paper will explore the exhibiting of orphan children in the Victorian era, demonstrating how these exhibits illustrate both the commodification of orphanhood and of race, and the unique position the orphan occupies at the intersection of contemporary discourses on race, science, childhood and visual culture. These exhibitions contrived to speak to emerging discourses: they were self-consciously constructed contributions to debates which were shrouded in quasi-scientific and imperial narratives of originality and discovery. The chapter will examine specific orphan exhibits as case studies including how literature contributed, offering exhibits or portraits of orphanhood which shared the staged visual nature of the exhibition. Considering these together, the chapter will argue for the key importance of these exhibits as challenges to mythologies of the family, community and emerging definitions of humanity. While posthumanism 'confronts us with our inhumanity – our animality, materiality, and irreducible alterity to ourselves' (Ellis 139), it has not always been the case that animality and materiality have been considered on a par with each other. Historically, associating races and classes with animals denied them humanity. The inclusion of these exhibited orphans in posthumanist discourse is important precisely because of the way the orphans embody the contestation of notions of humanity.

In August 1845, a handbill (Fig. 7.1) appeared advertising a new exhibition at Egyptian Hall, 'Extraordinary Exhibition! Bushmen

Figure 7.1 'Bushmen Children or Pigmy Race!' A handbill for the 1845 exhibition of San children. By kind permission of The Bodleian Libraries, The University of Oxford, John Johnson Collection: London Play Places 10 (47).

Children or Pigmy Race!' The handbill goes on to emphasise the extraordinary nature of the exhibition: 'Two Bushman Children from the interior of Africa, a most extraordinary Variety of the Human Race never before Exhibited in Europe'. But what was so extraordinary? The exhibition of humans stretched back three decades[1] to the 1810 exhibition of the Hottentot Venus, Sartje (real name: Sara Baartman). Between 1810 and 1845 there were exhibitions of Laplanders in 1822, Eskimos (Inuit) in 1824, and in 1843 Arthur Rankin's exhibition of nine Ojibbeways enlivened George Catlin's show of paintings and exhibits of North American Indians. Looking back further, these exhibitions grew out of a much earlier practice, stretching back to the fifteenth century, of displaying natural history specimens in cabinets of curiosity. This 'desire to collect and display' (Blanchard et al. 2) was the precursor to natural history museums. The human zoos played a pivotal role in this. The exhibitions of humans fed the increasing public appetite for science and understanding the world, particularly the different cultures that were being colonised as part of the British Empire. Crucially, the imperial expansion of trade fed these appetites through the commodification of humans and nature more broadly. It is this process of commodification which starts to feed the consumption of humans and nature that has led to the climate change emergency with which the chapter opened. Initially involved in the trade of human skulls and skeletons, the scientists who travelled out in empire gradually became involved in the trade of live humans for exhibition. The exhibition of orphan children this chapter considers came out of this interest and I will consider three exhibitions: the Bushmen children in 1845; the Aztec Lilliputians in 1853–4; and two Earthman orphans, a boy of sixteen and a girl of fourteen. These exhibits illustrate the commodification of both orphanhood and race; the loss of family has meant that these children have fallen into the hands of traders who seek to trade on their ethnic diversity.

Accompanying the developing scientific narrative on race and the rise of scientific racism was a developing visual culture. In the Victorian era illustrations and etched plates, predominately used for flora and fauna in the eighteenth century, increasingly focused on anatomy underscoring 'the imperative of carefully recording physical specificities so as to better demarcate the boundaries between races' (Bancel et al. 2). The human shows provided a live embodiment of race feeding this visual culture and the public appetite for the exotic and the savage. The exhibitions of orphan children provided 'living illustrations'[2] to accompanying scientific papers (Altick 280).

However, Robert Bogdan argues in *Freak Show: Presenting Human Oddities for Amusement and Profit* that these exhibits were not straightforward reflections of a new scientific knowledge. Rather, through understanding these exhibitions as part of a larger tradition of amusement and showmanship moving from circuses to human curiosities, Bogdan explores the constructed, fictional, even hoax, nature of these exhibits. As explorers and natural scientists brought back tales and specimens from distant worlds, there was money to be made. Thus, the exhibits were not transparently realistic; they were mediated interventions which in turn shaped the public understanding of difference be it racial, cultural or in terms of disability. These exhibits spoke to the developing discourses of the day, the interest in science and far-away lands, by offering a constructed contribution which largely aimed to pique public interest to sell tickets. The exhibits were 'part of development of mass culture constructed around the expansion of different modes of communication, including periodicals, expositions and specifically human exhibitions' (Bancel et al. 15). At the basis of this was a hoax of some sort, 'a fraud' with the exhibitor deliberately misleading the public in order to increase popularity and therefore revenue' (Bogdan 10). The significance of the expansion of communication based on a hoax (a precursor to fake news) has parallels with scientific discourses of the time which sought to obfuscate that they were mythic/constructed narratives rather than facts.

Central to increasing popularity of visual culture was the development of exhibition spaces, the most famous of which was the Egyptian Hall. The Egyptian Hall opened as the London Museum in 1812, a venue to house William Bullock's large collection of natural history specimens and curiosities. It quickly became known as the Egyptian Hall largely because of its architecture and because of the contemporary archaeological discoveries in Egypt which proved extremely popular when displayed in England. The Hall continued to host a range of exhibitions and panoramas from around the world and was host to the extraordinary exhibition of orphan children in 1845. The 1845 handbill tells us that the boy was sixteen years old and was 44 inches high while the girl, unrelated to the boy, was eight years old, 32 inches high and 'most elegant and delicate in proportion'. These figures have an obvious child-like physiognomy, their posturing modest and sedate compared to Sartje ('the Hottentot Venus'), who was sexualised both in the exhibition and in the visual materials which focus on her genitals. Both were 'characterised by remarkable intelligence and gentleness of disposition'. Neither had any memory of their parents who were 'murdered by the Kafirs, who pursue and exterminate the Bushmen Tribe with the most unrelenting ferocity'. The orphans were 'rescued' by a Dutch Boer trader and sold on, as a commodity. The children, like those that would come after them, were transported through the same networks that moved goods. As Sadiah Qureshi explains in *Peoples on Parade*:

> Managers recruiting performers relied on the same international networks of trade and export that governed the circulation of economically important goods such as spices and slaves. [. . .] Slavery provided a mass market for human commodities that were shipped along the same trade routes as flora and fauna. [. . .] Showmen exploited these existing networks of trade and travel. (Qureshi 108)

One of the legacies of the slave trade was the refinement of routes to move both people and goods as commodities. These orphans were a new commodity whose value lay in their exotic nature and in the increasing interest of the emerging scientific racism in defining and differentiating races. In fact, this exhibit captures this intersection powerfully. Identified as a most 'extraordinary Variety of the Human Race never before Exhibited in Europe', people paid one shilling each to come and view the San children who shared the billing with a baboon from the 'MONKEY TRIBE' from Port Natal. The exhibition's staging was deliberately symbolic placing these children between monkeys and humans: their existence seen as less than human, a missing link in an evolutionary schema which hypostatised the inferiority of their racial difference. Within the larger imperial arena the construction of orphanhood was a delegitimising discourse in which the colonial power (in this case Britain) operated as a parent to the developing (read underdeveloped) children, the colonial subjects. The move was an orphaning one, removing colonial subjects from their cultural genealogy, history and practice replacing this with those of the imperial power headed by the matriarchal figure of Queen Victoria. It is a metonymic substitution which replaces cultural specificity with a larger imperial (non)identity and family. The recently formed Ethnological society and the paying public alike asked: Are these children human or are they the missing link?

Following on from the 1845 exhibition of Bushman (San) orphans, 1853 saw two key exhibitions of orphans, the Aztec Lilliputians (Fig. 7.2) and the Earthmen (San) orphans. 1853 was also the year of the infamous Zulu Kaffir exhibition which prompted Dickens to pen 'On the Noble Savage' after visiting. The significance of Dickens's

Figure 7.2 Máximo and Bartola, the Aztecs. A handbill for an 1870 Crystal Palace 'extraordinary penny exhibition' of Máximo and Bartola. By kind permission of The Bodleian Libraries, The University of Oxford, John Johnson Collection: Human Freaks 4 (49).

visits to these exhibitions for his work will be considered later in the chapter. 'The Aztecs!' arrived with the handbill proclaiming 'A newly discovered Tribe of Human Beings' the exhibit of whom had been 'patronised by Queen Victoria, the Royal Family and Court of Great Britain on July 4, 1853'. The orphans exhibited were Máximo Valdez Nunez and Bartola Velasquez, advertised as the 'Aztec Lilliputians', purportedly representatives of a diminutive race only recently discovered by explorers in a remote, untouched community (Ixamaya). In reality, Máximo and Bartola were probably born in San Miguel, El Salvador to parents Innocente Burgos and Marina Espina (Bogdan 127). A Spanish trader Ramón Selva heard of their 'dwarfish and idiotic' appearance and proposed to their mother to take them to be educated and cured of 'imbecility' (quoted in Bogdan 128). They were then sold on to an American, Morris, who became their manager. The object of the exhibition was the racial, physical and cognitive difference they embodied. The 1853 UK exhibition followed on from a long-running, popular US exhibition which opened in 1849. The handbill celebrates:

> The most marvellous of all Human Beings ever seen by White people [...] They are totally unlike anything deemed Human – their Heads being formed like the head of an Eagle – Their Hair growing erect on the head, in form and dimensions of a huge grenadier's cap. Their frames are beautifully symmetrical, yet almost Lilliputianin [sic] size – eyes black and liquid – silky skin, of a deep olive colour – affectionate – amiable – intelligent – and pleasing in manner. (Fig. 7.2)

Key to the success of the show was engaging the scientific community which was achieved by shrouding their origin in mystery. Thus, it was important that Máximo and Bartola were presented as orphans – the mystery lay partly in being presented as from a particular race and worshipped as deities, so a discernible earthly genealogy which posed awkward questions to this presentation was elided. However, careful examination of Máximo and Bartola by various people, including the American doctor Dr J. Mason Warren, at the time of the American exhibition in 1851, cast doubt on the authenticity of the exhibit's claims. Warren published a paper in the *American Journal of the Medical Sciences* (April 1851) which both the *Athenaeum* and *The Illustrated London News* (*ILN*) reprinted on 8 October 1853 to accompany the London exhibition. This followed an earlier *ILN* column entitled 'The Aztec Children' (*ILN*, 9 July 1853, 11). Warren's conclusions were that Máximo and Bartola were children and not the adult representatives of 'a race of dwarfs [sic]'. In fact, they were special needs children whose disability was a source of fascination and commercial exploitation. Regardless, the exhibition was incredibly popular; the public flocked to see Máximo and Bartola and 'their presentations became prototypes for later exhibits' (Bogdan 121). In the US, they were received by members of Senate, House of Representatives and President Fillmore at the White House; in the UK they were viewed by the Royal family at Buckingham Palace and the Ethnological Society. After the exhibition in London, Máximo and Bartola then went on tour to the continent, and were seen by Emperor Napoleon, Emperor of Russia, leaders of Prussia, Bavaria, Holland, Hanover and Denmark (Bogdan 131). There are records of Máximo and Bartola being exhibited up to 1901, including a hoax marriage in 1867 to address falling audience numbers. One could argue that Máximo and Bartola achieved a status akin to celebrities; they were viewed by millions. However, the longevity of their exhibition underscores the fact that they were owned, managed and exhibited for virtually their whole lives.

At first glance, the *ILN* does appear to be naïve in referring to the narrative accompanying the exhibition which identified the children as gods celebrated by the remaining Aztecs who sought refuge from Cortez's invasion of Mexico in a remote isolated community. But in reality, this narrative formed part of a formulaic exhibition component in which the geography, flora and fauna would be presented as a background to the people being exhibited. In actual fact, the backstory for Máximo and Bartola was created from a popular two-volume travel narrative written by John Lloyd Stephens, *The Aztec Lilliputians or Illustrated Memoir of an Eventful Expedition into Central America* published in 1841 and 1843. The narrative purports to tell of the exploits of three men who travel to reach a forgotten Mayan civilisation:

> an eventful expedition into central America resulting in the discovery of the Idolatrous city of Iximaya in an unexplored region; and the possession of two remarkable Aztec children Maximo, (the man), & Bartola, (the girl), descendants and specimens of the sacerdotal cast, (now nearly extinct), of the ancient Aztec founders of the ruined temples of that country. (Stephens title page)

For the 1853 exhibition the narrative was prefaced by Professor Richard Owen, a leading comparative anatomist of the day and close friend of Charles Dickens, who testifies to 'the remarkable difference which these extraordinary children present, as compared with normal European children [ . . . yet] these children manifest no characters which ally them more closely than other human beings to the brute creation'. Here, while Owen resists classifying Máximo and Bartola as the missing link by insisting on their humanity, he is clear about both the racial difference embodied by these orphans compared to European children, and that they are children, not adults from a 'dwarf' race. Positioning itself as a scientific discovery, the exhibition pamphlet is dedicated to Prince Albert 'the Patron of Science and the Promoter of Whatever Tends to the Knowledge and Interests of Humanity'. Thus, the narrative provides two functions: it purports scientifically to prove the provenance of Máximo and Bartola while simultaneously announcing itself as an adventure narrative. Yet the only factual element of the exhibition was the presence of Máximo and Bartola: the accompanying memoir was fantastical, the backstory of Máximo and Bartola was revealed as a hoax/fiction. But this did not affect the popularity of the exhibition or the number of leading ethnologists and anatomists who seriously engaged with the exhibition. The Preface reveals that

> On Monday, July 4th, 1853, the Aztec Lilliputians had the honor to be presented to Her Most Gracious Majesty. Having previously visited the families of Sir James Clarke, Sir Benjaman Brodie, Doctors Latham, Guthrie, Hodgkin, and been seen by Professors Owen, Grant, and Faraday, and the heads of faculty generally, who considered them a curiosity so unique and extraordinary, as to warrant their commending them to the notice of royalty.

It is a moment when the construction of the scientific racial narrative is laid bare. What is acknowledged to be largely a hoax – there is no Lilliputian race, for example – feeds seamlessly into narratives of missing links, evolution and human belonging, the latter largely determined through racial belonging. It must be acknowledged that it is also a clever bit of marketing, as John Conolly, MD, DCL, wryly comments in 'The Ethnological Exhibitions of London' (1855):

> All the details of this romance were dwelt upon by the exhibitors of these children; and illustrated printed accounts of it were sold for one shilling. But the great city alluded to [. . .] remains [. . .] unverified, and must share the fate of all unverified marvellous statements. (Conolly 18)

The billing of Máximo and Bartola as the Aztec Lilliputians also recalls another marvellous story, Jonathan Swift's *Gulliver's Travels*, a precursor to the travel narrative genre. Likewise, it taps into a visual tradition of caricature parodying travel narratives.[3] The reference to Lilliputians did pose a concern for those who saw these as exhibits of serious scientific study. In the *ILN* (9 July 1853 issue) the author complains: 'Their diminutive stature may justify the children being termed "Lilliputians" but we had rather that a fabulous name had not been applied to the children, who are referred to in illustration of a great ethnological and historical question' (*ILN* 11). The concern expressed in the *ILN* insists on the scientific importance of the children to the general public testifying to a public appetite for ethnology, even in the face of the knowledge of the marvellous hoax. The extent to which the exhibitions, like the popular panoramas, allow the Victorian paying public to vicariously experience these travel narratives as a performance enacting diversity, is a pertinent question. Later in this chapter I will consider literary examples of the staging of orphan exhibits which share notable characteristics with these exhibits namely: the focus on the child, specifically the orphan child as the symbolic embodiment of an infantilised difference; the unknown parentage which translates into a genealogical break; the lack of memory translating into being outside history; the strong focus on the body as the embodiment of these discourses.

In the wake of the Great Exhibition of 1851, the second 1853 exhibition of orphans, was of 'Earthman' (San) orphans, Martinus, aged sixteen years and his sister Flora, aged fourteen years, from South Africa (Fig. 7.3). *The Illustrated Magazine of Art*, covering the exhibition in a piece entitled 'The Erdermänne, or Earthman of South Africa', identified them as 'representatives of a singular tribe' who were the 'last link in the human chain (the penultimate being the Bosjesman)'. Once again, the supposed evolutionary hierarchy is clearly stated: Martinus and Flora are the missing link. Next to them, down one link in the human chain, is the Bosjesman. Once again, these orphan children are denied human status because of their racial background. And once again the exhibition of the children encourages the viewer to see this race as in its infancy, yet to evolve fully into adulthood.

In similar circumstances to the San children exhibited eight years earlier, Martinus and Flora were found by a trader after being orphaned when their parents were killed by members of a hostile tribe. The trader then sold the children on to the 'agent of a mercantile house'

Exhibiting Colonial Orphans in Victorian Culture    153

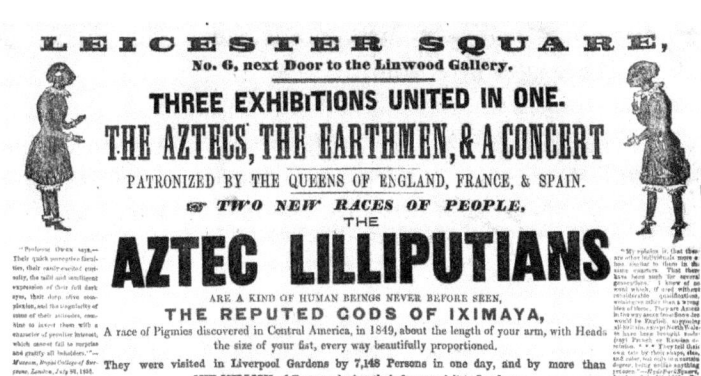

Figure 7.3  'The Aztec Lilliputians'. A handbill for the 1853 Leicester Square Exhibition of Máximo and Bartola. By kind permission of The Bodleian Libraries, The University of Oxford, John Johnson Collection: Entertainments Folder 9 (46).

who entrusted them to the care of Captain Wetherall to take them to England to be educated. Once in England they were consigned to the care of Mr George of Croydon 'who determined to educate them, in the hope that they might become ultimately useful as agents of civilization among their benighted countrymen'. The plan seemed to be working as the author reports:

> It is gratifying, however, to perceive, that in the short time in which they have been in England, the humanizing influence of civilized society has effected so complete a change in their moral and physical appearance, that they no longer present any of the disagreeable characteristics of savage life. ('Erdermänne' 23)

It appears, in receipt of civilising influences the 'last link in the human chain' can be evolved into humans. It also appears that once 'civilized' the orphan children are then to act as colonial agents to 'civilize' their countrymen ('Erdermänne' 23).

However, in spite of Mr George's plan, Martinus and Flora do not return to South Africa, or at least not immediately. Rather they are eventually exhibited with Máximo and Bartola once again promoted as a missing link: the 'Earthmen [. . .] a Race of People only 3½ feet high' and the 'Aztecs' a 'race of Pigmies' (Fig. 7.3). The joint exhibition underlines some key issues. First, these children were commodities, continually sold on 'like sheep' (Conolly 29). They were clearly popular, hence of commercial value to their promoters; the handbill advertising the combined show claims that Máximo and Bartola had over 1 million visitors to their last exhibition. They remain as the missing link, someone not quite human, fascinating Victorian audiences with images of their own savagery while confirming Victorian England's status as the most highly evolved.

Questions also remain over the care they received as children and ultimately their quality of life as adults; they moved from exhibition to exhibition for most of their lives, being continually sold on. Máximo and Bartola, for example, were exhibited in London, the US and around the world from 1849 until 1901, fifty-two years in total. As living exhibits the orphan children were frozen in this Peter Pan-like childhood state, never allowed to grow up. Although John Conolly commented that 'the four children seem happy, well fed, and carefully attended to, and that they are kept scrupulously clean [. . . and] vaccinated' (Conolly 28–9), he does raise concerns about their lives. 'One would hope that they all occasionally breathe fresh air, and enjoy liberty in grassy fields; for six or seven hours' exhibition, six days in the week, in ill-ventilated rooms, however large, cannot be very favourable to their health' (28–9). There is also the question of whether any provision has been made for the children once their popularity has waned. Rather than returning to their homelands on missions to 'civilise' their peoples, they were now alienated from home, country, culture and practices. It was a process of becoming doubly orphaned both from family/kin and from culture.

The exhibition did, however, lead to a differentiation between the perceived stage of development and hence positioning on the evolutionary scale of the pairs of children. Martinus and Flora, the San children, characterised initially by 'their gentleness, docility, and aptness for instruction'[4] were 'civilised' during their time in England, while Máximo and Bartola remain unaffected and untouched. Máximo and Bartola 'still have [. . .] the same love of play. But they have not learned even to use playthings; and, when not immediately addressed, they gaze on things about them with no expression above that of watchful domestic animals' (23). This leads the author to conclude: 'their faculties are evidently very low in the scale of animal intelligence' (24). This is in contrast to Martinus and Flora:

> whether at play or in repose, the difference is still strongly and undeniably marked, between the little South Africans, perfect in their kind, and the little Central Americans, arrested in their growth. In play, or in dancing, the African children act in concert, like any other children; they talk together, and are amused by each other's talk: of all which the Aztecs are incapable. (27)

Thus, Máximo and Bartola are viewed as immutable, unable to learn or develop. Here disability and diversity quickly become a larger metaphor for the great chain of human existence: those who are higher up the scale were perceived as more developed and those at the lower end of the scale more animalised. Often billed as the missing link, these orphan children were represented as being somewhere between human and animal. What posthumanism advocates, even celebrates, namely that humans are not privileged over animals in terms of development or consciousness was a source of contestation in the Victorian era. Those who were not considered of human status were seen as inferior, a bridge between animals and humans.

These three 'exhibits' discussed above were part of a wave of human exhibits, human zoos, in the nineteenth century. The exhibiting of children was part of a longer-established tradition of exhibiting 'wild children' from as early as 1161 in Poland. (Bancel et al. 188) However, the central concern of my argument is the way in which orphanhood spoke to a range of contemporary concerns. Orphanhood is particularly suggestive in exhibits which explore limits of human family and human kinship. The children's lack of memory of parents is suggestive of genealogical disruption or lack rendering the position of the children as unknown within a narrative of familial genealogy. For one whose genealogy is under question, the disruption of the familial narrative places them firmly outside the structures of civilisation and ultimately, humanity. While the children lack specific individual memory, as exhibits they are understood to embody a quasi-cultural memory: a memory of an earlier, more primitive state which places them just outside the human species but linking to it, the missing link. Therefore, they are neither human nor animal but simultaneously both. The shows contribute to contemporary discourses and produce knowledge based on racial hierarchies which consolidate the expansion of imperial domination even in the face of discourses of a shared humanity. It is an additional complication that the exhibitions were largely hoaxes hence positioning the orphans as vehicles of deception, the Bushmen (San) orphans passed off as a pigmy race, while in the case of Máximo and Bartola, children were passed off as miniature adults. In both cases the orphans are exhibited as remnants of some fantastical tribe the likes of which have only been seen in Swift's *Gulliver's Travels* and in widespread travellers' accounts of men with tails (Conolly 29).

Orphanhood made a unique contribution to these contemporary discourses which has not been fully recognised. In *Novel Politics: Democratic Imaginations in Nineteenth-Century Fiction,* Isobel Armstrong argues that 'illegitimacy becomes a nexus for democratic imagination because it challenges cultural certainties' (Armstrong 5). While there has been considerable work on illegitimacy and on foundlings, the particular condition of orphanhood has not been thoroughly explored. Orphanhood also offers a way of interrogating and reformulating kinship structures by problematising discursive notions of genealogy and inheritance in circulation with regards to community, the nation state and Darwin's 'family' of man. For the orphan figures explored in this chapter, the problematic relationship with genealogy and nation more broadly elides with discourses of miscegenation than with illegitimacy. Being outside geneaology offers the orphan a radical potential, challenging established structures and emerging discourses. However, the orphan is also one whose existence is on the margins of familial and kinship structures and whose challenge is to develop relationships and an alternative family/ kinship circle that would see them defined within the category of the human. The use of the figure of the child does allude to those of other races being infantilised. The helplessness of the orphan, without parents, does position imperial Britain in the role of wise parent, more highly developed/evolved and responsible for guiding the racial orphan into adulthood.

Orphanhood is as much a cultural construction as it is a biological one. Similarly, the family once identified as the cornerstone of society is the subject of extensive and productive critical inquiry[5] challenging its mythical status, extending its boundaries, and transforming understanding of what is often referred to as the social building block. Leonore Davidoff's *Thicker than Water* (2012) explores 'alternative models of kinship' in order to decentre linear structures which advance patriarchal principles and genetic ties. Davidoff argues for family as 'a process' rather than a fixed set of relationships and predetermined roles. In a similar spirit, the exhibited Victorian orphan-figure, can be explored in order to understand the challenges such a figure posed for notions of kinship, inheritance, the body, social reform, genre and the constitution of the human subject.

These exhibitions influenced key writers like Charles Dickens to consider issues of race and orphanhood in their own societies. They did so by exploring the burgeoning population of orphan street children, often referred to as 'street Arabs'. These children were the focus of widespread philanthropic and even ethnological endeavours such as found in the *Punch* satirical cartoon depicting the Ethnological Society's expedition into the East End of London. These endeavours shared the objectives of expeditions to colonial outposts, namely to civilise what were considered 'barbaric' peoples and to study people who were thus labelled as being sub-human or in an earlier evolutionary developmental state. While the expeditions to the East End shared the same civilising impulse, the population was considered sub-human by virtue of degeneration. It spoke to anxieties about maintaining a supposedly superior evolutionary state. Thus, class identity intersects the relationship between orphanhood and racial/cultural difference. As Peter Stallybrass argues, Marx, Engels and Victorian bourgeois society more widely often orientalised the poor as embodying racial difference that placed 'the lumpenproletariat' outside history, treating them 'as a distinct race [. . .] a nomadic tribe, innately depraved' (Stallybrass 84). The lumpenproletariat is the large group of people that existed on the margins, outside social structures, social processes and most importantly outside history.

Joey Kingsley's chapter in this collection (Chapter 6) examines how Thomas Barnardo used photographs to stage before-and-after exhibits of orphan children rescued from the street. Kingsley explores the extent to which these photos were constructed helping to mediate a discourse of redemption or reintegration into the larger family of the community. These 'street Arab' orphans were seen to embody a difference which was rooted both in class and in racial/cultural terms. Lydia Murdoch's *Imagined Orphans: Poor Families, Child Welfare, and Contested Citizenship in London* explores the interaction between the poor orphans and their families and the social institutions which increasingly took on their care in the nineteenth and early twentieth centuries. Murdoch's focus on Barnardo's use of before-and-after photographs of rescued children in his periodical *Night and Day: A Monthly Record of Christian Missions and Practical Philanthropy* identifies a larger narrative of degeneration and social inferiority in the photos' emphasis on physiognomy. The narrative of degeneration based on lack of social class intersects with the narrative of racial degeneration heightened by British imperial endeavours and arising from Darwin's evolutionary thesis. Hence, intersecting discourses of race, class and empire were embodied in the orphan child.

The focus on the orphan as exhibit informs key literary portraits of these figures. In the writing of Henry Mayhew and Charles Dickens these portraits share the same qualities as the exhibitions, focusing on the body of the orphan child to signify difference in an infantilising way, and focusing on the lack of genealogy to place the child outside history. Henry Mayhew's *London Labour and the London Poor*, published in serial form 1851–2, interwines the photo, exhibit and literary portrait. Mayhew recounts a number of excursions into various London neighbourhoods and locations with the aim of bringing to the reader's eye the poor population in London.

> I found the lad who first gave me an insight into the proceedings of the associated crossing-sweepers crouched on the stone steps of a door in Adelaide-street, Strand; and when I spoke to him he was preparing to settle down in a corner and go to sleep – his legs and body being curled round almost as closely as those of a cat on a hearth. [. . .] He was a good-looking lad, with a pair of large mild eyes, which he took good care to turn up with an expression of supplication as he moaned for his halfpenny.
>
> A cap, or more properly a stuffed bag, covered a crop of hair which had matted itself into the form of so many paintbrushes, while his face, from its roundness of feature and the complexion of dirt, had an almost Indian look about it; the colour of his hands, too, was such that you could imagine he had been shelling walnuts.
>
> He ran before me, treading cautiously with his naked feet [. . .] (Mayhew 264)

In capturing these moments for the reader, the guide Mayhew offers an orientalised portrait, one which constructs the poor in racialised terms, 'an almost Indian look', emphasising the difference his subjects embody. As Stallybrass argues, Mayhew and others of his time, view these marginalised subjects (lumpenproletariat) as becoming 'a distinct race' and/or 'a nomadic tribe'. These subjects share the same racialised representation as Máximo and the other orphan children exhibited in the human zoos. These subjects also face queries regarding their human status as they are seen as examples of degeneration.

Mayhew's exhibits offer a performance of the intersection of class and ethnicity of the poorest population in London, many of whom are orphans. The sections on 'Crossing Sweepers' establish that the role of the crossing sweep occupies the lowest of the social classes and this group is almost exclusively orphans. In the sketch, 'Of Two Orphan Girls', orphanhood is equated with 'friendlessness' and 'utter destitution' (Mayhew 166). In 'Asylum for the Houseless Poor' the homeless population are more often than not orphans; orphans embody homelessness. The portraits of 'the black crossing-sweep' (260) and the crossing sweep, referenced above, who has 'almost an Indian look about it' underline the intersection of poverty, orphanhood and ethnicity. The majority of those Mayhew interviews are Irish. Thus, orphanhood comes to represent loss of family and larger loss of nation with the orphans forming 'a ragged congress of nations' (440). The sweep's reference to circus ('suckus') (282) highlights the performative aspects of the sweeps' tumbling. In this their role shifts from lowly service to street entertainment. They become akin to the exhibits in the human zoos. Regardless of the skill on display ('there's one little chap, but he's very clever, and can tie himself up in a knot [. . .] I'm best at caten-wheels [sic]; I can do 'em twelve or fourteen times running' (279)), the crossing sweeps remain depicted as performing animals. They are ill-treated, the source of degrading humour and, at times, as they tell Mayhew, violent attack. What underpins Mayhew's portraits is the unspoken interrogation of whether these orphans can be understood as human; much like Jo in Dickens's *Bleak House*, the crossing sweeps appear at times to be spontaneously generated, 'I haven't got neither no father nor no mother – never had, sir' (*Bleak House* 271), and lacking in development. This lack of discernible genealogy does bring into question their humanity. This is reinforced by the 'do nothink' which profoundly questions the ability of reason, something which denotes humanity, casting the sweeps into the category of the sub-human.

Again, the phrase attributed to the crossing sweep, 'I do nothink' (*Bleak House* 267), anticipates Jo's character.

Charles Dickens was immersed in the discourse to which the shows contributed, namely the development of science, racial science and definitions of humanity. He was a great friend of Richard Owen, later reading and praising his *Memoir on the Gorilla* (1865). Dickens's visit to the 1853 Zulu Kaffir exhibition is well documented, not only in his letters but in the infamous 'The Noble Savage' essay to which it gave rise. Dickens returns to these ideas in his work, shaping it in discernible ways.[6] But his engagement started even earlier than this. As seen by his essay, 'On Duty with Inspector Field' Charles Dickens was immersed in the discourses of class, ethnicity and childhood throughout his life: his late-night walks introduced him to similar populations about whom Mayhew writes. On these walks Dickens and Inspector Field came across 'sickening smells', 'heaps of filth', 'the lowering foreheads, the sallow cheeks, the brutal eyes, the matted hair, the infected vermin-haunted heaps of rags' (Dickens, in Slater and Drew 381–2). It is clear that when creating the figure of Jo, the crossing sweep in *Bleak House* (published serially 1852–3), Dickens draws from Mayhew's portraits. From the onset, the narrator emphasises the visual display of Jo:

> Jo is brought in. He is not one of Mrs Pardiggle's Tockahoopo Indians; he is not one of Mrs Jellyby's lambs, being wholly unconnected with Borrioboola-Gha; he is not softened by distance and unfamiliarity; he is not a genuine foreign-grown savage; he is the ordinary home-made article. Dirty, ugly, disagreeable to all the senses, in body a common creature of the common streets, only in soul a heathen. Homely filth begrimes him, homely parasites devour him, homely sores are in him, homely rags are on him: native ignorance, the growth of English soil and climate, sinks his immortal nature lower than the beasts that perish. (*Bleak House* 513)

The stress on the homely does raise the issue of the unhomely or uncanny other, such as the orphans on display in the human zoos. Noting the etymological root of 'unfamiliarity' as family, Dickens identifies those 'foreign-grown savages' as outside the larger human family in order to make the distinction between those of other races and those 'home-made'. It is debatable whether, considering the earlier exhibitions, 'distance and unfamiliarity' 'softened' the perception of the exhibited orphans in the human zoos as they were billed as non-human, the missing link. Dickens seeks to distinguish between these orphans and the home-grown Jo embodying the condition of orphanhood within. Afflicted by 'homely grime', 'homely parasites' and 'homely sores', Jo asks 'What's home?' (*Bleak House* 119). Jo's lack of kinship is highlighted in his submission to court: 'Name, Jo [no surname] [. . .] No father, no mother, no friends. Never been to school. What's home? Know a broom's a broom, and know it's wicked to tell a lie' (119). Although Jo insists that he knows 'nothink' what he does know, like the earlier orphan exhibitions, is that he is 'scarcely human' (177): 'He is not of the same order of things, not of the same place in creation. He is of no order and no place; neither of the beasts, nor of humanity' (513). This is where the outrage lay for Dickens, curating his exhibit for a largely middle-class audience, much like the managers of the human zoos, Dickens implicitly argues for the possible humanity of the street children over the colonial subjects of the human zoos. On the basis of this essential humanity, Dickens argues for action for the home-grown poor over the colonial subject. Significantly, in preface to Franz Fanon's *The Wretched of the Earth*, Jean-Paul Sartre makes the point that bourgeois capitalism legitimised colonial exploitation by denying human status to the colonised subject. Thus, as both Mayhew and Dickens demonstrate, class narratives intersect with racial and evolutionary narratives to identify the orphans as not quite human. Whether this is because of a lack of evolutionary progress or because of the lack of family (civilisation) contributes to a narrative of degeneration is not clear. The examples point to both possibilities with the racially diverse exhibits having yet to achieve human status while the 'street Arabs' point to the precarious nature of development/civilisation and how quickly it can be lost.

At the end of his life, after having visited some of the human zoos, most notably the Zulu Kaffir exhibition in 1853, Dickens returns to the issue. In what was his last, incomplete novel, *The Mystery of Edwin Drood*, Dickens exhibits a set of orphan twins, the Landless twins. The fact that the issues are still resonating in his imagination can be seen in the introduction to Neville and Helena Landless:

> An unusually handsome lithe young fellow, and an unusually handsome lithe girl; much alike; both very dark, and very rich in colour; she of almost the gipsy type; something untamed about them both; a certain air upon them of hunter and huntress; yet withal a certain air of being the objects of the chase, rather than the followers. Slender, supple, quick of eye and limb; half shy, half defiant; fierce of look; an indefinable kind of pause coming and going on their whole expression, both of face, and form, which might be equally likened to the pause before a crouch or a bound. (*Mystery of Edwin Drood* 56–7)

From their introduction, framed by the character Crisparkle's query as to whether 'they were beautiful barbaric captives brought from some wild tropical dominion' (57), Neville and Helena Landless are positioned as an exhibit. Their journey to England from the former Ceylon (Sri Lanka) shares similarities to the exhibited peoples being considered in this chapter: although born in Ceylon to at least one British parent, the twins' orphanhood compounds their lack of family and homeland. They are willed to a guardian 'who grudged us food to eat and clothes to wear' and under whom they had a 'wretched existence'. The death of their guardian leads to them being passed capriciously to a man 'whose name was always in print and catching his attention' (60). More like commodities than human children, the Landless twins are outside kinship circles, community and nation. They belong to neither Sri Lanka nor England. The visual focus of the passage on the racialised bodies of the orphan twins, embodying a sense of racial mystery, is frozen in a 'pause'. It is also a pause which anticipates a leap, much like a dangerous animal from the East. The animalistic metaphors, and the notions of the hunter and the hunted, underscore questions about their non-humanity. Are they the big game trophies brought back from empire? Their name, Landless, compounds the mystery of their genealogy and origins. Being 'very dark', 'very rich in colour', 'almost of the gipsy type' speaks to miscegenation and a loss of originary homeland. Yet Helena is seen in the narrative as beautiful: she embodies the noble savage, while Neville is demonised. In the narrative Edwin Drood suggests that because of Neville's racial genealogy he has no place in white society. 'How should you know? You may know a black common fellow, or a black common boaster, when you see him (and no doubt you have a large acquaintance that way); but you are no judge of white men' (76). The language makes a distinction between the 'fellow' or 'boaster' of the non-white people *versus* the 'man' of the white race. The Landlesses are unassimilable because of their racialised identity and their 'un-English' (164) complexion. White culture is then inscrutable to the racialised other, emphasising their lack of belonging. The passage works to position Neville and Helena as not only outside this culture but as less than human, somewhere between animals and so-called civilisation.

What all the orphan exhibits share is an instability of identity due to lack of familial belonging or membership in a kinship circle. The lack of belonging is so profound that there are questions about their humanity and what it means to belong to the human species. These questions anticipate and/or contribute to developing evolutionary discourses of the day wherein specific races and civilisations were considered the most highly evolved. *In Dark Vanishings: Discourse on the Extinction of Primitive Races, 1800–1930,* Patrick Brantlinger argues:

> Throughout his writings Darwin emphasizes the great, chronological, and cultural distance between the savage and the civilized conditions of human existence. What has produced that distance is progress, although not all races seem capable of moving up the scale from savagery. (Brantlinger 168)

Beyond its centrality to the evolutionary narrative, the notion of progress more broadly is a central narrative running throughout the Victorian era. Celebrated as evidence of a highly evolved civilisation, progress, deeply intertwined with consumption, was used as an evidence base to decide on stages of racial development. Posing a challenge to this notion of progress is the figure of the orphan, a shadowy shape mired in the margins of society, family and nation, unchanging, unevolved, static:

> whether seen as antiquated or infantile, all savages were lost, misplaced in time. Darwin and his followers, of course, accepted geological 'deep time'; applied to humans, that meant a vast temporal difference between history and prehistory, and between civilization and savagery. (Brantlinger 168)

The constancy of the orphan figure belies the narrative of progress raising questions for the fast-evolving definitions of humanity at play. Is the orphan a fully evolved human? Or a sub-species? Or an example of degeneration? In examining this, the orphan figure anticipates contemporary debates surrounding posthumanism, accused of not engaging with race and the historical legacies of racism. Thus, it may be seen to elide those who have yet to achieve human status with those who have enjoyed the privilege of fully evolved human status. One resultant effect of this is the obfuscation of the cultural isolation and economic misery experienced by these people. It also obfuscates that not all humans were equally culpable in heralding the age of the Anthropocene. Paradoxically, those less responsible for climate change are the ones most adversely affected by it.

'Western liberal humanism has sorted biological humans along a racially and sexually coded spectrum from the "fully" human to the "nonhuman"' (Ellis 140). Notions of civilisation were closely entwined with western cultural practices. This chapter has sought to explore how the exhibited orphan child in Victorian times highlights the need for posthumanism to navigate issues of race and the historical legacy of racism. The orphan, at the intersection of contemporary discourses on race, science and childhood, spoke to emerging discourses of civilisation, racial superiority and the human/non-human/sub-human divide. As an exhibit, the orphan embodied the commodification of orphanhood and race which simultaneously challenged key mythologies of the family, kinship, community and humanity.

## Notes

1. For a full discussion of these, please see Richard D. Altick, *The Shows of London*. Harvard University Press, 1978.
2. Such as a November 1845 paper presented to the recently formed Ethnological Society.
3. For a full discussion, see David Taylor, *Politics of Parody: A Literary History of Caricature, 1760–1830*. Yale University Press, 2018.
4. *The Illustrated Magazine of Art*, 'The Erdermänne, or Earthman of South Africa': 23.
5. For a full discussion of the field of kinship/marriage studies, cf. Talia Schaffer, *Romance's Rival: Familiar Marriage in Victorian Fiction*, Oxford University Press, 2016; Mary Jean Corbett, *Family Likeness*, Cornell University Press, 2008; Rachel Bowlby, *A Child of One's Own*, Oxford University Press, 2013; Leonore Davidoff, *Thicker Than Water: Siblings and Their Relations 1780–1920*, Oxford University Press, 2012; *Victorian Review* [Special Issue], ed. Kelly Hager and Talia Schaffer, vol. 39, no. 2, Fall 2013.
6. For a full discussion, please see Laura Peters, *Dickens and Race*. Manchester University Press, 2013, pp. 54–81.

## Works Cited

Altick, Richard D. *The Shows of London*. Harvard University Press, 1978.

Armstrong, Isobel. *Novel Politics: Democratic Imaginations in Nineteenth-Century Fiction*. Oxford University Press, 2016.

Bancel, Nicolas, David, Thomas and Thomas, Dominic. *The Invention of Race: Scientific and Popular Representations*. Routledge, 2014.

Blanchard, Pascal. 'Human Zoos: The Greatest Exotic Shows in the West', in *Human Zoos: Science and Spectacles in the Age of Colonial Empires*, ed. Pascal Blanchard, Nicolas Bancel, Gilles Boëtsch, Éric Deroo, Sandrine Lemaire and Charles Forsdick. Liverpool University Press, 2008, pp. 1–49.

Bogdan, Robert. *Freak Show: Presenting Human Oddities for Amusement and Profit*. University of Chicago Press, 1988.

Bowlby, Rachel. *A Child of One's Own*. Oxford University Press, 2013.

Brantlinger, Patrick. *Dark Vanishings: Discourse on the Extinction of Primitive Races, 1800–1930*. Cornell University Press, 2003.

Conolly, John. 'The Ethnological Exhibitions of London'. 1855. http://access.bl.uk/item/viewer/ark:/81055/vdc_00000005376C#?c=0&m=0&s=0&cv=0&xywh=-530%2C-137%2C2595%2C2725 (accessed 12 November 2019).

Corbett, Mary Jean. *Family Likeness: Sex, Marriage, and Incest from Jane Austen to Virginia Woolf*. Cornell University Press, 2008.

Davidoff, Leonore. *Thicker Than Water: Siblings and Their Relations 1780–1920*. Oxford University Press, 2012.

Dickens, Charles. *Bleak House*. Chapman and Hall, 1892.

Dickens, Charles. *The Mystery of Edwin Drood*. 1870. Oxford University Press, 1989.

Ellis, Cristin. *Antebellum Posthuman: Race and Materiality in the Mid-Nineteenth Century*. Fordham University Press, 2018.

'The Erdermänne, or Earthman of South Africa'. Partial photographic reproduction of an article originally published in *The Illustrated Magazine of Art*, which includes an engraved image of Flora and Martinus, children of the Earthman tribe, accessed digitally from The Bodleian Libraries, The University of Oxford, John Johnson Collection: Human Freaks, 4 (79).

Hayles, N. Katherine. *How We Became Posthuman: Virtual Bodies in Cybernetics, Literature, and Informatics*. University of Chicago Press, 1999.

Jackson, Zakiyyah. 'Outer Worlds: The Persistence of Race in Movement "Beyond the Human"'. *GLQ*, vol. 21, nos 2–3, June 2015, pp. 215–18.

Mayhew, Henry. *London Labour and the London Poor*. Penguin, 1985.

Murdoch, Lydia. *Imagined Orphans: Poor Families, Child Welfare, and Contested Citizenship in London*. Rutgers University Press, 2006.

Peters, Laura. *Dickens and Race*. Manchester University Press, 2013.

Qureshi, Sadiah. *Peoples on Parade: Exhibitions, Empire and Anthropology in Nineteenth-Century Britain*. Chicago University Press, 2011.

Schaffer, Talia. *Romance's Rival: Familiar Marriage in Victorian Fiction*. Oxford University Press, 2016.

Slater, Michael and Drew, John (eds). *The Dent Uniform Edition of Dickens' Journalism*, vol. 4: *'The Uncommercial Traveller' and Other Papers, 1859–1870*. Dent, 1994–2000, pp. 381–2.

Stallybrass, Peter. 'Marx and Heterogeneity: Thinking the Lumpenproletariat'. *Representations*, vol. 31, Summer 1990, p. 84.

Stephens, John Lloyd. The *Aztec Lilliputians, Illustrated Memoir of an Eventful Expedition into Central America Resulting in the Discovery of the Idolatrous City of Iximaya, in an Unexplored Region; and the Possession of Two Remarkable Aztec Children, Maximo, (The Man), & Bartola, (The Girl) Descendants and Specimens of the Sacerdotal Cast, (Now Nearly Extinct), of the Ancient Aztec Founders of the Ruined Temples of that Country. Translated from the Spanish of Pedro Velasquez, of San Salvador.* https://books.google.co.uk/books?id=0tMTAAAAYAAJ&pg=PA3&dq=aztec+lilliputians+john+lloyd+stephens&hl=en&sa=X&ved=0ahUKEwjskfi567flAhXXSxUIHakHBoIQ6AEIKTAA#v=onepage&q=aztec%20lilliputians%20john%20lloyd%20stephens&f=false (accessed 12 November 2019).

Taylor, David. *Politics of Parody: A Literary History of Caricature, 1760–1830.* Yale University Press, 2018.

*Victorian Review* [Special Issue], ed. Kelly Hager and Talia Schaffer, vol. 39, no. 2, Fall 2013.

Chapter 8

# Getting the Father Back: The Orphan's Oath in Florence Marryat's *Her Father's Name* and R. D. Blackmore's *Erema*

*Peter Merchant*

At the moment when Heathcliff crows over him with 'we'll see if one tree won't grow as crooked as another, with the same wind to twist it!' (Brontë 186), Hareton in *Wuthering Heights* might stand for all orphans in literature. With necessarily shallow or severed roots, the orphan is peculiarly exposed to the winds of change. Adapting to changing fashions and patterns in fictional narrative has always been the lot of the orphan. In the 1870s, those fashions and patterns were of course not quite as they had been in the 1840s, when *Wuthering Heights* was written. The rise of sensation fiction was one significant new addition to the literary landscape; and a growing interest in heredity, soon to be explored by Zola and Ibsen, was another. Novels were becoming increasingly attuned to the rhythms of 'Retrograde Investigation', which had been one of the chapter titles in M. E. Braddon's *Lady Audley's Secret* (1861–2), and increasingly inclined to reason upward from the child to the parent. The energies of the detective story and the mystery thriller were therefore very often directed towards families harbouring skeletons in their cupboards and contending with a tainted inheritance, focused particularly on the figure of the father.

The Canadian writer and scholar James De Mille (1833?–80) soon sensed the way the wind was blowing, and used it to fill the sails of his 1874 novel *The Living Link*. The story opens in Cumberland with the heroine, Edith Dalton, who at the age of eighteen has already lost her mother, receiving reports of her father's death far away in Van Diemen's Land; so the pain of a fresh bereavement is added to the 'inherited infamy' (De Mille 158) of being the daughter of a man sentenced to transportation for life. Edith resolves to do all that she can to erase this 'stain of infamy' (45) and 'vindicate her father's memory' (18). Eventually it is shown that Frederick Dalton was neither a murderer nor a forger (but suffered for the misdeeds of another), and nor is he dead. He escaped and has hidden behind a disguise which he will not cast off, in a grand reunion with Edith, until his name is cleared. 'It was the one sweet hope of my life to redeem my name from its foul stain', he says, 'and then declare myself. I wanted you to get your father back as he had left you, without this abhorrent crime laid to his charge' (126). The father's hope is duly fulfilled, so that the story can end with 'the restoration of his name to its ancient honor . . . and the deep joy of Edith over such a termination to his sorrow' (170).

The bringing of the dead man back to life was perhaps one restoration too many, in the fevered cut-and-thrust of De Mille's plotting; the uncovering of a lineage more illustrious than could have been imagined is a more normal means of de-orphaning the fictional orphan (Simon 316–17). However, several later crime stories and sensation novels would revert to the essence of the situation which De Mille had imagined, that of a daughter left to clear the name of an unjustly convicted father. At the end of the line, at least so far as Victorian fiction is concerned, is the work of a fellow Canadian: Grant Allen's *Hilda Wade* (completed by Arthur Conan Doyle and published in 1900). Here, the heroine has 'a Plan to which [she has] resolved to sacrifice everything' (Allen 133), and we learn that she 'will never marry . . . till she has attained some mysterious object she seems to have in view' (6). As Hilda's real name is Maisie Yorke-Bannerman, her 'object' turns out to be rescuing the good name of her father, Dr Yorke-Bannerman, who is believed to have poisoned his uncle with aconitine. So she single-mindedly works her way from the crisis of 'I never will marry any one till I have succeeded in clearing my father's name' (189) to the closure of 'I have vindicated and cleared my father's memory. And now, I can live' (360). Her father of course, unlike Frederick Dalton, does not. In so far as a posthumous rehabilitation can constitute a restoration, however, Hilda – or Maisie – has still got her father back.

In 1876, two novels began to appear which put to use, one after the other, the same fictional mould that had already produced De Mille's heroine and would later produce Allen's. Florence Marryat (1833–99) used it for a novel entitled *Her Father's Name*, which between March and October was syndicated in various provincial newspapers; and R. D. Blackmore (1825–1900) followed immediately with his novel

*Erema; or, My Father's Sin*, which from the November number was serialised in *The Cornhill Magazine* under the editorship of Leslie Stephen. The two heroines, Marryat's Leona and Blackmore's Erema, follow closely parallel courses. Both find themselves, in their teenage years, orphaned in a double sense. Because their fathers were both suspected of murder and both had to flee overseas, where in the opening pages they die, the pain of a continuing character assassination throbs beneath a death that in itself is already a more-than-sufficient sorrow. The sorrows of both Leona in Brazil and Erema in California are reinforced by the experience of exile which they have had inflicted upon them, and are amplified again by their awareness that nothing is bequeathed them but ignominy. Both heroines dedicate themselves to repairing their fathers' tarnished reputations. Leona pledges her life to the sacred duty 'of clearing her father's name from obloquy and shame', and swears to heaven 'not to rest until [she has] done so' (Marryat 107, 273). Erema likewise sets herself to 'right [her] father's wrongs. And I never shall rest till I do so' (Blackmore 1: 261). By 'rest' they both mean the word spoken by Hilda Wade, 'marry'. Not until the disgrace that had haunted her father is entirely dispelled does Erema feel free to take Firm Gundry's hand and lead him away from 'the dismal, miserable, spectral desert' in which her fortunes reached their nadir (Blackmore 3: 306). Leona also postpones her own quest for love until 'the foul stain that rests upon the memory of a beloved parent' can be cleared away (Marryat 319–20). Only then is she able to stretch forth her hand to Don Christobal Valera and, by calling him her affianced husband, 'reward him at last for all his patient, faithful love to her' (321). They are able to marry now that she no longer risks bringing him, in place of the prize that she wanted him to have, only a dowry of disgrace.

\*

In Florence Marryat's *Her Father's Name* (1876), the ringing 'I will' to which (outside the limits of the text) we may imagine Leona Lacoste's story conducting resolves the despairing interrogative that set it in motion. The novel's initiating event was such as to draw from Leona, repeatedly, the same anguished cry that Bunyan's Christian had uttered two centuries earlier: 'What shall I do?' (Marryat 35) Her panic at this point is overwhelming. Having never known her Brazilian mother, who succumbed to 'a sharp fever' shortly after giving birth to her (32), Leona has suffered a loss which seems still more dire: that of her father. Ruth Perry's observation about eighteenth-century novels, '[t]he daughter's loss of her father is often represented as an extreme form of orphanhood' (86), is no less true of Victorian fiction. To compound the agony, Leona's father has just done what Trollope's Melmotte did the year before, in the seventeenth monthly number of *The Way We Live Now*: commit suicide by swallowing prussic acid. At seventeen, therefore, Leona is suddenly parentless. She is in a peculiarly exposed position because in Victorian times a parentless teenage girl is more plainly and permanently marked as an orphan than a parentless teenage boy. (Alaric Tudor in Trollope's *The Three Clerks*, of 1858, is not termed an orphan, despite being parentless at sixteen; but Lucy Morris in *The Eustace Diamonds*, of 1873, continues to be so defined throughout her teenage years.) Not only is Leona now very comprehensively orphaned by the loss of her father, but she has more to endure besides. She finds all that she ever believed about him challenged by a damning account of his having come to Brazil, and taken a false name, as a fugitive from the gallows.

The false name is Louis Lacoste; but in Britain Leona's father was known as George Evans. In Liverpool in his early twenties, a quarter of a century ago, he supposedly murdered a man called Abraham Anson; and then, with a signet ring engraved with 'A.A.' among his possessions, he fled abroad to avoid being hanged. The business and the wealth of their uncle Theophilus Evans, for whom Anson had worked, were inherited instead by George's younger brother Henry. For Marryat in 1876 no less than for H. Rider Haggard nine years later in *King Solomon's Mines* (1885), a pair of brothers called Henry and George and the dramatic disappearance of the latter add up to an arduous and hazardous quest. On this occasion, however, the quest is undertaken by George's daughter, and her father's good name – 'everything to me', she says, and 'far dearer to me than my own' (Marryat 28, 276) – is the treasure on which she is intent. Undoing the damage inflicted upon it by 'the injustice of public opinion' (167) becomes 'the object of her life' (205). What on her first appearance in the novel Leona dramatically declaimed in the character of Joan of Arc, 'In this extremity I throw myself into the breach . . . ' (5), now applies to a mission of her own. Her rededication of her life to this task, at the very centre of the text, is the fulcrum upon which the action is balanced:

> She had arrived at that scene in the life-drama she had sworn to play out by herself when . . . the plot was commencing to unfold itself . . . She had but one object in view. She looked upon her mission as sacred, and considered nothing underhand or dishonourable that was

necessary to forward the project she had pledged herself before high heaven to carry out – the clearance of her dead father's reputation from obloquy and reproach . . . Her eyes were steadfastly fixed upon one point, and she would have gone through fire and water to attain it. (Marryat 162–3)

The need to defend Leona against the imputation of dishonourable or underhand behaviour, as her actions undergo this searching midterm review, arises from the fact that she is currently in her uncle's home under false pretences. Christobal (or 'Tobalito'), her constant companion, was invited there on business, but was too unwell for so long a journey. His illness was an opportunity for Leona to take up the invitation in his place, and travel to London (the Evans family firm having moved from Liverpool to High Holborn) in the guise of the young Spanish gentleman to whom Henry Evans expected to be playing host. Leona's hidden agenda – ferreting out, if she can, the family's deepest and darkest secrets – travesties the obligations of a guest, even though some subterfuge is plainly 'necessary to forward the project she had pledged herself . . . to carry out'; and her cross-sex disguising, a travesty of a still more startling sort, is of course a clear challenge to Victorian gender norms.

When she first adopts an alias, female or male, Leona tends to play with the letters or the stress pattern of her own name. Leona Lacoste becomes Leon d'Acosta, Elena d'Acosta, Anita Silvano. Leona reinvents herself because a disguise 'is most convenient for travelling in' (48), or because – like Marryat herself, who was both a playwright and a performer – she is 'a born actress' (6, 47) and possesses the necessary skills, or simply because when she acts professionally in New York she needs a stage name. Later, the 'sacred mission' (220) of clearing her father's name gives Leona a compelling reason for more radical transformations: into the greying Jane Gibson (244) and above all, in the 'fraud' (198) on which her entire visit to England depends but for which she pleads an end so 'great and glorious' (199) as to justify fraudulent means, into Don Christobal Valera:

'Don Christobal – Miss Gibson – what have they to do with you?' said Mr. Evans, still more mystified.

'I am the false Don Valera – I am Miss Gibson,' replied Leona. 'I assumed those disguises for the purpose of entering your house. Forgive me, uncle! I know it was not a worthy part to play, but I had a purpose which trampled down every other consideration before it'. (Marryat 319)

Both Leona's experiences on the New York stage, where she found it 'much more natural ... to play a man's part than a woman's' (95–6), and the successful impersonation of Christobal, for which she here apologises, have had considerable collateral benefits. They have released her from the ordinary limitations of the female condition in the nineteenth century and saved her from a choice between demeaning evils: either dwindling into what she terms 'a stay-at-home, do-nothing woman' (6) or, if she resisted marriage, becoming 'a nonentity and a disgrace' (19). In the end, Leona transcends conventional gender roles in the same way as Joan of Arc, and is driven onwards by the same momentum 'that the Maid of Orleans must have experienced when the mysterious voices urged her to the field' (123); for she develops an ability not just to cross-dress but to take on male attributes. She is 'strong, energetic, and bold', 'impulsive, energetic, and determined' (18, 317). 'Her fiery untamed nature' (166) makes her true to her name, 'fearless as a lion' and 'lion-hearted' (111, 115). On four occasions she is seen as a beautiful panther (3, 17, 89, 255). Her gender identification hovers between emphatically female and effectively male; she is twice 'a tigress' (17, 317) but twice a tiger (240, 277). Thus, just as what Leona wears is 'a strange mixture of European and Spanish fashions' (4), and just as 'she has Brazilian blood in her, but ... mixed with European' (98), so she combines feminine qualities with masculine characteristics.

It is not just as a player of male parts that Leona exceeds what custom has pronounced necessary for her sex, but also as an international traveller. After her flair for acting – together with her need, following her father's death, to make her own way in the world without him – has taken her to New York, the higher purpose to which her life is then given over brings her across the Atlantic to London. By now the very opposite of 'a stay-at-home, do-nothing woman', she follows up leads in other British locations as well and goes wherever she might find something to counter the 'startling array of evidence against her father' (103). Like Elizabeth Gaskell's Mary Barton – who was also in search of the truth about a murder – Leona visits Liverpool Docks (237–8); and she beats a path to Brighton, changing her costume while the train is in motion (204–5). She is tireless in her sleuthing and her efforts to crack the case.

The mystery resists Leona's first attempts at unravelling it. She barks up the wrong tree when she becomes convinced that Henry Evans must be the true culprit. An already theatrical narrative, tracing 'the life-drama' of 'a born actress', appears at this point to be turning into a re-vision of Shakespeare's *Hamlet*. Leona has cast herself as a latter-day Prince of Denmark, with a dead father and a wicked uncle. As if seduced by this prospect, and under the orphan's characteristic compulsion to puzzle out in its entirety the jigsaw of the past, she constructs an alternative narrative about the crime which in chapter 17, 'The Acted Charades', is played out like 'The Mousetrap' before the man whose conscience Leona hopes to catch. In the end Leona's 'distorted imagination' (195) is seen to have run away with her, and Henry Evans is shown to be no Claudius: 'Oh, uncle, how I have misjudged you!' (321).

Leona has already made good her own errors of judgement, however, with a thorough retrograde investigation which ends with the other brother, George, shown to have been gravely misjudged by the world. He did not commit, years before Leona was born, the murder for which he has long been held responsible. All that he did at that time was father a daughter whom, without knowing whose child she was, his brother Henry eventually adopted. The girl's name was Lucilla (or Lucy), and the girl's mother was Rebecca (or Becky) Levitt. Abraham Anson was killed not by George but, because he defended George in an argument over the latter's relationship with Rebecca, by Rebecca's father Richard. Leona, when she learns all this, defends him too, portraying her father as not only guiltless of Anson's murder but blameless in his treatment of Rebecca (297–8).

When Rebecca expires in the novel's closing moments, Lucilla is left sharing the orphaned condition of her half-sister Leona, although because it is considered 'most advisable that the secret of her birth should not be revealed to her' (322) she shares it unawares. Lucilla, whose 'weak spine' (131) condemns her to being 'a stay-at-home, do-nothing woman', is far less robust than Leona in the emotional as well as the physical sense. What they have in common at the end of the story is the prospect of a fulfilling union. Lucilla, after her hopeless love for Leona masquerading as Christobal (194), is to marry Dr Hastings, who is 'a very clever and rising surgeon' but would have been no match for Leona because he is 'neither handsome nor tall' (137). Leona herself, after inheriting the money that should have been her father's (321), will finally be free to marry the real Christobal. These impending marriages would have been the crowning glories of most novels. Here, they are sideshows which the story suddenly finds it can sustain in the atmosphere of restrained celebration created by the main event: that is, the long delayed vindication of George Evans and the belated bearing out of the last words Leona ever heard him speak, *'your father was true!'* (22). Leona has kept her promise to restore his reputation, and so – she cries – 'My father's name will be purified again' (311). The father's disgrace is lifted at last, and the daughter's disguises are no longer needed:

> She was no more the Leona of Brazil – the actress of New York; she was ready to rush into her uncle's presence with the precious document she held in her hand, and proclaim in one breath her own identity and her father's innocence. (313)

\*

In the autumn of 1876, just as *Her Father's Name* came to the end of its run in the likes of *The Nottinghamshire Guardian* or *The Bolton Weekly Journal*, *The Cornhill Magazine* was printing the first monthly instalment of R. D. Blackmore's *Erema; or My Father's Sin*. There were some readers, therefore, to whom the *Cornhill* was bound to be giving the mixture very much as before: another serialised story about a heroine who desperately needs to believe that her father was true. Blackmore's heroine, like Leona, suffers a double paternal deprivation; not only does her father die while she is still in her teenage years but, since he dies a fugitive from justice and a suspected murderer, his good name appears forfeited for ever. Like Marryat, Blackmore calls the father George. He couples that forename with the aristocratic lustre of a surname, Castlewood, familiar from Thackeray's *History of Henry Esmond* (1852). His choice of name for the daughter is altogether more obscure. Greek *erēma* means 'bereft' or 'deserted' and is 'a word used of widows and orphans' (Ormand 41). Sophocles applies it to Deianeira, marooned by marriage to Heracles, in a passage which is printed on the title page of each of the three volumes in the 1877 book edition of Blackmore's novel. That the novelist had foreseen some of the difficulties which his heroine's name might cause is demonstrated when the dialogue signals its strangeness – 'Erema is popish and outlandish; one scarcely knows how to pronounce it' (Blackmore 2: 76) – but he probably underestimated them. In his immediate radius, at least, Blackmore was to find that not just the proper pronunciation but the correct etymology of 'Erema' had entirely eluded the reading public:

> We hear from our brother author, Mr. Blackmore, that he is annoyed to find that the Teddington young ladies *will* call his latest work 'Erema', and want to know what sin that is Latin for. He begins to think it was a stupid name for the book. ('Our Note Book')

The use in the title of a name so exotic, in apparent apposition to the word 'sin', diverted attention from what the daughter was called to what the father might have done.

The desolation of Erema – after her father's death, in the novel's opening instalment, leaves her bereft – is conveyed, if not by the name alone, then certainly by the setting in which Blackmore first places her. Appropriately, since Classical Greek designates wildernesses and desert places as *erēma* too (Liddell and Scott 524), the novel's curtain rises on the Californian Sierra Nevada; and it is here that George Castlewood dies. In search of 'a large, kind land' (Blackmore 3: 206) far from the cloud of suspicion which in England would have blighted her life as well as his own, Erema's father has brought her to America. The story therefore opens in the land of the free, whose citizens 'listen to no rumours . . . or malignant lies' and 'value people as [they] find them' (1: 211). But what Marryat's heroine found liberating – 'the free life of the Brazils has made *me* independent' (Marryat 121) – Blackmore's comes to find oppressive. In the *Cornhill*, Frank Dicksee's frontispiece image of daughter and father amid the Sierra Nevada mountains has two vultures or condors circling. To Erema, who narrates, the Sierra Nevada seems a 'desert of desolation' (Blackmore 1: 17). She cannot help transferring to it the desolation that she herself now feels, as a newly orphaned fifteen-year-old. 'I am nothing but a poor castaway,' she says (1: 208). Her father was the last surviving member of her immediate family. He is buried in a peach orchard beneath the mountains, beside a river with a mill-wheel. His grave is marked by 'a cross of white unpainted wood, bearing only his initials, and a small "Amen" below them' (1: 80). The aristocratic substance of Castlewood – which is not just Her Father's Name but Erema's own – is all dissolved away, in the 'Amen' of that bottom line, into nothing but an anagram of the word 'name'.

The predicament in which Erema now finds herself causes her to wonder whether any child was ever 'more thickly wrapped in mystery as well as loneliness' (Blackmore 1: 42). For the loneliness, the likeliest remedy appears to lie in the hands of the elderly sawyer Sampson Gundry ('Uncle Sam'), whom Erema's father trusted to look after her when he no longer could, and his grandson Ephraim (or 'Firm'), for whom Erema develops a fond regard. The solution to the mystery threatens to prove rather more elusive, because all of the clues lie hidden in the past. From the point in time in the late 1850s at which the action opens, Blackmore's story will move forward by five years – taking Erema from fifteen to twenty, and plunging some of its characters into the American Civil War – but it also faces having to go backwards by three, four and even ten times that distance. Erema will first need to look into her father's actions around the time of her birth, and it seems that there is nobody to help her in that. Sampson, she finds, is '(like every one else) reserved and silent as to my father's history' (1: 32).

The 'dark mystery' of George Castlewood's life (2: 66, 170) eventually emerges. He is supposed to have killed his own father, Lord Castlewood, and then, like Marryat's George Evans, fled abroad rather than face trial. Since the murder weapon was a pistol belonging to him, the guilt of Erema's father appears obvious. She struggles to fathom 'who could have done it instead' (2: 59). No suspicion can attach to the current Lord Castlewood, the cousin who inherited in George's place, as Erema hears that he is both 'an exemplary man' and a long-term invalid (2: 62). However, much like Leona 'painstakingly picking up . . . crumbs of information' (Marryat 197), Erema resolves that she will 'fish up every bit of evidence' (Blackmore 2: 150) which may contribute to the unmasking of the true culprit. This trawling for evidence is again necessarily an undercover operation; it is simply as 'Miss Wood', and thus 'shorn of two-thirds of [her] name' (1: 230), that Erema embarks on her fact-finding mission. In the course of it, even though Erema considers herself 'wrong of sex for doing any valiance' (1: 18), she has to knuckle down to 'man's work' – which 'a man would not have done . . . half so well' (2: 56) – and she also has to undertake a transatlantic voyage. These are remarkable initiatives despite the fact that, because she has more help from others, Erema does not launch into them alone in quite the way Leona had. Along with his wife Mary, Sampson Gundry's cousin Major Nicholas Hockin is present '*in loco parentis*' (1: 236) during the Atlantic crossing and throughout Erema's time in England. Much of the time, even so, her own inner resources suffice. Whatever gifts Erema lacks, she at least possesses 'the dull one of persistence' (3: 146). The Castlewood 'family fault of tenacity' (2: 172) makes her pursuit of the truth as single-minded as that of Grant Allen's heroine would later be in Hilda Wade (to which was added, as a subtitle, 'A Woman with Tenacity of Purpose').

After she reaches England, Erema still has a long road to travel before she can hope to erase the 'horrible slander and wicked falsehood' (Blackmore 1: 110) which have stuck to her late father's name, and 'establish truth and justice' (1: 271). From her base in the house the Hockins have taken at Bruntsea, 'a quiet little village on the south-east coast of England, in Kent or in Sussex, I am not sure which' (1: 242), Erema plans the expeditions that will best enable her to research her father's past life. She travels to London with the Major in search of Betsy Bowen (now Mrs Strouss), who nursed her in infancy. When Betsy and Erema then visit the place where the former Lord Castlewood was shot, there follows – in the words of one of the book's reviewers – 'the exquisite fragment of prose-poetry which brings before us the peaceful Hampshire village of Shoxford' ('New Novels'). Shoxford was once home to the Castlewoods, and the village churchyard is the last resting place not just of Erema's mother but of Erema's six brothers and sisters (George, Henrietta, Jack, Alf, Vi and Tiny), all of whom succumbed in very quick succession to a severe infection. Their 'fairy ring of rest' is also a moment of poignant pause in the narrative:

> Here were six little grassy tuffets, according to the length of children, all laid east and west, without any stint of room, harmoniously.
> From the eldest to the youngest, one could almost tell the age at which their burly stature stopped, and took its final measurement.
> And in the middle was a larger grave to comfort and encourage them, as a hen lies down among her chicks, and waits for them to shelter. Without a name to any of them, all these seven graves lay together, as in a fairy ring of rest, and kind compassion had prevented any stranger from coming to be buried there. (Blackmore 2: 193)

At this point Erema, now the sole surviving family member, thinks of the eighth grave, situated far from all of these in a Californian peach grove. The reader, of course, is likely to think of Philip, Georgiana, Alexander, Bartholomew, Abraham, Tobias and Roger, whose graves at the beginning of *Great Expectations* (1860–1) become such vivid markers of orphanhood for Dickens's Pip. Dickens had followed Mary Lamb in deploying a pair of motifs, the churchyard and the poor bereaved child, in which each reinforces the other (Merchant 244–5); and now Blackmore follows Dickens.

At Shoxford the plot thickens considerably. Volume 2 of the book edition ends amid mystery and menace, with a man whose face strikes Erema as 'the bad image of [her] father's' (Blackmore 2: 291) loitering and reconnoitring around the scene of the crime. The pieces of the puzzle then begin to fall into place in the third volume, in a manner reminiscent not so much of *Great Expectations* as of *Oliver Twist*. After Erema has resort to a 'little trick' (3: 26), a locket comes to light which is made of 'blue enamel and diamonds, with a back of chased gold' (3: 49), and which contains two wisps of hair. The locket reveals that in 1809 – which is the furthest reach of retrograde investigation in Blackmore's novel – 'George, Lord Castlewood, married Winifred, only child of Thomas Hoyle' (3: 109). The groom is Erema's grandfather, while the bride is a person previously unknown. Moreover, the couple had a son, although Lord Castlewood abandoned Winifred soon after the birth. Rather than finding her own half-sister, as Leona did, Erema has therefore found that her father had a 'wicked elder brother, by another mother' (3: 116). It was this half-brother, a second Thomas, who – albeit under enough duress to make his designation as 'wicked' disputable – shot his own and George's father. George was simply 'left . . . to bear the brunt of it' (3: 201), and in order to shield Thomas he allowed the finger of suspicion to point at himself.

This lays to rest, at last, the threat that the locket had posed to Erema's position. The alarming prospect with which it had confronted her was the possibility that '[her] own dear father was a base-born son' (3: 110–11). In fact, Thomas and not George was the base-born son, because Winifred was 'married' without benefit of clergy and Lord Castlewood's improvised 'attestation and certificate' were all that she and her father ever had from him (3: 182). If that stigma had attached to George, it would have destroyed Erema's previous proud sense of who she was: 'when I saw myself sprung of low birth, and the father of my worship base-born, down fell all my arduous castles, and I craved to go under the earth and die' (3: 146). She seems visited by the same catastrophe that Leona once faced, discovering herself to be 'a nameless, parentless, base-born outcast!' (Marryat 237). In Erema's case the matter is resolved by means familiar from Blackmore's most successful novel, *Lorna Doone: A Romance of Exmoor* (1869). In *Erema*, just as in *Lorna Doone*, the orphaned heroine has her aristocratic credentials confirmed while the outlaw and pretender goes under. There, Carver Doone was swallowed by a black bog; here, a storm causes Thomas to drown – along with his mother Winifred – in 'the merciless water' off Bruntsea (3: 244–5). Metaphorically, however, Erema herself bobs safely to the surface. Far from being disinherited, she is now entitled to 'the fair estates of Castlewood' (3: 172), and her father's good name is also fully restored. After Thomas has drowned, a letter found on his person establishes that he had 'no compact of any kind' with Erema's father (3: 251), who can be duly exonerated. The heroine's work is accomplished, and she is able to return to America with all of the bleakness which beset her there before banished altogether now. The title of the first chapter, referring both to Erema's environment and to her condition, had been 'Desert'. The title of the final chapter is 'Beyond Desert, and Deserts'. Just as the 'sin' of the novel's subtitle is now wiped away, for what appeared George Castlewood's sin 'was not his own, but fell on him' (3: 308), so the heroine's melancholy and ignominious name no longer defines her. The final five words of the narrative (3: 308) are 'I am no more Erema.' She is no more the Erema of the Sierra Nevada, at least – just as Marryat's heroine, at the corresponding moment of vindication, 'was no more the Leona of Brazil' (Marryat 313).

\*

'Never seed a double-barrelled one before', says Joe the fisherman in the storm scene of Blackmore's novel (3: 239). He was expecting to be handed a standard spy-glass and is bamboozled by the binoculars given him instead. In late 1876, when the final stages of Leona's quest for the truth – as played out in the pages of *The Bolton Weekly Journal* or *The Nottinghamshire Guardian* – and the first phase of Erema's came close to overlapping, any reader of both books would have been in the same situation, and had the same sense of seeing double, as Joe the fisherman. All of a sudden, on a crowded literary horizon, there were two seemingly identical dots on which to train the telescope. While one barrel continued to pick out a heroine of Marryat's devising, on the point now of fulfilling her solemn promise to set the record straight about her father, a heroine of Blackmore's just about to embark on a matching mission began to come into focus in the other; and the latter's trail led back to the same literary hinterland, the sensation fiction of the 1860s, from which the former had arisen. More particularly, in so far as each was both a devoted daughter and a female crusader for justice, they might claim descent from the characters created by Wilkie Collins. Magdalen Vanstone in Collins's *No Name* (1862–3) is one of two orphaned sisters who find themselves debarred by illegitimacy from an £80,000 inheritance, their father's fortune; and into her attempts to recover it she pours the same 'knack of disguising her own identity in the impersonation of different characters' (Collins, *No Name* 178) that would be seen in Leona. A later Collins novel, *The Law and the Lady* (1874–5), has a heroine called Valeria Woodville who challenges on her husband's behalf a verdict deeply damaging to his good name. For Valeria the end in view, erasing a stain of infamy, is the same as for Edith Dalton in the De Mille novel, *The Living Link*, with which Collins's happens to coincide; but the means, taking her 'out of the common way' and beyond 'the ordinary limits of a woman's thoughts and actions' (Collins, *Law* 121, 243), anticipate the unfeminine 'valiance' that will characterise the heroines' actions in Marryat and Blackmore. Greta Depledge in her introduction to *Her Father's Name* (Depledge xxii) compares Leona with Valeria, and a connection with Erema would be equally valid.

Very few of those who read *Her Father's Name* or *Erema* in 1876, or who wrote about either in 1877, appear to have recognised the common provenance of the books' plotlines or observed the strong resemblance between the two which results. This is in spite of the fact that several periodicals – including *The Academy*, *The Athenæum* and *The Spectator* – published reviews of both, nine or ten months apart. The writers generally gave less space to *Her Father's Name* but, perhaps because the fame which Blackmore had won with *Lorna Doone* inflated expectations, thought less well of *Erema*. On both counts, the differences were most marked in *The Spectator*. Marryat's allocation is just over 200 words of qualified commendation; although there is 'nothing original or striking' about its characters, goes the verdict, the story 'holds the reader with a genuine interest' ('Current Literature' 22). Exactly nine months later, *Erema* rates more than 2,000 words but (except on the measure of column inches alone) emerges much less well. '[T]he story would have been greatly improved had it been condensed into one volume', considers the reviewer; and, despite containing 'several passages of real feeling and beauty, of which perhaps the best is the description of the little village of Shoxford', it is in the final analysis 'unworthy of Mr. Blackmore's talents ... he has only produced a third-rate magazine fiction, loose and wildly improbable in construction and incident, and most tedious in narration' ('*Erema*' in *Spectator* 20, 21). Other reviewers were similarly inclined to admire the parts (especially the Shoxford interlude) but find the whole defective. One redeeming exception was the review carried by *The Morning Post*:

> Mr. Blackmore possesses very strongly the faculty of story-telling, and is able to combine the picturesque, the sensational, and the realistic in such a way as to command and to retain the reader's interest, intensifying with every page the power of his narrative. ('*Erema*' in *Morning Post*)

Whatever interest either novel commanded then, in 1877, was not such as could extend beyond the authors' lifetimes. By the century's end it appeared exhausted, and there have been few signs of any revival. Although *Her Father's Name* has been available since 2009 in Greta Depledge's edition for Victorian Secrets, *Erema* has attracted so little scholarly attention, and remains so emphatically excluded from the nineteenth-century literary canon, that its title could almost describe the book's own 'bereft' and 'deserted' condition. The prospect of seeing these two novels somehow plucked from the merciless water that has now submerged them therefore seems remote; but the rewards, if that ever came about, could be considerable. Not only is the conjunction of the two novels highly suggestive, but, separately considered, each one is an invaluable index of its age. For, if the orphan is a *tabula rasa*, so too is the orphan text. Wherever it thrives, it tends to take some tincture of comparable or contemporaneous forms of literary production, whose extracted traits it then exposes to a more compact and convenient inspection. The emergence of the female detective – shown in Greta Depledge's account of the figure (xxi–xxvi) to be becoming, 'from the 1860s', ever more prominent and pivotal – is clearly one of the characteristic mid-Victorian and late Victorian developments that leave their mark upon *Her Father's Name* and *Erema*. Another, strongly led by Tennyson's *Idylls of the King* (1859–85), is the reinvention of the knight-errant, or his present-day equivalent, as the bringer of social salvation. These two figures are fused in the investigative, and ultimately rehabilitative, projects that Leona and Erema pursue. When Erema resolves that in order to 'do some good' with her 'grown-up age, and health, and buoyant vigour' she will 'right the wrong of [her] own house' (Blackmore 3: 195), and when Leona – with her father likewise in mind – feels called upon 'to avenge his wrongs' (Marryat 166–7), they reflect the keen sense that Tennyson's Arthurian poems were communicating of the high heroic endeavour of those who 'ride abroad redressing human wrongs' (Tennyson 1736).

Leona and Erema, even so, are riders of an altogether new kind: the kind who, because the foreign country ridden into is a largely forgotten and stubbornly mysterious past, may not be in control of the ride. Both Marryat's heroine and Blackmore's must delve into the events of so many years ago that they can have no memory of them. Neither they nor their counterparts in backward journeying, those pioneers of the nineteenth-century sciences of mind who now had childhood experience in their sights and were starting out on the royal road to the unconscious, could quite know where the ride would take them. Valeria Woodville feels like the horseman who rode unwittingly across Lake Constance: 'what I had done, I had, so to speak, done blindfold. The merest accident might have altered the whole course of later events' (Collins, *Law* 396). Erema likewise has to rely on sheer accident, as when a 'monster nugget, transcending the whole of creation' (Blackmore 3: 131), is uncovered in the bed of the Sawmill River by her dog Jowler; and it was 'by no exertion of my own, but by turn after turn of things, to which I blindly gave my little help,' she says, that 'the mystery of my life was solved' (3: 203). There are occasions when Marryat's heroine, too, benefits not by her own exertions but by pure chance; George Saintsbury, in a review for *The Academy* which is quoted by Depledge, pointed out that 'everybody tells Leona everything she wishes to know in a charmingly obliging and communicative manner' (Marryat xxvi, 339). This is not to devalue in any way the efforts of either heroine. Detectives of the conventional sort might be expected to reach the truth through the exercise of their deductive powers rather than through serendipitous discovery; but for Erema and Leona the defining achievement, which in each case is perfectly secure even before the 'life-drama' is half played out, is their having come from California and Brazil to place themselves in a position where discovery is possible. In order to rise to be 'a mighty finder' (Blackmore 3: 83) the heroine must first become 'a great traveller' (Marryat 160), and the experience of each is that it is this globetrotting – 'riding abroad' in a genuinely international sense – which empowers and emancipates her. It affords her a means not just of becoming a citizen of the world but of vaulting audaciously over the perceived obstacle of her femininity. It allays the regret, and even resentment, of a heroine wishing 'that Providence had not seen fit to issue [her] into this world in the masculine form' (Blackmore 2: 141), or that she might have been 'made . . . a man, instead of a stay-at-home, do-nothing woman' (Marryat 6).

Any thought of a conclusion that would see the heroine settling into a sedate life on what could finally count as home soil is bound, then, to be decisively dispelled. After the heroine's journey in search of her father's past has brought her across the Atlantic she chooses to cross back over again. The Americas were where both Erema and Leona first found themselves orphaned – '[o]rphanhood, one might argue, is a characteristically American condition' (Stahl 209) – and both now feel impelled to return. Leona could 'take up . . . residence in England' (Marryat 322), but instead insists that she and Christobal should go first to Spain and then to New York. Erema could become 'the Right Honourable Baroness Castlewood', but, as if to stress that her previous horror of being shown to be 'base-born' was felt solely on her father's account, resolves 'neither to claim nor acknowledge' that title (Blackmore 3: 175); 'I am nobody's ladyship' (3: 289), she says, and she decides that her future lies in America with Firm Gundry. Erema's reunion with her childhood companion, like Leona's, can be transferred overseas because it is only an adjunct to what in each case is plainly presented as the principal source of the heroine's (and reader's) satisfaction: the reclamation of the name of the father, 'purified again' (Marryat 311) or 'cleared from all stain' (Blackmore 3: 265). The daughter's reconnection with the mother country need not be permanent so long as out of it there comes a very conclusive reinstatement of the father. If 'parentalian' works are to be defined – in the words of Douglas Brooks-Davies – as 'works which . . . honour and in a way raise a memorial to the dead father' (Brooks-Davies xiv), both of these novels plainly warrant being classed as such. The 'parentalian' impulse so powerfully felt in each provides the nineteenth-century orphan text, whose peculiar properties and problems are known today from the work of Laura Peters, with a possible path towards resolution. The end of all Erema's exploring, accordingly, is the recovery of 'the father of [her] worship' (3: 146), who once more stands 'blameless and heroic' (3: 203). The figure of the father is given his full due at last; and, since the same has already happened in Marryat's novel, he is given it with both barrels.

In reverting from the daughter to the father, when everything earned by the energy and tenacity of the former is made a posthumous prize for the latter, and in reverting equally from Britain to America, each of these novels moves in a perhaps surprising direction. 'We do not quite relish the shifting from California to England, and then from England to California', wrote one reviewer of *Erema* ('*Erema*' in *Contemporary Review* 1107). Both Marryat and Blackmore disrupt the typical rhythm of the orphan narrative, which consists in the movement of the orphan from the margins into the social mainstream, and simultaneously into a marriage that will more than make up for the loss of the parent or parents. Erema and Leona still of course progress from the periphery to the centre of society, because in superintending the rehabilitation of her father each daughter also brings about her own. In that sense Blackmore and Marryat both have recourse to the re-legitimation plot, which, as Ruth Perry observes (41–2), is the customary way of resolving the problem of the dispossessed daughter. Crucially, however, each novelist dispels the dullness of familiarity by contriving a kind of retrograde re-legitimation, which puts the posthumous honouring of the father into main focus and far ahead of the elevation of the orphaned daughter. The infamy which seemed all that the father could hope to hand down to the daughter is turned into a glory which redeems him completely and in whose reflection she too can inconspicuously bask. That done, neither Marryat nor Blackmore needs to be tempted by the miraculous physical resurrection with which De Mille had accompanied these repairs to the father's reputation. It is enough that, thanks to the refreshing late Victorian variations which they have played upon its essential elements, both writers effect a modest resurrection from potential staleness of the orphan text itself.[1]

### Note

1. For a number of generous and constructive suggestions of which this chapter avails itself, particularly in its fourth and final section, I am much indebted and deeply grateful to the anonymous reader of my submitted manuscript.

### Works Cited

Allen, Grant. *Hilda Wade*. Grant Richards, 1900.
Blackmore, R. D. *Erema; or, My Father's Sin*, 3 vols. Smith and Elder, 1877.
Brontë, Emily. *Wuthering Heights*. Oxford University Press, 1981.
Brooks-Davies, Douglas. *Fielding, Dickens, Gosse, Iris Murdoch and Oedipal 'Hamlet'*. Macmillan, 1989.
Collins, Wilkie. *The Law and the Lady*. Oxford University Press, 1992.
Collins, William Wilkie. *No Name*. Oxford University Press, 1986.
'Current Literature: Her Father's Name'. *The Spectator*, week ending Saturday 24 February 1877, pp. 22–3.
De Mille, James. *The Living Link*. Harper, 1874.
Depledge, Greta. 'Introduction'. *Her Father's Name*, by Florence Marryat. Victorian Secrets, 2009, pp. i–xxxii.
'Erema'. *The Contemporary Review*, vol. 30, 1 June 1877, pp. 1106–7.
'Erema'. *The Morning Post*, Tuesday 30 October 1877, p. 6. British Library Newspapers. http://tinyurl.galegroup.com/tinyurl/4vVHn0
'Erema'. *The Spectator*, week ending Saturday 24 November 1877, pp. 20–1.
Liddell, Henry George, and Scott, Robert (eds). *A Greek–English Lexicon*, 4th edn. Oxford University Press, 1855.
Marryat, Florence. *Her Father's Name*. [1876]. Victorian Secrets, 2009.
Merchant, Peter. '*Great Expectations* and "Elizabeth Villiers"'. *Dickens Quarterly*, vol. 14, no. 4, December 1997, pp. 243–7.
'New Novels'. *Graphic*, Saturday 10 November 1877, p. 11. British Library Newspapers. http://tinyurl.galegroup.com/tinyurl/4vVJ30
Ormand, Kirk. *Exchange and the Maiden: Marriage in Sophoclean Tragedy*. University of Texas Press, 1999.

'Our Note Book'. *The Sporting Times*, Saturday 11 May 1878, p. 4. 19th Century UK Periodicals. http://tinyurl.galegroup.com/tinyurl/4vVJSX

Perry, Ruth. *Novel Relations: The Transformation of Kinship in English Literature and Culture, 1748–1818*. Cambridge University Press, 2004.

Peters, Laura. *Orphan Texts: Victorian Orphans, Culture and Empire*. Manchester University Press, 2000.

Simon, Leslie S. 'The De-Orphaned Orphan: *Oliver Twist* and Deep Time'. *Dickens Quarterly*, vol. 34, no. 4, December 2017, pp. 306–30.

Stahl, John Daniel. 'American Myth in European Disguise: Fathers and Sons in *The Prince and the Pauper*'. *American Literature*, vol. 58, no. 2, May 1986, pp. 203–16.

Tennyson, Alfred, Lord. *The Poems of Tennyson*, ed. Christopher Ricks. Longmans, 1969.

# Chapter 9

# Girlhood and Space in Nineteenth-Century Orphan Literature

## Jane Suzanne Carroll

Before the development of a public health system and before vaccinations, antibiotics and modern diagnostics became widespread, orphans were commonplace. It should come as no surprise then that the orphan figure has been a standard in children's literature since its modern inception with texts like Newbery's *The History of Little Goody Two-Shoes* (1765) and that orphaned children continue to be stock characters throughout modern children's literature. Although there are some ensemble casts in children's orphan stories – for instance, the two waifs at the heart of Brenda's *Froggy's Little Brother* (1875) – the orphan in children's literature is most often a single child outside, or teetering on the margins of, family life. Even when the child protagonist is part of an established family group they may be symbolically orphaned or isolated from the core family unit for extended periods of time. In many cases, the child protagonist removes themselves voluntarily from the family home, as Jim Hawkins does in R. L. Stevenson's *Treasure Island* (1883) and Huckleberry Finn does in Mark Twain's novels of 1876 to 1896, in order to experience life beyond the limits of the domestic space. In such cases, the absence of parents, or at the very least the absence of attentive, nurturing parents, is a neat narrative trick performed in the opening chapters of the book, allowing the child character unprecedented levels of freedom, increased agency and the opportunity to have meaningful adventures free from adult oversight. These adventurous orphans and pseudo-orphans are almost exclusively male and although they seem to turn aside from established social orders, their travels and experiences actually prepare them to attain a more secure position within society. Christopher Parkes has argued persuasively that '*Treasure Island* grooms its hero, Jim Hawkins, to take his place in [an] emergent class' (332) of modern civil servants, clerks and imperial administrators. While these adventures initially appear to distance Jim from his homeland and his society, they ultimately prepare him to become even more tightly integrated within middle-class British society.

The 'preparatory lone adventure' narrative is not normally available to female protagonists, who must instead attain the knowledge, agency and awareness to become meaningful players within wider society while operating within the confines of the domestic space and the family circle.[1] Orphan girls in children's literature of the long nineteenth century usually begin their stories by joining a new household and their narrative arcs focus on their integration within this household. These narratives are centripetal; everything acts to draw the female protagonist deeper into the unmoving centre of the home space. As Perry Nodelman notes, such narratives can almost appear to be 'a story without a plot' (31). That is to say that these are not dramatic narratives whereby a character's old identity is erased by or cast aside in favour of a new adult identity; the sort of narrative based on crisis, violence, struggle and masculinity has no place within the domestic novel that has its roots in a sentimental tradition. The female orphan narrative revolves around the family and the home space and the struggles she faces are internal, both in the sense that they are largely played out within the domestic environment and in the sense that they are emotional and personal. The absence of external conflict means that there is rarely a true crisis of identity for these female protagonists and, as a result, the orphan girl 'does not change much in the course of the events that follow' (Nodelman 30) in these stories. They do not change their identities but rather consolidate them. I argue that the orphan girls of the long nineteenth century begin and end their narratives as marginal figures. They are socially, spatially and imaginatively liminal and their narratives are not about their assimilation into an established society, but about a confirmation and consolidation of their liminality. These characters are liminal in the sense that they are both associated with physical thresholds and boundary spaces, most notably garrets and attics, and in the sense that they occupy conceptual thresholds: they exist on the margins of the family and are in the process of transitioning from childhood to adulthood. In addition, they exist in the intermediate space between the real and the imaginary, the earthly and the supernatural.

Though there is a large pool of female orphan texts to draw from, especially if one widens the net to include narratives about half-orphans and pseudo-orphans, in this chapter, I limit my study to six classic novels: Joanna Spyri's *Heidi* (1880); Frances Hodgson Burnett's *A Little Princess* (1905) and *The Secret Garden* (1911);

L. M. Montgomery's *Anne of Green Gables* (1908) and *Emily of New Moon* (1923); and Eleanor Porter's *Pollyanna* (1913). Each book features a pre-pubescent orphan girl who is adopted or taken into a new household but who nevertheless remains a liminal figure on the margins of family life. While it may seem that *Heidi*, as a German-language text, is an outlier within this group, Joanna Spyri's two novels *Heidis Lehr- und Wanderjahre* (1880), and *Heidi kann brauchen, was es gelernt hat* (1881) were quickly assimilated into the Anglophone market, with the first translation appearing in England in 1882 and a second, American translation by Louise Brooks hard on its heels in 1884. Susan Stan identifies over 100 distinct Anglophone editions of Heidi between 1882 and 1959, a clear sign of the book's popularity and prominence within an English-language market and its canonical status (Stan 1–23). Like *Heidi*, the other texts in my selection have parallel histories in North America and Canada and in Western Europe, with near-simultaneous publications on both sides of the Atlantic. Each of these books has proved influential on the development of children's literature and they have proved especially influential on the books produced by female authors for female readers in the early and mid-twentieth century. These texts span what is commonly termed the 'first golden age' of children's literature, a period lasting between the mid-nineteenth century and the first three decades of the twentieth century (Carpenter ix). Several of these texts have been thematically linked before, and Perry Nodelman also highlights the narrative correspondences among *Anne of Green Gables*, *Heidi*, *Pollyanna* and *The Secret Garden*, arguing that these orphans 'all live the same story, and they come to seem like variations of an ideal of female childhood that transcends national boundaries, and even the boundaries of time – for we still find the story enticing' (Nodelman 30). The six texts discussed here provide a small but representative sample of the ways that girls' literature developed its own unique concerns in parallel to but distinct from children's literature about male orphans. While the male orphan journeys towards integration within a broader society, these female orphans move towards a greater acceptance of their own status as outsiders. While their male counterparts move decisively away from the family unit, these female orphans operate around the margins of the family; never quite assimilated, never quite excluded. This social liminality is echoed and reinforced by their spatial and imaginative liminality too. The narratives I discuss here draw powerfully from both the Romantic and the Gothic tradition and present the figure of the orphan girl as one who slips lithely – and blithely – between the boundaries of childhood and adulthood, the real and the imaginary, the natural and the supernatural, the living and the dead.

Perhaps surprisingly, the orphan girl narrative does not have a long pedigree: Joe Sutcliff Sanders identifies Susan Warner/Elizabeth Wetherell's *The Wide, Wide World* (1850) as 'the genre's foundational text' (24) and it is only in the later part of the nineteenth century that the orphan girl narrative develops as a distinct genre with recognisable narrative and thematic patterns of its own. Significantly, this new prominence coincides exactly with the rise of new concepts of 'girlhood' in the *fin de siècle* and, in particular, with the new identification of girlhood as a 'distinct cultural category in late-nineteenth century literary and print culture' (Rodgers 1). Beth Rodgers argues that the liminality of girlhood resonates deeply with the mood of the *fin de siècle* itself, a period when the social, cultural and artistic preoccupations of the nineteenth century were beginning to shift and merge and give way to a new set of values. Rodgers, like Michelle Smith, Kristine Moruzi and Claudia Mitchell, has drawn valuable critical attention to the texts written by women for young female readers which have been often overlooked in scholarly investigations into the period which problematically equate 'adolescence' and 'youth' with male adolescence and male youth. Rodgers argues that 'there is [. . .] something special and noteworthy about girlhood and its "constantly shifting" nature' (5) in the long nineteenth century. For Rodgers, girlhood in the late nineteenth century represents that confluence of an especially ambiguous phase in a young woman's development and an especially ambiguous moment in history. It is absolutely appropriate, then, that the orphan girls at the centre of these narratives are introduced to the reader just as they reach this particularly liminal period in their life, right on the verge of adolescence, poised to begin the transition between the apparently stable categories of 'child' and 'woman'.

The prepubescent orphan girl is rendered further liminal, not only because she exists on the margins of the categories of 'child' and 'woman', but also because she exists outside or on the margins of heteronormative family structures. Many of these characters live comfortably within non-traditional family units. Heidi lives happily with her grandfather. In both of Montgomery's works discussed here, Anne and Emily live with sets of siblings rather than with a married couple. Pollyanna lives with a maiden aunt, Mary Lennox with a widower-uncle and his son. And before Sara Crewe is reunited with her father – for she is not an orphan at all, only presumed to be one – she lives in a household entirely composed of women and girls. In many modern children's narratives, the absence of a stable and satisfactory family unit provides a motivation for those characters who yearn for, and journey towards, a new home and a new family unit where they will gain acceptance and love (Dewan 8) but these orphan narratives are not about a quest to join a stable family, but about blending or merging existing, fractured family units to create new hybrids. Even though she may be formally adopted as, for example, Anne is in Montgomery's *Anne of Green Gables* (1908), or brought to live with relatives, as Mary Lennox is in *The Secret Garden* and Emily Byrd Starr is in *Emily of New Moon* (1923), the orphan girl is never fully integrated within the family. She remains something of an outsider no matter how much time she spends with her new family. No matter how much Marilla and Matthew grow to love Anne, she retains the identity that she had before she came to them. Mary Lennox may come to speak 'broad Yorkshire' (Hodgson Burnett, *Secret* 211), but she continues to draw upon her life experiences in India and allow these experiences to shape her understanding of the world. These orphan girls are not fully subsumed into existing heteronormative families but rather play an important role in extending the boundaries of the family unit.

The orphan girl's personal identity also remains ambiguous. In contrast to the male adolescent protagonist at the heart of the traditional *Bildungsroman*, the female protagonist does not seek out, nor attain, a single and fixed identity. This fictional trope reflects the gendered social dynamics of the period. Carol Dyhouse observes that in the late nineteenth century 'for the boy, [adolescence] was a time of ambition, growth and challenge. For the girl, it was a time of instability [. . .] During adolescence, boys grew towards self-knowledge. Girls, on the other hand, could never really attain self-knowledge' (122). Though Dyhouse frames the distinctions between male and female growth in terms of absence, suggesting that the girl somehow fails to attain what the boy achieves, I argue that there is a more optimistic way of understanding this distinction. A close examination of Anne Shirley reveals how her character is fundamentally unstable and how she retains and revels in this sense of instability and her status as an outsider throughout her life. This, I argue, is not condemned in Montgomery's novel, but is rather presented as something to celebrate. From the very outset, the reader is given to understand that Anne is a shifting and fluid character. The various names and variations of her name – Anne, Anne Shirley, Anne Shirley Cuthbert and Anne of Green Gables – are an indication of this plurality and potentiality. Katherine Slater suggests that these various identities, along with the imaginary friends Katie Maurice and Violetta, and her *nom de plume* Rosamond Montmorency, are born 'out of trauma' (171–2) and are signs of Anne's dissociation from herself and from her troubled, unhappy reality. Slater proposes too that Anne's admission that she 'has always imagined that [her] name was Cordelia' (Montgomery, *Anne* 34) indicates a continued dissociation even after she begins her new life at Green Gables. Slater reads Anne's narrative as a journey towards acceptance and integration within the community, arguing that 'it is only through her capitulation to the established law of the community that she will achieve the affection denied her since the death of her parents' (172) and, in doing so, become whole. I suggest that we should not see Anne's journey as a simple one of integration and assimilation, but rather as a complex journey of self-discovery and the various names that she gives herself allow us to chart her progress on that journey. It is particularly significant that she eventually names herself 'Anne of Green Gables', uniting personal and geographical identities. Slater argues this is an indication 'that she has so foregrounded her need to be interpellated by the community that it becomes part of the signification that is Anne' (175). But, I argue, this integration within the community is not total, nor does it come at the price of Anne's rich and imaginative inner life. Just as she has 'come to the conclusion that it is no use trying to be romantic in Avonlea' (Montgomery, *Anne* 315) Matthew Cuthbert advises her not to 'give up all your romance, Anne [. . .] a little of it is a good thing' (316) and so Anne learns to strike a balance between her inner world and the world around her. It is a delicate balancing act and sometimes Anne tips too far one way or another – usually with humorous or dramatic effect – but she manages to find this balance and to retain her imagination and her sense of individuality throughout her life. In sequels to this first narrative, Anne is seen to seek out and identify with other liminal figures and to offer them nurture and support. This, in turn, lends Anne an agency and a power that the other girls – and women – in Avonlea lack. Her quest is not to discover and fix a singular identity but rather to find a way to maintain a fluid and multi-faceted identity within Avonlea. When she gives up her chance to go away to College in favour of staying to care for Marilla, Anne is careful to remind Mrs Lynde that she intends to continue her studies (Montgomery, *Anne* 422) making it clear that she does not see her options as starkly black or white, nor her decision to stay with Marilla as some awful sacrifice that comes at the expense of her career. Anne regards this as a compromise: she can be both a student and a teacher in Avonlea, she can stay at home while also continuing her studies, she both acts as a caregiver within the home and maintains a professional role outside the home. In opting to stay in Green Gables, her identity is not stymied but multiplied.

The orphan's social status as outsider is indelibly connected to her spatial movements within these texts. Just as 'children's identities are constituted in and through particular spaces' (Holloway and Valentine 765) so too are these fictional characters' liminal identities reinforced through their association with boundary and threshold spaces. In nineteenth-century children's literature, where the domestic space is synonymous with the family, the orphan's status as a liminal figure is often made known through the ways orphan characters are relegated to or drawn towards border zones and marginal spaces in the home. Rodgers has noted the myriad references to borders and thresholds in the literature written for young female readers in the latter part of the nineteenth century (1) and it is appropriate that the social and ideological liminality of these heroines is mirrored by their spatial and geographical liminality. These spatial dynamics are especially apparent in the depictions of domestic spaces in these books. The house in children's literature, as I have argued elsewhere, is characterised by strict boundaries and a strong central focus: the hearth and the central areas of the house where the family gather together are often given prominence (Carroll 19). Frequently, a character's decision to absent themselves from these central rooms is a sign of an underlying tension or dissonance between them and the other family members. Characters who are drawn towards the margins of the house – the windows and the thresholds – or to transitional areas – like corridors and stairways – may be trying to escape from the confines of the family unit and the restrictions of routine. Emily often escapes to the garret of New Moon to write her letters and journals. In Spyri's *Heidi*, Hodgson Burnett's *A Little Princess* and Porter's *Pollyanna*, the orphan girl lives in an attic room, away from the rest of the household. This physical marginalisation functions as an outward and visible sign of an ideological separation from the rest of the household. Heidi chooses this lofty space for herself, but both Sara and Pollyanna are exiled to the furthest reaches of the house.

In Hodgson Burnett's *A Little Princess*, the first sign that Sara Crewe's status has changed from pampered heiress to penniless orphan, is her exclusion from her 'bower of luxury' – a comfortable private bedroom and sitting room in Miss Minchin's school – and her exile to a lonely bedroom in the attic of the building. For Sara this attic 'was another world' (105), a far cry from the comfort and colour of the rooms downstairs. The attic is a place for unwanted things, furnished with items 'too much worn to be used downstairs' (Hodgson Burnett, *Princess* 105). The shabbiness of the attic stands in stark contrast to the brightness and comfort of the rest of the building. Sara's movement from the school to attic is both a spatial one and a social one:

> [Sara] felt as if she were walking away and leaving far behind her the world in which that other child, who no longer seemed herself, had lived. This child, in her short, tight old frock, climbing the stairs to the attic, was quite a different creature. (Hodgson Burnett, *Princess* 105)

Here, the shift in the social order and Sara's status within it are mapped on to and made visible to the reader through spatiality. Though she ascends the stairs, we understand that this is paradoxically a lowering of her position: she moves up in the house but down in the household. The attic bedroom at the extreme limits of the house is viewed by Miss Minchin as an appropriate location for the orphan girl.

Similarly, when Miss Polly is first confronted by her overwhelmingly cheerful niece, Pollyanna, she feels

> glad [. . .] that she had put the child in the attic room. Her idea at first had been to get her niece as far away as possible from herself, and at the same time place her where her childish heedlessness would not destroy valuable furnishings. (Porter 24)

Although Pollyanna initially feels 'frightened' by the attic space, with its 'bare wall, the bare floor, the bare windows' (Porter 26) she soon comes to feel 'sure it – it's going to be a very nice room' (27). It is interesting that the feature that most appeals to Pollyanna is this bare window – which Porter notes several times as lacking screens or blinds – which affords her a view over the town. Just as Anne delights to see a '*radiantly* lovely' (Montgomery, *Anne* 44) tree outside her bedroom window, Pollyanna is particularly delighted that there is a tree very close to her bedroom window:

> against this window a huge tree flung great branches. To Pollyanna they looked like arms outstretched, inviting her.
> Suddenly she laughed aloud.
> 'I believe I can do it', she chuckled. The next moment she had climbed nimbly to the window ledge. From there it was an easy matter to step to the nearest tree branch. Then, clinging like a monkey, she swung herself from limb to limb until the lowest branch was reached. (Porter 28–9)

Pollyanna's affinity with nature is established here as well as her liminality. She moves fluidly from interior to exterior space, from architectural ledge to organic branch, and even slips from human to animal as she moves 'like a monkey'. Pollyanna's escape from the confines of the house foretell her ability to evade Miss Polly's attempts to control and restrict her in other ways too. Miss Polly's decision to push her niece to the furthest margin of the house only encourages Pollyanna to explore and express her liminal tendencies. Likewise, when Emily is locked in the spare room as punishment for disobedience, she absconds, literally and figuratively breaking free from the confines of the house (Montgomery, *Emily* 134).

Some of the spaces in other narratives examined here seem to be almost entirely symbolic and the authors make little attempt to render them in anything other than the broadest brushstrokes. The Frankfurt townhouse Heidi stays in only matters insofar as it offers us a clear sign of the repression and restriction of the urban space in contrast to the beauty and freedom of the mountains. Similarly, as Peter Hunt notes, the landscapes presented in Hodgson Burnett's *The Secret Garden* are symbolic rather than realistic. He writes:

> The house represents repression, the garden, growth, and the moor, freedom [. . .] The actual location does not matter – it is vaguely Northern England – but as a landscape it is strikingly artificial [. . .] Similarly, Misselthwaite Manor may be based on Fryston Hall in Yorkshire, but it is no more than a collection of Gothic stage-props. (Hunt 26)

Among this collection of 'stage-props', the garden is the most significant. It is a threshold space, one enclosed within the Manor property and carefully sheltered from the true wildness of the moor, yet it is a space that permits growth and a degree of freedom that is impossible inside the house itself. It is both a space of cultivated growth and a space of spontaneous growth. Ruth Y. Jenkins notes 'there is visual fluidity as well as uncertain states of being' (432) in the garden, calling attention to the way Hodgson Burnett describes the space as a 'hazy tangle', a 'fairy place' and 'a queer, pretty place' (Hodgson Burnett, *Secret* 89, 101, 115) that suggests this space is on the edges of what can be perceived and what can be tamed and controlled. I suggest that in this text, the garden serves as an interstice, a boundary between the wild and the contained, the natural and the cultural, the living and the dead. And so it becomes an appropriate space for Mary – as an orphan girl poised between childhood and adulthood, between the known and the unknown – to cultivate her own sense of identity.

The social and spatial liminality of girls contributes to a further sort of liminality, what I will term imaginative liminality. The characters examined here are all a little otherworldly, they all border on the supernatural and the sublime. Sanders has identified the roots of the orphan girl narrative in sentimental fiction that draws heavily on the tropes of Romanticism, but other critics including Kathleen Ann Miller and Kate Lawson have also identified the later narratives in this period as engaging closely with Gothic tropes. A close examination of these texts reveals that many they have both Romantic and Gothic elements; Spyri, Hodgson Burnett, Porter and Montgomery engage knowingly with the literary tropes of both genres. The protagonists often embody Romantic notions about childhood – Ann Alston notes the 'Romantic trope where the child revives the adult' (45) is present in both *Pollyanna* and *Anne of Green Gables*. Arguably, it may also be seen in *Heidi*, *The Secret Garden* and *A Little Princess*, where a child who is more completely in tune with nature and with their own innocence may revitalise a child who has been stifled by adult culture and may suffer from both emotional and physical restrictions. Gothic tropes are present too; the young heroines may uncover family secrets or reveal lost heirs, encounter weird, ghostly presences in strange houses, and brush with death. These intertextual connections to the Gothic may be playfully invoked, as they are when Sara Crewe imagines herself as a princess shut up in a tower, or when Emily is left for the night in a pink room that parodies the red room Jane Eyre is forced into by her cruel aunt. Though Emily is thrilled to think of herself as 'one of the heroines in Gothic romance' (Montgomery, *Emily* 283), the comparison makes us aware that Emily's fears are a much-diluted version of the horror that Jane experiences in Brontë's novel, her aunt is spiky but by no means abusive, her room is merely pink rather than red. Just as these authors engage with both Romantic and Gothic tropes, the orphan girls are poised between Romantic ideals and Gothic ones: on the one hand, a rich internal imaginative life and a delight in nature is common across each of these characters, and on the other, these characters echo a distinctly Gothic image of the thin, pale child shut away in a gloomy old house who has a strange relationship with death, the ghostly and the haunted. Whether we see these orphan girl narratives as engaging with Romantic tropes or with Gothic ones, it is abundantly clear that the supernatural and sublime qualities associated with these genres are, in the orphan girl narrative, focalised upon and located within the person of the orphan girl herself.

The germinal text in the genre, *Heidi*, demonstrates how the orphan girl, rather than the narrative itself, is the locus of the uncanny tensions of the text. Heidi herself makes much of the beauty of the mountains of her homeland and her emotive responses to the landscape echo the impassioned responses to nature of Romantic poetry and painting. Charles Wharton Stork's introduction to the 1919 edition draws clear connections between Spyri's work and Wordsworth's poetry, and establishes Elizabeth P. Stork's suitability to translate the work because she

> was born and reared in a region closely similar to that of the story. Her home was originally in the picturesque town of Salzburg, and her father, Franz von Pausinger, was one of the greatest landscape painters of his country and generation. (Stork 8)

Yet, the locus of Romantic sentiment within the text is undoubtedly Heidi herself. Early in the narrative, the reader is shown her joyful response to nature:

> The old fir-trees were rustling and a mighty wind was roaring and howling through the tree-tops. Those sounds thrilled Heidi's heart and filled it with happiness and joy. She danced and jumped about under the trees, for those sounds made her feel as if a wonderful thing had happened to her. (Spyri 46–7)

The narrative also draws on ghost stories and later Heidi is mistaken for a ghost haunting the Frankfurt townhouse of her adopted family. The orphan girl is central to the sense of the uncanny within the text. Playfully drawing on the tropes of the nineteenth-century Gothic narrative, Spyri builds a sense of dread and suspense by introducing Heidi's nocturnal wanderings as a mystery to both characters and readers: 'Something strange and weird was happening in the house. Every morning, when the servants came down-stairs, they found the front door wide open' (154). The fact that the front door is left open threatens the sanctity and security of the house, breaching the barrier between the private and public, the domestic and the strange. These events are uncanny, unhomely, because they create an uncomfortable convergence of the familiar and the unfamiliar. Appropriately, these 'weird' events are concentrated around liminal spaces: the hallway, the stairs, the threshold of the front door itself. These strange occurrences come to a head when some of the staff decide to wait up all night in a little room beside the hall and, to their horror, the men see that: 'On the threshold stood a motionless white form, lighted up by the moon' (160). The eerie presence is revealed as nothing more than the orphan girl. It is significant that Heidi has not been transmuted or enchanted in any way: the nocturnal wanderings are the result of her own powerful but repressed desire to return to the mountain. This repression, identified by the kindly doctor as homesickness, points to an uncanny repression and revelation, and to the power of this strange child's secret imaginative life (163). But this darker side of the orphan girl is rendered benign once Heidi returns to the mountains and uses her deep connection with the natural world to guide others, notably Clara, towards the restorative power of nature.

Spyri's text makes use of the term *unheimlich* (and its many variants) which is often rendered as 'weird' or 'eerie' in translations but could also be understood to mean 'uncanny'. This uncanniness offers a fruitful way to understand the imaginative liminality of these orphan girls. As Laura Peters notes:

> In German, Heimlich, meaning familiar deriving from the Latin *familiaris*, is that which 'belongs to the house, not strange, familiar, tame, intimate, friendly'; in a more general sense *heimlich* is 'belonging to the house of the family, or regarded as so belonging'. In contrast then, one outside of this family home, like the orphan, would be regarded as *unheimlich*, meaning unhomely or uncanny. (Peters 19)

While *heimlich* and *unheimlich* are often interpreted as dialectical opposites, in fact the terms blur together. Freud's discussion of the term contains the observation that 'among its different shades of meaning the word *heimlich* exhibits one which is identical with its opposite, *unheimlich*. What is *heimlich* thus comes to be *unheimlich*' (4). The word both means and connotes uncertainty and the hesitation it inspires in the reader or translator mirrors the 'intellectual uncertainty' (2) caused by the presence of the uncanny. The orphan girls in these narratives are not merely uncanny because they originate from outside the family home, they are uncanny because they are strangers who are present within the family home. They are uncanny because they unite the strange with the familiar and occupy the boundary between the known and the unknown. This uncanniness is expressed through the spatial dynamics of the texts. I have discussed how the orphan girl's position on the boundaries of the domestic space subverts and unsettles the primacy of the home. Though the home space is often assumed to be the locus of both personal and familial identity, the children who originate outside this space and who are never fully and completely accepted within it, build their identities on other foundations. These orphan girls look to spaces outside the home for their sense of personhood. These orphan girls are, therefore, 'unhomely' – the home space is not their only source of self-worth and self-reflection. Just as they toy with the spatial borders of the domestic space, they also unsettle the ideological and spiritual boundaries within the texts, playing along the margins of what is considered normal or natural. The orphan girl may connect the natural and the cultural and move agilely between the two. They may also express their essential uncanniness through powerful imaginations or unusual powers of insight, or through a deep, instinctive connection with an imaginative world. Their ability to see beyond the ordinary is often presented as unsettling, as something that disturbs the rigid order of the world around them.

The unsettling presence of the orphan girl is sometimes stated explicitly within these texts. For Rachel Lynde 'it seems uncanny to think of a child at Green Gables' (Montgomery, *Anne* 11) and it is especially uncanny for that child to be a girl rather than the boy Marilla and Matthew Cuthbert expect to join the household. Anne thwarts their expectations and unsettles the fine balance of the household and, by extension, the neighbourhood. But Anne's presence is disordering rather than disturbing, and some of the upset she causes comes from being utterly ingenuous about her feelings. Like Heidi, she has rapturous responses to the natural world:

> Overhead was one long canopy of snow, fragrant bloom. Below the boughs, the air was full of a purple twilight and far ahead a glimpse of painted sunset sky shone like a great rose window at the end of a cathedral aisle.
>
> Its beauty seemed to strike the child dumb. She leaned back in the buggy, her thin hands clasped before her, her face lifted rapturously to the white splendour above. (Montgomery, *Anne* 24–5)

And, like Heidi, Anne's imagination can take dark and unsettling turns too, as when she decides to re-enact the death and river burial of Tennyson's Elaine. These moments of imagination, even more so than her guileless speech and impulsive behaviour, are central to Anne's ability to disturb and subvert the everyday. Her imaginative power has both positive and negative effects: Thomas MacLulich suggests that 'Anne's flights of fancy are [. . .] an important source of the renewed life she brings to Green Gables' (466) but, as Elizabeth Epperly argues, these moments of 'excessive imagination' also lead to mishaps and misunderstandings (Epperly 25–6). These moments when imagination overrules reality are crucial to Anne's ability to push up against the limits of ordinary life and to display her true uncanny nature.

In contrast to the effusive Anne and the irrepressibly 'glad' Pollyanna, Hodgson Burnett's heroines are not as openly emotional as their North American counterparts and they do not often reveal their imaginative inner lives to other characters. But even so, Mary and Sara's reserve and self-control is regarded as peculiar. Because they are more in control of their emotions and their expressions than children are expected to be they challenge pervasive ideological assumptions about childhood. Sara Crewe, for instance, does not behave in the manner expected of a young girl and the result is unsettling. Sara's classmate, Jessie, observes that '"She's different from other people [. . .] Sometimes I'm a bit frightened of her"' (Hodgson Burnett, *Princess* 242). Sara's nemesis throughout the book is Miss Minchin who is described as a 'worldly' woman – as her opposite, it seems fitting that Sara is an otherworldly child. Even before news of her father's death reaches London, Sara is described in terms of the otherworldly. She is 'a rose-coloured fairy' (60) who speaks 'dreamily' (61). The news that she has been orphaned does not induce her to become more ordinary and practical but rather transforms her into 'a strange, desolate, almost grotesque figure' (100). Though Sara has always been a little different from the other children, her new status as an orphan confirms and deepens this strangeness, exaggerating it to the point that she becomes an almost fantastical character. Sara had initially been regarded as a sort of princess by the other pupils because she was the heiress to great wealth, but when she is orphaned, she becomes more like a princess in a fairy tale, locked up in a tower and forced into servitude, though Becky points out that her journey from riches to rags to riches again does not alter her strangeness nor makes her more like the other children in Miss Minchin's school. Sara remains ethereally strange and in the attic gives free rein to her powerful imagination.

Mary Lennox is a further extreme, serving as a ghostly presence within the house. Though readers of *The Secret Garden* may be more accustomed to viewing Colin Craven as the ghostly presence within Misselthwaite Manor, Mary's spectral presence in the bungalow in India, and later at Misselthwaite should not be overlooked. In India, she is a mere rumour, 'the child no one ever saw' (7) and many did not even know about. When she is discovered by British officers as the sole survivor of a cholera outbreak, the men are initially shocked to see her:

> The first man who came in was a large officer she has once seen talking to her father. He looked tired and troubled, but when he saw her he was so startled that he almost jumped back.
>
> 'Barney!' he cried out. 'There is a child here! A child alone! In a place like this! Mercy on us, who is she?' (Hodgson Burnett, *Secret* 7)

The presence of a child in a house of the dead is disturbing; her loneliness and singularity are the initial – and understandable – cause for the officer's concern. But this scene also disturbs the usual power dynamic between adult and child here that contributes to his uneasiness: Mary has watched him, and seen him while remaining unseen. She knows him but he does not know her. Her unexpected knowledge and her unexpected presence renders her both canny and uncanny in this moment.

Mary continues to be both canny and uncanny throughout the novel, observing those around her while slipping out of their sight into hidden gardens and through forgotten passageways, quietly holding back her secrets while at the same time encouraging others to divulge their knowledge to her. Her close relationship with the secret garden itself is the best expression of her uncanny nature: because she controls the borders to that space, she has some measure of control over life and death. She is the one who decides to revive the secret garden and to raise it from the dead. Her desire 'to see them [the flowers] come alive' (134) is mirrored in her ability to revitalise Colin and to bring him from his sick bed to the garden and there to transform him into a strong and healthy boy. When Colin first sees her, he asks '"Are you a ghost?"' (141) and in some senses she might be: she remains in the bungalow when everyone else has died or left, and at Misselthwaite, she haunts the corridors and forgotten rooms. The experience of this isolation 'makes [her] feel queer' (63) but this feeling only serves to match what others already know about her: she is a strange, contrary child who moves along the margins and forgotten spaces of the house. As Colin is brought into central focus, Mary seems to fade into the background. She is present throughout the final chapter but significantly says nothing at all and so she remains strange and unknowable to the very end, hiding her secrets even from the reader. In this novel, positions on the centre and on the periphery are gendered. As Colin moves into the centre of the narrative attention, his physical strength is increasingly linked to positive, masculine qualities and his emerging 'boyish' nature. The climax of the novel sees Archibald Craven reunited with his son in the secret garden and throughout their joyful reunion, Mary remains silent. Mary's girlhood allows her to evade – or perhaps condemns her to remain on the edge of – both the other characters' and the narrator's attention and to become, once more, a child that nobody sees or hears.

Perhaps the most imaginatively and spiritually liminal of the orphan girls discussed here is Emily Byrd Starr. She is identified, by both the narrator and by other characters within Montgomery's novel, as a queer creature (*Emily* 26). She has pointed ears and eyes that seem to change colour depending on her mood. Like Anne and Sara, Emily has a rich imagination and a penchant for day-dreaming. But she is also subject to something more powerful and uncontrollable. Emily calls this sudden surge of imaginative insight the 'flash' and it is by turns a sort of rapturous reaction to the natural world, and a sudden, overwhelming insight. For Kate Lawson, the 'flash' is indicative of Montgomery's movement away from sentimental fiction with neat, romantic plots towards something darker and more subversive. She writes: 'the *Emily* trilogy as a whole hints at darker forces of personality and identity than are evident in *Anne of Green Gables* and its immediate successors' (71). Miller agrees, noting that in this late trilogy, 'Montgomery privileges the uncanny and suggests that characters cannot navigate their world without having access to the Gothic imagination' (127). Miller identifies this imagination as explicitly Gothic but I argue that Emily's powerful imagination has less to do with generic conventions than with the liminality and uncanniness of the orphan girl herself.

Significantly, Emily thinks of the 'flash' in spatial terms, as a moment that allows her to come close to and even peep through the boundaries between this world and something else entirely.

> Between it and herself hung only a thin curtain; she could never draw the curtain aside – but sometimes, just for a moment, a wind fluttered it and then it was as if she caught a glimpse of the enchanting realm beyond – only a glimpse – and heard a note of unearthly music. (Montgomery, *Emily* 7)

The 'flash' allows her to feel that her body and soul are separate entities and that in these rare moments of ecstasy, her soul might 'cast aside the bonds of flesh and spring upward to the stars' (96). When the 'flash' comes, Emily is endowed with supernatural insight and awareness. Her bodily senses are heightened too and though Emily most often experiences the 'flash' in private moments, the effects of it, and the changes it brings to her, can be seen by those around her too.

Another uncanny quality Emily possesses is her ability to connect with the dead. While Mary Lennox's love for the secret garden links her to her deceased aunt, Lilias, she does not channel the dead woman's spirit. Emily, however, can embody the dead. In moments of heightened emotion, she channels the spirits of her dead ancestors and may even seem to wear their features. Her Aunt Elizabeth is frightened by this 'transformed or possessed child' (127) and tries to explain to her sister: 'I saw – father – looking from her face', gasped Elizabeth, trembling. 'And she said "let me hear no more of this" – just as *he* always said it – his very words' (128). Emily ventriloquises or perhaps even seems to serve as a medium who speaks with the voice of the dead. After a second such moment of possession, the narrator tries to explain exactly why this unsettles Elizabeth so much:

> The thing might not have been so uncanny if Emily had resembled the Murrays. But to see the Murray look superimposed like a mask over alien features was such a shock to [Elizabeth's] nerves that she could not stand up against it. A ghost from the grave could not have cowed her more speedily. (176)

Here, Montgomery explicitly links Emily with images of the grave and with the alien and the unknowable. She also makes it clear that we should consider Emily as uncanny. Here, Emily combines the familiar (the image of the father's expression) with the unfamiliar (the father's expression on a strange girl's features). She is at once a stranger to Elizabeth and a blood relation, a child and an adult, both girl and man. Like Mary, Emily possesses a dual uncanniness and canniness that is frightening to the adult onlooker. Emily defies expectations of how a child should look, sound and behave and, as a result, becomes ideologically and imaginatively liminal.

The climax of Emily's liminality comes when this connection with the dead is combined with an unusually powerful moment of insight. While delirious with fever brought on by measles, Emily 'sees' into the past and sees the accidental death of Ilsa's mother:

> she opened her eyes and looked at Aunt Laura – looked through her – looked beyond her.
> 'I see her coming over the fields', she said in a high, clear voice. 'She is coming so gladly – she is singing – she is thinking of her baby – oh, keep her back, keep her back – she doesn't see the well – it's so dark, she doesn't see it – oh. She's gone into it – she's gone into it'.
> Emily's voice rose in a piercing shriek which penetrated to Aunt Elizabeth's room and brought her flying across the hall in her flannel nightgown. (382–3)

Emily is granted this vision in a moment of unusual spiritual liminality – she herself is close to death, closer than her aunts ever let her realise, and in this interstice between life and death, Emily can see beyond the quotidian. Looking 'through' and 'beyond' what stands in front of her, Emily is able to see something that happened years before she came to Blair Water. Her vision proves to be disturbingly accurate and leads to the discovery of the remains of Ilsa's mother at the bottom of a disused well. As a stranger to Blair Water, Emily should not know the story of Ilsa's mother's disappearance and so her aunts know that her information she provides comes from a supernatural source. Emily's vision leads to a recovery of the past, to that which has been hidden (kept secret), being brought out into the open (and secreted). Her vision brings together the known and the unknown, the familiar and the strange, the living and the dead and is a perfectly uncanny ending to this phase of her narrative.

At the beginning of *Jane Eyre* (1847), an orphan girl takes refuge from her adoptive family and hides behind a curtain to read a book:

> A breakfast-room adjoined the drawing-room, I slipped in there. It contained a bookcase: I soon possessed myself of a volume, taking care that it should be one stored with pictures. I mounted into the window-seat: gathering up my feet, I sat cross-legged, like a Turk; and, having drawn the red moreen curtain nearly close, I was shrined in double retirement. (Brontë 1)

In this moment, Jane is absolutely liminal. While Jane considers this a 'double retirement' there are actually three layers to her liminality: socially, she is excluded from the nuclear family and positions herself as a lone figure away from the rest of the household; physically, she is poised on the very margins of the house, in the window-seat; and imaginatively, she is captivated by a book and her mind is on something far distant from her actual surroundings. Brontë's heroine is an important touchstone for the orphan girls at the centre of narratives aimed at young readers in the long nineteenth century and the social, spatial and imaginative liminality that marks Brontë's character at the very start of her story is developed and given full expression in the books I have discussed here and many like them. What makes these children's texts distinct from Brontë's work and other contemporary texts like Wetherell's *The Wide, Wide World* (1850), is that the characters at the centre of these narratives might grow but they do not grow up. The orphan girls I discuss here, Heidi, Sara, Anne, Mary, Pollyanna and Emily, remain children within these texts (though Anne and Emily do indeed grow to womanhood in the longer sequences of books about them). They begin and end their narratives as liminal figures. Though they cultivate fulfilling relationships with those around them, they remain as orphans. Though their narratives are centripetal, they move around the edges of the domestic space because they are both drawn towards and excluded from the centre of the home. These characters have rich imaginative inner lives and are deeply connected with nature and with a spiritual world beyond the everyday. Their position on the edges of the household and on the edges of the ordinary affords them the ability to unite the strange and the familiar, the mundane and the remarkable. While the uncanny is often understood in terms of the eerie or the unsettling, these orphan girls demonstrate a liminality that has proved powerfully attractive and engaging for audiences in the long nineteenth century and beyond.

## Note

1. See Peter Merchant's chapter in this volume (Chapter 8) for a contrasting discussion of female orphan adventure narratives.

## Works Cited

Alston, Ann. *The Family in English Children's Literature*. Routledge, 2010.
Brontë, Charlotte. [1847]. *Jane Eyre*. Penguin, 2010.
Carpenter, Humphrey. *Secret Gardens: A Study of the Golden Age of Children's Literature*. Houghton Mifflin, 1985.
Carroll, Jane Suzanne. *Landscape in Children's Literature*. Routledge, 2012.
Dewan, Pauline. *The House as Setting, Symbol, and Structural Motif in Children's Literature*. Edwin Mellen Press, 2004.
Dyhouse, Carol. *Girls Growing Up in Late Victorian and Edwardian England*. Routledge, 2012.
Freud, Sigmund. 'The "Uncanny"'. Trans. Alix Strachey. *Sammlung*, Fünfte Folge, San Diego State University, 1919. https://web.mit.edu/allanmc/www/freud1.pdf
Hodgson Burnett, Frances. [1905]. *A Little Princess*. Puffin, 2007.
Hodgson Burnett, Frances. [1911]. *The Secret Garden*. Puffin, 2010.
Holloway, Sarah and Valentine, Gill. 'Spatiality and the New Social Studies of Childhood'. *Sociology – The Journal of the British Sociological Association*, vol. 34, no. 4, 2000, pp. 763–83.
Hunt, Peter. 'Unstable Metaphors: Symbolic Spaces and Specific Places', in *Space and Place in Children's Literature, 1789 to the Present*, ed. Maria

Sachiko Cecire, Hannah Field, Kavita Mudan Finn and Malini Roy. Routledge, 2015, pp. 23–38.

Jenkins, Ruth Y. 'Frances Hodgson Burnett's *The Secret Garden*: Engendering Abjection's Sublime'. *Children's Literature Association Quarterly*, vol. 36, no. 4, 2011, pp. 426–44.

Lawson, Kate. 'The "Disappointed" House: Trance, Loss, and the Uncanny in L. M. Montgomery's *Emily* Trilogy'. *Children's Literature*, vol. 29, 2001, pp. 71–90.

MacLulich, T. D. 'L. M. Montgomery's Portraits of the Artist: Realism, Idealism, and the Domestic Imagination'. *ESC: English Studies in Canada*, vol. 11, no. 4, 1985, pp. 459–73.

Miller, Kathleen Ann. 'Haunted Heroines: The Gothic Imagination and the Female *Bildungsromane* of Jane Austen, Charlotte Brontë, and L. M. Montgomery'. *The Lion and the Unicorn*, vol. 34, no. 2, 2010, pp. 125–47.

Montgomery, L.M. [1908]. *Anne of Green Gables*. Puffin, 2015.

Montgomery, L. M. [1923]. *Emily of New Moon*. Virago Press, 2013.

Nodelman, Perry. 'Progressive Utopias or, How to Grow Up without Growing Up', in *Such a Simple Little Tale: Critical Responses to L.M. Montgomery's* Anne of Green Gables, ed. Mavis Reimer. The Children's Literature Association and The Scarecrow Press, 1992, pp. 29–38.

Parkes, Christopher. 'Treasure Island and the Romance of the British Civil Service'. *Children's Literature Association Quarterly*, vol. 31, no. 4, 2006, pp. 332–45.

Peters, Laura. *Orphan Texts: Victorian Orphans, Culture and Empire*. Manchester University Press, 2000.

Porter, Eleanor H. [1913]. *Pollyanna*. Scholastic, 2017.

Rodgers, Beth. *Adolescent Girlhood and Literary Culture at the Fin de Siècle: Daughters of Today*. Palgrave, 2016.

Sanders, Joe Sutliff. *Disciplining Girls: Understanding the Origins of the Classic Orphan Girl Story*. Johns Hopkins University Press, 2011.

Slater, Katharine. '"The other was whole": *Anne of Green Gables*, Trauma and Mirroring'. *The Lion and the Unicorn*, vol. 34, no. 2, 2010, pp. 167–87.

Spyri, Joanna. [1880]. *Heidi*. Trans. Elizabeth Stork. J. B. Lippincott, 1919.

Stan, Susan. '*Heidi* in English: A Bibliographic Study'. *New Review of Children's Literature and Librarianship*, vol. 16, no. 1, 2010, pp. 1–23.

Stork, Charles Wharton. 'Introduction'. Joanna Spyri, *Heidi*. Trans, Elizabeth Stork. J. B. Lippincott, 1919.

Chapter 10

# 'The accumulated and single': Modernity, Inheritance and Orphan Identity

*Diane Warren*

> From the mingled passions that made up his past, out of a diversity of bloods, from the crux of a thousand impossible situations, Felix had become the accumulated and single – the embarrassed. (Barnes 9)

This is how the narrator introduces Baron Felix Volkbein, the orphan whose narrative opens *Nightwood* (Djuna Barnes, 1936). Felix is preoccupied throughout the novel with locating himself in the cultural fabric, via his researches into the 'great past' (37) and his attempts to found a dynasty. Yet the narrator's comments position Felix's search for origins as an ever-receding project, which can never be accounted for, as it comprises 'mingled passions', 'a diversity of bloods' and 'a thousand impossible situations', none of which escape the plane of generalisation. The detail of kinship bonds therefore eludes him, remaining just out of reach, much as he thinks of the circus as 'a loved thing that he could never touch' (11). Nevertheless, subjectivity forms from these contrasting and conflicting fragments, and Felix becomes the 'accumulated and single' (9), in a manner which recalls the identity bricolage seen in Pound's 'Portrait d'une Femme':

> No! there is nothing! In the whole and all,
> Nothing that's quite your own.
>     Yet this is you. (34)

Felix's predicament: the 'embarrassment' caused by the tension between accumulation and singularity, resonates with modernist writers' tensioned reception of inheritance, and its relationship to originality. Consider, for example, the rival representations of the past seen in Woolf's criticism. The rejection of the conservative and passive inheritance seen in 'Modern Fiction' (1919) and 'Mr Bennett and Mrs Brown' (1924), contrasts sharply with the dynamic relationship to inheritance, seen in Woolf's analysis that 'a woman writing thinks back through her mothers' (*A Room of One's Own* 88). Since *A Room of One's Own* begins the process of piecing together a tradition of women's writing, to create literary place, it implies that the woman writer is a species of cultural orphan, and that orphanhood can be ameliorated by awareness of the work of other women writers. Tradition, in this more dynamic sense, offers access to an imaginative home through literary inheritance.

T. S. Eliot also distinguishes between an imitative (and hence subservient) approach to literary inheritance and an organic and metamorphic understanding of tradition, the whole of which changes with each new work produced ('Tradition' 85–6). In each of these cases, what inheritance is, and how it may relate to present and future work is actively contested, and this contestation is closely related to the tension between inheritance and self-fashioning which informs the readings of *Nightwood* (Barnes) and *When I Lived in Modern Times* (Grant) which follow.

The interplay between individual and collective experience seen in the epigraph is important: this interplay is also illustrated by the works' interest in genealogy. The readings which follow explore the ways in which nineteenth-century scepticism about genealogy,[1] and the awareness of the cultural discourses of inclusion and exclusion which accompany this, is examined and intensified by the focus on the orphan in my focal texts: Djuna Barnes's *Nightwood* (1936) and Linda Grant's *When I Lived in Modern Times* (2000). Both texts anatomise the ways in which the interface of culture and biology render the orphan 'the accumulated and single' (Barnes 9): burdened by inheritance, yet searching for kinship. I shall also examine the ways in which imaginative inheritance, in the form of what Gaston Bachelard calls 'the poetry of the past' (16) inflects the orphan's search for kinship, belonging and a sense of cultural place, offering a personal imaginative genealogy.

*Nightwood* is usually read as novel primarily concerned about (failed) love between women, or in terms of its stylistic complexity.[2] Here, however, I want to focus on the orphan elements of the work, mediated by the Felix Volkbein narrative thread, which opens the work and then acts as a complementary narrative. Born (and immediately orphaned) in Vienna in 1880, Felix's genealogical researches reveal much about the temper of the times, in a society where cultural orphanhood was becoming an increasingly politicised issue, as Jews found themselves more frequently socially marginalised.[3] *When I Lived in Modern Times* is set some years later. Most of Grant's novel is set in London and Mandatory Palestine, and focuses primarily on the time of cultural change in the aftermath of the Second World War. The narrative follows the orphan protagonist Evelyn Sert, from Soho to Mandatory Palestine, in her search for kinship, and in the process illustrates the ways in which nineteenth-century understandings of orphanhood continued to hold sway until well into the twentieth century. Like Felix, Evelyn is keen to find home and kinship. Partially aware of her complex inheritance as an orphan of the diaspora, she hopes to find home in the 'new Zion' (Grant 4) of Mandatory Palestine. There (ironically, as it turns out) she considers that she shall be able to escape dissimulation and reinvent herself amid the clean lines of the newly built New Internationalist buildings of the White City of Tel Aviv.

In this chapter I shall argue that Evelyn and Felix represent two contrasting modernist reactions to inheritance, and the inheritance of the long nineteenth century in particular. Where Felix seeks to embrace the past in order to create the future, Evelyn attempts to reject the past in order to 'Make it New!'[4] Both novels suggest ultimately that the past cannot be escaped, but must be negotiated while establishing agency, although both also absolutely reject an essentialist quest for origins. In the following analyses, I shall tease out the contested reception of inheritance and the search for cultural place in my readings of *Nightwood* and *When I Lived in Modern Times*. For these novels, the past functions as both resource and burden: the tension between the two is negotiated in differing ways by the orphans in each case.

The readings which follow are dependent upon the awareness that orphanhood may be understood in both biological and cultural terms.[5] I shall argue that the texts employ orphans to question 'the codes of inclusion and entitlement that generate exclusion' (Armstrong 8) which shape the genealogies (or lack thereof) of their protagonists. Both also question the role of inheritance in the formation of identity and its relationship to kinship structures. In a sense then, they can be read as inheritors of the nineteenth-century genealogical narrative. The texts also examine the important role played by elective kinship structures, in the orphan's search for a sense of belonging and cultural placing. Although, of course, those choices are often limited by the pressure of conservative inheritance and convention, also reflected in the constricting cultural frameworks of gender values and anti-Semitism.

Rereading orphanhood as a discursive practice resonates with Judith Butler's analysis of the processes which create cultural understandings of the body. She observes that 'performativity must be understood not as a singular or deliberate "act", but, rather, as the reiterative and citational practice by which discourse produces the effects that it names' (2). Similarly, Simone de Beauvoir's analysis that 'one is not born, one rather becomes a woman' (*The Second Sex*) is also pertinent to the orphan condition. The changes in state that often accompany the cultural construction of orphanhood accentuate the trials and tribulations of the development of agency, and begin to explain why orphans in all guises were so important to the development of the novel.[6] It follows, then, that individuals (or ethnic/religious groups) may also be culturally orphaned: a term that Kuo Pao Kun uses to articulate Singaporean identity, but which has many resonances for the analysis of the displaced adult orphans discussed in this chapter.[7]

Although Felix is orphaned at birth, and Evelyn is not completely orphaned until she is a young adult, the novels are chiefly preoccupied with orphanhood as a process of othering, frequently defined from without or otherwise influenced by the dominant culture: a process which results in an orphan state of mind. For example, Evelyn identifies herself as a migrant and a Jew – although she has 'no religion' (Grant 60),[8] and Felix is represented as a Jew although his father had 'adopted the sign of the cross' (Barnes 5) and his mother was Christian.[9] The sense of identity in flux which both of them experience resonates with Kuo Pao Kun's work. Having defined Singaporeans as cultural orphans, he observes that:

> At the confluence of several great civilisations and in the international flow of information, Singaporeans sense the richness of interacting with every place but also feel the pain and frustration of not belonging anywhere. Boundless space, boundless bewilderment, boundless loss and boundless hope – there naturally emerges an orphan mentality and a condition of marginality. Even if we were able to trace back and return to our respective cultural parentages, we would still not be at home in the past. (Kuo)

Kuo's words emphasise the extent to which orphanhood can be read as a highly marginal state of being, which informs the individual's whole life. They stress the longing for belonging, much as they position the possibility of a return to a home in the past – a golden age of wholeness – as an impossible dream, since belonging has already been irrevocably lost. Both Felix and Evelyn strive to find a sense of cultural parentage. Born in Vienna, 'at the confluence of several great civilisations' (Kuo) Felix's researches into 'the great past' can be read as an attempt to find home. By contrast, Evelyn consciously seeks to reject the material past by reimagining herself as 'a daughter of the new Zion' (Grant 4) in line with her childhood fantasy. Both Felix and Evelyn face cultural bewilderment, and are forced to successively examine and renegotiate their aspirations as they seek to find cultural place and a sense of kinship to 'resolve the orphan's dangerous isolation' (Schaffer 170). The longing for the locatedness of home, or for a sense of cultural placement, is one of the main tropes of orphan narratives, and it informs both *Nightwood* and *When I Lived in Modern Times*, often becoming intertwined with the narrative of inheritance and the mystery of origins trope (which has been examined in other chapters in this volume). It is also an important component of the development of orphan subjectivity and agency, which in turn, resonates with modernist writers' processing of literary inheritance.

In each of these texts, the search for cultural place is complicated by the orphans (secular) Jewish inheritance. For Yuri Slezkine, there is a special relationship between Judaism (secular and otherwise) and modernity. Slezkine's analysis reads society through the lens of an Apollonian/Mercurian split, where (in broad terms) the Apollonian is associated with farming and nationalism, and the Mercurian, with the mentally agile modern professions of 'service nomads' (22). Slezkine argues that nineteenth-century Europe was the birthplace of nationalism, but that ironically (as he argues that nationalism is based on tribalism), Jews were excluded from 'the Age of Nationalism' (1). He observes that 'the most successful of all modern tribes, they were also the most vulnerable' (1–2).

> More desperate than any other European nation for state protection, they were the least likely to receive it because no European nation-state could claim to be the embodiment of the Jewish nation. Most European nation-states, in other words, contained citizens who combined spectacular success with irredeemable tribal foreignness. The Jewish age was also the age of anti-Semitism. (Slezkine 2)

In this context, Slezkine argues, Freudianism, Zionism and Marxism can also be seen as 'solutions to the Jewish predicament' (2): a predicament which, I would argue can be seen as a species of cultural orphanhood. It is however an orphanhood which reaches far beyond Jewish culture. Slezkine continues to argue that 'Freudianism [. . .] proclaimed the beleaguered loneliness of the newly "emancipated" to be a universal human condition' (2): a comment which correlates neatly with Auerbach's observation that

> Although we are now 'all orphans,' alone and free and dispossessed of our past, we yearn for origins, for cultural continuity. In our continual achievement of paradox, we have made of the orphan himself our archetypal and perhaps only ancestor. (416)

In this context then, Marxism and Zionism seem to offer solutions to that isolation: either in terms of socialist collectivism, or in the search for cultural place or 'home'. In the discussions that follow, home is often more of an imaginative construct than a material place.

The continued psychological importance of the role of home, in the form of the imaginative imprint of the first house, is explored by Gaston Bachelard. In *The Poetics of Space*, Bachelard explores the relationship between memory, physical space and imaginative renditions of space, and he argues that the memory of the first house is fundamental to the imaginative well-being of the individual. Consider for example: 'The house that we were born in is more than an embodiment of home, it is also an embodiment of dreams' (15). Bachelard goes on to argue that:

> If a compact centre of daydreams of repose had not existed in this first house, the very different circumstances that surround actual life would have clouded our memories. Except for a few medallions stamped with the likeness of our ancestors, our child-memory contains only worn coins. It is on the plane of the daydream and not on that of facts that childhood remains alive and poetically useful within us. Through this permanent childhood we maintain the poetry of the past. (16)

For Bachelard then, the imaginative ideal of the first house is far more significant than the empirically verifiable existence of the house. Nonetheless, it is, I would argue, the sense of stability provided by that first home, which facilitates the creation of the house 'on the plane of daydream'.[10] For literary orphans, this unconscious relationship to 'the poetry of the past' (16) is often complicated, or interrupted altogether, by dislocation from that first house. It is not therefore surprising that the orphan's yearning for wholeness can be understood, in part, as an imaginative quest. Consider Felix Volkbein, comprehensively orphaned moments after his birth, as his mother Hedwig 'named him Felix, thrust him from her, and died. The child's father [Guido] had gone some six months previously, a victim of fever' (Barnes 3). The house that he was born into 'became a fantastic museum of their [his parents'] encounter' (6), emphasising the emblematic role that the house played in their relationship, and endowing the objects within it with high levels of symbolic significance, as museums tell history through the preservation of exemplary objects.

The narrator reveals that Felix still owns items from the family home, namely, two portraits, which he believes represent his grandparents,[11] although the reader is not informed whether Felix still has access to the physical house.[12] The imaginative influence of the house as 'fantastic museum' is, however, central to Felix's sense of self, along with the impulse to reach into the past to attain coherence and belonging, crystallised in his observation that 'to pay homage to our past is the only gesture that also includes the future' (38).

As he grows older, the influence of the 'fantastic museum' continues to inform Felix's actions as he widens his search for a sense of kinship. He finds 'that sense of peace that formerly he had experienced only in museums' (Barnes 11) in 'the splendid and reeking falsification of the circus' (11): a synergy that implicitly underscores the fabricated nature of Felix's family history. Felix empathises with the ways in which the circus performers 'had seized on titles for a purpose. [. . .] It brought them together', even though their desires are different. However, much as Felix identifies with the circus performers and their overtly fabricated world, his initial encounter with them is unable to create intimacy, and he remains isolated. The narrator observes that: 'The circus was a loved thing that he could never touch, therefore never know' (11), a distancing which at this point in the novel 'produced in Felix longing and disquiet' (11) thus further exacerbating the desire for a sense of cultural place, or home.[13] Felix's craving for the 'loved thing that he could never touch' marks an absence which resonates with his orphanhood, while prefiguring his marriage, and its failure. It also recalls his father's attempt to 'span the impossible gap' (4) in his own marriage, and the narrator's comments about the milk Felix received from his wet nurse which 'was his being but which could never be his birthright' (10). The novel circles around such losses, marking the enduring effects of cultural and biological orphanhood.

Like his father before him, Felix identifies the aristocratic system as scaffolding within which he may be able to locate himself.

The narrator has however already suggested that this is a loss that can never be mediated, observing that the process is 'futile' (4). In a complicated sequence peppered with rhetorical shifts and turns, the narrator reveals that Guido was like other Jews who were 'cut off from their people by accident or choice' (4): a moment in which he becomes a cultural orphan. To remedy his orphanhood, Guido

> adopted the sign of the cross; he had said that he was an Austrian of an old, almost extinct line, producing, to uphold his story, the most amazing and inaccurate proofs: a coat of arms that he had no right to and a list of progenitors (including their Christian names) who had never existed (5)

In some ways, this performance is successful as it secures him the wife he had dreamed of since 'Hedvig had become a Baroness without question' (6). Yet, she intuits that something is wrong, and thus the difference between them, the 'impossible gap' that Guido had attempted to 'span' (4) remains. This gap functions in three main ways: to underscore the isolation of the cultural orphan, to suggest that there was no real intimacy in the marriage, and to underscore what the text represents as the insurmountable difference between Christian and Jew.

It is important to recall the location of Felix's birth in 1880 Vienna at this point. Carl E. Schorske argues that by the *fin-de siècle*, the once liberal city was becoming increasingly anti-Semitic (5–6). Scott Spector argues that there was a 'standoff between pastness and futurity cohabiting in the empire's present' (53). Both Guido and Felix are poised at the point of this standoff, and both attempt to resolve it. Guido overwrites his inherited memories of persecution with an alternative genealogy, and Felix desires to father 'a son who would feel as he felt about the "great past"' (Barnes 37) since, 'to pay homage to our past is the only gesture which also includes the future' (38). Where Guido is motivated by concealment as he wishes to create 'an alibi for the blood' (8), Felix is driven by a recuperative impulse: he hopes that the past 'might mend a little'.[14] There is a distinct echo of the curative orphan trope seen in *Jane Eyre* here, although the recuperatory impulse is frustrated in *Nightwood*'s case, by the conservative elements of late nineteenth-/early twentieth-century Viennese culture, which block the transformations that each of the orphans attempt. The narrator still positions both men as 'Jews', even though Felix would not necessarily have been seen as such in orthodox terms, since his mother was Christian.[15]

Ironically, the narrator suggests that it is Guido's cultural and emotional legacy to the child he shall never meet, that marks him as an outsider, and which marginalises the boy more than his biological orphaning:

> Guido had prepared out of his own heart for his coming child a heart, fashioned on his own preoccupation, the *remorseless* homage to nobility, the genuflection the *hunted body* makes from muscular contraction, going down before the *impending and inaccessible* as before a great heat. It had made Guido, as it was to make his son, heavy with *impermissible blood*. (Barnes 4; emphasis added)

The extent to which Guido has internalised his own abjection is marked in the lexis here: the traumatic effect is such that homage becomes 'remorseless'. The purely reactive nature of this process is then stressed in the image of the presumably involuntary 'contraction[s]' made by the 'hunted body'. Yet the 'impending' is also 'inaccessible', implying that the veneration shall never be able to create community between the venerated and the veneratee: the implied hierarchy here is immovable and irreversible. It is this this internalisation of cultural pressures, which renders the blood 'impermissible'. The close proximity between Guido and the 'impending and inaccessible' also recalls Butler's analysis of the abject. Consider her observation that: 'this exclusionary matrix by which subjects are formed thus requires the simultaneous production of a domain of abject beings, those who are not yet "subjects", but who form the constitutive outside to the domain of the subject' (3). While both Guido and Felix attempt to escape cultural orphanhood and hence abjection, the narrator suggests that it is the desperate intensity of their desire for social acceptance, which most forcibly marks their otherness and thereby perpetuates the subject/abject dichotomy, ensuring their continued abjection and cultural orphanhood. In this way *Nightwood* marks 'the reiterative and citational practice by which discourse produces the effects that it names' (Butler 2).

Felix appears to be unaware of the complexity of his paternal inheritance, since he observes that the narrative of his familial past he has been told by his aunt is 'single, clear and unalterable' (Barnes 94) as it is received from one source. This apparently transparent observation further complicates analysis of Felix's awareness of his inheritance, since it implies that the reader knows far more about his past than Felix does. His interlocutor observes that Felix's '"devotion to the past"

[. . .] "is perhaps like a child's drawing"' (94): the analogy evokes the imaginative and evocative 'poetry of the past', which Bachelard notes in the enduring memory of the first house. In Felix's case, even that memory is a construct: not his own memory, but an image conjured by his aunt, which he yearns to appropriate and inhabit, through his researches into the 'great past' (37). In an attempt to more fully understand his familial past, Felix seeks out the 'officials and guardians' (9) of venerable houses: a slow and painstaking process, which risks revealing the fictive nature of his family history and title, and hence his 'disqualification' (9).

The novel's interest in genealogy draws attention to the ways in which genealogical narratives are constructed, and encourages sceptical responses to the hierarchies Felix works so hard to outline. Writing on the importance of genealogy to novels of the long nineteenth century, Isobel Armstrong observes that: 'genealogy in fiction hints, overtly or covertly, at scepticism about social hierarchy, family lineage and the permanence of the law, and both exposes and imagines the codes of inclusion and entitlement that generate exclusion' (8). The Volkbein narrative offers ample opportunity for the critique of 'the codes of inclusion and entitlement', and questions whether such codes have any value (Armstrong 8).[16] The novel also employs its analysis of titles more generally to suggest that the pursuit of authenticity is a delusion, which also calls into question the search for origins. Thus, in the closing stages of chapter 1, as Felix and his friends are leaving Count Onatorio Altamonte's house, Felix (ever keen to locate the right thing to venerate) asks his friend the circus performer Frau Mann whether Altamonte is 'really a Count?' prompting the response: '"*Herr Gott!*" said the Duchess! "Am I what I say? Are you? Is the doctor?" She put a hand on his knee. "Yes or no?"' (Barnes 21).

Felix spies a chance to 'make a destiny for himself' (40), and thereby to locate himself in culture, by marrying a young American woman, Robin Vote. Reflecting that he had anticipated that making a destiny would require 'laborious and untiring travail' (40), he decides that 'with Robin it seemed to stand before him without effort' (40). This perception is fuelled by his belief that 'with an American anything can be done' (37). Cheryl Plumb's manuscript work reveals that Robin was initially imaged as an orphan (Plumb 192), and I would argue that in this alliance two contrasting tropes of orphanhood meet (at least in Felix's imagination). The search for origins meets the self-fashioning narrative: a moment which Felix misconstrues as offering an easy resolution to his complex narrative of origins. It is also a moment at which the orphan narrative meets the narrative of nationhood.

When Felix first sees Robin, she is surrounded by luxuriant foliage, in the miniature Eden she has constructed in her hotel room in Paris (Barnes 33–5):[17] a moment which, by implication, allows Felix to vicariously access the myth of the American Adam: the protagonist of his own American Dream fantasy. It is an interesting moment because the fantasy permits access to an alternative myth of origins, in which there is no burdensome past.[18] It is as though the 'fantastic museum' in the 'poetry' of Felix's past has been replaced by a *tabula rasa*. As with Bachelard's discussion of the first house, there is a tension between the imaginative and the empirical. Felix's image of Robin is shown to be no more than 'a stop the mind makes between uncertainties' (Barnes 93), the marriage based on illusion can only fail, and Robin leaves Felix, soon after their son (who is also called Guido: a naming which underscores recurrence) is born.

When the narrative returns to Felix, some years later, he drinks heavily, is still obsessed with the 'great past' and observes that Guido 'does not grow up' (Barnes 101) At this point, it may appear that Felix has failed in his attempts to find peace. However, a closer interrogation reveals that Felix has constructed his own kinship structure, through his care for his son and his companionate relationship with the circus performer Frau Mann. Although described by the narrator as an 'odd trio' seen in 'many cafés' (103), the three of them form an effective social unit capable of warmth and care. This care is illustrated in their return to Felix's native city: 'Felix rode into Vienna, the child beside him, Frau Mann, opulent and gay, opposite, holding a rug for the boy's feet' (103). The chapter closes with an act of gentleness, as Felix rubs oil on Guido's cold hands. The physical closeness of this scene contrasts with the longing piqued by the circus as 'a loved thing which he could never touch' (11). Felix has finally found kinship: through his relationships with Guido and Frau Mann, he has resolved what Talia Schaffer calls the orphan's 'devastatingly dangerous isolation' (170). Felix's final acts of solicitous care once more recall the trope of the healing orphan seen in *Jane Eyre*. Unlike Jane, however, the sense of peace and cultural place Felix finds is not in the private domestic domain, but in interpersonal relations played out in the metropolitan spaces of Vienna. This is appropriate since throughout the novel Felix's identity is performed in the public spaces of European cities: we have little perception of his domestic setting, a point that underscores the extent to which his identity, as cultural orphan, is defined in and by the gaze of others. Nonetheless, Felix has managed to create a sense of home on the public stage, in the city of his birth.

The orphan's complex negotiations between inheritance and self-fashioning seen in Djuna Barnes's *Nightwood* are also at issue in Linda Grant's *When I Lived in Modern Times* (2000). The narrative opens with Evelyn Sert's arrival in Mandatory Palestine, then an analepsis traces her early years in Soho, as a prelude to a closer focus on her time in Palestine: a place where she hopes to create an identity liberated from the burden of the past and released from dissimilation (much as Felix hoped to reinvent himself in marriage). Inevitably, this process does not play out as Evelyn intended: she is expelled from Palestine as the British leave and the state of Israel is born. The novel closes with an older Evelyn, who has returned many years later, to the flat that she rented in the White City of Tel Aviv, still in search of a sense of home.

Evelyn was born in an institution for 'wayward women of the Jewish faith' (Grant 7), which 'suppl[ied] the contents of the cots at the Norwood orphanage' (7). Her mother had been in love with an American (Arthur Bergson), and he had gone home without ever returning and fulfilling his promise to marry her. Evelyn 'suppose[s] he never knew that he had a daughter somewhere in the world' (5). Even worse, when she asks her mother to tell her about him, Evelyn gains only the briefest of commentaries, (8) which reveals little more than the photograph of her parents in Trafalgar Square, taken in 1923 (5). Evelyn considers that this is remarkable, observing that: 'I had a Jewish father with the shortest story in the world' (8) emphasising the importance of narrative inheritance for diasporic peoples.

Orphaned from her father, born in an institution, and travelling to a new land to re-fashion herself, Evelyn bears many of the stamps of nineteenth-century orphanhood. In especial, Laura Peters argues that poor nineteenth-century orphans could be migrated by the Parish to cleanse the family and thereby also spread the imperial seed (79–121). Middle-class orphans might voluntarily migrate to escape the stigma of illegitimacy, often associated with orphanhood. Evelyn migrates on the prompting of 'Uncle Joe', her mother's lover and benefactor. Her mother 'came to the attention' of Uncle Joe at the home (Grant 5), and she became his mistress. He set her up in a hairdressing business and funded Evelyn's convent school education (on the grounds of its high quality, not as an attempt to convert her). After the death of her mother, the salon is sold, 'Uncle Joe' checks that Evelyn has no other ties in the UK, suggests she travels to Palestine and gives her some of the sale proceeds to make the journey. Although she considers this very generous, she is uncertain of his underlying motivation, and wonders whether this should be read as an expression of his Zionism, or of his desire to 'get rid of' (26) her, by removing her from London and hence from his wife and family, comfortably settled in the Hampstead Garden Suburb. Both possibilities (and the circumstances of her birth) evoke nineteenth-century practices, although the role of the Parish has been replaced by a wealthy individual, who is interested in his own pleasure, not moral containment.

Evelyn's access to 'home' is repeatedly problematised from the moment of her birth. As the child of a single woman, she narrowly escapes the orphanage by virtue of Uncle Joe's interest in her mother. Since it appears that the financial security of mother and daughter is dependent upon Uncle Joe's generosity (despite the fact that her mother works hard to run her hairdressing business), both carefully manage their interactions with the man. Evelyn notes that her mother 'learned the arts of a minor courtesan' (8), in a way which both 'fascinated and appalled' (9) her daughter. Evelyn comments on her own relationship with him:

> Was he like a father to me, Uncle Joe? Well, we sized one another up and he saw me as the child he had to keep in with if he wanted the mother, and I saw him as someone to manipulate for my own ends, for God knows, my mother was incapable of manipulating anyone. (Grant 9)

This sharp awareness of the transactional nature of relationships is borne out of Evelyn's orphanhood, and accompanies her throughout her life. She grows up in Soho, a place which she frames as a tolerant space of many 'little colonies' (11). Her mother does not have to try to 'avoid unwanted attention' as 'an unmarried mother with a child', because in Soho, 'it was acceptable to be different, it was *normal*' (11; emphasis original). The language is important as, although she thinks that some of the other inhabitants 'felt sorry for us at Christmas' (9), she nevertheless feels a sense of empathy and heterogeneous kinship. This scene of cultural diversity is complemented by the family (hi)stories of Poland and Latvia that her mother and Uncle Joe tell, which complicate and laminate the notion of home, and develop Evelyn's awareness of the importance of narrative in shaping identity, especially for migrants. She observes that:

I was looking around to find out who exactly I was. In the end, all I had to know myself by was a fragment of something and I was trying to find out what was the main whole it had broken off from.

It turned out that the fragment was part of a story. I was part of a grand narrative that had started before I was ever born. (Grant 10–11)

Evelyn's search for identity is initially driven by her paternal orphanhood, but as she grows older and begins to understand that she is part of a 'grand narrative', in a sense then, she begins to see herself self-reflexively as an orphan in narrative terms also. This is also the point at which her sense of her orphanhood is complicated by her gender and her Jewishness. Both of which, in differing ways, also make her a cultural orphan, and recall Felix's experiences. In this context then, the lack of her father's story accentuates her sense of bereavement, and complements her sense of self as a fragment 'broken off [or orphaned] from' the grand narrative.

Uncle Joe's propagandistic narratives of a Zionist homeland in Palestine are also woven into her early years, and become intertwined with her sense of self, to create an imaginary homeland, in effect creating a fantastic narrative of 'the poetry of the past'. Thus, on her birthday, 'Uncle Joe pushed through the slot' in the box for the Jewish National Fund, which sits on the Sert's mantelpiece, 'a whole half a crown' (15). He explains that this is '"so [that] part of little Evelyn [. . .] will make things grow in the earth of the Jewish home"' (15). The phrasing of the sequence emphasises Uncle Joe's wealth and agency, the money penetrates the box in the women's home, implicitly stating his financial and sexual power in the household, although he does not live there. Since he insists that 'part of little Evelyn' will fertilise the homeland, 'pushing the money through the slot' might be read as an act of metaphorical generation, implying that his cash can father her in the Jewish homeland. It explains the origin of Evelyn's sense that she is, 'a daughter of the new Zion' (4), as she steps onto Palestinian soil at the opening of the novel. The annual ritual also causes Evelyn the child to imagine herself 'as a flower or a tree in the hands of some Jewish farmer' (16). This image, however, underscores her lack of agency, and hence her vulnerability: a pattern that I would argue is played out in a series of relationships with men, each new attraction causing her to redefine herself.

The trope of the imaginary homeland is complemented by her complex relationship to Britain. In tolerant Soho, she lives through the Blitz, an experience which involves her in an iconic British cultural moment. Conversely, she experiences anti-Semitism from the staff at the convent school. It is not, however, until her mother dies, and precipitates her migration, that Evelyn fully realises her cultural orphanhood. Walking from the Foreign Office, having been granted permission to travel to Palestine, Evelyn strolls into a stylised scene of Britishness, staged in the heart of London, its cultural significance distilled in the 'artful arrangement of cricketing paraphernalia in the window' (26) of Lillywhites. This is also, emphatically, an imperial moment, as she reaches St. James's Park she observes:

> I saw one [bird] rise from the water and take wing against the bare black twigs, and turning saw it fly over Buckingham Palace with the flag ripping against the wind to tell us that our King and Queen and princesses were at home. [. . .] The might of the British Empire was burnished in the frail sunshine of this morning in February 1946, when London had never looked lovelier. The grandeur and majesty of England *bore down on me*. (Grant 26; emphasis added)

The sequence appears to position Evelyn as a loyal subject, as she reflects on 'our' royal family and comments on the 'loveli[ness]' of the scene, although the predatory overtones of 'bore down on me' suggest that Evelyn feels culturally isolated. They also recall the narrator's description of Felix. Evelyn's sense of alienation develops as the walk continues and she attempts to 'feel' like the 'modest Christian girl' (26) that she 'appeared to be'[19]: it becomes clear that the gap between feeling and semblance is unbridgeable. This is the moment at which Evelyn becomes aware of her status as a cultural orphan, and she reflects that:

> Inside my head the Kings and Queens of England were stacked like pancakes in chronological order, going back to the Wars of the Roses but no-one I was related to had ever set foot on English soil until forty-five years ago. What could an immigrant child be except an impersonator? I felt like a double agent, a fifth columnist. And I knew that as long as I lived in this country it would always be exactly the same. I walked among them and they thought they knew me, but they understood nothing at all. It was *me* that understood, the spy in their midst. (Grant 27; emphasis original)

Evelyn's awareness of her difference resonates with Woolf's analysis of split consciousness, which is also catalysed by a walk in the city. Woolf remarks:

if one is a woman one is often surprised by a sudden splitting off of consciousness, say in walking down Whitehall, when from being the natural inheritor of that civilization, she becomes, on the contrary, outside of it, alien and critical. (*Room* 88)

It also recalls Laura Peters's observation that the orphan is 'of the nation but simultaneously outside it' (142).[20] Evelyn's response to her multi-valent orphanhood is to use the performance of Englishness, in order to migrate to Mandatory Palestine and to access her own cultural space, where she imagines that dissimulation would no longer be needed because she would be at home. She thinks of this as 'a place without artifice or sentiment, where life was stripped back to its basics, where things were fundamental and serious and above all modern' (Grant 1). This is why she poses as a Christian tourist, to gain access to 'the Holy Land', telling herself that: 'I had come to the place where no Jew need ever invent himself again or pretend to be someone he wasn't [. . .] We would cease to be composite characters' (30). For Evelyn, whose expectations have been coloured by Zionist propaganda, the 'new' city of Tel Aviv is the place where this authentic selfhood shall be revealed, not just for herself, but for all of the diasporic Jews who migrate there. This is an idealised vision of a kind of collective *tabula rasa*, a collective imaginary homeland, where cultural orphanhood is once and forever sloughed off. In this place the pamphlets tell her that 'the elemental nature of the Jew, stripped of the accents of a foreign language and its customs was going to reveal itself for the first time since the Exile' (30).

Evelyn's first impressions of Tel Aviv are rapturous, and it appears that she has found her imaginary homeland:

> I was in the newest place in the world, a town created for the new century by its political and artistic ideologues: the socialists and Zionists, the atheists and feminists who believed with a passion that it was the *bon ton* to be in the forefront of social progress and in a place where everything was new and everything was possible, including a kind of rebirth of the human spirit. (Grant 72)

Still informed by her idealist vision, heady with visions of the 'rebirth of the human spirit' (72), Evelyn chooses to live in a newly built apartment block, designed in the New Internationalist style. In its newness, the building resonates with her fantasy of the imaginary homeland: a fantasy of inheritance that she has projected into the future. However, her experience of living in the block emphasises that the past cannot be so easily escaped. A range of migrants, with sharply differing political views and cultural inheritances, inhabit the block. Her landlord is keen to accentuate, when she objects to his charging multiple fees, that there is no conceptual kinship between them. He remarks: 'as the saying goes among my circle. I did not come here from conviction. I came here from Germany. [. . .] I am not a socialist, but a capitalist' (88). While the Zionist rhetoric suggests homecoming, Evelyn's experiences suggest that a sense of kinship remains out of reach.

Like the inhabitants of Soho, the migrants have brought their 'little colonies' with them: unlike the inhabitants of Soho, their difference does not appear to be tolerant or harmonious, and it does not offer kinship opportunities. This is important on both personal and cultural levels: for Evelyn's orphanhood, and for the novel's reading of the emergent Israeli state. Evelyn's fantastic narrative of home and kinship, fuelled by her fantastic 'poetry of the past', is based on the yearning for the impossibly idealised hope of the *tabula rasa*. As with Felix's marriage to Robin, the orphan narrative of self-fashioning is shown to be an illusion. What she finds in her own experiences, in her apartment block, and by implication, throughout the country, is the accumulation of too many clashing and irreconcilable inheritances. Like the past, cultural orphanhood is not so easy to escape.

Thus, when Evelyn steps off the boat, she experiences not recognition and homecoming, but a scene of absolute difference, as she recognises none of the vegetation (2). The scene resonates with the experiences of other colonial settler cultures, and accentuates her sense of cultural orphanhood.[21] Later that day, she craves 'a *cup* of tea, made properly in a pot, with milk and two spoons of white sugar' (Grant 32; emphasis original). The initial lack of recognition, combined with the craving for sweet milky tea, marks her as stereotypically English, yet she considers herself disqualified from this kinship possibility also, observing: 'what kind of English girl doesn't look at a tree and know what type it is, by its bark or leaves? How could I be English, despite what was written on my papers?' (2). Ironically, Evelyn's lack of understanding that her image of the 'English girl' is not fully representative, but narrowly class-bound, and emphasises that she has limited knowledge of 'English girls': so the sequence doubly underscores her sense of cultural orphanhood. This sense of isolation and bereavement is then further developed as she is taken into the countryside, to work on a kibbutz:

> The city of Haifa receded and now we were driving north across stony ground, through what they later said were olive groves, to nothing I understood, though they kept on saying I was home now.
> Earth. Smells. Hills. Dust. I was speechless. (Grant 33)

The one-word sentences underscore the extent of Evelyn's perplexity, and the dislocation between her experiences and the 'the poetry of the past' in the fantastic narrative of the imaginary homeland that she had created for herself as cultural insulation. Salman Rushdie writes that:

> It may be that writers in my position, exiles or emigrants or expatriates, are haunted by some sense of loss, some urge to reclaim [ . . .] But if we do look back, we must also do so in the knowledge – which gives rise to profound uncertainties – that our physical alienation from India almost inevitably means that we will not be capable of reclaiming precisely the thing that was lost; that we will, in short, create fictions, not actual cities of villages, but invisible ones, imaginary homelands, Indias of the mind. (10)

Rushdie's analysis of the 'imaginary homeland' resonates with Evelyn's complex 'poetry of the past' and the fantasy of the Jewish homeland that it creates. However, Rushdie's awareness of the difficulty of 'reclaiming precisely the thing that was lost' is intensified in Evelyn's experience, as she attempts to gain access to a homeland which had only ever been imaginary. The disparity between her idealised vision and her lived experience underscores the difficulty of finding a cultural home, echoing Kuo Pao Kun's analysis that: 'Even if we were able to trace back and return to our respective cultural parentages, we would still not be at home in the past' (Kuo).

The 'home for wayward women', tolerant Soho, the earth of the Jewish home and the narratives of migrants, are interlaced in Evelyn's imagination to form a very potent kaleidoscopic image of the first house. The complexity of her inheritance colours her relationship to 'the poetry of the past'. She has observed that her mother changes their familial name to Sert, because it 'was brief' and 'did not seem to come from anywhere' (Grant 8), and thus eludes any invocation of kinship or association. Evelyn's decision to re-make herself as a 'daughter of the new Zion' (4) is an attempt to evade dissimulation and in this to liberate herself from the past. She rapidly discovers, however, that Mandatory Palestine is not the 'land without people for the people without land' (33) that the Zionist propaganda has led her to anticipate. Lulled into the expectation that she shall find home and kinship in this land where 'everything [is] Jewish' (16), she finds instead that her inheritance is more complex than she had supposed. Much as she rationally despises them as colonialists, she empathises emotionally with the British people living in Tel Aviv, not least as they share many formative (if rather stylised) experiences, having survived the Blitz in London.

Although Evelyn returns to her apartment in Tel Aviv at the end of the novel, it seems to me that the feeling of home and kinship remain just out of reach. Her illegitimacy and her orphan inheritance are still affecting her status, as she needs to produce her mother's marriage certificate, to prove her Jewishness, so that she may 'rest her bones in the Promised Land' (237), finding a home in death. There can be no certificate, as there was no marriage, so the female orphan's desire for cultural place is once more obstructed by gender codes. Evelyn resorts to hiring a private detective to 'search [. . .] the burial sites of the East end of London for the graves of my grandparents' (237) in an attempt to link herself to a kinship structure, and thereby grant herself a final home. Her daughter Naomi (who has become an academic), is also interested in the narrative of origins. Where Evelyn hoped that Zionism would give her access to this, Naomi considers Zionism to be an imperialist project, and seeks instead to trace the family's past in Latvia. The quest for origins seems to be infinitely deferred for them both however, in a manner which recalls Deleuze and Guattari's idea of the rhizome they are: 'always in the middle, between things, interbeing, *intermezzo*' (27; emphasis original).[22] A sense of identity in progress is neatly coded in Evelyn's observation that when she reached Palestine:

> I felt like was a chrysalis, neither bug nor butterfly, something in between, closed, secretive and inside some great transformation under way as the world itself – in that strangest of eras just after the war was over – was metamorphosing into something else, which was neither the war, nor a return to what had gone before. (Grant 2–3)

Although Evelyn imagines that the state which was 'neither the war, nor a return to what had gone before' would be the brave new world of the daughter of Zion, the wider span of the novel suggests that homecoming in its fullest sense is eluded, and that this metamorphic condition persists, as interbeing. For Evelyn and for her daughter Naomi, what stands in place of a fully articulated sense of home, is an awareness of interconnection with the ever-developing past, and with female inheritance.[23] For, while the novel explores the implications of paternal absence, Evelyn has access to her mother's stories, at least until they are lost to illness, and these are then more formally accessed by Naomi's Latvian research, or the search Evelyn commissions for her grandparents' graves, as the orphaned daughter gains formal access to the past.

'Home', then, becomes not a static construct, but one which is informed by 'the poetry of the past' and which is, like T. S. Eliot's conceptualisation of an organic poetic tradition, always open to new modulations. So, although neither Evelyn nor Naomi can be at home in the past, in Kuo Pao Kun's terms, opening a conversation with the past can give them access to an imaginative home, which they may share. This is in some ways akin to Nina Auerbach's analysis that 'we have made of the orphan himself [. . .] our only ancestor' (416) as they settle themselves in the awareness that the quest for origins must remain open ended. Evelyn plays on this as she ironically remarks of the climate in Tel Aviv: 'being a Latvian, I'll never get used to this damned climate' (Grant 260). Latvia is a place that Evelyn only knows from her mother's stories, and even her mother was not born there. At this point, we might recall Frau Mann's comment: 'am I what I say, are you?' (21) or Pound's 'there is nothing [. . .] in the whole and all that's quite your own,/ Yet this is you' (34).

And yet: Auerbach's comment can also be contextualised in relation to the history of the novel, which persistently returns to orphan-figures, to examine the ways in which subjectivity is structured. In the recurrent analysis of fracture and disconnection, the orphan figure stands as a constantly changing reference point, which yet creates a sense of interconnectivity and literary kinship across the long development of the novel. As Isobel Armstrong reminds us, the novel form maintains a scepticism for the grounds of genealogical 'inclusion' and 'exclusion' (8). Perhaps then, 'the poetry of the past' (Bachelard 16) as teased out in the orphan novel, allows for a collective fantasy of loss, and in this, the recurrent possibility of recovery.

## Notes

1. See Isobel Armstrong's *Novel Politics* for a broader discussion of nineteenth-century genealogy.
2. See the Djuna Barnes special issue of the *Review of Contemporary Fiction*, 13: 3 (1993), *Silence and Power*, or more recently, Daniella Caselli's *Djuna Barnes' Bewildering Corpus*. Joseph Allen Boone is

one of the few critics to comment more extensively on orphans in *Nightwood*, although for Boone, this forms part of a wider reading of the work's queer poetics.
3. Readings of Felix's Jewishness have tended to focus on the extent to which it may or may not be read as anti-Semitic or as a way of ventriloquising lesbian history. See the work of Meryl Altman, Lara Trubowitz, Karen Kaivola, Mairéad Hanrahan or my discussion of the critical reception of *Nightwood* (*Djuna Barnes* 124–7).
4. For a thoughtful analysis of the concept of the new, see Jed Rasula's 'Make it New'.
5. As Peters notes, in the nineteenth century, a child might be deemed orphan on the death of one parent (1).
6. In work by Ian Watt, Nina Auerbach, Christine van Boheemen and Isobel Armstrong, among others.
7. For example, Diana Pazicky explores the ways in which indigenous American peoples became culturally orphaned.
8. Charles Bernstein notes the established nature of secular Jewish culture: 'my children go to a Jewish camp for those who have no religious Jewish beliefs, a camp with a seventy five year history of secular Jewish commitment' (12).
9. Since Jewish inheritance follows the maternal line, he would not necessarily have been seen as a Jew in orthodox terms.
10. Bachelard argues that the image of the house is not one of precise detail, but accessible instead through a meditative state. The manner in which the image resists detailed representation recalls Freud's sense of the dream's navel: a point beyond interpretation. The resonance between the two underscores the extent to which the imaginative idea of the first house exists in a pre-conscious state as a very early image of home.
11. Portraits are a recurrent trope in nineteenth-century narratives, and often provide clues as to the orphan's true identity. *Nightwood*'s portraits, by contrast, point to the constructed nature of discourses of origin.
12. Michael D. Schmidt reads a related sequence, discussing Nora's flat as a 'museum of her encounter with Robin' as evidence of *Nightwood*'s exploration of commodity capitalism (108), arguing that once inside the museum, objects lose their radical potential and become 'ossif[ied]'(108). I shall argue that in Felix's case the objects he inherits function as emblems of intimacy and inscribe his yearning for kin and community. Although he is offered money for the portrait of his 'grandmother', he refuses to sell it because he is emotionally attached to it, not because the price is too low (98).
13. Michael D. Schmidt argues that in this sequence creates 'social attachment' between Felix and the circus performers (115). I would argue however that, although his identification with the circus performers is apparent, they still function as emblems of loss and longing at this point. Since they remain as visual indicators only, they cannot satisfy

Felix's need for belonging and cannot therefore resolve his sense of orphan isolation. The visual nature of the connection parallels both the portrait of Felix's grandmother, and his reflections on his lack of understanding of Robin as merely 'an image' (93). I would argue that Felix craves tactile consensual intimacy, not merely the spectacle of intimacy. Later in the work, and as a parent, he understands that Robin had not wanted to be with him- (although she had remained silent on the topic), as he notes that "she is with me in Guido, they are inseparable, and this time' the Baron said, catching his monocle, 'with her full consent" (99). The catching of the monocle prefigures Felix's paternal care in rubbing oil into his son's hands at their last appearance in the novel.
14. Judith Butler's analysis of the repurposing of terms like 'queer' and 'nigger' underscores the difficulty inherent in recuperatory processes. Butler asks: 'can the term overcome its constitutive history of injury? Does it present the occasion for a powerful and compelling fantasy of historical reparation?' (223). For Butler, attempts to repurpose 'nigger' are 'capable only of reinscribing its pain' (223). Similarly, Felix remains trapped in his anxiety.
15. Arnold Schoenberg's experiences of Viennese life reflect the dominant culture's refusal to accept Jewish conversions to Christianity. As a composer he was lauded in the city, and yet he was unable to spend the summer of 1921 with his family at Mattsee (a resort near Vienna), because he was perceived as a Jew, despite his conversion to Christianity (MacDonald 60). Schoenberg's experiences reflect the narrator's failure to accept Guido's 'adop[tion]' of Christianity (5): he remains a cultural orphan, as he is represented as 'a Jew' throughout, despite all of his attempts to change his cultural location and to create alternative kinship structures.
16. Armstrong correctly observes that genealogy tends to trace the patriarchal line: this is also the case in *Nightwood*. There is an irony here, however, as it is this practice which marks Felix as Jewish in terms of the dominant Christian perspective, expressed by the narrative voice. For orthodox Jews, inheritance flows through the female line, implying that Felix would not necessarily be Jewish from that perspective. I would argue, however, that the narrator's insistence on Felix and Guido's Jewishness acts to focus attention on the process of cultural orphaning and abjection, which has little care for the status of the other.
17. See Michael D. Schmidt's chapter for a very engaging analysis of the intertextual interpretation of this passage.
18. This resonates with Evelyn Sert's fantasy of new beginnings in Mandatory Palestine: where Felix tries to access the fantasy through marriage, Evelyn envisages rebirth.
19. There is a further irony here as Evelyn borrows Catholic Christian paraphernalia (a cross and rosary beads) from her friend Gabriella,

without realising that these mark not kinship with, but difference from the Church of England.
20. Evelyn's assessment that she is an 'impersonator' recalls Luce Irigaray's analysis of the subversive potential of mimicry: 'To play with mimesis is thus, for a woman, to try to recover the place of her exploitation by discourse, without allowing herself to be simply reduced to it' (Irigaray 76).
21. Evelyn's bewilderment in the face of the vegetation recalls Les A. Murray's poetic explorations of Scottish settlers in Australia.
22. The way in which the search for origins complicates all sense of a recoverable origin is also put into play in the textual apparatus which surrounds T. S. Eliot's *The Waste Land*, which directs the diligent reader to *From Ritual to Romance*. Rather than provide an origin *per se*, however, Weston's text offers a number of possible origins for the mythical material and the sense of origins retreats into the very distant past, rather as Freud employs the image of the navel, to explore the point at which the dream goes beyond interpretation (*The Interpretation of Dreams*).
23. Much as Woolf famously argues that 'a woman writing thinks back through her mothers' (*Room* 88).

## Works Cited

Altman, Meryl. 'A book of repulsive Jews?: Rereading *Nightwood*'. *The Review of Contemporary Fiction*, vol. 13, no. 3, 1993, pp. 160–71.

Armstrong, Isobel. *Novel Politics: Democratic Imaginations in Nineteenth-Century Fiction*. Oxford University Press, 2016.

Auerbach, Nina. 'Incarnations of the Orphan'. *ELH*, vol. 42, no. 3, 1975, pp. 395–419. http://www.jstor.org/stable/2872711 (accessed 10 September 2016).

Bachelard, Gaston. *The Poetics of Space*. Trans. Maria Jolas. Beacon Press, 1994.

Barnes, Djuna. *Nightwood: The Original Version and Related Drafts*, ed. Cheryl J. Plumb. Dalkey Archive Press, 1995.

Beauvoir, Simone de. *The Second Sex*. Trans. H. M. Parshley. Picador, 1988.

Bernstein, Charles. 'Radical Jewish Culture/Secular Jewish Practice'. *Radical Poetics and Secular Jewish Culture*, ed. Stephen Paul Miller and Daniel Morris. University of Alabama Press, 2010, pp. 12–17.

Boheemen, Christine van. *The Novel as Family Romance: Language, Gender and Authority from Fielding to Joyce*. University of Tulsa Press, 1987.

Boone, Joseph Allen. *Libidinal Currents: Sexuality and the Shaping of Modernism*. University of Chicago Press, 1998.

Broe, Mary Lynn (ed.). *Silence and Power: A Reevaluation of Djuna Barnes*. Southern Illinois Press, 1991.

Butler, Judith. *Bodies that Matter: On the Discursive Limits of 'Sex'*. Routledge, 1993.

Caselli, Daniela. *Improper Modernism: Djuna Barnes's Bewildering Corpus*. Ashgate, 2009.

Deleuze, Gilles and Guattari, Félix. *A Thousand Plateaus: Capitalism and Schizophrenia*. Trans. Brian Massumi. Athlone Press, 1987.

Eliot, T. S. 'Tradition and the Individual Talent', in *A Modernist Reader: Modernism in England, 1910–1930*, ed. Peter Faulkner. Batsford, 1986, pp. 84–90.

Grant, Linda. *When I Lived in Modern Times*. Granta, 2011.

Hanrahan, Mairéad. 'Djuna Barnes's *Nightwood*: The Cruci-Fiction of the Jew'. *Paragraph*, vol. 24, no. 1, 2001, pp. 32–49.

Irigaray, Luce, 1985. *This Sex Which is Not One*. Trans. Catherine Porter. Cornell University Press, 1985.

Kaivola, Karen. 'The "beast turning human": Constructions of the "Primitive" in *Nightwood*'. *The Review of Contemporary Fiction*, vol. 13, no. 3, 1993, pp. 172–85.

Kuo Pao Kun. Excerpt from: *Images at the Margins: A Collection of Kuo Pao Kun's Plays (1983–1992)*, trans. Teo Han Wue. Times Books International, 1995. http://kuopaokun.com/pdf/kpk-thoughts-orphans.pdf (accessed 27 April 2018).

MacDonald, Malcolm. *Schoenberg*. Oxford University Press USA, 2008. http://ebookcentral.proquest.com/lib/portsmouth-ebooks/detail.action?docID=415745 (accessed 28 April 2018).

Pazicky, Diana Loercher. *Cultural Orphans in America*, University Press of Mississippi, 2008. http://ebookcentral.proquest.com/lib/portsmouth-ebooks/detail.action?docID=680056 (accessed 24 April 2018).

Peters, Laura. *Orphan Texts: Victorian Orphans, Culture and Empire*. Manchester University Press, 2000.

Plumb, Cheryl. 'Textual Notes', in *Nightwood: The Original Version and Related Drafts*, ed. Plumb. Dalkey Archive Press, 1995, pp. 187–210.

Pound, Ezra. 'Portrait d'une Femme'. *Selected Poems 1908–1969*. Faber, 1977, p. 34.

Rasula, Jed. 'Make it New'. *Modernism/modernity*, vol .17, no. 4, 2010, pp. 713–33. Rushdie, Salman. 'Imaginary Homelands'. *Imaginary Homelands : Essays and Criticism 1981–1991*. Granta/Penguin, 1992, pp. 9–21.

Schaffer, Talia. *Romance's Rival: Familiar Marriage in Victorian Fiction*. Oxford University Press, 2016.

Schmidt, Michael D. '*Nightwood* as a Way of Life: Queer Aesthetics, Capital, and Sociality'. *Feminist Modernist Studies*, vol. 2, no. 1, 2019, pp. 104–20, DOI: 10.1080/24692921.2019.1573785 (accessed 26 March 2019).

Schorske, Carl, E. *Fin-de-Siècle Vienna: Politics and Culture*. Cambridge University Press, 1992.

Slezkine, Yuri. *The Jewish Century*. Princeton University Press, 2006.

Spector, Scott. 'The Habsburg Empire', in *The Cambridge Guide to European Modernism*, ed. Pericles Lewis. Cambridge University Press, 2011, pp. 52–74.

Trubowitz, Lara. 'In Search of "the Jew" in Djuna Barnes's *Nightwood*: Jewishness, Anti-Semitism, Structure and Style'. *MFS*, vol. 51, no. 2, 2005, pp. 311–34.

Warren, Diane. *Djuna Barnes' Consuming Fictions*. Ashgate, 2008.

Watt, Ian. *The Rise of the Novel*. University of California Press, 2001.

Woolf, Virginia. 'Modern Fiction', in *A Modernist Reader: Modernism in England, 1910–1930*, ed. Peter Faulkner. Batsford, 1986, pp. 105–11.

Woolf, Virginia. 'Mr Bennett and Mrs Brown', in *A Modernist Reader: Modernism in England, 1910–1930*, ed. Peter Faulkner. Batsford, 1986, pp. 112–28.

Woolf, Virginia. *A Room of One's Own*, in *A Room of One's Own and Three Guineas*, by Virginia Woolf. Penguin, 1993, pp. 3–116.

Chapter 11

# 'Something worse than the past in not being yet over':[1] Elizabeth Bowen's Orphans, Exile and the Predicaments of Modernity

*Ann Rea*

Like ghosts,[2] orphans in Elizabeth Bowen's fiction represent what domesticity and the family cannot accommodate, whether in Anglo-Ireland, upper-middle-class England or wartime London. Laden with a variety of simultaneous meanings, these orphans are distilled remnants of the persistent past, evidence of repressed family scandal, often the result of uncontrolled sexual passion, and often of a family's lack of control over women's sexuality. In Bowen's short stories the misunderstood past emerges as ghosts: in the novels it persists as orphans.[3] While literary orphans throughout the nineteenth century signalled change, breaks from tradition and disconnections from the community that provoked moral confusion, Bowen's orphans drift in modernity, severed from a troubling past, even while serving as symbols of it, while they struggle with disjunctions from not only cultural history and family traditions, but also because the future is uncertain. Reading Elizabeth Bowen's many central orphan protagonists in the post-colonial context allows us to see that they embody her sense that the early twentieth century consists of historical and temporal traumas in Ireland and in England. This chapter will also argue that modernity's reluctance to acknowledge the past, in the eagerness to make everything new, appears for Bowen in her depictions of orphans who stand for unassimilated aspects of the past.

Whether adults or children, Bowen orphans metonymically represent disruptions of links with the past by being the last in the line of their family amidst the dispossession that typifies the experience of modernity. For modern Anglo-Irish Bowen, history's movement severs people from their tradition yet persists in repressed memory in ghosts, heirlooms and in the figure of the orphan, disconnected from the past, and yet powerless over the future. The Anglo-Irish people, in general, come to seem orphaned in the post-colonial era, as in *The Last September* where the protagonist, orphan Lois, becomes the distillation of the predicament of her extended family's orphanhood, and the orphanhood of her extended family, class and ancestors. At the end of the novel she is at art school in Paris while Danielstown, the Big House, burns to the ground. This severance of Anglo-Irish ties to Ireland invalidates their culture, and obliterates their social and political authority: they become historical remnants. Lois is a vestige of her class and culture, whose geographical upheaval means she has no home country. Disconnection from the family's, colonials' and culture's past appears in Bowen to be the central predicament of modernity, even beyond Anglo-Ireland, with many of her protagonists showing ignorance of even their country's recent past, such as Louie in *The Heat of the Day* (1948), who cannot remember how the Second World War started even though she lives in its midst. Similarly, Portia in *The Death of the Heart* (1938), grows up without knowing about her family's history. Severance from family homes entails severance from family and cultural history, and post-colonial exile, and increasingly, throughout her fiction, Bowen characters have to leave their homes. Increasingly, Bowen seems to embrace the dislocation of modernity, preferring the uncertainty in disinheritance and deracination to the false certainties that modernity can also offer. Nels C. Pearson observes, 'Bowen heroines are usually in process of negotiating belonging relative to one or more adoptive families, past affiliations, or foreign communities, and they are just as likely to cherish separation from these as to seek attachments' (324–5). As Pearson suggests, the separation and re-negotiation of connections are intricately tied, with separation paradoxically providing the context in which to forge new connections. Consideration of Bowen's central orphan protagonists' representation throughout her career therefore allows a deeper understanding of her fiction and is itself a commentary on the experience of the predicaments of modernity and the post-colonial era.

Emblematic of modern turmoil in Ireland, and suburbanising or wartime England, orphans in Bowen resemble her ghosts who demand that other characters confront their century's traumas and upheavals.[4] This chapter will consider the orphan protagonists in four Bowen novels, each of whom exemplifies specific predicaments of modernity that were important to their author: Lois in *The Last September* (1929), who stands metonymically for the orphanhood of the Anglo-Irish people as a whole, faces an uncertain future as her aunt and uncle, and the Anglo-Irish generally, confront exile and loss of their Big House culture. Leopold in *The House in Paris* (1935) and his cousin Henrietta are both orphans and wait at the house in Paris for Leopold's mother's arrival, which never happens. Leopold is the illegitimate offspring of his mother's illicit passion for Jewish Max, and his birth is unacknowledged, openly at least, by his mother's family, who give him up for adoption. Critics[5] have noted that in 1934 these parentless children moving around Europe, one of whom has a Jewish parent, suggest the growing numbers of refugees and orphans as political extremism increases. After her mother's death, Portia in *The Death of the Heart* (1938) goes to live with her modern brother Thomas and his wife Anna, who typify Bowen characters who are, as Hermione Lee observes, 'people disinherited from a past rich in emotions and certainties, and prisoners to a future which requires "genius" to be lived in at all.'[6] If modernity sought to break with the past, the price was the atrophy of the feelings the past would evoke, as Thomas and Anna show, in their quest for elegant respectability that Thomas's lower-middle-class orphan step-sister Portia threatens, in part because she was the result of his father's infidelity. *The Heat of the Day*'s (1948) Louie, shows a different aspect of the predicament of modernity. Orphaned when her parents died during the Battle of Britain, Louie is left unmoored in wartime London lacking the history and rootedness that a family would have provided. Because of her ignorance of the recent past, she is particularly susceptible to wartime propaganda as morally and historically deracinated.

Most of Bowen's fiction's protagonists are orphans and each one represents particular version of modernity's difficulties.[7] The fact that her fiction portrays so many orphans may depend on the fact that Bowen herself became an orphan after leaving Ireland and her mentally ill father, to spend, as Selena Hastings describes, 'a peripatetic period alone with her mother in a series of rented houses; then her mother died when she was thirteen after which she was brought up by what she always referred to as "a committee of aunts"'.[8] Bowen insisted that her childhood was happy, and that she enjoyed the independence of boarding school although, as Victoria Glendinning observes, 'One of the words at which her stammer consistently baulked was "mother"' (28). She left behind Bowen's Court, the family Big House, when the Anglo-Irish lost their political and social power with Irish independence in 1922, and became exiles, either in Ireland or abroad, with many of their houses burnt to the ground. Bowen's own Anglo-Irish post-colonial sense of exile extends into the fiction that takes place elsewhere, written after she left Ireland, but nevertheless carries over this sense of what Sinéad Mooney observes when she says that Bowen's ghosts, 'thrive on and colonize a modern world perceived as fractured, dislocated, precarious' (78). The sense of instability in modernity applies equally to her orphans and to her ghosts, and indeed amid the tumult of modern experience, the orphan is the exemplary modern protagonist.

The loss of family, culture and home requires a renegotiation of belonging and meaning that becomes existential, amidst which orphans also, although sometimes unwittingly, disruptively reassert the past that others try to forget or wish to keep secret, even as they simultaneously end the family line. Bowen lost her home, her culture and community, as well as her mother, and then lived in wartime London, with the growing sense that exile and deracination were typical of modernity. And although Bowen is not from the oral peasant culture that David Lloyd describes, his account of the uncanny vestiges of pre-colonial Ireland that persisted after colonisation helps explain Bowen's fascination with the domestic uncanny and orphans. Recalling that the German *'heimlich'* or 'homely' is the antithesis of *'unheimlich'* or 'uncanny', we can see how orphans, vestigial and supplementary to the family, are like the 'spectres' that Lloyd describes:

> Its [the uncanny's] potentials are not the petrified remainders of economic and social forces that have consigned them to irrelevance if not oblivion, but unsubsumed resources for alternative imaginaries, drawn not from abstract principles but from the damages and disregarded forms of useless life. (18)

The 'damages' of the past produce these 'disregarded' residues, orphans or ghosts, holding repressed memory, serving as persistent evidence of what must be excluded from the family, the home, and the tradition. Lloyd's uncanny represents, '"something that one does not know one's way about in"', but that '"leads back to what is known of old and long familiar"', and is therefore both known, on some level, as part of the family's repressed memory, but also ignored (63). Both uncanny figures, in this respect, the orphan and the ghost are also unhomely in their incomplete assimilation into the families that inherit them. Lloyd continues,

> For ghosts are not merely the tattered remnants of our unpacified history, the unquiet afterbirths of our unpacified history. They may also represent the survival, in unexpected times and places, of unexhausted possibilities, of potentials that exceed the confines of common sense or verisimilitude. (50)

Similarly, Bowen's orphans and ghosts signify what might have happened in a family, its rejected possibilities, thereby threatening to disturb the family's peace. Leopold, for example, in *The House in Paris*, is kept out of sight in Italy with his adoptive parents because of his illegitimate birth. When his mother, Karen, fell in love with Max and conceived Leopold while each of them was engaged to someone else, her family deemed continuation of their relationship as an affront to many social decencies, not least because Max is Jewish. The result is Max's suicide, and since acknowledgement of Leopold as legitimate is socially impossible, Karen marries her fiancé, and Leopold is brought up by adoptive parents.

Leopold then symbolises a betrayal of friendship and social proprieties, even miscegenation, as well as Karen's infidelity and uncontrolled sexuality, and he also embodies the 'unexhausted possibilit[y]' of the passion that Karen and Max could never realise. Instead of acknowledging the 'vestige' Leopold, Karen's family is determined to shake off the past he evokes, which shame he continues to embody. Under this enormous weight of meaning that others see in him, there is little room for his own agency. Leopold evokes the 'mysteries of birth' marking the past as complex and troubling social propriety, evoking shame and guilt, like Lloyd's reference to the 'unquiet afterbirths of our unpacified history' (50). *The Death of the Heart*'s Portia and *The House in Paris*'s Leopold, both conceived outside marriage, symbolise their mothers' scandalous, unruly sexuality. Similarly, Lois, in *The Last September,* evokes her mother's 'liveliness,' a word that implies inadequately contained sexuality, of which she serves as a reminder, in part because of her resemblance to her mother. So like Lois, Portia and Leopold thwart their families' attempts to erase scandal from the past by serving as reminders of it.

The events that produced these orphans create unavoidable predicaments and disruption in the family's continuity. Orphans in Bowen's fiction are often passed to the care of other family members, like heirlooms, forcing these relatives to confront the 'unsubsumed' story behind the orphan, in Lloyd's words. As a result, the orphan often serves as an heirloom, even when he or she, as the last in the family's line, is also its heir. For *The Last September*'s orphan Lois, 1920s eviction of the Anglo-Irish Protestant Ascendancy from their Big Houses, with their loss of cultural and political authority in Ireland, ruptures ties to the past. Yet as the last of her family's line, Lois's main heirloom is the Ascendancy's lack of future. With only marriage or finishing school as options, she temporarily disposes of her future by engagement to English soldier Gerald, thereby gaining a brief 'sense of being located', as she thinks, in familial, cultural and psychic ties, as well as a home. The choice also means life in middle-class England, which evokes the 'fears of illegitimacy and miscegenation' which Laura Peters associates with orphans (Peters 143). Peters notes that, 'the presence of the orphan unsettles notions of belonging for both family and nation' (143). Lois, then, does not merely face an existential purposelessness because of her orphanhood, her gender and her class, but represents these threats to the Anglo-Irish people around her. Even this possible future is eradicated when Gerald dies in an IRA attack (171). On many levels Lois lacks agency: her gender compounds her predicament since, as a woman and a pseudo-aristocrat, her role in life is to arrange the flowers, marry someone from her own background and do little else. Although her cousin Laurence, a student at Cambridge, seems equally purposeless, he can be excused as an 'intellectual'. Laurence thinks,

> Today four weeks, Term would have begun again: [. . .] there was nothing for *her* to go on with. [ . . . H]e suggested she should go on with her German. He gave her two grammars, a dictionary, and a novel of Mann's, which she took from him doubtfully. (161)

But Lady Naylor thwarts this makeshift purpose, observing that German, 'still offends so many people: Italian is prettier and more practical', suggesting art school instead (164). Lady Naylor prevents the marriage to Gerald to assert Anglo-Irish belief in their superiority to the English middle-class, at the time of heightened anxiety about the fragility of these distinctions as the Ascendancy class faces its demise. And while her guardians watch their Big House burning, Lois is already exiled by her aunt in Paris. Orphan Lois is, as Peters says of orphans generally, 'of the nation but simultaneously outside it', and her aunt prevents her from witnessing her historical deracination (142). The predicament of the loss of inheritance and the eradication of her people's future marks the experience of Bowen orphans.

In *The Death of the Heart*, Thomas and Anna Quayne inherit Thomas's step-sister, Portia, on her mother's death, although she embodies her father's social decline into vulgarity, which is anathema to elegant Thomas and Anna. Effectively, Portia will replace the child that they cannot have because of their infertility, an inability to carry on their lineage, which serves metaphorically to represent the ruptures in tradition and breaks with the past that Bowen sees in modernity. Portia's incomplete assimilation into Thomas's and Anna's affections exemplifies Bowen's orphans' objectification by the family members who inherit them. As Anna Teekell notes, in Bowen's fiction, 'The orphan child is the ultimate piece of baggage. [. . .] Leftover (in literary terms, perhaps, from the Gothic novel),[9] the orphan embodies at once the past and the future' (Teekell 148). The orphan becomes an object with singular tangibility as others impose their interpretations of what he or she means. Portia's repressed and eminently respectable step-brother Thomas and his wife Anna, her guardians since the death of her mother and father, would prefer to ignore her existence since she reminds them of the shame of Mr Quayne's infidelity, and Portia's mother's social inferiority.

As an object, defined by others, with little agency, and handed down as an heirloom, Portia becomes like the family's other objects, such as the furniture, which Matchett the housekeeper curates. As part of the tradition of the literary housekeeper as the repository of family secrets[10] in the Victorian fiction that Paula Krebs describes, Matchett attempts to rectify Portia's ignorance of the past, and thereby maintains the family history, telling Portia about the day she was born, for example, and encouraging Thomas and Anna to acknowledge Portia as a remnant from the past, and a connection to it. For Portia, Matchett's body is 'a vaseful of memory that must not be spilt', which places her among the old wives of folklore, those who retain culture from before 'rational' modern life, the repressed irrational, uncanny vestiges that modernity eschews (77). Like David Lloyd's uncanny pre-colonial traces, the past persists in the housekeeper's tales and superstition, or as Krebs says, 'the haunting of the Victorian middle classes by fear of the people they designated as 'the folk; [. . .] a cultural past that the English had transcended' (41). Anna and Thomas believe they are modern enough to ignore the vulgar past Portia embodies, that Matchett has maintained with the furniture. We even read that Matchett came into the household *with* the furniture, knowing the family guilt, and knowing what 'proper' moral actions would be. She strives to rectify Thomas's disconnection from the heart, urging that he and Anna acknowledge his father's infidelity, which in itself arose from the fact that he was 'all feeling' (80). Matchett tells orphan Portia about the heirloom furniture's metonymic ability to represent family memory, saying,

> Furniture's knowing all right. Not much gets past the things in a room, I daresay, and chairs and tables don't go to the grave so soon. Every time I take the soft cloth to that stuff in the drawing-room, I could say, 'Well you know a bit more'. [. . .] Unnatural living runs in a family, and the furniture knows it, you be sure. Good furniture knows what's what. [. . .] Oh, furniture like we've got is too much for some that would rather

not have the past. If I just had to look at it and have it looking at me, I'd go jumpy, I daresay. But when it's your work it can't do anything to you. Why, that furniture – I've been at it years and years with the soft cloth: I know it like my own face. (81)

Matchett sees the family memories – including the 'unnatural living [that] runs in a family' – stored in these fine pieces, which are heirlooms, like Portia. Supplementary and vestigial, orphans serve as objectified remnants of unadmitted responsibility from the past, simultaneously outside the family and yet irrevocably linked to it. When Leopold in *The House in Paris* is brought to Paris to meet his mother for the first time, he meets his cousin Henrietta, another orphan, who lives with her grandmother, having lost her mother and then been rejected by her father. She tells Leopold, '"we're children, people's belongings"', reiterating the idea of the orphan as an heirloom, and as baggage (55). Without agency, they are moved around like inanimate objects that, nevertheless, no one fully owns. Leopold says, '"No one knows I'm born"', suggesting that, with the exception of his sinister grandmother, his birth has been eradicated from his family's consciousness just as he has been exiled from his family and his country (54). What he and Henrietta lack, as objects, is the full assimilation into a family that creates belonging and ties of affinity that would connect them to a family's past and their feelings.

Matchett can provide access to the past for Portia. The uneasy intimacy between brusque and unsentimental Matchett and Portia relies on the fact that 'they talk about the past [ . . . t]heir great mutual past', that makes them 'so knit up' (311). She disparages Thomas and Anna's preference to 'not have the past' and observes, 'No wonder they don't rightly know what they're doing. Those without memories don't know what is what' (80). Matchett strives to overcome Thomas's and Anna's modern detachment from tradition and family memory, and detachment from ties of affinity to Portia, dismissing their 'airy, vivacious house', commenting, 'there was no place where shadows lodged, no point where feeling could thicken' (42). The past that she curates, like Lloyd's oral culture and Paula Krebs' old wives' tales, evokes the uncanny, dark residues of past scandal, like the adulterous affair that orphan Portia unwittingly embodies, even more unwelcome in modern, refined London. Like the furniture, and herself another kind of heirloom, Portia evinces her parents' passion and a threat to Thomas's respectability, against which he and Anna have deadened their modern, refined hearts. And while Thomas and Anna retain the heirloom furniture, the family's handed-down possessions, they do not fully 'own' them, leaving their care to Matchett, just as they have not fully developed ties to Portia, but merely shoulder some of the responsibility for her upkeep. In the midst of modern fervour for making everything new, Anna and Thomas prefer to accept their historical dispossession that Matchett allows by her maintenance of the heirlooms and her role in forging familial ties for Portia.

But when she learns of Portia's flight to Major Brutt's hotel, Matchett waits 'to see whether [Thomas and Anna] do the right thing', enforcing that Thomas and Anna behave with responsibility and moral propriety (304). Anna points out that Thomas cannot treat Matchett as a mere employee, but that 'Matchett stays with the furniture' and that Portia and the housekeeper must remain in the family, as a result of which Thomas confers on Matchett the power to bring Portia back (312). In so doing, Thomas appears willing to reintroduce the family's past into his house, and suggests a potential reconciliation with the family's history, and with feelings. The novel ends, '[Matchett] pushed on the brass knob [of Major Brutt's hotel] with an air of authority' that suggests she can assert Portia's importance to Thomas and Anna as a family member (318). Matchett privileges Portia's father's passion over the absence of feeling, saying, 'Mr. Quayne was all nature', while Mrs Quayne 'had no nature' (76). And although Anna concedes that Portia was '[T]he child of an aberration, the child of a panic, the child of an old chap's pitiful sexuality', she also observes that Portia, 'has inherited everything', while, ironically, Thomas and Anna seem disinherited (246). As the last of the family line and its heir, Portia has inherited little more than her parents' shame unless Thomas and Anna acknowledge her fully, with the family history she embodies, and their ties of affinity to her. To do so could return Anna and Thomas to feeling, revive their hearts, and introduce the past into their sterile modern lives, instead of perpetuating modernity's rupture with and disdain for the past. But the novel, typically for Bowen's orphan stories, leaves the ending undefined and without resolving its orphan's future.

*The House in Paris* ends with even less certainty about Leopold's future. When Henrietta childishly tries to read Leopold's fortune in his cards, the children wonder whether this will 'ma[ke] things happen', whether they have the power to discover the future, or change it. Like other Bowen orphans, Henrietta and Leopold lack agency over the future, instead passively being moved according to the strongest will around them. As Teekell comments, these novels leave their orphaned subjects on the verge of something happening' (151). Leopold's abandonment by his mother at the end, after which we assume that he will return to his adoptive parents, also signifies Karen's repudiation of her maternal responsibilities, even though Leopold's existence prevents a repression of those memories. While he and Henrietta wait in the house in Paris for Karen to arrive, Henrietta imagines Karen as embodying, '"every desire, not only his own"', suggesting the orphan's longed-for mother, one that Bowen may well have imagined herself (56). A rare moment of agency, if only in the imagination of a desire, it is thwarted because, poignantly, Karen never comes, in a refusal, or inability, to acknowledge or accept blame for the past. Like the *pharmakon,* of whom Laura Peters writes in the Introduction to *Orphan Texts*, Leopold serves as 'a promise and a threat, a poison and a cure' (Peters 2). Anathema, for the reminders he carries and the shame he symbolises, especially in Karen's husband's judgement of her, he might nevertheless catalytically create a reconciliation and healing if Karen had the moral determination to let this happen. Instead, she never arrives. As Anna Teekell observes, 'None of Bowen's orphan novels properly "answer" the question of the orphan at their centers' (150). Instead each orphan ends the novel in the midst of the specific predicament of their experience of modernity, and for each of them, orphanhood has severed ties to the nation.

Mr Quayne can perceive that Portia has 'grown up exiled not only from her own country but from *normal, cheerful* family life' [sic], seeing a profound connection between her orphaned exile from the family and from her country (15). Orphans have lost their ties to their nation in *The Last September, The Death of the Heart, The House in Paris* and *The Heat of the Day*. Portia and her parents wander in the colder, cheaper parts of the Riviera, a story similar to Bowen's own biography and her familial, historical and national dispossession. Like Lois in *The Last September,* Bowen was forced to embrace a cosmopolitanism[11] that replaced Anglo-Irishness, and resulted from her foreign travel with her mother and the demise of the Ascendancy class, leaving her with a rootless, orphaned nationality. But in the midst of the growing tide of nationalism in 1930s Europe, unspecified nationality might have seemed attractive. Modernity brought, variously, post-colonial exile for the Anglo-Irish, but also deracination and dispossession for the Second World War's refugees, whom Leopold evokes. And Louie in *The Heat of the Day* undergoes dispossession in her orphanhood, which the Blitz and war culture intensify until she finds in propaganda a more conventional version of femininity, and a means of inventing affinity ties and clear moral prescriptions.

As evidence of a different form of modern predicament, Louie becomes orphaned and evicted from her family's home by the war, losing her family, community and connection to the past, when her parents die in a bomb, 'wiped out during the Battle of Britain', becoming exemplarily susceptible to propaganda and war culture (13). Like Lois, Portia, Leopold and Henrietta, she is exiled from family life and by extension her country, because of the loss of historical memory that her family might have provided. With no sense of the past, she absorbs the Ministry of Information's messages uncritically, coming to represent an alarming example of the effects of modernity's severance from the past. Oblivious to even recent history, she has, 'with regard to time, an infant lack of stereoscopic vision; she saw then and now on the same plane; they were the same. To her everything seemed to be going on at once' (15). Louie's modern, kaleidoscopic, synchronic perception of time collapses the past and the present, effectively removes her agency in a war culture which offers moral certainty and the law's patriarchal restraint of new legislation, to replace family tradition. Louie enjoyed the early war years' sexual freedom in London until the introduction of the Emergency Powers Act (Defence) 1939 and 1940 sought to reassert restraints and rules, especially on women's behaviour. Louie observes, 'You saw [. . .] where it says how war in some ways makes our characters better?' (170). But the propaganda intrudes further as she consumes it in newspapers until she

> now felt bad only about any part of herself which in any way did not fit into the papers' picture: she could not have survived their disapproval. They did not, for instance, leave flighty wives or good-time girls a leg to stand on: and how rightly – she had romped through a dozen pieces on that subject with if anything rather special zest, and was midway through just one more when the blast struck cold. Could it be that the papers were out with *Louie?* (168)

Newspapers now decide Louie's sexual ethics, defining her as 'a flighty wi[fe]' and 'good-time girl' who requires redefinition according to propaganda's proffered roles, its acceptable definitions of women.

While Louie's birth did not result from inadequately controlled behaviour by women, wartime and orphanhood result in her promiscuity, which newspaper propaganda serving as internalised surveillance, corrects. Newspapers come to define her *moral* behaviour and character, showing that, in Louie's case, propaganda can extend dangerously into her very subjectivity. We read,

> Left to herself, thrown back on herself in London, she looked about her in vain for someone to imitate; she was ready, nay, eager to attach herself to anyone who could seem to be following any one course with certainty. (13)

Orphaned and uprooted from her home, Louie lacks a place in time, totally severed from her past, willing to take on any prescriptions for behaviour. Propaganda provides the 'national character' that Peter Mandler observes as 'simultaneously [. . .] the means of war fighting – its principal weapon – and the ends' (73). Propaganda simultaneously creates a distinctively British character, and promotes its defence, and the Emergency Powers Act mandated the intrusion of surveillance into private behaviour, including women's sexual behaviour, which becomes subject to what Adam Piette calls 'self-watching censorship' (2). Propaganda offers an apparent certainty to malleable orphan Louie, unprotected, uprooted, living in exile, in a wartime London that effectively exiles all its citizens. Louie typifies the predicaments of wartime life, and becomes propaganda's exemplary citizen. She returns to Seale-on-Sea at the novel's end, with her illegitimate baby, after her husband's death in the war, to create fictional roots for herself and her child in the absence of real ones, continuing wartime propaganda's subsumption into its fictions.

Newspapers permeate Louie's consciousness and take over her flimsy subjectivity, displayed masterfully by Bowen in free-indirect discourse. Louie's propaganda-infused language *is* her character, and shows a collapse of her subjectivity in a profound syntactical dislocation in the news she absorbs. Critiquing the press manipulations of the British public, Bowen depicts Louie as searching for certainty amidst modernity's deracination and the obliteration of her sense of the past. Newspapers resolve her wartime confusion by offering the illusion that she has mastery of contemporary history, as we see when we read, 'if you could not keep track of what was happening you could at least take notice of what was said' (167). Louie asks her flatmate, ironically, 'Still you'd surely not rather be like the Germans, Connie? I was told how they swallow anything they are told' (171).

Bowen brilliantly evokes communal discourse and the passivity of the collective consciousness, under the Ministry of Information's influence. Modern newspaper propaganda substitutes for the recent history that family ties might ordinarily offer. We read,

> With the news itself she was at some disadvantage owing to having begun in the middle; she never quite had the courage to ask anyone [. . .] how it had all begun – evidently one thing must have led to another, as in life; and whose the mistake had been in the first place, or how long ago, you would not care to say. (167)

Newspapers take over her consciousness, until, 'Louie, after a week or two [. . .] discovered that she *had* got a point of view, and not only *a* point of view but the right one' (168).

Propaganda horrifyingly impinges on Louie's ability to determine truth from fiction, replacing her perceptions with its fictive ones. On the epistemological level, modernity undermines trust in the reliability of perception, but total war's penetration of the Home Front creates an epistemological crisis, Bowen infers, for a character like Louie, who accepts the fictional identities for women offered in the newspapers: 'worker, a soldier's lonely wife, a war orphan' and ultimately widow and single mother of an orphan child (168).[12] Unmoored in the epistemological chaos of total war, she allows newspapers to define an acceptable wartime persona for her: the fiction of widowed motherhood. Comforted by the wartime narrative, oblivious to the impossibility that her child 'Thomas Victor' could be her soldier husband's child, since she conceived him in her husband's absence, and becoming 'an orderly mother', Louie is the sole Bowen orphan with a definitive ending. We see her deluded, but happy, returned to Seale-on-Sea, seeing baby Tom looking like his 'father' and regaining her old family: we read 'Then, [. . .] she took Tom straight round to his grandparents'. The thin air which had taken the house's place was, now that she stood and breathed in it, after all full of today and sunshine' (372). Although her parents are dead, as is her husband, she embraces the historically current and sanctioned role: 'orderly mother'. While she cannot do this without delusion, yet she finds in it what she wants.

Propaganda has effectively allowed her to use her orphanhood to negotiate new but disturbingly unreal social belonging. When Matchett instigates the negotiation of an appropriate relationship to the Quaynes that acknowledges their father's past and Portia's birth, she connects Portia to her family's real history. Yet Pearson might argue that Bowen's depiction of Louie's contentment with the conventional role that propaganda can provide arises from, 'The need to recognize new associations beyond the homeland while also accounting for the *unresolved* status of one's prior national belonging: the feeling that one has yet to belong to a stable consensus of nationhood' (322). This search for 'a stable consensus of nationhood' began with Lois, evicted from an already 'unresolved' Anglo-Ireland facing an uncertain future in exile and symbolising her Ascendancy class's impending demise. Sharing the predicament of unstable nationhood, Henrietta has no parents to define her nationality clearly, and Leopold's combination of English, Anglo-Irish and Franco-Jewish paternity, is consummately unstable and undefined, and results from his mother's refusal to accept responsibility for her lineage. Portia's father, exiled from his family and home because of his infidelity, at least recognises Portia's exile, 'from her own country' (15). These familial, cultural and historical disruptions cause psychic deracination but, Bowen ultimately suggests, may be preferable to propaganda and nationalism's false national certainties, such as the propaganda to which *The Heat of the Day*'s orphan Louie is supremely susceptible. Louie evinces 'a lack [of] historical sense and [. . .] the absence of a notion of change over time if not, indeed, an inveterate resistance to progress and development' (5). Although the orphan's exclusion from domesticity, which Dickens portrayed as a national scandal undermining the sanctified Victorian family, stands as the source of the orphan's greatest suffering, it sometimes offers the modern Bowen orphan an escape from stifling bourgeois constraints, which might particularly impinge upon women: even though the result is uncertainty and lack of definition.

For Bowen herself, as a 'cosmopolitan', 'dislocation becomes relocation, mobility beyond cultural borders becomes movement between them', as Pearson would say (323). Adapting to the necessities of history's reality for the Anglo-Irish, Bowen espoused deracination and an alternative national location, one she would embrace as preferable to the distorted certainties of either anachronistic pseudo-aristocratic Ascendancy tradition, or wartime nationalism either in fascism or in wartime propaganda. As consummate moderns, for Pearson, Bowen protagonists

> do not possess an orientation that precedes their disorientation. They live in the present of disruptions and historical crises, but they have not previously experienced a stable mode of belonging that was, 'botched' by the sudden and seismic turmoil of modernity. (325)

Their orphanhood is the very source of this 'disorientation', and provides the fertile ground for modernity's "seismic turmoil', compounding their deracination and unmooring. An orphan Bowen protagonist is 'ultimately subject to the manifest pressures of history and place', as was Anglo-Irish Bowen herself (328).

Bowen's personal stake in orphanhood lay in her own loss of parents and home, and Anglo-Irish exile and dispossession, and she portrays orphans who search for definition and belonging, as Portia, Henrietta, Leopold, Lois and Louie exemplify, in the *potential* in the absence of national, familial or cultural affiliations. As deracinated moderns, her protagonists are ultimately liberated in their exile even if they endure pain in the process. Their cosmopolitanism resists nationalisms, and their separation from society facilitates the renegotiation of social ties. Dislocation can become relocation. These orphans develop, then, throughout Bowen's career, from the Anglo-Irish Lois, constrained by Ascendancy traditions, with an uncertain future, to *The Death of the Heart*'s Portia, who forces Thomas and Anna to confront her meaning, and the atrophy of their hearts. Linked with the old wives' tale and the uncanny, orphans disrupt orderly, domestic life, although *The Heat of the Day*'s Louie afloat, rudderless, linguistically disenfranchised and vulnerable to propaganda, can nevertheless appropriate fictions to create a role for herself as a war widow and 'orderly mother' precisely because she has no inherent history or language. Early Bowen orphans, like Lois, inherited constraining traditions of which they knew nothing, or lacked knowledge of the traditions within which they lived, as did Louie, Henrietta and Leopold. But the formula works in reverse too: Bowen's deracinated orphans exemplify the predicaments of modernity itself, with its tumultuous post-colonial disruptions, and its potential for cosmopolitan rejection of national certainty, preferable, Bowen suggests, to the certainties that totalitarian nationalism and wartime propaganda offered, even if cosmopolitanism asserted a form of national orphanhood as the modern alternative to a fictive sense of belonging.

## Notes

1. Elizabeth Bowen, *The House in Paris* (42).
2. Victoria Glendinning observed, 'the absence of ghosts is the "big divide" between Bowen's novels and the short stories', although one ghost, Guy, does appear in *A World of Love* (80). Bowen plays with

the ghost story genre in many of her short stories, notably 'The Demon Lover', 'The Cat Jumps', 'Attractive Modern Homes' and 'Green Holly.'
3. One novel, *A World of Love*, has a ghost that represents an unresolved family conflict.
4. Critic Sinéad Mooney observes that in Bowen's work, haunted houses 'are more likely to be newly built villas, bourgeois weekend retreats, or bomb-threatened London terraces than the solitary castles of traditional Gothic' (78).
5. See Teekell 139–55; Lassner 202–4).
6. See Lee, *Elizabeth Bowen*.
7. Because of restrictions of space, this study does not include *To the North* (1932) and *Eva Trout* (1968), both of which have orphan protagonists.
8. Selena Hastings, Introduction to *A World of Love*, 5.
9. It is worth noting the Gothic roots of the Anglo-Irish Big House novel.
10. Krebs considers specifically *Jane Eyre* and *Wuthering Heights*, both of which have housekeepers who are the repositories of folklore, ghost stories and superstition, as well as knowledge of family secrets.
11. Another Bowen orphan protagonist, Eva Trout, in the 1968 novel that bears her name, is the ultimate cosmopolitan, living in many countries, moving peripatetically.
12. For Bowen protagonists, motherhood is as fraught as childhood is. Few Bowen women display uncomplicated motherly roles, many cannot have children, and increasingly her fiction portrays orphans as mothers in Louie, whose child is illegitimate and her husband dead, and *Eva Trout*'s eponymous orphan protagonist becomes a mother by paying for a child to be abducted from its parents. This child then shoots Eva at the end of the narrative, effectively bringing about his own orphanhood.

## Works Cited

Bennett, Andrew and Nicholas Royle. *Elizabeth Bowen and the Dissolution of the Novel*. St Martin's Press, 1995.
Bowen, Elizabeth. *The Death of the Heart*. Penguin, 1962.
Bowen, Elizabeth. *Eva Trout: Or Changing Scenes*. Penguin, 1982.
Bowen, Elizabeth. *The Heat of the Day*. Alfred A. Knopf, 1949.
Bowen, Elizabeth. *The House in Paris*. Anchor, 1998.
Bowen, Elizabeth. *The Last September*. Penguin, 1942.
Bowen, Elizabeth. *To the North*. Penguin, 1945.
Bowen, Elizabeth. *A World of Love*. Vintage, 1995.
Corcoran, Neil. *Elizabeth Bowen: The Enforced Return*. Clarendon Press, 2004.

Craig, Patricia. *Elizabeth Bowen*. Penguin, 1986.

Ellmann, Maud. *Elizabeth Bowen: The Shadow Across the Page*. Edinburgh University Press, 2003.

Glendinning, Victoria. *Elizabeth Bowen: Portrait of a Writer*. Weidenfeld and Nicolson, 1977.

Ho, Janice. *Nation and Citizenship in the Twentieth-Century British Novel*, Cambridge University Press, 2015.

Krebs, Paula. 'Folklore, Fear, and the Feminine: Ghosts and Old Wives' Tales'. *Wuthering Heights*. *Victorian Literature and Culture*, vol. 26, no. 1, 1998, pp. 41–52.

Lassner, Phyllis. *British Women Writers of World War II: Battlegrounds of Their Own*. Macmillan, 1998.

Lee, Hermione. *Elizabeth Bowen: An Estimation*. Barnes and Noble, 1981.

Lloyd, David. *Irish Culture and Colonial Modernity, 1800–2000: The Transformation of Oral Space*. Cambridge University Press, 2011.

Mandler, Peter. *The English National Character: The History of an Idea from Edmund Burke to Tony Blair*. Yale University Press, 2006.

Mooney, Sinéad. 'Unstable Compounds: Bowen's Beckettian Affinities'. *Modern Fiction Studies*, vol. 53, no. 2, Summer 2007, pp. 238–56.

Moynihan, Julian. *Anglo-Irish: The Literary Imagination in a Hyphenated Culture*. Princeton University Press, 1995.

Osborn, Susan. *Elizabeth Bowen: New Critical Perspectives*. Cork University Press, 2009.

Pearson, Nels C. 'Elizabeth Bowen and the New Cosmopolitanism'. *Twentieth Century Literatur*, vol. 56, no. 3, Fall 2010, pp. 318–40.

Peters, Laura. *Orphan Texts: Victorian Orphans, Culture and Empire*. Manchester University Press, 2000.

Piette, Adam. *Imagination at War: British Fiction and Poetry 1939–1945*. Macmillan, 1995.

Teekell, Anna. 'The Orphan Decade: Elizabeth Bowen's 1930s Novels'. *Etudes Irlandaises*, vol. 42, no. 2, 2017, pp. 139–55.

Tillinghast, Richard. 'Elizabeth Bowen: The House, the Hotel & and the Child'. *Contemporary Literary Criticism Select*, Gale, 2008. Literature Resource Center. https://link.galegroup.com/apps/doc/H1100004425/LitRC?u=upitt_main&sid=LitRC&xid=323d1755 (accessed 2 July 2019). Originally published in *The New Criterion*, vol. 13, no. 4, December 1994, pp. 24–33.

Walshe, Eibhear. *Elizabeth Bowen*. Irish Academic Press, 2009.

Chapter 12

# Orphans, Money and Marriage in Sensation Novels by Wilkie Collins and Philip Pullman

## Claudia Nelson

The orphan frequently appears in mid-nineteenth-century fiction as pathetic, fragile and helpless in a worldly sense.[1] Archetypal Victorian orphans of this species include Charles Dickens's Little Nell and Jo (1841 and 1853), the motherless Helen Burns in *Jane Eyre* (1847; Jane herself, though a full orphan, is more tenacious of life), and the fatherless title character in Hesba Stretton's *Jessica's First Prayer* (1865). These iconic figures lack both natural protectors and natural defences, and thus, as Elisabeth Wesseling observes, 'Orphans are ideally suited to melodramatic sentimentalism, as they embody the powerless and meek that the reader should take pity on' (211). Yet just as Jessica's drunken mother and Helen's distant and lately remarried father illustrate that the Victorian understanding of 'home' encompassed much more than the kind of home idealised within sentimental domestic fiction, the sentimental orphan is of course not the only kind of orphan to be found in Victorian settings. Studies such as Laura Peters's *Orphan Texts: Victorian Orphans, Culture and Empire* (2000) and Elizabeth Thiel's *The Fantasy of Family: Nineteenth-Century Children's Literature and the Myth of the Domestic Ideal* (2008), among others, explore alternative visions of nineteenth-century orphans, with Peters arguing that parentless children 'played a pharmaceutical function in Victorian literature: the orphan embodies a surplus excess to be expelled to the colonies' (19) and Thiel that stories of the 'transnormative' household, a family missing one or both of the original parents, 'are often subtly subversive' and 'challeng[e] the verisimilitude of the domestic ideal' (10, 8).

The idea of subversion and challenge is one that I take up in this chapter, but with a specific focus on how stories of Victorian orphans may function to highlight the subversive interplay of domesticity and money. The novelistic genre dominant during much of the Victorian period, namely domestic fiction, tends to see finance and domesticity as adversaries or at least opposites, so that Silas Marner, say, cannot possess his hoard of gold during the time that he is bringing up the golden-haired adoptive daughter who replaces it. Yet this vision is far from unitary, especially once one leaves the boundaries of that genre. Sensation fiction, in particular, often posits that cold cash and warm domestic idylls are two sides of the same coin – and counterfeit coin at that, since the form specialises in revealing the shocking secrets, often financial by nature, lurking within seemingly respectable homes. Laurence Talairach-Vielmas remarks that 'the sensation novels of the 1860s embedded their narratives within a capitalist society where the construction of "woman" subversively depended upon the market economy' (57), while in writing of *East Lynne* (1861), Vicky Simpson explores how that novel 'think[s] of the family in terms of property, commodification and ownership [as] a corrective to the sentimentalization of family in much Victorian literature' ('Not-So-Happy' 585). Indeed, Ann Cvetkovich posits that Karl Marx's *Capital*, written at the height of the popularity of the sensation novel, should be understood as an example of this genre, a work structured 'as the revelation of a secret' that involves a ghastly connection between factory and human: 'As the capitalist system becomes alive with the energy of the worker's labor-power, the worker himself is like an object whose resources can be exhausted just as a machine gets worn out' (180, 185).

The status of 'corrective' or 'oppositional' literature is one that Victorian sensation fiction shares with a later genre that often draws inspiration from it, namely the neo-Victorian novel. One of the 'defining features of the Victorian period', as Sonya Sawyer Fritz and many others have pointed out, was the insistence that home and marketplace should not be understood to overlap (40).[2] Yet that comfortable boundedness was not stable at the time; Rebecca Stern sums up 'two decades of scholarship in feminist and cultural studies in taking the Victorian ideology of separate spheres as precisely that – an ideology, one that operated alongside, and crucially depended for its popularity on, a reality that offered no such clear separation' (4). Nor is it stable in retrospect today. Nadine Boehm-Schnitker observes that neo-Victorian studies as a field of study presumes that the neo-Victorian novel is best 'understood as an uncanny doubling, a double of the Victorian text which mimics "its language, style, and plot" and repeats its "tropes, characters and historical events" as well as its genres, thus sometimes defamiliarising "our preconceptions of Victorian society"' (94). As the example of the sensation novel helps to illuminate, however, it does not do to forget that this project of the defamiliarisation of the Victorians was initiated by the Victorians themselves.

In this chapter I consider a neo-Victorian text, Philip Pullman's Sally Lockhart trilogy (1985–90, supplemented by the related volume *The Tin Princess* in 1994), alongside a Victorian sensation novel, Wilkie Collins's *No Name* (1862). My purpose in juxtaposing these two oppositional texts from different moments is to throw into relief what they share. Both approach their project of questioning standard notions of family by focusing on a young female orphan – Sally Lockhart is sixteen when we first meet her, while Collins's Magdalen Vanstone is eighteen – who learns that she can achieve and maintain domestic security only if she also has financial security, and vice versa. Both fictions depict domestic ties as commodities that can be purchased and forged, and the law as incapable of keeping pace with a domesticity represented as contingent and fluctuating in value and values. Both protagonists respond to their unusual family circumstances by becoming tough, assertive and clever entrepreneurs who direct their energies towards the acquisition of money in a way that illustrates money's connection to family. And that finally both texts opt to erase their protagonist's demonstrated earning power, providing her instead with a happy marriage, suggests the extent to which, as Thiel puts it, 'as late Victorians we have [. . .] implicitly inherited and internalized various and diverse ideologies spawned during the nineteenth century' (1). If works such as Pullman's Sally Lockhart trilogy use the figure of the orphan and the context of the earlier century to illuminate problems in our inheritance of the past, they also demonstrate that the fiction of our more recent memory may not have devised satisfactory solutions to those problems.

*

The Sally Lockhart trilogy, composed of *The Ruby in the Smoke* (1985), *The Shadow in the North* (1986) and *The Tiger in the Well* (1990), focuses on the adventures and tribulations of a young female financial manager in the 1870s and early 1880s. Upon Captain Lockhart's death, shortly before the opening of the first novel, Sally is forced to confront the fact that not only has his money – her presumed inheritance – mysteriously disappeared at the moment of her orphaning, but she also lacks the feminine accomplishments that might enable her to enter the Victorian job or marriage market in a conventional way. She has no musical or artistic skills, no aptitude for the life of a governess or paid companion or (despite her beauty) compliant wife and attentive mother; indeed, she realises in volume 3 that she doesn't even know how to play with her own child, to whom she is more father than mother, since she is breadwinner and protector rather than primary caregiver. On the credit side of the ledger, however, she is an expert accountant, a knowledgeable picker of stocks and a shrewd and imaginative developer of business opportunities overlooked by her male friends. Living by her wits, in the inaugural volume she solves the mystery of the deaths of her birth father and her adoptive father, in the process choosing between two modes of economic being: dependent heiress or independent entrepreneur. She also shoots the novel's villain, Ah Ling, leaving him for dead – yet he is resurrected in the third volume, now a quadriplegic because of Sally's bullet, as the mastermind behind a diabolical plot that seeks to strip Sally of her business, her bank account and her daughter, whom he hopes to enslave and turn into his body servant. The antagonism between Ah Ling and Sally, then, and indeed between Sally and all the trilogy's villains, is always located in both the domestic and the financial spheres. Thus Ah Ling's greed for money both orphans Sally and threatens to deprive her of a daughter who, he hopes, will be transferred, as payment for the debt that in his view she has incurred by attacking him, into a nightmarish alternative family as its lowest-status (or least valuable) member.[3] Sally, however, resists this transaction.

In creating a young nineteenth-century orphan who does not run true to the fragile feminine type, Pullman is simultaneously battling the stereotype of 'the economically incompetent Victorian woman' – a stereotype that George Robb has provocatively termed a mere convenient fiction, the invention of 'ideologues [. . .] who wanted to shore up separate spheres' and keep women out of the professions in the twentieth century as well as the nineteenth (8). In this regard, the trilogy appears to participate in what Margaret Stetz identifies as a standard project of contemporary neo-Victorian fiction for young female readers:

> to introduce audiences composed mainly of young girls to feminist ideologies, both in nineteenth and in [late twentieth- or] twenty-first-century terms, and to represent the individual and collective political [or in Pullman's case economic] actions of women in a positive light. (141)

But this positive note is tempered by its opposite. Although Pullman's deployment of familiar melodramatic tropes such as the

Moonstone-like gem 'of incalculable value' 'responsible for deaths too many to list' (*Ruby* 29, 41) or the subterranean room slowly filling with water and threatening the life of a captive heroine is lighthearted and witty, the Sally Lockhart saga is also gloomily didactic: in the third volume, a newly 'woke' Sally falls in love with a socialist agitator and decides that in her attention to investment and profit, she has been complicit in

> the gnawing poison cancer destroying and eating and laying waste at the heart of it all [. . .] All this time, all the money we've made so cleverly by buying and selling and buying again – we never knew what it meant. (*Tiger* 350)[4]

Before exploring the implications of the overt ideological agenda of such moments, I want to examine a more subtle aspect of the trilogy's approach to economics, namely, how Pullman creates in these novels a complex web of associations between money and domesticity such that money – like the figure of the orphan herself – is made to stand both for familial love and for its absence. In a telling use of cliché, the saga opens in what the first sentence describes as 'the financial heart of London' (3), and this juxtaposition of economics and sentiment establishes the keynote for what will follow. Thus in volume 1 Sally discovers that she is not, as she has believed, the daughter of the recently deceased merchant and ex-Army officer Matthew Lockhart and his long-dead wife, a role model described to her throughout her childhood as 'a wild, stormy, romantic young woman who rode like a Cossack, shot like a champion, and smoked (to the scandal of the fascinated regiment) tiny black cheroots in an ivory holder' (*Ruby* 13). In fact, no such mother existed, and paternity is exploded as well. It turns out that Captain Lockhart was a lifelong bachelor who acquired Sally in her toddlerhood from her biological father, opium addict and fellow English officer Major Marchbanks, in exchange for the legendary Ruby of Agrapur; Marchbanks's endeavour to make amends by trying to ensure that Sally will inherit the ruby after his murder puts her and many other characters in the novel in mortal danger. Although astonished by these revelations and initially shaken in her sense of her own parentage inasmuch as she briefly starts referring to Marchbanks as 'father', Sally comes to terms with the idea that Lockhart is at once her adoptive father and her true parent. Associated in the novel with both romantic love and paternal love, the ruby is also a symbol of a monetary value that proves to be inseparable from emotional ties.

Indeed, in a more openly patriarchal text, Sally's renewed confidence in the Captain might depend upon her discovery that he literally valued her above rubies. As Nadine Muller – echoing Luce Irigaray, among others – notes in a discussion of the 'gender economics' of another neo-Victorian text, Sarah Waters's *Fingersmith* (2002),

> Feminist critics, philosophers and anthropologists of previous decades have agreed that in patriarchal societies women usually serve as commodities within transactions between men [. . .] in such a structure, they are unable to act as autonomous transaction partners themselves. (116)[5]

Under these circumstances, the best that a commodified woman could hope for might be to fetch a high price. After all, in Irigaray's words, 'A sociocultural endogamy would [. . .] forbid commerce *with* women. Men make commerce *of* them, but they do not enter into any exchanges *with* them' (172). To invoke Adam Smith, then, one might say that Victorian cultural practices were arranged in such a way as to discourage middle-class women from profiting from their own use value and to encourage the inflating of their exchange value; they were to be seen as like rubies, beautiful rather than functional.

Sally, however, rejects this way of being valued. At the end of *The Ruby in the Smoke* her position *vis-à-vis* patriarchy has changed, in that she escapes from her initial commodification into financial agency, an escape demarcated through her contrasting inheritances from her two fathers. After a lengthy search for the ruby that culminates in her flinging the stone into the Thames so that neither she nor the other woman who has been bought for this price, the villainous Mrs Holland, will have possession (213), she is eventually united with Captain Lockhart's legacy to her. The latter proves to consist of a small chest of banknotes and a letter advising her that 'with cash, you have freedom. Look for a small business, one which needs capital to expand.' Reading this statement of trust in her financial acumen, Sally breaks down over her inheritance:

> Everything had come to this now: to a box full of money, and a letter. She was crying. She had loved him very much, real father or not [. . .]
> And he had made everything safe; there would be a future.
> 'Daddy,' she whispered. (*Ruby* 230)

In this moment, the chest of banknotes effectively substitutes for 'Daddy' in both emotional and practical terms; simultaneously, Captain Lockhart lives up to two sets of expectations, the Victorian requirement that the good father provide for his daughter and our own era's requirement that such provision include the trust that having been properly equipped for life, the daughter will use her advantages to secure her own financial independence and agency.

And Sally does so. Earlier in the novel she has been rescued and sheltered by an unconventional young photographer, Frederick Garland, and his bohemian family; not wishing to occupy the passive role of needy damsel in distress, Sally has in turn offered them her accountancy skills and creative marketing ideas, commercial assets that gain her an invitation to become a permanent member of the Garland family. With her father's legacy, she can also offer monetary backing, causing the photographic business owned by Frederick and his uncle to prosper and enabling the participants to diversify: in volume 2, Frederick opens a private detection agency, while Sally sets up as a financial consultant. As sole proprietors of small businesses whose cases sometimes turn out to be related, Sally and Frederick see themselves as equals, a perception that at once enables and complicates their romantic attraction to each other. For Sally is reluctant to become a wife in Victorian England:

> [S]he'd never marry anyone else, but she wouldn't marry him. Not until the Married Women's Property Act was passed [. . .] As a matter of fact, it wasn't as simple as she claimed. There had been a Married Women's Property Act passed in 1870, which had removed some of the injustices, though not the worst ones; but Frederick knew nothing of the law and didn't know that Sally's property could legally remain hers under certain conditions. But because Sally was uncertain of her feelings, she stuck to this principle – and rather dreaded the passing of a new act, since it would force her to decide one way or the other. (*Shadow* 13–14)

Sally, then, is comfortable with the family of interlocking businesses that has been born of her connection with Frederick, but she is less comfortable with more conventional ideas of family, a discomfort that comes from her reading of the power dynamics of domesticity. Late in the second instalment, antagonist Axel Bellmann explains his philosophy that money, 'which is financial power', can be connected to mechanical power, electrical power and so on to create a system of infinite dynamic change (*Shadow* 304–5). That Sally is profoundly disturbed by his outlook seems allied to her reluctance to connect financial to domestic power in her own life. Yet while Bellmann too overlooks the emotions as a source of energy, a central theme of all three volumes is that these elements are always already connected and that neither Sally nor anyone else has the luxury of opting out. The trilogy makes clear that the commodification of women within as well as beyond the idealised domestic setting is rife in Victorian society. Negotiating with his prospective father-in-law for a bride whose ownership of large graphite deposits will advance his business interests, for example, Bellmann says silkily, 'We agree that the value of your daughter is six hundred and fifty thousand pounds' (*Shadow* 88). His statement is offensive but not inapposite, since the young woman's father has indeed been wondering just how large a sum she might fetch. And for all the confidence that Sally derives from being around 'her balance sheets and her files' (80), she is as vulnerable as anyone to being turned into an item in balance sheets or files controlled by hostile interests.

This point is driven home in volume 3, in which Sally is threatened with the confiscation of her home, business, assets and illegitimate daughter by the now deceased Frederick, when a man she has never met (later revealed to be an accomplice and subordinate of the scheming Ah Ling) produces faked evidence of their marriage and sues for divorce and child custody. Under British law, Pullman makes clear, Sally has no recourse largely because, as an orphan and spinster, she has no male protector; Frederick's uncle and her friend Jim, the two men best positioned to intercede on her behalf, are making an extended trip to South America. She is unable to prove the truth of her case through her own efforts, and she lives in a world in which, despite the Married Women's Property Acts, the default assumption is still that women's efforts at financial autonomy are socially transgressive. And, of course, she is presumed transgressive on the domestic as well as the economic level, because even if she is not the rebellious and badly behaved wife that the mysterious Mr Parrish accuses her of being, she is an unrepentant unmarried mother who has invaded the masculine sphere of finance.

That these two roles are interdependent is made clear throughout the volume. For instance, while Sally is more concerned with the prospect of losing her child than with the prospect of losing her business, it is in the economic realm that her worry is first manifested, as an early sign of the avalanche that is about to descend upon her is her discovery 'that she'd made a mistake in a letter she'd sent to her stockbrokers, which had resulted in a client's money being wrongly invested' (*Tiger* 112). While that error has no serious consequences, it is an early link in a chain of events that will, within a few dozen pages, see Sally musing bitterly,

> Me, the great independent woman – oh, I used to be so proud. I cruised along earning money and organizing businesses and thinking I was so clever, and then *this* comes at me and all of a sudden I'm huddling on a bench with only seven shillings in the world. (178)

Sally's instinct to conflate her financial status with her continued ability to mother her daughter is not merely excused but mandated by her status as orphan devoid of family and by the novel's plot. Once a source of pride to Sally, independence must in the absence of funds be redefined as vulnerability.

Sally has been forced to redefine her own identity and position in the world earlier in the trilogy, most notably in volume 1 when she must come to terms with her status as adoptee. Yet at that moment, as discussed above, her adoptive father's loving message and cash legacy restore her original sense of self as the daughter of Captain Lockhart rather than of Major Marchbanks. In the financial and social deconstruction that she undergoes in volume 3, in contrast, her allegiances undergo a radical and seemingly permanent transformation. Having explored multiple ways in which money or objects of value are tied symbolically and practically to the emotional life of the family, the trilogy ends with sixty pages that show Sally experiencing a sudden revulsion against her way of earning a living. Although she regains her rights to daughter, business and self-determination, she turns her back on these earlier priorities in order to embrace an anticapitalist, collectivist project. Her attitude towards work and individualism has changed:

> [T]here was so much for her to do. Not single-handedly: she'd learned that lesson. Things got done in the world when you worked with other people. There were movements to join, things to learn, groups to organize, speeches to make. How strange it was [. . .] she'd seen at last the work she was born to do. She felt absurdly lucky. To have real, important work to do, and to know it! (*Tiger* 406)

The preceding volume ends on a note of feminist solidarity when Sally's redoubtable client Miss Walsh insists on investing the money that Sally has recovered for her from Bellmann in Sally's firm, remarking that 'If female emancipation meant anything [. . .] it meant the right of one woman to support the work of another in any way she chose' (*Shadow* 324). In sharp contrast, *The Tiger in the Well* replaces this stance with the claim that Sally's hard-earned financial position, her symbolic eldest child, is not a sign of her vitality and intelligence, not 'the work she was born to do', but part of a 'gnawing poison cancer' on society. The memory of her investment activities shames her, and by extension, the reader too is to regard Victorian prosperity as a monument to greed.

In denigrating her financial acumen as contributing to social evils, Pullman reduces Sally's agency by making her embrace the idea of being dependent – not financially but ideologically – on a supposedly wiser man. It is noteworthy that this move reverses the pattern established in volume 1 by Sally's inheritance from her adoptive father, presented as a nest egg that the sixteen-year-old is expected to increase through the deployment of her independent judgement, and in volume 2 by Sally's partnership with Frederick, presented as a relationship in which she is the more knowledgeable about the supposedly masculine realms of money and law. In retrospect, then, that both these egalitarian bonds are ended by the man's death implies that they were ultimately not sustainable, whether because socialist doctrine locates power in the collective rather than in the individual or because, in Pullman's view, the stereotypically Victorian dependent relationship needs to constitute the heroine's happy ending even in a neo-Victorian novel that elsewhere uses finance to critique Victorian shibboleths of domesticity and gender.

Tracing matrilineal narratives, in which 'a daughter's awareness of her mother's past and her consciousness of being her mother's progeny can have a significant impact on the way a daughter performs her own present identity', through the pages of fiction by Waters and other writers, Muller notes that 'matrilineal genealogies have not only become a significant issue in feminist theory and a recurring motif in contemporary women's writing, but they have also become an increasingly prominent theme in neo-Victorian fiction' (109–10). For Muller, 'matrilinealism [offers] a metafictional comment on neo-Victorian fiction's relationship to the (nineteenth-century) past' (111); she considers that in Waters's novel *Fingersmith* (whose two female protagonists, like Pullman's Sally, have each been imbued with false knowledge about their mothers' identities) and elsewhere in neo-Victorian fiction, this comment could be said to advocate a symbolic matricide as a way of urging the renegotiation of inherited narratives (130). Pullman's manoeuvre in revealing in volume 1 of his trilogy that Sally's supposed mother, that convention-defying champion shooter, rider and smoker, was an invention of

Captain Lockhart's may thus be understood on one level as engaging in a narrative trope that is often to be found in this genre. Yet seen in conjunction with the requirement that Sally abjure the economic foundation on which her livelihood is built, the manoeuvre is also part of a pattern in which sources of female agency are made suspect. In *The Ruby in the Smoke*, Sally's real biological mother is revealed to have been a 'sickly thing' rather than a dashing heroine (210), while the most powerful (and least nurturing) woman in the novel, Mrs Holland, is an arch-villain whose many crimes include impersonating a mother.

In this light, the final lines of the trilogy, an exchange between Sally and her now-recovered young daughter (whose language reflects a recent sojourn in the underclass), are appropriately ambiguous:

> [Sally] said, 'And we won't let anyone be bad to us again, will we?'
> 'Not bloody likely,' said Harriet. (*Tiger* 407)

For judging by the connection that the trilogy has consistently established between economic power and domestic agency, Sally's relinquishment of money-making as a shield against her own helplessness makes it entirely 'likely' that her ability to keep the 'bad' away from the family has been diminished in favour of masculine authority. If the trilogy's first volume causes Sally to reassess her past to come to a new, agentive understanding of who 'Sally Lockhart' might be, its conclusion calls that renegotiated identity into question once more. Significantly, she makes only a cameo appearance in the companion volume, *The Tin Princess*, which refers to her not as Sally but by her married name; she is now 'Mrs. Goldberg' to the narrator, and instead of delving – as she longs to do – into the mystery presented to her, she will accompany her husband to the US. The effect of her conversion is to turn her from a monument to feminist self-determination into something of a ghost, a memory haunting the final volume of a series that formerly focused on her ability to profit from her individual financial talents and enterprise.

\*

The descriptions above should have made evident that like many other neo-Victorian texts for young readers, the Sally Lockhart trilogy is designed in part to counter ideals conventionally associated with 'Victorianism': most importantly in this case, the innocent and vulnerable young orphan, the ideology of separate spheres, and the principles of laissez-faire capitalism and individual striving. In what remains of this chapter, I use Wilkie Collins's *No Name* to suggest that the 'Victorianism' to which Pullman's work opposes itself was understood even during the nineteenth century as a construct, a pleasing or maddening fiction that could be upended as readily as it could be reproduced. Significantly for the purposes of the collection in which this chapter appears, the vehicle that Collins employs to interrogate identity formation and demonstrate the economic and legal underpinnings of domestic virtue is again the teenaged girl orphan, here depicted as an accomplished mimic who, having in law no identity of her own, can take on any that suit her in order to pursue her own ends. Although the novel concludes with an assertion of the value of truth, the sincerity that is crucial to the sentimental project has for many readers been rendered irredeemably suspect.

*No Name* traces the efforts of its young protagonist, Magdalen Vanstone, to regain her share of the family fortune lost to her through her father's misunderstanding of English law and the effect of illegitimacy upon inheritance rights; her infractions against the moral code considered appropriate to young ladies include running away from home, earning her living by giving public performances upon the stage, masquerading under multiple false names and with the help of disguises, and ultimately (again under an alias) seducing into marriage a cousin whom she despises in order to regain her patrimony and her right to the Vanstone name. Meanwhile, Magdalen's Christian name, with its connotations of repentance, invokes the idea of redemption in both its moral and its financial sense.[6] The work is, in Deirdre David's judgement, the Collins novel that most 'interestingly conflates resistance to dominant aesthetic and sexual ideologies' (34), and in Sundeep Bisla's, a text in which 'far from accommodating a newly emergent popular Victorian domestic taste [Collins] is actually covertly attacking that taste at its very foundations' (1). Inasmuch as its project seems to bear a close (family) relationship to that of Pullman's trilogy, it helps to undermine the implicit claims of neo-Victorianism to be boldly staking out new terrain.

Moving from socially approved amateur theatricals to scandalous engagements as a paid entertainer and then to still more scandalous private appearances in disguise in order to further her schemes, Magdalen allies herself to the self-described 'Rogue' Captain Wragge so that he can help her contract the loveless union with Noel Vanstone. Half marriage, half parent–child tie, the connection between Magdalen and Wragge is formed for avowedly fraudulent purposes and involves the impersonation of a family that does not exist. Like fiat money, in which paper currency (for instance) is assigned value purely on the issuing government's say-so, the individuals now calling themselves the Bygraves constitute a kind of 'fiat family', backed not by blood or virtue but by mere assertion. Wragge is not the bluff, honest character that he creates for Noel; Magdalen, posing as Wragge's niece, is not the loving innocent who attracts Noel's interest. In effect, these personalities have been brought into being by Noel's bank account and are given their power by Magdalen and Wragge's skill at connivance, their cynical awareness that the characteristics that they affect are among those to which Victorian society assigns particular value. Thus in *No Name* just as in Pullman's trilogy, domestic ties are susceptible to forgery. It seems emblematic that for much of the narrative, Wragge steals from Magdalen and seeks to betray her trust in other ways, this being his understanding of how 'business' with a 'fair relative' should naturally be conducted (Collins 185).

Yet over the course of their association, as Simpson points out, Magdalen, Wragge and the moronic Mrs Wragge – herself married for her money by her unscrupulous and abusive husband – do in fact form an odd but real family bond based on sympathy and respect. The counterfeit family here

> may be seen as more genuine than any other model in the novel because of the depth and sincerity of its relationships, and because it is a genuine partnership, one in which each puts up with the shortcomings of the other in order to realise a mutually desirable goal. (Simpson, 'Selective' 127)[7]

The perverse appeal of this union of muddled roles, in which the giant Mrs Wragge functions as ingenue, Magdalen as Mrs Wragge's chivalrous protector, and Captain Wragge ultimately as disinterested doctor and Cupid, underscores the undesirability of most of the more conventional male–female partnerships in the novel. Surveying, say, the mercenary marriage that Magdalen's erstwhile fiancé, Frank Clare, contracts with 'the elderly widow of a rich colonist' (Collins 601) or the bond between Noel Vanstone and his housekeeper Mrs Lecount, whom he continues to employ primarily because he is too parsimonious to pension her off, the reader may well find Magdalen and Wragge's joint venture preferable; if Wragge is accustomed to embezzle from her, she is at least aware of the fact and indifferent to it.

Over the course of the narrative, like many other Victorian orphans from Oliver Twist to Jane Eyre, Magdalen loses and gains multiple family identities. Her parents are taken from her not only by death but also by the discovery that they were not legally married at the time of her birth, but she then gains the Wragges as parodic surrogate parents who provide cover and social protection for her socially unacceptable endeavours. Similarly, she loses her original fiancé, whose exposure very early in the narrative as financially helpless is a major motivation for her own financial hyperassertiveness, but at the end of the novel she gains a replacement partner whose sterling worth helps the reader to identify his predecessor as, in effect, a gimcrack imitation of a desirable man: Frank Clare was neither 'frank' nor 'clear', but a counterfeit of those qualities. Finally, Magdalen's rebelliousness over her newly equivocal and impoverished position prompts her to separate herself from her sister, Norah, so that she can better pursue her schemes to retake possession of her money, yet the ironic denouement of all these schemes is that the more principled sister is the one to regain her inheritance. Nevertheless, and despite all her adventuring, Magdalen recovers a permanent and non-mercenary family at novel's end, like Sally Lockhart undergoing a near-death experience that leaves her in a happy marriage while simultaneously shutting down discussion. *No Name*, then, prefigures the Sally Lockhart books in establishing a pattern in which family is first undone and then redone, based on the young female protagonist's changing relationship to money.

That Magdalen, like Sally, is an orphan is clearly an important factor facilitating the formation of new families; that she is a teenaged girl is another. Alison Milbank notes Collins's perennial 'interest in the destabilisation of female identity' (52), and the protagonist of *No Name*, who is both an actress and an individual desperate to reconstitute a social being that has been eradicated by death and by law, is both responding to and seeking to exploit her own 'destabilisation'. Andrew Smith, meanwhile, identifies yet another important factor in the identity erasure that he terms 'render[ing] characters ghostly', namely, a particular relationship to economics: 'it is Magdalen's association with financial scheming that makes her ghostly', he contends (55). Marginalised by orphanhood, by illegitimacy, and by her sex and age, Magdalen is also necessarily othered by her understanding of herself as a person who has to operate by subterfuge if she is to achieve the bank balance that she thinks will allow her to recoup her erstwhile identity; 'The self', Smith adds, 'is thus performed by money', and in turn, 'Money supplants affection' (55, 56). Like Pullman's neo-Victorian trilogy, then, Collins's nineteenth-century text is using finance to critique the conventional economies of Victorian gender.

*No Name* contains an overt ghost story of a sort, inasmuch as Mrs Wragge, encountering on the stairs a Magdalen disguised as an elderly lady, takes the apparition for a ghost and refers obsessively to the encounter thereafter, a tic that eventually has significant effect upon the plot by enabling Mrs Lecount to expose his wife's true identity to Noel Vanstone. Yet the narrator also employs the word 'spectre' metaphorically on multiple occasions that do not make reference to Magdalen. The term is used of Magdalen's mother, who 'stood, the spectre of herself. With a dreadful vacancy in her eyes, with a dreadful stillness in her voice', upon hearing of the train accident that has killed her (now lawfully wedded) husband (92–3). It is used of Mrs Lecount when she has tracked down Noel Vanstone after having been separated from him by Wragge's machinations: 'Was it the spectre of the woman, or the woman herself?' Noel wonders, struck by the change that 'sickness and suffering' have wrought (447). And finally, it is used of Noel's relation Admiral Bartram, who has taken to sleepwalking as a response to the anxiety of overseeing the secret trust that Noel sets up to conceal how he has left his money:

> He passed Magdalen slowly, his lips whispering without intermission, his open eyes staring straight before him with the glassy stare of death [. . .] The terror of seeing him as she saw him now was not the terror she had felt when her eyes first lighted on him – an apparition in the moonlight, a spectre in the ghostly Hall. (551)

What these three examples have in common is the combination of emotional stress, a riven domestic arrangement and a connection to an effort to direct the flow of money. Significantly, however, all three characters involved also enjoy a considerably more secure social position than Magdalen does, with the most ghostly of the descriptions being applied to the respectable and benevolent elderly admiral. By implication, when questions of money and its inheritance enter a household, no identity is too stable to be erased into spectrality.

With this point in mind, we may wish to return to the question of what happens to Magdalen at novel's end. Most critics of *No Name* see Magdalen's final identity transformation, her forthcoming marriage to Captain Kirke, as an eradication of her subversive energy, akin to the eradication of Sally's individualistic and capitalistic drive at the end of Pullman's *The Tiger in the Well*. Debra Morris writes:

> Having restored a father figure in her life, Magdalen becomes completely passive. She is silenced in the last words of the text, this time with a kiss[,] and thus finally succumbs to her place in society [. . .] Magdalen has no choice but to embrace her assigned role as her steps outside the law only draw her closer to its terms. (284–5)

For David, somewhat similarly, having 'marrie[d] in a symbolic reconciliation with the father figure who left her [. . .] she is enfolded within patriarchy's embrace by the end' (36), while for Talairach-Vielmas, 'the closure of the story reasserts male supremacy over female transgressiveness, using medical discourse as a way of enforcing gender relationships' (71). Simpson is the dissenter here, finding that Magdalen remains

> active and independent [. . .] taking the lead in her relationship with Kirke. She recognises his desire long before he sees hers and, in the final scene, encourages him to speak if he has any reservations; Kirke silences himself by kissing Ma[gd]alen instead. ('Selective' 120)

The exchange as described by Collins's narrator in the last four lines of the novel is as follows:

> 'Tell me the truth!' she repeated.
> 'With my own lips.'
> 'Yes!' she answered, eagerly. 'Say what you think of me with your own lips.'
> He stooped and kissed her. (609)

Examining only these lines, indeed, one may readily see them as a silencing of the woman, who here opens herself to masculine judging while acknowledging her moral inferiority to her future husband. Yet Simpson's point that it is Kirke, not Magdalen, who refrains from speech is well taken. Perhaps considering the terms in which the narrator's own judgement is rendered may be of help in interpreting the (presumably deliberate) ambiguity on display. Noting that Magdalen has told Kirke '[t]he whole story of her life', concealing '[n]othing that she had done, nothing even that she had thought', the narrator reports that Kirke 'knew the priceless value [. . .] of a woman who speaks the truth' (608). This phrasing returns us to the question of money, but with the proviso that whereas the novel's scheming women, Magdalen herself and Mrs Lecount, have both named specific sums (£5,000 free of legacy duty for Mrs Lecount,

£80,000 for Magdalen) as what they hope to extract from Noel, we now understand that as a commodity in the marriage market, Magdalen herself is of 'priceless value'.

Moreover, Magdalen and Kirke's conversation next turns to a matter of 'business which he believed that he had concealed from her', namely, the question of whether he will return to the ship that functions as her rival: 'He little knew that she had learned already to be jealous of his ship' (608). From this 'business', Magdalen emerges triumphant, since Kirke will reject the invitation to return to his ship in favour of marrying. Kirke, then, will now have no business beyond his domestic life, which will be carried out in tandem with his 'priceless' wife. The woman who has subverted domesticity by counterfeiting a family and marrying for money has now, as Morris notes, 'reclaim[ed] her role within family' (284) in a more genuine sense – but as it was this genuineness that Magdalen has craved throughout the novel, Collins is clearly presenting this outcome as a happy ending while simultaneously indicating that trickery and the selling of her innocence need not render a woman ineligible for such a reward. Readers of both *No Name* and *The Tiger in the Well* may thus be justified in concluding that while both texts are profoundly interested in economic underpinnings to domesticity that the Victorian sentimental tradition might have preferred to keep silent about, the ending of the Victorian novel is potentially more subversive than the neo-Victorian novel's forcible conversion of its heroine to an ideology that undermines the very principles that initially defined her. Arguably, Magdalen's identity is rather more stable than Sally's.

But perhaps the same cannot be said of the identity of domesticity itself in these two works, as Collins's and Pullman's texts may both be described as exceptionally ready to question the stability and genuineness of the family. In both the nineteenth-century sensation novel and the twentieth-century young adult thriller, family ties are shown to be as much a matter of assertion as they are a matter of fact. Parent–child and husband–wife relationships, readers learn, can be constructed by the individual's fertile imagination, sometimes aided and abetted by the law and sometimes entirely privately, but never without some important economic motivation. In this project, both Collins and Pullman suggest, the figure of the orphan readily becomes central – perhaps because the orphan always already stands as evidence of family's impermanence. And this vulnerability, it turns out, can be staved off neither by fabulous rubies nor by £80,000, whether or not free of legacy duty.

## Notes

1. I thank Susan Egenolf, Emily Johansen, Anne Morey, Larry Reynolds, Sally Robinson, Justin Rogers, Shawna Ross and Deanna Stover for their valuable comments on an early draft of this chapter, and Ginger Frost, George Robb, Gail Savage and (especially) Anne Morey for feedback on the Interdisciplinary Nineteenth-Century Studies conference paper on Sally Lockhart, in which the chapter began.
2. This is not to suggest that money is unimportant in Victorian domestic fiction – far from it – but rather that Victorian novels are typically reluctant to see finance and domesticity as connected by likeness rather than as adversaries or opposites.
3. Little Harriet is not to be a replacement child but a replacement service animal, as Ah Ling presently employs a trained monkey to do the tasks that he envisions reassigning to Sally's daughter.
4. My colleague Emily Johansen has suggested to me that one might usefully contemplate the trilogy's rhetorical approach to high finance, exemplified by comments such as the one just quoted, within the context of the 1986 'Big Bang' caused by the deregulation of the London Stock Exchange. Christopher Bellringer and Ranald Michie observe that the 'Big Bang' is sometimes viewed as 'an ideological revolution engineered by the Conservative government of Mrs Thatcher in the 1980s with the deliberate aim of restoring the City of London to its position as the leading international financial centre' and sometimes as an instance of politicians acting 'as mere pawns being manipulated by powerful City interests seeking to establish the primacy of finance over manufacturing industry'. While by the moment of *The Tiger in the Well*'s publication in 1991, a full understanding of the repercussions of the reform had not yet emerged, left-leaning commentators were always more inclined than their right-leaning colleagues to view the transformation of the London financial market in a negative light.
5. See, e.g., Irigaray's 'Women on the Market': 'The production of women, signs, and commodities is always referred back to men (when a man buys a girl, he "pays" the father or the brother, not the mother [. . .]), and they always pass from one man to another, from one group of men to another. The work force is thus always assumed to be masculine, and "products" are objects to be used, objects of transaction among men alone' (171).
6. While readers of this chapter may wonder whether Magdalen's shady behaviour undermines my decision to pair her with the more upstanding Sally Lockhart, I propose that in naming her, Collins directs his audience's attention towards her ultimate restoration to the ranks of 'good women'. While the narrative makes the requisite gestures at condemning her behaviour, it also emphasises that Magdalen is acting out of frenzied anger and frustration at what she sincerely regards as a

miscarriage of justice brought about by the shortcomings of English inheritance law.
7. Simpson's is a minority view; other critics, including Talairach-Vielmas, Debra Morris and Collins's biographer Lillian Nayder, see Wragge as nearly as controlling, patriarchal and exploitive towards Magdalen as he undoubtedly is towards his wife.

## Works Cited

Bellringer, Christopher and Michie, Ranald. 'Big Bang in the City of London: An Intentional Revolution or an Accident?' *Financial History Review*, vol. 21, no. 2, 2014, pp. 111–37. DOI: https://doi-org.srv-proxy2.library.tamu.edu/10.1017/S0968565014000092.

Bisla, Sundeep. 'Over-doing Things with Words in 1862: Pretense and Plain Truth in Wilkie Collins's *No Name*'. *Victorian Literature and Culture*, vol. 38, 2010, pp. 1–19.

Boehm-Schnitker, Nadine. 'Neo-Victorian Gay Fictions: A Critique of Stereotyping and Self-Reflexivity', in *Neo-Victorian Literature and Culture: Immersions and Revisitations*, ed. Nadine Boehm-Schnitker and Susanne Gruss. Routledge, 2014, pp. 93–107.

Collins, Wilkie. *No Name*. [1862]. Dover, 1978.

Cvetkovich, Ann. *Mixed Feelings: Feminism, Mass Culture, and Victorian Sensationalism*. Rutgers University Press, 1992.

David, Deirdre. 'Rewriting the Male Plot in Wilkie Collins's *No Name* (1862): Captain Wragge Orders an Omelette and Mrs. Wragge Goes into Custody', in *The New Nineteenth Century: Feminist Readings of Underread Victorian Fiction*, ed. Barbara Leah Harman and Susan Meyer. Routledge, 1996, pp. 33–44.

Fritz, Sonya Sawyer. 'Double Lives: Neo-Victorian Girlhood in the Fiction of Libba Bray and Nancy Springer'. *Neo-Victorian Studies*, vol. 5, no.1, 2012, pp. 38–59.

Irigaray, Luce. 'Women on the Market'. [1978]. *This Sex Which Is Not One*, trans. Catherine Porter with Carolyn Burke. Cornell University Press, 1985, pp. 170–91.

Milbank, Alison. *Daughters of the House: Modes of the Gothic in Victorian Fiction*. Palgrave Macmillan, 1992.

Morris, Debra. 'Maternal Roles and the Production of Name in Wilkie Collins's *No Name*'. *Dickens Studies Annual*, vol. 27, 1998, pp. 271–86.

Muller, Nadine. 'Not My Mother's Daughter: Matrilinealism, Third-Wave Feminism and Neo-Victorian Fiction'. *Neo-Victorian Studies*, vol. 2, no. 2, 2009/2010, pp. 109–36.

Nayder, Lillian. *Wilkie Collins*. Twayne, 1997.

Peters, Laura. *Orphan Texts: Victorian Orphans, Culture and Empire.* Manchester University Press, 2000.

Pullman, Philip. *The Ruby in the Smoke.* [1985]. Dell, 2000.

Pullman, Philip. *Shadow in the North.* [1986]. Knopf, 1997.

Pullman, Philip. *The Tiger in the Well.* [1990]. Dell, 2001.

Pullman, Philip. *The Tin Princess.* [1994]. Knopf, 2008.

Robb, George. 'Inventing the Economically Incompetent Victorian Woman.' Paper presented at the Interdisciplinary Nineteenth-Century Studies Association, Dallas, TX, 22 March 2019.

Simpson, Vicky. 'Not-So-Happy Homemakers: Women, Property and Family in Ellen Wood's *East Lynne*'. *Women's Writing,* vol. 19, no. 4, 2012, pp. 584–601.

Simpson, Vicky. 'Selective Affinities: Non-Normative Families in Wilkie Collins's *No Name*'. *Victorian Review,* vol. 39, no. 2, 2013, pp. 115–28.

Smith, Andrew. 'Money and Machines: Wilkie Collins's Ghosts'. *The Ghost Story 1840–1920: A Cultural History.* Manchester University Press, 2010, pp. 25–53.

Stern, Rebecca. *Home Economics: Domestic Fraud in Victorian England.* Ohio State University Press, 2008.

Stetz, Margaret D. 'The "My Story" Series: A Neo-Victorian Education in Feminism'. *Neo-Victorian Studies,* vol. 6, no. 2, 2013, pp. 137–51.

Talairach-Vielmas, Laurence. 'Victorian Sensational Shoppers: Representing Transgressive Femininity in Wilkie Collins's *No Name*'. *Victorian Review,* vol. 31, no. 2, 2005, pp. 56–78.

Thiel, Elizabeth. *The Fantasy of Family: Nineteenth-Century Children's Literature and the Myth of the Domestic Ideal.* Routledge, 2008.

Wesseling, Elisabeth. '"Like Topsy, We Grow": The Legacy of the Sentimental Domestic Novel in Adoption Memoirs from Fifties America'. *Neo-Victorian Studies,* vol. 5, no.1, 2012, pp. 202–33.

Coda

# Rereading Orphanhood

*Diane Warren*

The process of writing must always also be a process of reading: the process of editing one of rereading. From the very first encounters with literary orphans (and orphan texts) which prompted the idea for a collection of essays, the cultural importance of those orphan-figures has been notable. Our initial sense that the orphan figure, placed on the margins of the family, always needing to negotiate their relationship to kinship structures, often distilled the cultural mores of their day, has broadened and deepened as we read, reviewed and commissioned essays. From the first chapter in this volume (by Cheryl L. Nixon) to the last (by Claudia Nelson), it is clear that the orphan draws attention to the processes by which kinship structures are made. Nixon and Nelson's chapters are also not alone in underscoring the ways in which familial and kinship bonds (both biological and constructed) are closely allied to financial bonds, which themselves form part of a wider examination of the cultural construction of value. As Nixon observes, the Fitzherbert case is underpinned by the 'obvious' argument that those who can offer emotional support are the best caregivers for a child. At the point at which the case was brought, however (and as Nixon shows), the argument was far from obvious, as convention favoured legal and financial understandings of 'care', underpinned by the validation of paternal right. It follows then, that, right from the outset, these chapters, and the orphans that they discuss, cause us to examine and question the presumptions we bring to the concept of inheritance, adoption and even the nature of being human.

The chapters emphasise that being orphan is far more than a matter of bereavement, although it is, of course, that too. Our contributors demonstrate that being orphaned is a state of mind, which informs the perceptions of the individual and remains throughout life. Thus, Kevin Binfield shows how bereavement colours the actions of Charlotte Smith Richardson, from her earliest poems to her last will and testament. This is then also part of a larger interrogation of the role of charity and patronage, which informs many other chapters including those by Harriet Salisbury, Joey Kingsley, Laura Peters, Jane Carroll and Claudia Nelson. Many of these chapters, therefore, pose important questions about the motivation of benefactors, and the impact of charity and patronage upon the lives of the recipients.

The question of the orphan's status is frequently debated within the volume: not just as the recipient of 'charity', but also in terms of gender, agency and even humanity: issues that are foregrounded in Peter Merchant's, Jane Carroll's, Claudia Nelson's and Laura Peters's chapters. As Merchant notes, and other chapters show, the female orphan is often especially affected by the death of the father: a point that underscores the extent to which the conventions of orphanhood are affected by patriarchal values. It is no surprise, then, that the questioning of the role of inheritance (both personal and colonial), including the extent to which it may be understood as a resource or a burden, is at issue in chapters by Peter Merchant, Diane Warren, Ann Rea and Claudia Nelson.

These chapters, and the texts which they discuss, also chart and examine the important (and frequently redemptive) role played by caregiving as the orphans they discuss flex, challenge and amend the family, to produce new kinship structures, based on taste, affinity and adoptive reading. This last is engagingly demonstrated in Kelly Hagar's chapter, although many of the chapters explore the operation of adoption and other elective kinship bonds, in harmony with Leonore Davidoff's analysis of the breadth of kinship structures in the long nineteenth century. Read collectively then, the chapters of *Rereading Orphanhood* prompt a thorough reassessment of the role of the literary orphan, and in the process, shed new light on the construction of social, cultural and literary bonds.

# Index

abject (the), 214
abjection, 73, 214, 227n
adoption, 4, 25, 56–60, 62, 64–70, 72–3, 75–80, 233, 267–9
Adoption of Children Act, 67, 78n
adoptive reading, 5, 83–4, 90, 91
advertisement(s)/advertising, 95, 125, 126, 128, 133, 139, 143, 146, 154
agency, 6, 7, 23, 37, 38, 39, 40, 45, 48, 49, 53n, 128, 186, 187, 191, 208, 209, 210, 219, 235, 236, 237, 238, 239, 240, 241, 253, 254, 257, 258, 269
alienation, 37, 40, 51, 73, 82, 112, 220, 223
Allen, Grant, *Hilda Wade*, 168, 169, 176
ancestor(s), 201, 211, 225, 232
Armstrong, Isobel, *Novel Politics: Democratic Imaginations in Nineteenth-Century Fiction*, 1, 3, 9, 58, 70, 73, 77, 78, 106, 119, 156, 208, 215, 225–7
Auerbach, Nina, 'Incarnations of the Orphan', *ELH*, 3, 9, 57, 76, 78, 211, 225, 226, 228
Austen, Jane, *Mansfield Park*, 4, 10, 12–14, 16–19, 27, 30–2
Auyoung, Elaine, *When Fiction Feels Real*, 84, 90, 96, 97

avuncular, 85, 88
Aztec (Lilliputians), 145, 147–55, 166

Baartman, Sara (Sartje), 145, 146
Bachelard, Gaston, 207, 211, 215, 216, 225, 226n
Barnardo, Dr Thomas, 6, 121–36, 138, 139, 157, 158
Barnes, Djuna, *Nightwood*, 8, 206, 207, 208, 210, 212–17, 225
bastard/bastardy, 17, 33, 34, 49, 50, 52n; *see also* illegitimacy
bereavement, 33, 37, 39, 41, 42, 48, 49, 50, 51, 52n, 53, 167, 219, 222, 268, 269
*Bildungsroman*, 56, 60, 62, 65, 66, 190
Blackmore, R. D.
  *Erema*, 7, 167, 168–9, 174–84
  *Lorna Doone*, 178, 180
blood(s), 5, 22, 39, 51, 74, 82, 86, 89, 117, 172, 202, 206, 213, 214, 260
body, 1, 4, 6, 14, 24, 116, 117, 126, 127, 129–39, 152, 157, 158, 160, 201, 209, 214, 237, 251
Bogdan, Robert, *Freak Show: Presenting Human Oddities for Amusement and Profit*, 146, 146–50

Bowen, Elizabeth, 231, 233, 234, 240, 244, 246
  *The Death of the Heart*, 8, 232, 233, 235, 236, 240, 245
  *The Heat of the Day*, 8, 232, 233, 240, 242–5
  *The House in Paris*, 8, 235, 239, 240
  *The Last September*, 8, 232, 235, 240
Bowlby, Rachel, *A Child of One's Own*, 2, 9, 61, 78, 79, 164, 165
Braddon, Mary Elizabeth
  *The Fatal Three*, 5, 57, 59, 73–6
  *Lady Audley's Secret*, 167
'Brenda' (Mrs Castle Smith), 6, 102, 103, 119
  *Froggy's Little Brother*, 101, 111, 112, 114, 115, 117, 118, 186
  *Nothing to Nobody*, 114, 115
British Empire, 69, 129, 145, 220
Brontë, Charlotte, *Jane Eyre*, 68, 73, 74, 77, 195, 203, 213, 216, 246n, 248, 260
Brontë, Emily, *Wuthering Heights*, 78n, 167, 246n
Brooks-Davies, Douglas, 183
Bunyan, John, 97, 169
Bushman children, 144, 145, 147
Butler, Judith, 209, 214, 227n

Cappe, Catherine, 34, 35, 36, 37, 40, 44, 52n
charity, charitable, 5, 6, 33, 34, 35, 40, 41, 48, 49, 51, 60, 62, 68, 69, 70, 123, 125, 129, 130, 132, 133, 138, 269
child custody law, 12–16, 18–23, 26, 31, 132
child labour, 60

childhood, 6, 12, 35, 39, 62, 65–8, 73–6, 84, 105, 125, 127, 143, 154, 160, 164, 181, 182, 187–9, 194–5, 199, 210–11, 233, 246, 252
children's literature, 2, 4, 6, 7, 77, 84, 100–2, 104, 120, 140, 186–8, 192, 204–5, 248, 267
circus(es), 146, 159, 206, 212, 215, 216, 226n
civilisation, 6, 125, 150, 156, 161–4, 209, 210
Cleere, Eileen
  *Avuncularism: Capitalism, Patriarchy and Nineteenth-Century English Culture*, 2, 9
  'Reinvesting Nieces: *Mansfield Park* and the Economics of Endogamy'. *Novel: A Forum on Fiction*, 19, 32
Collins, Wilkie, 5, 8, 70, 266
  *The Law and the Lady*, 179–81
  *No Name*, 8, 179, 250, 259–61, 263–5
colonisation, 4, 234
commodity/commodification, 147, 154, 162, 226, 250, 253, 264–5
community, 2, 4, 6, 8, 82, 84, 109, 143, 149, 150, 156, 158, 162, 164, 191, 214, 226, 231, 234, 241
Conolly, John, 151, 154, 156
Corbett, Mary Jean, 2, 164
*Cornhill Magazine*, 169, 174
counterfeiting, 264
Craik, Dinah Maria Mulock, *King Arthur*, 57, 58, 68, 69
crossing-sweep, 135, 158–60
Culler, Jonathan, 84
Custody of Children Act, 132

Darwin, Charles, 156, 158, 163
Davidoff, Leonore, *Thicker Than Water: Siblings and Their Relations 1780–1920*, 2, 9, 103, 114, 119, 157, 164, 165, 269
degeneration, 143, 157–9, 161, 163
DeMille, James, *The Living Link*, 167, 179
detective story, 7, 167
Dickens, Charles, 5, 6, 91, 122–5, 133, 134, 138, 139, 150, 157, 158, 244
  *Bleak House*, 56, 60, 62–4, 66–7, 74, 75, 135, 136, 159, 160–1
  *David Copperfield*, 60, 64, 127–30, 132, 133, 135, 137
  *Great Expectations*, 76, 126, 130, 132, 137, 177, 248
  *Little Dorrit*, 74, 78
  *The Mystery of Edwin Drood*, 161–2
  *Nicholas Nickleby*, 59
  *Oliver Twist*, 56, 63, 66, 77, 131, 133, 137
  'On Duty with Inspector Field', 160
  'On the Noble Savage' 147, 160
Dickens, Charles and Collins, Wilkie, 'No Thoroughfare', 56, 70–2, 76
disability, 122, 146, 150, 155
disguise(s), 72, 168, 171, 174, 259, 262
disinheritance and re-legitimation, 168, 178–9, 183
domestic (the), 7, 8, 20, 40, 41, 56, 73, 82, 84, 88, 90, 92, 93, 102, 103, 105, 109–11, 116, 122, 126, 155, 186, 187, 192, 196, 197, 198, 204, 216, 231, 234, 244, 245, 248–52, 254, 255, 257, 258–60, 262, 264, 265

*Doppelganger*, 58
Doyle, Arthur Conan, 168

Earthman (orphans) (Martinus and Flora), 145, 152, 154–5
East End Juvenile Mission, 128, 138
Edgeworth, Maria, 95
Egyptian Hall, 143, 146
Elegy, 36, 37, 38, 39, 42, 46
Eliot, George, 1, 77n, 78n, 97
Eliot, T. S., 207, 225, 228n
ethnicity, 2, 159, 160
Ethnological Society, 147, 150, 157, 164
evolution, 7, 135, 143, 147, 151, 152, 155, 157, 158, 161, 163, 265, 266
exhibit/exhibitions, 6, 92, 141–62, 164, 197
experience, 8, 19, 60, 76, 83, 95, 96, 103, 105, 108, 112, 114, 116, 127, 133, 136, 143, 152, 169, 181, 182, 186, 200, 207, 209, 219, 221, 223, 231, 232, 234, 236, 240, 261

fairy tale, 64, 83, 88, 93, 199
fantasy, 66, 71, 78n, 93, 210, 216, 221, 223, 225, 227n, 248
Felski, Rita, *Uses of Literature*, 90, 92, 94, 95, 96, 97
Foundling Hospital, 56, 61, 70, 71, 72, 78n
Freud, Sigmund/Freudianism, 197, 210, 211, 226n, 228n
Fridays for Future, 142–3

gender/gendered, 2, 4, 7, 118n, 171–2, 190, 200, 209, 219, 224, 236, 253, 257, 261, 263, 269
genealogy, 1, 3, 4, 7, 73, 147, 149, 156, 158, 159, 162, 207, 213, 215, 225n, 227n

genre, 1, 3, 4, 7, 58, 76, 77, 84, 101, 102, 152, 157, 189, 195, 246, 249, 250, 258
ghost(s)/the ghostly, 195, 196, 199, 200, 202, 231, 232, 234, 235, 245n, 246n, 258, 261, 262
Golden Age (children's literature), 5, 83, 84, 98, 188
Gothic literature, 75, 188, 194–6, 201, 237
Grant, Linda, *When I Lived in Modern Times*, 8, 207, 208, 210, 217–25
Gubar, Marah, 98

Hager, Kelly and Schaffer, Talia, 'Introduction: Extending Families', *Victorian Review*, 57, 102, 164, 166
Haggard, H. Rider, 170
Hemans, Felicia, 83, 96
Hocking, Silas, *Her Benny*, 6, 102–4
Hodgson Burnett, Frances, 195
  *A Little Princess*, 5, 187, 192, 193, 199
  *The Secret Garden*, 7, 77, 82, 94, 95, 187, 190, 194, 199
homeland, 162, 187, 196, 219, 221, 223, 244
homeless(ness), 6, 60, 121, 128, 159
homes, Dr Barnardo's, 121, 122, 124, 125, 126, 128, 129, 136, 138
Howitt, Mary, 6
  *The Story of Little Cristal*, 101, 102, 103, 104, 113, 116, 118n
human, 1, 2, 4, 6, 7, 41, 47, 48, 51, 106, 114, 120, 131, 134, 142–3, 145–9, 151–7, 159–65, 181, 194, 211, 221, 229, 249, 268, 269
human zoo, 4, 145, 155, 159, 160, 161

illegitimacy, 1, 3, 58, 60–2, 64, 66, 67, 70, 73, 74, 76–9, 106, 122, 156, 179, 217, 224, 236, 259, 261; *see also* bastard/bastardy
illness, 33, 35, 38, 39, 41, 43, 44, 46, 47, 122, 124, 125, 136, 137, 171, 225
*Illustrated London News (ILN)*, 149, 150, 152
inheritance, 1–4, 7–9, 11, 13, 23, 62–5, 68–7, 77–8, 156, 157, 167, 179, 206–10, 214, 217, 221–7, 236, 250, 253, 257, 259, 261, 262, 266, 268–9

Jewsbury, Geraldine, 67

kinship, 1–7, 155, 156–8, 161, 162, 164, 206–8, 210, 212, 216, 218, 222–5, 227, 228, 268, 269
Kuo Pao Kun, 209, 223, 225

land, 113, 117, 167, 175, 217, 221, 223, 224, 228
landscape, 61, 131, 134, 167, 194, 196
legacy, 8, 25, 164, 214, 253, 254, 256, 263, 264
liminal, 7, 8, 187–9, 191, 192, 194–7, 200–4
Lumpenproletariat, 7, 157, 159
Lynch, Deidre, 95, 97

Mackintosh, Mabel, *Dust, Ho!*, 102
Marryat, Florence, *Her Father's Name*, 7, 167–84

masculinity, 187
Máximo and Bartolo, 148–56, 159
Mayhew, Henry, *London Labour and the London Poor*, 102, 158–61
Meade, L. T., 6, 101, 102, 103, 111, 115, 117
*Medical Pickwick: A Monthly Literary Magazine of Wit and Wisdom, The*, 136
memory, 1–4, 8, 9, 34, 52, 71, 74, 76, 146, 152, 155, 156, 168, 169, 181, 211, 215, 231, 234, 237, 238, 241, 250, 257, 258
miscegenation, 156, 162, 235–6
modernity, 8, 210, 231–4, 236, 237, 239–45
money, 8, 9, 63, 69, 74, 89, 95, 108, 117, 118n, 130, 132, 146, 173, 219, 226n, 248–64, 265n
Montgomery, Lucy Maud
  *Anne of Green Gables*, 5, 7, 83, 88, 188–91, 193, 198, 201
  *Emily of New Moon*, 7, 188, 194–5, 200–2
morality, 13, 17, 49, 103, 134, 137, 138
Morris, Sir Lewis, *The Works of Sir Lewis Morris* (containing the cited poems 'Meliora' and 'A Plea for the Children'), 125, 132
Murdoch, Lydia, *Imagined Orphans: Poor Families, Child Welfare, and Contested Citizenship in London*, 61, 63, 121, 124–5, 158
museum(s), 145, 146, 212, 216, 226n

nation, 3, 8, 67, 156, 159, 162, 163, 210, 221, 236, 240
nationalism, 210, 240, 244, 245
nature, the garden, 86, 110, 112, 117, 194, 200–1
neglect, 6, 13–14, 17–20, 25, 28, 31, 62, 67, 77n, 82, 89, 113, 122, 124–5, 128–9, 131, 133, 139
Neo-Victorianism, 2, 259
Nesbit, E., 77, 88, 108
  *The Story of the Treasure Seekers*, 5, 81, 85, 95, 99
  *The Wouldbegoods*, 5, 81

origins, 1, 4, 5, 32, 56, 57, 59–65, 67–75, 162, 206, 208, 210, 211, 215, 216, 224, 228
Owen, Professor Richard, 150–1, 160, 177

paternal absence, 167–84
Peters, Laura
  *Dickens and Race*, 164
  *Orphan Texts: Victorian Orphans, Culture and Empire*, 2, 60, 97, 101, 183, 197, 217, 221, 236, 248, 269
philanthropy, 6, 52, 62, 135, 138, 158
photography, 123–4, 127, 134, 139, 141n
poetry, 35, 45, 47–8, 51, 52n, 83, 87, 98n, 177, 196, 207, 211, 215–16, 219, 222–3, 225
Poor Laws, 63, 128
Porter, Eleanor, *Pollyanna*, 7, 188, 192, 193, 195
posthumanism, 2, 142–3, 155, 163, 164–5
Pound, Ezra, 206
poverty, 35, 37, 43, 49, 61, 102–4, 109, 115, 118, 123, 125–6, 129, 132, 136, 159

prisons, 122
propaganda, 221, 223, 233, 240–5
Pullman, Philip, *Sally Lockhart Trilogy*, 8, 250–2, 255, 257, 259, 260–2, 264

Qureshi, Sadiah, 147

race, 7, 122, 142–5, 147, 149–52, 154, 156–60, 162–5
reading *see* adoptive reading
rehabilitation, 6, 123, 129, 133, 135–6, 168, 183
rhizome (the), 224
Richardson, Charlotte Smith
  'child of sorrow', 44–5
  'The Tawny Girl', 41, 48–9
Romantics/Romanticism, 143, 195
Russell, Margaret, 41, 48–9

Schaffer, Talia, *Romance's Rival: Familiar Marriage in Victorian Fiction*, 2, 3, 102, 164, 210, 216
Scott, Sir Walter, 99n
sensation fiction, 7–8, 56, 58–60, 67, 70–3, 75–6, 78n, 135, 167–8, 179–80, 249–50, 264
sentimentality, 30, 58, 65, 71, 73, 75–6, 187, 195, 201, 248–9, 259, 264
separate spheres ideology, 20, 248, 251, 258
servant, 3, 48, 77n, 82, 93–4, 112, 127, 186, 196, 251
*Seymour v Euston*, 4, 10–12, 14–15, 18, 20–6, 31–2
Shaftesbury, Lord, 105–8
Shakespeare, William, 172–3
Slezkine, Yuri, 210, 211
slums, 102–3, 109–10, 112–14, 116
Spyri, Joanna, *Heidi*, 7, 187, 188, 192, 195, 196, 197

Stauffer, Andrew, 'An Image in Lava', 5, 83–4, 90–1
Stephens, John Lloyd, *The Aztec Lilliputians or Illustrated Memoir of an Eventful Expedition into Central America*, 150
Stevenson, R. L., 186
street Arabs, 61, 118, 157, 161
Stretton, Hesba, 6, 101, 102
  *Alone in London*, 106
  *Jessica's First Prayer*, 107–9, 118, 248
  *Little Meg's Children*, 111, 112, 116
  *Lost Gip*, 103, 110, 115, 117
  *Pilgrim Street*, 112, 113, 11, 117
supernatural, 8, 187, 189, 195, 201, 203

*tabula rasa*, 181, 216, 221, 222
Tennyson, Alfred Lord, 181
Thackeray, William Makepeace, 174
Thompson, Flora, 113
Thunberg, Greta, 142
tradition(s) 73, 146, 207, 152, 155, 187, 188, 225, 231, 234, 236, 237, 238, 241, 244, 245, 264
transformation, 6, 125–6, 136–8, 171, 213, 224, 256, 262, 265n
translation, 188, 197
Trollope, Anthony, 170
Tuke (family), 46, 48
Twain, Mark, 186

uncanny (the), 160, 196, 197, 198, 200, 201–4, 234, 237, 238, 245, 249

Vienna, 207, 210, 213, 216, 227n

waif, 6, 60, 61, 63, 65, 74, 77, 101–6, 109–10, 112–14, 116–18, 124, 125, 134, 186
Walton, Mrs O. F., *Christie's Old Organ*, 6, 102, 103
Wandsworth Prison, 133
Watts, G. F., 116
widow, 16, 33, 41–3, 44, 47, 51, 52n, 60, 74, 85–6, 174, 189, 243, 245, 260
Wiggin, Kate Douglas
*Christie's Old Organ*, 101, 104, 106, 113
*Rebecca of Sunnybrook Farm*, 5, 82, 86, 88
Wilde, Oscar, *The Importance of Being Earnest*, 69
will(s), 86
Woolf, Virginia, 207, 220, 228n
workhouses, 43, 59, 69, 122, 128, 131–3, 135–6
working-class, 6, 77, 117
Wynne, May, *Mollie's Adventures*, 102, 104

York, 33–5, 41, 46–8, 49–51

EU representative:
Easy Access System Europe
Mustamäe tee 50, 10621 Tallinn, Estonia
Gpsr.requests@easproject.com

www.ingramcontent.com/pod-product-compliance
Lightning Source LLC
Chambersburg PA
CBHW071830230426
43672CB00013B/2799